ST HELENS LIBRARIES

D0261233

STRICTLY ANN

STRICTLY ANN

The Autobiography

ANN WIDDECOMBE

Weidenfeld & Nicolson

LONDON

First published in Great Britain in 2013
by Weidenfeld & Nicolson

3 5 7 9 10 8 6 4 2

© Ann Widdecombe 2013

All rights reserved. No part of this publication may be
reproduced, stored in a retrieval system, or transmitted,
in any form or by any means, electronic, mechanical,
photocopying, recording or otherwise, without the
prior permission of both the copyright owner and
the above publisher.

The right of Ann Widdecombe to be identified as the
author of this work has been asserted in accordance
with the Copyright, Designs and Patents Act 1988.

Every effort has been made to trace the owners of copyright material.
In the event of any omissions, the publishers will be pleased to
rectify any errors in future editions.

A CIP catalogue record for this book
is available from the British Library.

ISBN- 978 02978 6643 5

Typeset by Input Data Services Ltd,
Bridgwater, Somerset

Printed and bound by CPI Group (UK) Ltd,
Croydon CR0 4YY

Weidenfeld & Nicolson

The Orion Publishing Group Ltd
Orion House
5 Upper Saint Martin's Lane
London, WC2H 9EA
An Hachette UK Company
www.orionbooks.co.uk

The Orion Publishing Group's policy is to use papers that are
natural, renewable and recyclable products and made from wood
grown in sustainable forests. The logging and manufacturing
processes are expected to conform to the environmental
regulations of the country of origin.

In memory of my father,
without whose unfailing support and encouragement
much of what follows would not have happened.

ST HELENS LIBRARIES	
380551494140	
Bertrams	12/06/2013
941.085	£20.00

CONTENTS

CONTENTS

Author's Note and Acknowledgements

Many people have helped with the preparation of this autobiography. Without Edward Winstanley, who researched among the chaos of boxes still unpacked from when I left Parliament, this book would still be unwritten. Many thanks also to the House of Commons Library, whose staff saved a great deal of Whitehall time and public money by dealing with a last-minute query for which I might otherwise have needed to burrow in the archives of a government department. Harriet Bastide, my secretary, somehow managed to carve out enough time in the diary for me to produce this work and my agent and publishers have been unfailingly patient.

My thanks also to numerous civil servants, former members of my office in Parliament, friends and family who have contributed, sometimes unwittingly, their own memories.

Finally I owe a huge debt of gratitude to many who may not appear in this book at all, not least to Kay Killick, Ruby Bhundoo and Sarah Mitchell who have kept my surroundings clean and tidy and my fridge stocked. My political agents, Peter Currie and Brian Moss, my literary sleuth Mark Coote, my ever-patient technological advisors Nick Roberts and Danny Corder together with so many friends and colleagues have been squeezed out only by my selection of events rather than by any lack of gratitude on my part. My apologies to any who are offended by the omissions but it will not have been deliberate. Were I reproducing a daily journal they would all be there, but my guiding principles for this book have been digestibility and accessibility.

Ann Widdecombe
Dartmoor 2013

INTRODUCTION

This is not one of those tomes which former politicians often produce, detailing every last consideration behind every clause of every bill. Nor have I gone into detail about the results of every leadership contest or general election because that is well enough covered elsewhere. Inevitably I have had to explain the events surrounding my disagreements with Michaels Howard and Portillo but I wish both well. Rather, instead of trying to contribute to political scholarship, I have endeavoured in this book simply to give a flavour of a life which began in the austerity of post-war rationing and progressed to the glamour and glitter of *Strictly Come Dancing* via twenty-three years as MP, minister and Shadow Secretary of State.

It is, I think, better to paint the bigger picture than to worry about the clauses in the Associated British Ports and Killingholme Cargo Terminal Bill or what I ate for breakfast.

Bearing in mind that many who will be reading this little volume will not be acquainted with the minutiae of daily political life I have explained terms which may cause others to feel patronised, and the same is true of my references to theology. The apostolic succession is reduced here to almost absurd simplicity but I would have left too many baffled had I not explained it at all.

I was born into a world in which Britain still ran an empire and families were scattered around the globe, went to a strict Convent School in the swinging sixties and into Parliament while Margaret Thatcher was still Prime Minister but the aftermath of my career was perhaps the most extraordinary sequence of events in a highly eventful life.

Much that happened before, I could have either predicted or

hoped for when I was still in my teens: to be a politician and a writer were always cherished dreams. If however somebody had said to me in 2010 as I was retiring 'Well, this is how it is going to be, Ann. You will spend three months dancing on prime-time television, then you will tour the country in a live dance show with Craig Revel Horwood appearing at venues such as Wembley and the O2, then you will go into pantomime and, oh, by the way, you will be appearing in an opera at Covent Garden,' my response would have been: 'Lie down and have an aspirin.'

Yet that is what happened and one of the pleasures of my retirement is that I have no idea what may happen next.

Chapter One

ARRIVING (1)

Twice in recent years the makers of the television programme *Who Do You Think You Are?* have approached me to see if my ancestry might be sufficiently interesting for one of their programmes and have concluded that it is not, which is a pity as I was hoping they might help me to distinguish between the facts and the myths of family legend.

The facts are simple enough: my parents were of solid West Country stock, seasoned with a sprinkling of Irish and Scots. My father was born in Saltash, Cornwall and my mother in Plymouth, Devon and they met on Plymouth railway station in 1926, in the latter years of their schooldays, where one was catching a train for Saltash and the other for St Budeaux, an area in the north-west of Plymouth.

My mother is said to have asked a boy from Devonport High School: 'Who's that chap over there with the prefect's hat?' and received the reply 'Murray Widdecombe, but you won't catch him. He's far too ambitious to bother with girls.' And the rest is my history.

In January 2006 *Family History* magazine traced my father's ancestry back to 1747 when John Whiddecombe married Mary Martin. I was disappointed they could not get back a hundred years further as I have always wanted to know what the family did in the Civil War, fervently hoping they supported the King rather than ghastly Noll Cromwell. There was, however, a legend within this timescale that could not be verified. My father always told me that he had it from his grandfather, who in turn heard it from his grandfather, that we had wreckers in the family.

Wreckers were the characters immortalised in Daphne du Maurier's *Jamaica Inn*, who lured ships on to the rocks at night by flashing lanterns to confuse the sailors into believing they were seeing a lighthouse. When the ships were helpless, aground or broken upon the rocks, these charming fellows looted and sometimes killed. If any of my ancestors were involved on those dark nights then I am obliged to wish them hanged. Perhaps they were.

Other ancestors made rather more legitimate use of the sea. My maternal grandfather, Jim Plummer, was a master mariner, a great-grandfather on my father's mother's side was a ship's engineer with the Navy for thirty years and my own father was a naval captain in World War II, thereafter spending his entire career in the Admiralty.

'You looked all at sea,' an older lady once said to me after my performance on *Strictly Come Dancing*. I murmured, to her incomprehension, that it was a family tradition. So was baking, the trade of both my grandfather and great-grandfather of the Widdecombe line. They had a shop in Fore Street, Saltash, which was occupied by Widdecombes for some sixty years.

Family History magazine established that it had been the last Tudor building left in Fore Street until 1941 when it was bombed and destroyed by the Luftwaffe, who made regular sorties over Plymouth Docks. Meanwhile another Luftwaffe bomb played a significant part in my own, as yet unrealised, life. My grandmother was bombed out of her Plymouth home and, being a widow, took refuge with her only child, my mother. She lived with our family from then until she died when I was fourteen so that I grew up with a granny always resident.

On my mother's side we had Henry Doidge Rundle, a Cornish sailor with a propensity for the odd bit of smuggling and who has an entire website devoted to him. My great-grandmother, Maria, was one of his daughters but I never heard tell of his exploits until they were unearthed by *Family History*. What I did hear a great deal about was my grandfather, James Henry Francis Plummer, my mother's father who died of throat cancer when she was eighteen.

Jim Plummer came from Ireland, a son of a large Catholic family in County Cork. He ran away to sea at thirteen years of age and nothing is known of his family. However there was a tradition that an uncle on the Plummer side founded the store Plummer's, which became Plummer Roddis, which was subsequently hoovered up by Debenhams. Plummer's was a fashionable chain of department stores in my youth and the legend stated that the uncle had started it with a small haberdashery stall. If so it was a fortune which never came our way.

My mother also said that we might be related to the famous actor, Christopher Plummer, but that she thought not. Given the general prevalence of Plummers throughout the British Isles, I also think not, but I would have liked to have traced some members of Jim Plummer's family.

The Scottish element was provided by my father's mother, Alice Murray, whose own ancestors hailed from Glasgow.

The courtship between my mother, Rita Noreen Plummer, and my father, James Murray Widdecombe, lasted ten years. My grandfather had made a fortune from his bakery business during the First World War, feeding the troops that flocked into the area, and was able to afford private education for his sons. His second son, Donald, became a vicar and my father turned down a place at Cambridge to join the Admiralty.

It was a decision that I think he may have regretted although he never had any regrets about his choice of career which culminated in his becoming Head of Naval Supplies and Transport and being awarded the CB. He left Saltash for the naval base at Rochester, where in June 1936 he and my mother finally married, and never returned, his career taking him all round the world. Uncle Donald also left and, after spending the war as an army chaplain, became the vicar for the quaintly named parish of Yetminster and Ryme Intrinseca.

Ambition was considered best left to the boys and my father's sisters stayed in Saltash. The younger one, Molly, died there recently at the age of ninety-one.

In September 1937 my parents were stationed in Gibraltar and expecting twins a couple of months later but the birth was premature and went badly wrong. My brother's twin, James Patrick, was stillborn at the Military Hospital and my brother,

Malcolm Murray, was born temporarily paralysed and weighing two pounds. In an age without the incubators and apparatus which do not always guarantee survival even today, he lay in his cot struggling for life, willed on by my mother.

Decades later I came upon a minute vest in a drawer in my mother's dressing table and asked her to which of my dolls it had belonged. She replied it was my brother's, the one he wore while that fight for life was going on, and which she had faithfully preserved. After she died I searched among her possessions, intending to give it to him, but I failed to find it and sadly concluded that it had been lost in the clear-out and move when she came to live with me on being widowed.

My brother lived but was a weak child, with a congenital eye defect. Gradually he grew stronger and by the time he was in his teens was a keen rower. My mother sent him first to Captain Olsen's Gym School and doctors covered up his good eye to try and strengthen the bad one, while forcing him to write with his right hand instead of his natural left. He bore it all quite stoically while my mother mourned the dead twin: 'I used to look at one all warm in his cot and think of the other cold in his grave.' Even now I pause when I remember those words.

When my brother was two the Second World War necessitated a return to Britain. 'Well, we got through France before it fell,' my mother commented matter-of-factly, when recounting the train journey on which the only food offered to the tiny Malcolm was a large corned beef sandwich.

By now Malcolm was nicknamed Joe. He was very good and well behaved (unlike his sister at that age) but had a habit of sticking his jaw out provocatively when trying to get his way. The family dubbed this his 'Musso' look after Mussolini, but now the Italian dictator was allied to Hitler and it was decided to drop the joke. A worse one followed when my father commented sarcastically that they could always call him Joe after Stalin and Malcolm said delightedly 'Joe!' It stuck and in later years I would tease him with 'Look who *you* were named after!'

My mother had been advised to have no more children for three years and my father resolutely refused to have a child in the war. Nobody could tell what the future held and a wife and child at home while he was at sea or at various depots abroad looking after naval armaments were more than enough to worry about, he proclaimed. Thus Malcolm and I were born pre-war and post-war or, as he used to say, he was quality and I utility.

I arrived, ten years and one month to the day after my brother, he being born on 4 September 1937 and I on 4 October 1947. In later years we had a ritual that I would ring him up when he reached forty and gloat that I was still twenty-nine and so on each decade whenever he reached a big O.

The birth took place at eight o'clock in the morning at the Forbes Fraser Nursing Home in Bath where my mother, brother and grandmother had spent most of the war and where my father was now stationed. This time everything was straightforward and I emerged weighing six pounds and healthy, but there had been a scare during my mother's pregnancy when, at the height of the danger period, she had contracted rubella.

Today the pressure to have an abortion would have been huge but then it was both illegal and unthinkable. Indeed my mother told me that she never gave the possible consequences of her German measles a moment's thought but Doctor Love, the family GP, was perturbed and when I proved a slow talker actually feared I might be tongue-tied!

As Rita Noreen Widdecombe lay back exhausted from a night's labour, Ann Noreen Widdecombe was being carried about the nursing home to be admired for her beauty because my eyelashes were so long that they produced shadows on my cheeks and the eyes behind them were an unusual shade of dark blue. That was probably the only time in my entire life that I was acclaimed for my looks, although make-up artists still comment on my long lashes.

Meanwhile Malcolm Murray Widdecombe said 'damn' on learning he had a sister instead of a brother and James Murray Widdecombe departed for the pub. My paternal grandmother, Granny Wid, was staying with us and began to ring up all the relatives to announce my birth while Gran Plum kept the house in order.

Granny Wid spent the years from the death of her husband until her own death circulating between her four children, although living with one of my father's sisters. So each year we received what felt a bit like a state visit and which lasted for a month or six weeks. My other grandmother called her Al, short for Alice, but she never used Christian names in return and determinedly stuck to Mrs Plummer.

My mother spent ten days at the Forbes Fraser before bringing me home. In those days mothers were not routinely discharged, as now they are, the day after the birth and it was normal for grandparents to converge to take charge of any siblings and of course the husband who could not possibly be expected to cook or wash up, let alone manage his laundry, ironing and cleaning.

Home, in the south-west of Bath, was a rented house in Bloom-field Park, called Megohm, because the owner was an electrician. It was years before I realised that it was not Meg Home and when I did it somehow seemed to lose its special warmth. I remember very little about it because we left when I was three and my father was posted to Portsmouth. I do recall that the next-door neighbours were called Sidwell and they were on the other side of the fence, so I suppose the houses must have been semis but Megohm is the only one of my childhood homes to which I have never returned and I can recollect no more.

Ordnance House, Gosport, was the first of the big houses in which we lived during my father's many admiralty postings. It had five bedrooms, a lawn tennis court and large grounds which were tended by the two gardeners, Grayle and Compton. It seems odd now to recollect that in infancy I would address grown-ups by their surnames alone but this was the class-conscious Britain of the middle of the last century when the distinction between officers' daughters and those of other ranks was meticulously preserved.

My mother did not preserve it in my choice of friends and I always brought home to tea whomever I liked. It was not only the right attitude for a world which was about to change but the right grounding for making friends throughout my life in which the only factor that mattered was: did I like them?

This seems to me so obvious a basis for friendship that I have never understood why supposedly intelligent interviewers express surprise that I have gay male friends. As I point out, if I chose my friends on the basis that I must first agree with all their views and choices then I would have to exclude not only homosexuals but all those who are divorced, living in sin, having children out of wedlock, having abortions (that one is quite difficult), known to have taken drugs, holding strong left-wing views and certainly unbelievers. And assuming, under this scenario, that others would judge me and everyone else also by their own moral criteria, then we would all be living in little lonely bubbles of our own.

Yes, I do oppose gay marriage but so do plenty of gays because it will give not one extra right to homosexuals which they do not have with civil partnerships but will take away from heterosexuals the right in law to be called husband and wife. Certainly gay marriage does not promote equality because a heterosexual couple cannot elect to have a civil partnership but must choose between full marriage or having none of the protections of a legally recognised union. Opposition to this politically driven measure is not anti-gay: it is anti-redefining an institution that is recognised across the globe, is intuitively unique and has been the bedrock of society for millennia: one man and one woman in a union open to procreation.

Friendship is founded upon liking, loyalty and reliability not upon shared opinions and should be capable of surviving being let down and disappointed. It is as disloyal to abandon someone for falling by the wayside or deserting a cause as it is to abandon someone for losing all his money. True friendship can survive almost any test except betrayal. If my epitaph were to be 'she was a good friend' I would not consider my life to have been wasted.

However let us go back to Portsmouth and the gardeners. Compton was young while Grayle, whom I adored, seemed quite old. He used to come to work on a bicycle and when sweet rationing ended he sat me on the saddle and pushed me to the shops to buy Smarties. There was also Stamp, the driver, who used to chat to me as he stood by the car, waiting for my father, and who sent me *Uncle Mac's Children's Hour Story Book* for Christmas when we had left for Singapore.

I was surrounded by benign grown-ups and felt like an only child because by then my brother was at weekly boarding school. My mother, like most women of that period, did not work, and there was also Gran Plum, who taught me all my tables before I went to school. She loved to read with me and we used to listen to children's programmes on the wireless. I suppose the main entertainment must have been *Listen with Mother*, but I do not remember it.

Gran always made sure I said my prayers before going to bed and then we waved goodnight to the garden. There was a sundial on the lawn and in spring I would be wildly excited by the pink cherry blossom which carpeted the ground and which my father cursed.

In addition to the humans there were Jimmy the black cat and Shaun the wire-haired terrier. Jimmy was sadly killed on the road but I was told that he had 'gone to live in the woods', which I imagined populated with woodcutters and old ladies collecting firewood. Jimmy was replaced by Tibby the Tabby who really did flee to the woods when we went to Singapore.

There was a great deal of excitement when the Queen, who had not long acceded to the throne following the death of her father, George VI, came to review the fleet. My brother sat on my bed and taught me the words of 'God Save the Queen' which came in handy for the coronation preparations a year later. By then I was at school and hating it.

Bridgemary was the only school of the five I attended before the age of eleven in which I was unhappy. Ironically, I almost did not go there at all, as by then we knew we had been posted to the Far East and my parents were of the view that it would be confusing for me to start at one school and then almost immediately move to another, but I was five and the law said I must be in full-time education so off I went to Bridgemary.

In those days there was none of the gradual acclimatisation that there is now when children go to nursery and then build up towards a full day. One day I was at home with Mother in the usual way and the next was dropped at the school gates. It did not cause any trauma until I came to go home and left through the wrong gate. I could not understand why my mother was not there and began to wander uncertainly off while my poor parent fretted with anxiety at the right exit. We finally arrived home to find my grandmother beside herself because we were so late. No mobile phones in 1952!

I had not been there long before the bullying started. It was trivial stuff really but to my five-year-old self a group of girls making menacing faces at me each and every playtime was frightening. Then one of them pinched me clandestinely in assembly and I slapped her away not at all clandestinely. Naturally I, not she, was the one who was reprimanded and my sense of justice was outraged even further when my mother finally went to the school to complain and was told I had been 'unkind' to the girl concerned.

Years later when, as an MP, I recounted this story publicly I received a profoundly silly letter from the then headmistress of what had been Bridgemary but had since been renamed, in which she protested about my criticising the school. As the incident had happened more than four decades earlier and the school did not even have the same name, I thought her indignation was ludicrous.

It was a government requirement that each afternoon younger schoolchildren had to lie on mats and rest. Inevitably some actually fell asleep and usually were then left until they woke naturally. I always hoped I would drift off and sleep till home time, but it never happened.

While I was enduring the petty tormenting at school, the family was facing the biggest upheaval of its existence. My father had been posted to Singapore for three years and my brother and grandmother were to be left behind. In 1953 left behind meant just that for the entire three years: there were no assisted passages for family members out and back during tours of duty. By the 1960s when I was at boarding school the girls in the dormitory whose parents were stationed abroad with the forces could go out once a year for the summer holidays.

It is now mercifully unthinkable that children should be separated from their parents for so long, but then we took it for granted. That is not to say that we were particularly reconciled to such arrangements but, in an age when we were still running an empire, they were regarded as neither cruel nor unusual.

The silver lining in the dense black cloud of knowing it would be years before you saw your parents was the role of the extended family. Children left at school in Britain stayed with grandparents, aunts, uncles and godparents in the school holidays and at half-term. These sturdy characters also turned up for speech days, sports days and the school play.

Appalling? Yes, but it is a deep irony that today, when such arrangements would be thought barbarous, there has never been so much family breakdown, so little involvement of the wider relations. Dad may be living only a few miles away with his own new family but you don't live with him on a daily basis. Children live with one parent all week and go off to the other at weekends. 'Access' has replaced daily parenting, 'quality time' has replaced Mum-at-home, 'partners' have replaced Dad. It is the State rather than her own children that is expected to provide a home for Granny.

I prefer what we had fifty years ago.

My grandmother had to remain in England on health grounds. In those days civilian airflights were few and the journey out to Singapore was to take three weeks by ocean liner. There was, of course, no air conditioning other than fans, and the doctor was of the opinion that my grandmother would not make it 'through the Red Sea with all the heat'. I suspect that was nonsense but it represented the medical opinions of the time.

So it was arranged for Gran Plum to stay with a cousin of my father, Mona Dunkerley, a war-widow whose husband had died when the ship on which he was serving was sunk with all hands, and who was now an optician. She was also my godmother and had two children of her own, Peter and Janet, of a not too dissimilar age from Malcolm's.

My brother was at boarding school, Monkton Combe, a minor

public school near Bath. He had been sent first to prep school there, and had then, after we left for Gosport and Ordnance House, boarded first weekly and then full time. He was fifteen and approaching O levels and it was decided he should stay on, spending holidays with Auntie Mona and Gran, with some other godparents known as Auntie and Uncle Pick, and with yet others who were called Auntie Dora and Uncle Mit. Of these only Mona was a real relative, the rest being godparents.

He also stayed with my father's brother, the vicar, who had a daughter, Daphne, of approximately the same age. As by now Malcolm was determined to become a vicar, staying with one had advantages!

Thus it was that my grandmother and brother were consigned to various members of the extended family. Uncle Donald also took Sean the dog and a home was found for Tibby the Tabby, who stayed with a neighbour for a few days shortly after we left but when Malcolm came to collect her, she spat, scratched, jumped out of his arms and fled towards the woods and, sadly, was never retrieved. We did not, despite extensive enquiries by those still in the area, find out Tibby's fate.

I can only begin to imagine now what my poor mother must have been feeling as the day of our departure approached and she was faced with seeing neither her mother nor her beloved son for three long years, but I was shielded from all of it. Children were not then embroiled in adult traumas and when we set sail I had no idea that this was to be a major parting. When I asked where Gran and Malcolm were I was told they were still in England and I think I had some notion that they would catch us up, until gradually, with the adaptability of childhood, I just got used to their not being around and ceased to question their absence.

Might my parents have taken a different decision had Malcolm been a girl? In the 1950s it was considered de rigueur for middle-class sons to be sent to public school and the colonies offered no equivalent, although the junior education was outstanding. There was, however, less pressure on girls. My parents always assumed, even then, that I would be properly educated and go to university, but it was somehow less vital and the plan was for me to go through state primary schools and then to grammar.

Indeed, in later years, when it became obvious that I was vastly more ambitious than Malcolm, my father shook his head in bewilderment and observed to my mother that 'Ann should have been the boy'! Considering how keen he was on university for me, how he cheered on the first woman newsreader, Angela Rippon, backed Thatcher from the start and was the only member of the family to support the proposal for women priests, it seems something of a contradiction but somehow he could not quite overcome the conventional expectation which had been there in his own family: boys were ambitious, girls were home-makers.

Yet, as I have observed above, by the time I was at a girls' boarding school in the 1960s my fellow pupils were seeing their parents only once a year. Of course, many of them were there only because their brothers were at the nearby major Catholic public school of Prior Park and their parents, having carefully selected a school for their sons, looked round for the nearest appropriate one into which to place their daughters! But still they were there and not abroad with their parents.

Why? Stability is the answer. No matter how good day schools abroad might be, postings came every two or three years and moving about was not exactly the best way to secure a reliable secondary education with its different syllabuses and plethora of public examinations.

I do not remember a great deal about the three-week voyage out. We left a Britain gripped by coronation fever and one of my last memories of Bridgemary is receiving a coronation mug with a bag of sweets in it.

Now people pay a fortune to spend three weeks on a cruise to the Far East but for us it was all in the line of duty. The ship was the *Canton* and we must have called at many ports, but whereas I remember the return journey on the *Asia* quite vividly the *Canton* is a blur, which is odd given that the voyage was so unlike anything I had previously experienced.

For the adults it was a highly social event with lavish dinners and entertainments and, of course, the port stops. Now, we see the far ends of the earth portrayed daily on our television screens until no corner of the globe is a mystery, but then each new experience was startling: the flowing robes and camels at Aden, the desert on either side of the Suez Canal, the smells and spices of Bombay, the colour and cacophony of different languages, of different people. I recall being disappointed that the Red Sea was not a vivid scarlet and even more disappointed that the Chinese were not bright yellow.

Much of what we saw is captured in the old black-and-white photos of the time but the vividity, the movement, the strange-ness and the overpowering heat live best in the memories of those of us caught up in the excitement as we sailed slowly towards a new life.

Chapter Two

EMPIRE'S CHILDREN

Number 300 Kloof Road in Singapore was a large black-and-white house built on concrete pillars. It was still there unchanged in 1998 but had gone by the time of my visit in 2000. Instead of windows the house had long interior balconies on either side with shutters which were closed only in the monsoon season when the rain was severe. The rooms within had saloon-style doors and every bed a mosquito net, with the house functioning on one floor as a bungalow. Downstairs were only box rooms and the boiler room, in which lurked Nadisan, the gardener.

The garden was large but not vast. At the back was a belt of bamboos and in the front were banana bushes and, of course, keng hua.

The beautiful flower of the keng hua, which blossomed only at night with its distinctive, pungent scent, was a source of fierce but friendly competition among the naval wives, who vied to see who had the most out. When, some years after their return to England, my parents bought their first house they called it Keng Hua and a neighbour, Mr Wakelin, who was a commercial artist painted a picture of the spectacular flower, which he obtained from a book. That picture hangs in my own house now.

The garden had an old, disused air-raid shelter, which my parents forbade me to enter because of snakes but it became an irresistible source of adventure. At the back of the house a long flight of steps ran up to the kitchen entrance and the front had a circular drive big enough for the school bus to turn round in, which was convenient as we were the last house in the road and there was nowhere else for the bus to go. My incredulous mother took a picture of the manoeuvre and sent it home to be marvelled over by Gran and Malcolm.

For me the main attraction was the long, low house at the back where the staff lived. The cook was called Hoon and was immensely fat. He was with us throughout my time in Singapore but I do not think I exchanged more than half a dozen sentences with him in three years. He spoke no English but cooked English food with skill and ease.

The amah, or housekeeper, also spoke no English but used to communicate with my mother through signs and actions, which were the source of great hilarity in the household. Meng, the houseboy, who seemed to fill the role of general help, alone spoke enough of our language to communicate.

My mother, who had always run her own home with the help of only my grandmother and a twice-weekly cleaner, told me in later years that she used to wonder how on earth it needed so many people to run a house until she discovered the debilitating effect of the Singapore heat, relieved only by fans, and the relentless round of entertaining which was expected of her.

'When we had a free evening, your father used to write BED in huge letters in the diary and we would collapse early and sleep for nine hours!' Indeed my own routine always included a visit from my mother, wearing a rustling evening gown that made her seem to my childish eyes like a princess, to check that I was asleep before the night's parties were under way. If I woke I would hear the loud buzz of conversation and the clink of glasses from the drawing room where colleagues of my father and their wives, officers from visiting ships and personnel from the naval base were gathered. Later the roar of cars and snatches of grown-up conversation from the departing guests would drift up to my room.

Meanwhile if my mother was wondering at the size of the staff, Amah and Meng were aghast at the size of our family. The previous occupant was not only childless but also a bachelor and the thought of a wife and child about the place, the one doubtless interfering and the other making noise and mess, was decidedly uncongenial. Three years later they were to be distraught when we left.

Amah had three children: a son, Ah Gee; a married daughter, Wee Jong; and her youngest, a daughter four years older than me, Ah Moi. On my very first day at the house in Kloof Road I met Moi, who was playing in the back garden. She had long dark hair, large black slanting eyes and an air of fun. We became friends on the spot and remain so sixty years later. Incredibly, at the time of writing, Amah has only just died at the age of 103.

My mother treated Moi as if she were my sister and she was always included in family outings. One of the most regular of these was a trip to Seletar Island, a wild place which we reached by boat and where we would lunch on the beach and swim. We never went beyond the beach because the place was so wild and overgrown and there was the ever-present danger of snakes. Today Seletar Island is a commercial resort with water sports and hotels.

On such an outing one of my parents' friends, a Mr Powell, fell overboard and there was a mighty panic before he was safely back in the boat. I did not understand the fuss. He could swim, couldn't he? Thus it was that I learned about sharks. His daughter, Janet, must have already known because she cried throughout the drama.

Most of Singapore's social life revolved around the water: swimming at HMS Terra (which for years I thought was terror), going to the sailing club, picnicking from boats. The children came home proficient swimmers and divers and, where they could keep up the activity, often went on to compete at county level.

Used to a full day at school, I now found my time organised differently. School took place in the mornings only, although they were long mornings and started earlier. There were no school lunches and the afternoons offered no shortage of activities. I had swimming lessons twice a week and Brownies once. My mother also enrolled me in ballet classes but I rebelled after the third lesson and never went again. Not even the pictures of

little girls in fairy-tale white dresses at the end-of-year performance could lure me back, much to Mother's disappointment.
She was probably thinking of Gran receiving the photos and
saying 'Ahhhhh!'

Most of us went to the Monday elocution classes run by
Mrs B. Lumsden-Milne, a rather fierce-looking woman of buxom
proportions. I used to recite a poem called 'The Good Bad Child'
but never quite breathed in the right places. I failed to see that it
mattered how I breathed as long as I could memorise the words
but I enjoyed the classes because I loved learning poetry by
heart.

After the afternoon's activities I did my homework and played
with Moi. Sometimes my parents took us swimming in the early
evening and then it was bed.

Moi did not attend the Royal Naval School, which was solely
for the English children of the Navy and Admiralty. Instead she
went to a school in which she was taught both in English and
Chinese. I used to look in wonder at her Chinese books and tried
to practise some of the figures. Of course nobody encouraged the
learning of Chinese because there was no general perception that
China was to become one of the most powerful nations on earth.
Being British was all that mattered. We had won the war and
thought no country had as much right to regard itself as destined
to rule others.

Certainly this was reflected in the celebrations every year
on Empire Day, which fell on 24 May, when we were lined up
under the Union Jack to sing patriotic songs. Moi's favourite
name was Elizabeth, after the Queen. The more far-sighted could
see the coming of a different world but then Britain stood for
order, stability, stiff upper lips and reticence. Egad!

I look back to those times and wonder that I noticed so
little the difference between Moi and me. My dolls had more
by way of cots, clothes and tea-sets than did Wee Jong's many
babies. I had more dresses, a cupboard full of toys and a swing
in the garden. At Christmas my gifts filled a large pillow case
and I spent hours in play, while Moi increasingly had to help
her mother cook and clean. I simply took it all for granted then

but now I wonder how I might have viewed matters had I been older.

When Moi cooked meals for the staff I used to join her in sampling the food as it was being prepared but once I found Amah plucking a live chicken and I ran away with a mixture of terror and pity for the poor struggling bird.

In addition to the Chinese there were Malays and Indians. Nadisan was an Indian and the driver, Ballay, was from Malaya. The different nationalities had their own festivals and customs and Mrs Lumsden-Milne taught us a poem:

The Christians they have Christmas,
The Chinese have New Year,
The Hindus have Deepavali,
And once in every year,
Comes Hari Raya Puasa,
A time Malays await,
Throughout the months of fasting,
With joy to celebrate.
So whether we are Christians, Hindus, Chinese, Malays,
We wish them all with all our hearts,
The happiest of days.

Doubtless I failed to breathe in the right places while reciting it, but perhaps the reason I remember it so fluently six decades later is that it expresses a sentiment which we would do well to recapture in this age of religious and racial tension.

A popular holiday for the colonials was to go up to Kuala Lumpur for a week or so and, very occasionally, to Hong Kong. The latter involved a longer stay and my mother went for six weeks, during which time it became my father's lot to read me *The Wind in the Willows* and cut my toenails, but largely that of Amah and Moi to look after me. My father himself did not manage such a vacation but once went to Australia on business and brought me back a cuddly koala bear, which we named Kroo.

Many people reading this will wonder why we did not all go to

Honkers or KL, as these places were nicknamed, but the concept of an annual family holiday was more limited then. People generally used breaks to visit relatives or grandparents, but these were living 8,000 miles away. The Kuala Lumpur trip involved a long, tiring train journey which was unlikely to be enjoyed by a young child any more than was the hill walking which formed part of the attraction, and the fares to Hong Kong were prohibitive for an entire family. As for beaches and swimming, we had them all in Singapore where they were part of the daily experience rather than an annual treat.

While the children were at school the Admiralty wives occupied themselves with good works, my mother being involved in the Soldiers, Sailors, Airmen and Families Association (SSAFA) and also in health promotion among the local population. Wee Jong quickly became known to us as Wee June and by then had five children: Ah Ching, Ah Fong, Ah Nee, Ah How and Ah Yong. The three girls made a wonderfully attractive little group with their identical black fringes and dark eyes as they stood in order of height. The two boys were but babies and Wee June wanted a break. Was there, she asked, a pill to stop any more?

There was not, nor would there be for years to come.

The heat overwhelmed the adults but we children quickly became acclimatised, running, competing and climbing trees with no less energy than would have been natural back home. We were, however, regularly laid low with a procession of childhood illnesses, some of which, such as measles and whooping cough, would be taken seriously today. I escaped both scarlet fever and mumps and was twenty-three before I caught chickenpox, but German measles, real measles, whooping cough, urticaria and other diseases took their turn in putting me out of action for anything up to three weeks. By then there were vaccinations against diphtheria but the sight of a child in callipers as a result of polio was not unusual.

Singapore posed its own health hazards and my mother was fastidious about my mosquito net being tucked in all the way round, while I was never allowed to go outside barefoot on account of the dreaded hookworm. Meng got hookworm and my mother used his resulting disappearance to hospital as a cautionary tale.

Children were often off school because of germs. The term seemed to cover everything from colds to stomach upsets to unspecified infections. 'Margaret cannot come to Brownies today. She has a germ.' 'Fiona missed the nativity play. We think she caught a germ from Penny.' 'Don't share ice lollies – it will give you germs.'

Our parents dosed us with Minadex and Virol but fruit was abundant and no child lacked vitamins. A favourite was the pomelo, a large variety of citrus with white flesh, which I did not see from 1956 until 1964 when a girl in the dormitory at Bath Convent, whose parents were stationed at RAF Changi, brought some to school after she had visited them for her summer holiday. When I went back to Singapore for the first time in 1983, I fairly lived on pomelo.

Papaya was a staple at breakfast and even now its taste will remind me of those far-off days when I would be sitting at the table in my white school tunic, swinging my legs to and fro as I watched Meng clearing up, and waiting for the school bus. My father would have already left for the armaments depot, which he managed for the Admiralty, clad in the uniform of the British civil servant posted to hotter climes: white, short-sleeved shirt, white shorts and white knee socks. As late as 1966 when I visited friends stationed in Malta, this was still the norm. Whether it was the advent of air conditioning or simply the propensity of natives in newly independent states to dress in suits and ties, as symbols of authority, that changed this custom I do not know.

Mr Wong Kwee Yong was the local tailor who looked after most of the Brits. He ran a shop in the village of Sembawang where there were also a cold store and a NAAFI outlet, while Ah Lim ran a cigarette and sweet shop near Kloof Road. To get to his tiny emporium I had to cross a stream which used to swarm with tadpoles and I rarely went without a jam jar but my tadpoles never became frogs.

We were taught to avoid snakes and I recall the great excitement when one got into the staff quarters and Meng evicted it with a stick. Yet, for all the warnings, this was a rarity and I was never once alarmed by a snake. A much greater peril was the harmless lizard which crawled along ceilings and occasionally fell off on to the bare arm of a woman below. As the fashion was for heat-defying sleeveless dresses it was a common event at a cocktail party to hear a sudden shriek.

Once, when the guests had departed and the house was still, I crept out from my mosquito net and stood on the verandah by my room, listening to the crickets and smelling the keng hua. My mother found me and concluded, wrongly, that I must have been sleepwalking but it was while I was in Singapore that the first episode of somnambulism really did occur when I walked, fast asleep, into a dinner party.

My mother successfully got me back to my bedroom without waking me up whereupon I announced 'my pyjamas have gone wrong'. She obligingly changed them and put me back to bed, but in the morning I had no recollection of the incident.

As my father had sleptwalked in his younger days and had even woken up outside it was assumed I was likely to have inherited the tendency but it did not manifest itself with any frequency until my teens. Once I woke up trying to get into the unmade twin bed in my room but usually I returned without waking and could hardly believe it when told I had been wandering around in the night. At Bath Convent I gave myself a jolt when I woke to find myself staring in the mirror in which my dark reflection was just discernible and on several occasions the nuns followed me in case I should go out on the fire escape.

With no recorded incidents at university it appears that, as had my father before me, I had grown out of this somewhat disconcerting habit, which does not appear to have ailed any of the next generation.

The child is the father of the man or in this case the mother of the woman and when I look back to my time in Singapore I can see the beginning of character traits and interests which were to define me in later life. I was sociable enough, with children round to play nearly every day, but I did not really enjoy parties (although my seventh birthday was memorable for the entire Brownie pack coming to tea) and I was perfectly happy to play for hours alone.

Much of that play took the form of making up or writing stories and I had some vague notion that when I grew up I might be like Enid Blyton. Or perhaps I would be a teacher, I thought, as lining up my dolls and bears, I delivered lessons from my blackboard. I never entirely lost either ambition.

Ah Moi was a regular playmate, despite the gap in our ages, and she too liked playing schools but also hospitals, which I was less keen on, but which I remembered in years to come when she began her nurse's training. She was amazingly talented at art and my mother was keen for her to become a commercial artist. Indeed when the time came for us to return home there was some debate as to whether Moi should come with us and be educated in England but she was then only twelve and there was no certainty as to when she would see her mother again.

Some families did take their amahs' daughters home to Britain, especially in cases where they were somewhat older, and I noticed several on the ship as we were returning but in later years I wondered if they were all about to enjoy an expansion of their education or if some were simply cheap nannies. I suspect now that, like the children of the *Kindertransport*, or the British children who were sent to Australia, it all depended on the luck of the draw with individual families. It is difficult to see on whom such a young Chinese girl could have relied had things gone wrong.

With no television in Singapore, children made their own entertainment but when I hear complaints now that children spend too much time cooped up with television or computers as opposed to how they were all outside and healthy in the golden age, I do not recognise the picture.

We swam, sailed and picnicked, certainly, but when left to our own devices we were often indoors. Painting, stencils, Fuzzy Felts, board games and reading were major pastimes for my generation. Their superiority over the preoccupation with the small screen lies in the latter being a largely passive hobby while the former demand active thought and effort. Both however are indoor activities, demanding no physical energy.

The absence of television made it easy to shelter us and there was no sex education. Divorce was actively frowned upon and most of us spent our years in primary education feeling utterly secure in our families where the adults went out of their way to protect our innocence.

It was certainly with complete innocence and absence of understanding that many of us coped with the horrible tragedy of a small child, Mark Crighton, drowning in Terra despite the presence of lifeguards and the pool being full of adults as well as children. His sister, Susan, was in my class and we had to buy her a book and write her a letter. This we did but I do not think that any of us had a clue as to what she was going through. Death was an unsuitable topic for a child. Had I not been told that Jimmy the cat had 'gone to live in the woods'?

'We mustn't say "poor Mark",' observed my friend and regular playmate, Zillah Pettit. 'Because he's in Heaven. But we can say "poor Susan" because it will be ages before she sees him again.' I have no doubt that would have been the teaching in most homes in the naval base.

God was presented to us as a fact not as a belief. On Sundays families went to the naval base church, run by Padre Leonard, with whose son, Tom, I occasionally played. The children went to Sunday school and afterwards a group of us would be invited to the house of Admiral Shattock, a friend of my parents, where we swam in the pool and drank cream soda.

Moi apart, none of my friendships from Singapore became lifelong. Many of the families we knew in the naval base were subsequently also posted to Bath but the only children I saw again were those I had known but vaguely at the Royal Naval School. My regular playmates, Fiona Sivier, Deirdre Kedge, Margaret Machin, Gilly Potts and Zillah Pettit never crossed my path again. Occasionally, when I was an MP and therefore easily traceable, someone from those days would get in touch but now

I look back at the photos and would be hard put to name half a dozen of those pictured.

We came home in 1956 on the *Asia* run by the shipping line Lloyd Triestino. Three years earlier I had embarked upon the outward voyage with no appreciation of the length of separation from my brother and grandmother which would follow but now I did understand that I might never see Moi, Meng and Amah again. I flew about wildly excited, looking forward to the return and the new adventure ahead, but I was also sad and that was to be the pattern of most of the moves we made. I never minded the prospect of a new school and new friends and never ceased to be excited by a new house but from this age onwards there would always be something I knew I would miss.

People often now comment that so many moves must have been difficult for a child but mine never were and I do not recall any other child finding them particularly unsettling. It was simply a way of service life and we took it as much for granted as the air we breathed. Indeed when we finally did settle into a permanent abode I grumbled as much as my long-suffering mother rejoiced.

On the journey home I would pretend that Moi was with us on the ship and, when I passed through a door would hold it open long enough for the imaginary her to join me. The ship was one of the last to get through before Nasser closed the Canal at the beginning of what was to become known to history as the Suez Crisis.

The three-week return is as clear in my mind as the earlier voyage is fuzzy. The ship had a swimming pool which occupied us on days at sea and when we were in port we visited the local attractions, among which the hanging gardens at Bombay stand out in my mind. In 1994 I was visiting India and went back to see them, only to be disappointed.

My father took me each day to see our position on the ship's map and suggested I keep a journal, but I preferred writing stories. I did some sums which my parents gave me but there were no formal classes on board and our education consisted of the voyage itself.

Lifeboat drill was given in both English and Italian and for years afterwards I claimed to know Italian because I could say *zattera due* or lifeboat number two. At eight the possibility of having to use such boats was exciting rather than disturbing, but whenever I looked down at the sea I thought only of Moi and Meng and of how far off they must now be. My parents could have been thinking only of Malcolm and Gran and of how much closer they were becoming.

Our last port was Genoa and we visited Pompeii, that city for ever frozen in time by the molten lava of Vesuvius in AD 79. I looked at the figures of men shielding their eyes from the dust, at ruins of dwellings, at the paths for carts and something, which was the beginning of my fascination with Roman history, stirred.

From Genoa we travelled by train through Italy and Switzerland to Calais and thence to England by ferry. Presumably we must have been exhausted but all I remember is that, just as the Chinese were not bright yellow and the Red Sea not scarlet nor was England cold for we had arrived in the summer and I did not have to wear the coats, scarves and gloves which I had seen in pictures of life in England.

My father was now posted to Whitehall and we had to live within London's commuting belt. We were due to rent a cottage in Haslemere, Surrey, from a family friend, Admiral Elkins, who had himself been posted abroad, but he was not going to depart for six months so we roosted temporarily in a six-bedroomed house in Tunbridge Wells. Its greatest attraction from a child's point of view was the railway line which ran at the back of it. There was but one track, which I think was still used by the very occasional steam train, but we were there only six months and my recollection may be faulty and it may have been by then disused.

I had not read *The Railway Children* then or the old track might have become the source of great imaginary adventures. The other big attraction was a room in which the landlady, Mrs Copeland, had stored all her children's toys, among which was a rocking horse and doll's pram. I was allowed to take the pram out very occasionally but absolutely forbidden to climb on to the rocking horse because my parents feared that if I were to damage it replacement would have been impossible. My own toys arrived back at intervals in tea chests, which Gran and I unpacked together.

We had gone to Chichester to collect Gran and to the station to meet Malcolm, who was now leaving school and ambitious to enter theological college. I regarded my grandmother with enormous enthusiasm as her re-emergence in my life meant the doting attention of an adult was always at my beck and call, but for a while my relationship with my grown-up brother was uneasy.

For three years I had been effectively an only child but now I had a contender for my parents' interest and affection. Inevitably, not having seen him for so long, they gave him vastly more attention than me and my understanding of the situation was sufficiently limited for me to be jealous. Furthermore I remembered him as a playmate, who brought home other big playmates, but now he was recognisably one of the adults as were his friends who came to visit.

Meanwhile I was probably a bit of a shock to him. I had left as a small five-year-old whom he could spoil or boss about as the mood took him, but returned as a wilful eight-year-old with opinions, likes and dislikes of my own. Perhaps also he felt some subconscious resentment that I had been with my parents while he was 8,000 miles away.

My parents must have handled the situation effectively because gradually he and I became close again but it took time, not least because he went off to train for the priesthood at Tyndale Hall in Bristol and I saw him only in the holidays. He was always what my friends described as 'good fun', playing tricks on us and teasing us so that I never failed to hope he would be there when they came.

He had been born in Gibraltar and I had spent a chunk of my formative years in Singapore but there were to be no more foreign postings. Within seven years Singapore would be independent and the empire rapidly dwindling. Moi and I were both empire's children but, as we grew up on different sides of the world, our fates were shaped by the diverging paths our countries took when the Union Jack came down.

Chapter Three

GROWING UP

We were due to be in Tunbridge Wells for so short a time that my mother refused to buy me a uniform for St Mark's, the school I attended for one term. I wore my Royal Naval School uniform, a white tunic, instead of the brown and white check dress which the others wore but, by a happy coincidence, I had a brown check dress which I wore as often as I could, resisting fiercely when my mother took it to wash, a process which then took two days. I hated being the odd one out and one or two of the teachers frowned whenever I appeared in my RNS tunic but I loved the school.

I was a bit surprised at the frequency with which children had to hold out their hands to be slapped, as at Singapore Juniors I had never seen a child smacked. It was common in the infants' school but I never saw either my form mistress, June Allen, or the headmaster Jack Cordner, so much as tap a pupil once we had moved up to juniors. In my next school there was the occasional caning of a boy and at the Convent prep school one of my fellow pupils received a ruler across her hands but at St Mark's light corporal punishment was an almost daily event.

I was also puzzled when, on the first day, a fellow pupil was told to show me the offices and they turned out to be the loos. These facilities were always called 'the offices' at St Mark's but it was a piece of nomenclature I had to forget in a hurry at my next school where the very suggestion met with hilarity.

At the end of term I played a bird, which I think must have been a canary because the wings were bright yellow, in a school production of Robin Hood. While the other children were being given their form allocations for the following year I was facing yet another school.

I think if I had been a bit older my friend next door, Popsy Thomas, would have appeared somewhat unconventional but at that age I accepted uncritically her odd style of dress, her education at a progressive boarding school and the tendency of her father to use what I knew to be swearing. I did however find it disconcerting that she called her parents by their Christian names, Dick and Eleanor. She was immense fun as a playmate and introduced me to tin shoes.

We took two matching food tins and pierced holes in the tops through which we threaded string. Then we stood on the cans with the string pulled tight around our feet and walked on them. Apparently at Sunninghill, her school, everybody in the playground walked about on tin shoes.

Popsy was not acceptable in the homes of some of my friends from St Mark's. One of them, Sally, told me Popsy was a gypsy, to which I retorted that gypsies lived in caravans and Popsy lived in the house next door. My own parents maintained their policy of letting me choose my friends on the basis of kindness and fun, and Popsy supplied both in large measure. I hope that she has had a good life.

I often walked home with Sally and envied her the small dog which used to wait for her every day by their gate, tail wagging with excitement when it saw her coming. I was also in love with Tim, the dog in Enid Blyton's Famous Five stories, and began to importune my parents for such a pet.

In Gosport we had Shaun, the wire-haired terrier who had gone to live with my vicar uncle when we went to Singapore, but my father had steadily refused me any pet while we were overseas, not relishing putting the animal through quarantine on return. I was told we would get both a dog and a cat when we were settled.

Settled meant moving to Haslemere, Surrey and spending two years in the home of Admiral Elkins. Quell Cottage was a delightful little house which I instantly declared my favourite of them all. It had two small ponds, one covered in lilies, a stream with primroses on its banks and the house itself was in the middle of a wood. As we were about three miles from my school and none of the near neighbours had children, my schoolfriends came to stay most weekends and we would go off exploring the fields, woods and lanes all day, taking Enid Blyton-style picnics and pretending we were having great adventures.

My generation was probably the last to do that and we do tend to be a bit wistful when reminiscing but it is true that childhood was vastly more carefree and less supervised than would be considered safe today. We had no mobile telephones then but our parents did not worry if we were away from morning till night as long as we came back at whatever time had been stipulated. The sole warning was not to take lifts from strangers and occasionally we broke even that rule, when it was raining, without too much parental rebuke.

One of the results of this approach was that leaders emerged among us and we sorted out our own grievances. There was no adult to whom to appeal when quarrels occurred, no authority figure to say that X was at fault and must apologise to Y, no arbiter of justice. Complaints in retrospect were despised and 'sneaking' was derided.

Today children are encouraged to tell their parents every small grievance with the parents then often complaining in turn to teachers or other parents. Any normal childhood name-calling is inspected for 'racist' or 'homophobic' abuse and children of kindergarten age find themselves on council registers. Pushing and shoving are regarded as 'assaults', childish confrontations as 'bullying' and any teacher grabbing hold of a misbehaving child will probably find himself on gardening leave while the 'abuse' is investigated.

'Johnny hit me' would once invite the adult response 'Well, go and hit him back.' Now the result is an inquisition. The consequences have worked their way through to the grown-up world where people are regularly 'offended', sue for 'hurt feelings' and expect tribunals to resolve what are often nothing more than workplace personality clashes. Anybody losing self-control and raising his voice will be warned about 'bullying', which diminishes recognition of the real bullies who may deliberately set out to intimidate subordinates.

We learned to deal with these issues from an early age and, regarding intervention from authority as a last resort, took that independence into adulthood. Now I dread to think of the trees which have been cut down in their thousands to provide the paper mountain which is the average HR office. Health and safety. Grievance procedures. Satisfaction surveys. Appraisal forms. Disciplinary procedures. Workplace hygiene. The forty-eight-hour working week.

Furthermore very few of these forms are designed to elicit much that is useful. Let us consider satisfaction surveys, the collated results of which do not much more than enable firms to boast about the high level of approval their services generate among the public and which are designed in the first place to produce exactly that result.

BT sends out a survey every time you complain which asks you about 'the last person you spoke to'. What that means is that the person who finally solves your problem is the one you are being asked to assess while the twenty who abjectly failed do not feature at all.

Then there are the wretched hotel surveys which pop up on your pillow alongside the complimentary square of chocolate. These have innumerable boxes for you to tick and a tiny space for 'additional' comments. In other words the hotel bosses are deciding the criteria for your satisfaction. Was the bathroom clean? Yes? Oh, good, the customer is satisfied, despite there being no flannels provided, no space for laying out toiletries beyond the perimeter of the washbasin and bath, too high a mirror and a shower, the mechanics of which are more challenging than a medium Sudoku puzzle.

Even worse are the forms which come in the sheep's clothing of helpfulness while in reality being the wolves of intrusion and personal information storage. Take out a library book and the chances are you will be given a form asking for your sexual preferences and racial origins, presumably on the basis that the local council can decide whether you are a consumer of detective fiction or romance or non-fiction just by the colour of your skin and what you do in the bedroom. It is so ludicrous that it should be a joke but instead is taken so seriously that an army of public servants, paid and pensioned by the rest of us, spend millions of man hours analysing the results.

Indeed the State is now more powerful and intrusive than it has been in my lifetime. Even George Orwell in his wildest imagination did not think up microchips in wheelie bins. The State, heaven help us, is actually in our rubbish. It prescribes the type of lightbulb with which we may illuminate our own homes, it censors our speech and despatches the police to our doors if we utter views which conflict with State orthodoxy, it monitors whole journeys on cameras and every day the database on which it keeps our most personal details swells.

When I was not exploring the countryside I had a new diversion – television. I did not so much as see a set until I was nine. There had been none in Singapore and our house at Tunbridge Wells did not have one, but now, at Quell Cottage, I was glued to children's hour every day: *Crackerjack*, *Playbox*, *Champion the Wonder Horse*, *Funbook*, a weekly play, *The Appleyards*, and then at weekends the *Six-Five Special* and *Dixon of Dock Green*. There was just one channel and the set took a couple of minutes to warm up but I was wild with enthusiasm and, indeed, one of those weekly plays was to have an impact on my own writing decades later.

It was called *The Watch Tower* and was set in the Second World War. So clearly can I remember it that I even recall it was produced by Shaun Sutton and starred Barry Letts and Garth Adams, a feat of recollection which astounded a BBC team a couple of years ago.

A German pilot crash-lands in a field in which stand the ruins of an old watchtower. Two children (the girl is called Jo) come to play there and discover an unexploded bomb which endangers their lives when they become trapped behind it. The German pilot deals with the bomb at huge risk to himself and is taken prisoner afterwards. He asks Jo if her name is short for Joanna and when she says it is, he remarks that he also has a daughter of the same name.

I do not know why but the story caught my imagination.

Perhaps it was my first introduction to the concept of the 'good German' as opposed to those devils who had killed Uncles Ronnie, Jack and Eric and who had bombed out Gran Plum. Whatever the reason for its impact it caused me to graduate from Enid Blyton to Biggles, where good Germans were often to be found.

As a teenager I discovered *All Quiet on the Western Front* and *The One that Got Away*. I read, at the age of eleven, Desmond Young's biography of Rommel and decided that Montgomery was not such a genius after all: he arrived at a time when Rommel was low on supplies. My father regarded such a view as little short of blasphemy, Montgomery being something of a god to his generation.

Of course the terrible aspects of Nazism, the persecution and the genocide, were unknown to me because children were not then exposed to horror as young as they are now but by the time I began to appreciate the evil of that ghastly regime I had a fixed view that ordinary, kindly human beings stayed ordinary and kindly whether they wore British or German uniforms.

So far I have published two books of a trilogy which explores the theme of the ordinary mortal caught up in conflict with other ordinary mortals. When I came to write the first, *An Act of Treachery*, I paid private tribute to *The Watch Tower* by naming the daughter of the good German Johanna.

In 2010, I became quite hopeful and excited that I might actually see *The Watch Tower* again, when I was invited to contribute to a training programme on the influence of television and, enthused by the tale, the producer made a determined effort to track down the work but, alas, though it is mentioned in the index of the National Film Archive, no copy of it could be found.

I did not, however, merely watch television at Quell Cottage: I featured on it. There was a weekly religious programme for children run by the Reverend Elphingstone-Fyffe in which one could put a question to him and be invited to do so on air. I was not thus invited but asked to supply a photograph which filled the screen and I have both it and his letter to this day.

The question was 'What does Selah mean?' Selah is a word which appears at the end of some verses in the Psalms and means, roughly, Pause and Think. It speaks volumes that a child of ten could put such a question and that it was considered of enough general interest to broadcast, but scripture, in the form of The Authorised Version of the Bible, was taught in schools and to all ages, children routinely attended church and Sunday school, and to have read the psalms and noticed an odd word would have been a perfectly normal experience, even if I were not growing up in a household of practising Anglicans. Today it would be looked upon as at best nerdish and at worst eccentric.

The loss of scripture as a basic subject in schools has contributed not only to the decline of Christian belief but also to the decline of an understanding of our Christian heritage and culture. It is beyond me how any student of mediaeval history can even begin upon the subject without a grounding in the teaching and practice of the Church but, when I was making my programme on the Reformation in 2008, a professor of history at a major university told me that he had students who believed they could dispense with any examination of the influence of the Church and that it was irrelevant.

Worse still, generations of children now read Shakespeare or Milton without recognising the references to verses from the Bible and are oblivious to the origins of very common sayings.

I once teased a male acquaintance who was complaining in a friendly fashion that his burgeoning girth was due to his wife's wonderful cooking. 'Ah,' I replied, 'men's excuses don't change much down the years, do they? *The Woman tempted me and I did eat.*' He looked as blank as if I had just spoken in Chinese.

School, Shottermill County Primary, was some four miles away and the journey was made in the family's baby Austin. The car was the first new one my father had owned and had been bought in Tunbridge Wells in preparation for our move to the Surrey–Sussex border. It was very shiny and black and its registration number was YKE which we pronounced 'Why-Key' and which became its name. Nobody said 'Is the car in the garage?' but always 'Did someone put YKE away?'

With Quell Cottage situated at the end of a two-mile drive through a narrow country lane and well away from any bus route, that car was essential to us, but two problems arose. The first was my mother's driving test. My father had obtained a licence in his youth, before any such test became law, and drove hair-raisingly all his life, but my mother had learned and passed in Singapore and now had to retake the test in order to qualify for a British licence.

Unwisely and with the confidence of someone who had been driving for three years, she simply drove normally on the test instead of by the book and was promptly failed. It was a catastrophe for us because, with my father at work all day, she was all that could provide transport between Quell Cottage and the rest of the world. Riddled with nerves, my mother took the test a second time and passed.

The second problem was provided by Colonel Nasser who had, as already noted, closed the Suez Canal, thereby forcing Britain into petrol rationing. We could just get by if the car made no more than four journeys a day along Fernden Lane and into Haslemere to the station from which my father commuted and the school I attended.

My brother had failed his National Service on the grounds of his eyesight, one eye having never recovered from his premature birth. He was therefore filling in the time between school and college by working on a chicken farm. Throughout the petrol rationing he and my father would give a lift to a man from the other end of the lane whom one morning they passed as he walked along. Thereafter they gave him a lift each day but my brother told me whimsically, years later when we both made a return to Fernden Lane, that they never found out his name.

Some days, in order to save petrol, I would go to a friend's house and stay there until it was time for my mother to collect my father from the station. Her name was Janet Wilcox and we used to go to Brownies together and she would often spend weekends at Quell Cottage, as would Rita Blake, another friend from the same school. We kept in touch for some years after I left Haslemere but then lost contact altogether until only a few years ago when I was being interviewed by a Midlands radio station and Janet suddenly popped up among the callers!

A third hazard at Quell Cottage was the winter. Snow and ice could leave us isolated and everybody would set to with shovels and sand. My parents put chains on the car, which had the somewhat surprising side effect of curing the dog's travel sickness.

In my early days at Shottermill school I was surprised to find how ahead I was of my classmates, not a feature I had noticed at St Mark's, and perhaps that should have alerted my parents, but the school had been recommended and we all liked the headmaster, Mr Oldham, and my form teacher, Mrs Spooner. I excelled at essays and English in general and there was no doubt in anybody's mind that I would pass the 11-plus but Mrs Spooner, who had only just come to the school from another, was always telling the class that we were not up to the mark and that only one or two of us could hope to pass.

The 11-plus was important to me because my parents made a distinction, then quite common, between the educational needs of a boy and of a girl. My brother was in private education from the day he first went to school to the day he left public school at eighteen. By contrast I was expected to go through grammar school, but the plan went awry.

At the end of the school year in 1958 my father had been posted back to Bath and we were facing yet another move. That October I would be eleven and would take the exam in the following Easter term at whichever school I was then attending. There was some discussion about the desirability of a move at such a time and whether I should stay with Janet Wilcox and move schools only after the exam was over, but then came an event which rendered all the discussion redundant.

In the course of that summer I developed what was diagnosed as whooping cough. I was breathless, coughed in great whoops and was sick after the smallest exertion. Given that one cannot get whooping cough twice and that I had already had it in Singapore, it seems an odd diagnosis but my parents accepted it. Whatever it was, it lasted not for a few weeks but for months and, upon moving to Bath, I missed the entire autumn term and then the next, being first still infectious and then still coughing and sick. When I was finally pronounced no longer infectious I was taken to the cinema to see Charlton Heston in *The Ten Commandments* as a celebration and two children, Christine and Catherine Davies, the only ones within easy distance, who had called during my illness were at last allowed to meet their new neighbour.

Christine and Catherine lived in a small house which had no bathroom and each Friday the four children were washed in turn in a huge tin bath. In between Fridays the children would wash in an outside stream and clean their teeth at the kitchen sink. Many years later when Catherine and I revisited the area we found a rather magnificent house which probably had several bathrooms!

It was at the village school, which they attended, some two miles along the lane in which we now lived, that I took – by special arrangement and in a room all by myself – my 11-plus without having sat in a classroom for nearly two terms. My parents attributed the subsequent failure to the whooping cough, if whooping cough it really were, but I am not sure. A letter from Rita Blake told me that only one girl in our form at Shottermill had passed and she had private tuition.

Whatever the reason, the grammar school plan was no longer operative, my parents would not consider a secondary modern and the hunt for a private school began. My name had been down at Bath High School since my earliest days in Bath and the headmistress Miss Blackburn had a formidable reputation but she said the school was full. My parents were not too disappointed, having decided that they wanted a school with the option of boarding later in case of another posting.

The school selected was La Sainte Union Convent, a Catholic day and boarding school, and I joined the last year of the prep school before successfully taking the entrance exam to the senior school. By the time I began my secondary education both my health and academic performance had fully recovered and at the end of my first term I scored 92 per cent in Latin, a subject with which I had fallen in love.

Home was a large, somewhat uncared-for house called The Mead at St Catherine's, near Batheaston. Once it had been tea gardens and a huge sign overhung the drive which, for some reason, the council would not let us take down. The inevitable result was that we were plagued by people turning up for tea. Once a family arrived looking so bedraggled that my grandmother could not bear to turn it away so two parents and three children sat in our dining room and devoured a Madeira cake to which I had been looking forward. My subsequent protest was met with the biblical injunction 'to give and not to count the cost'.

To a child The Mead was exciting. Unlike the tiny Quell Cottage, it was large and rambling, with six bedrooms, including two attics. Through one of these was access to a large loft which, being unlit, unused and a bit unsafe seemed to promise Famous Five-style adventure, which disappointingly never materialised into anything more than encounters with cobwebs and loud creaks.

The house was reputed to be very old and in the dining room the chimney had footholds for child sweeps, while outside was a boarded-up well and huge greenhouses where food had once been grown for the tea gardens. The grounds were extensive but had been divided into plots with a chalet in one and a caravan in another. Our own garden provided challenge enough, for it had been untended a very long time and the grass was taller than me.

Throughout the first weeks of our tenure my father and brother attacked it with scythes and every so often one would call out that he had found a path or a bank but, to my great sorrow, no one found a pond.

Beyond the garden was an orchard and then fields. The Davies children and I spent our free time in the country, roaming and exploring, and, when I had acquired a bicycle for my twelfth birthday I often went off alone. Catherine Davies and

I discovered a large lake a couple of miles away and we made a den between our houses which we called 'leaf canopy' in a space between some trees bordering a field, well away from the road.

It was on my bicycle that I came to appreciate the beauty of an early summer evening when the weakening sun is spreading its rays across the English countryside. In later years I savoured the same spectacle from the back of a horse and today it is my favourite time to walk on Dartmoor.

I once asked my mother why we always chose such isolated places to live with all the inconvenience of inaccessibility and she told me it was because she did not want to live among the rest of the Admiralty families 'with their gossip and cocktail parties'. It must have been hard on my grandmother who did not drive.

The Mead was situated in the tiny community of scattered farms and houses called St Catherine's which would have been described as a little hamlet but for having a church, albeit a very small one which was part of St Catherine's Court, a grand house. The vicar of Batheaston, the Reverend, later Prebendary, Reggie Evans used to conduct services there on a Sunday afternoon and, often, we children went along. For the most part though we worshipped at Batheaston and Reggie Evans used to come back for a drink occasionally. When my father was church treasurer the large farmhouse table in the kitchen would be covered with the contents of that Sunday's collection and we would all arrange the coins into piles for counting.

It was a happy, secure, sunny existence. Then the dog went mad.

Tim was the wire-haired terrier we had purchased while still at Quell Cottage. He was a pedigree and had always been a bit excitable. He had a particular hatred of the telephone and whenever it rang he would run round in circles barking wildly. Once my grandmother flapped a tea towel at him while he was doing this and he bit her so badly that she had to be taken to hospital for stitches.

The family took this in its stride as a one-off. After all, the dog had been provoked when already stressed. It had always been good natured and got on with the cat and visiting children so surely there could be no cause for alarm. About a year after we arrived at The Mead, Tim began to growl and bark at my father every suppertime. Then he took to attacking.

I was forbidden ever to be alone with him and our walks and ball-throwing abruptly ended, while my parents resorted to hugely expensive veterinary treatment. If visitors came, Tim was shut away. Once I was handing something to my mother and Tim jumped up between us and nipped my arm. It was a very fleeting and trivial pain but my feelings were hurt. I knew it to be unreasonable but I reacted as if the dog had rejected all the love I had given it.

Eventually Tim went to the vet for a make-or-break operation and died during the surgery. My parents never owned a dog again. The dog was mine and the cat my brother's but Tim had attached himself to my father and Monty, the cat, attached himself to me, which perhaps was unsurprising as I did not spend months away, unlike my brother at college in Bristol.

The night before we were due to move to The Mead, Monty, who had arrived at Quell Cottage on the back of my brother's bicycle from the chicken farm, had been shut in what was to be my bedroom with both door and window firmly closed. The latter had two catches, one at the bottom and one at the side. He opened both and escaped.

The next day we hunted high and low, in the lane, the surrounding fields and amidst the untamed grass of our own garden. We were alarmed and bereft but above all baffled. How on earth had he done it?

Monty returned, unruffled, that evening. I took him up to bed with me, secured the window and went to sleep. The next morning the window was open and the cat once more gone. Eventually my mother watched him in action: he lifted up the lower catch with his paw and then used both paws to release the side catch. And there are those who claim cats are not intelligent!

In my last year at The Mead, Monty caught cat flu and, despite the best and prolonged efforts of the vet, he died. For the first time since I had come back from Singapore we were petless. I missed Monty dreadfully but my parents were unwilling to get another cat until the future was settled because in 1961 we were on the move again.

Chapter Four

CONVENT GIRL

This time the posting was to London and at first my father considered a weekly commute from Bath. Today Bath is easily commutable on a daily basis but then the journey was by steam train and as he worked long hours it was regarded as too much. I was settled at school, my brother was at college in nearby Bristol and The Mead, redecorated throughout and with a now beautiful garden, was a pleasant enough pasture.

However the landlady, Mrs Smith, who lived in Ireland, wanted a higher rent. Additionally my father was now the Director of Victualling at the Admiralty and it seemed unlikely that he would ever be posted away from London again. Eventually my parents decided the future was stable enough for them to buy their own house somewhere in the commuter belt and chose the village of Normandy, near Guildford.

Today fifty would be a decidedly late age at which to be buying one's first home but renting was common enough then and particularly among service personnel. My parents were hugely excited but I am ashamed to say that I turned my nose up when I saw the house. It was a very ordinary three-bedroomed house in a row of six similar ones in a small road called Mariners' Drive and to my mind the only redeeming feature was the disproportionately large garden which backed on to a small field where horses were kept.

Megohm would have been as small but I had left when too young to take much notice of my surroundings. Our two Admiralty residences, Ordnance House in Gosport and 300 Kloof Road in Singapore had been large, as was The Mead and the house in Blatchington Road, Tunbridge Wells, had enough bedrooms for me to use a big one solely as a playroom. Only Quell Cottage had been small but what it lacked in size it made up in character and location and, anyway, at least we all had our own bedrooms. Now it was a squash. Huge quantities of our furniture had to go and I was reduced from two rooms to one. I am afraid I grumbled mightily.

I was thirteen and had begun to transform my playroom at The Mead to a more grown-up space. An old table served as a desk and I put two deckchairs by the fireplace, pretending they were armchairs. Books were arranged on the large, deep window-sills and against one wall was the piano which my mother had from childhood. I had no ear for music, as fans of *Strictly Come Dancing* will have discerned, and played entirely by reading the notes from a score, but I was enthusiastic enough and having private lessons from Madam Pascal at school. There was however no room for the piano at Mariners' Drive and it suffered the ignominy of being housed in the garage. I often wonder if I would have kept up my music if the piano had continued to occupy a more central space.

Worse, my brother had no bedroom of his own but had to sleep on a divan in the dining room in the vacations. My parents, grandmother and I took the three rooms upstairs. The house itself was renamed Keng Hua after the beautiful, scented flower of Singapore.

My grandmother was now in declining health. She was in her mid-eighties and had suffered from arthritis since before I was born. On the eve of the move from Bath to Guildford my mother, grandmother, brother and I were staying in a hotel because The Mead had been emptied. My father was not with us so I think he must have been looking after the move from the Bath end or perhaps my mother had shooed him away for a couple of days while she settled us in the new house.

My mother took my brother and me out to dinner but Gran was too tired from the journey and, in any event, had for some time not been keen on going out. When we returned it was to find that she had caused a disturbance at the hotel, having become disorientated and uncertain where she was. From then on her mental as well as physical health went downhill.

The only money Gran had was her old-age pension but every week she insisted on giving my brother a sixpence and me a threepenny bit. Then one day she gave me a shilling for 'the other one'. My mother told me not to worry, her mind was wandering and we could just put the shilling back when she wasn't looking. Don't contradict her, I was told. When she talks rubbish, go along with it.

On another occasion, when she was sitting outside, she fell off her chair twice. My brother, who was planting a row of cypresses, which is there till this day, rushed to pick her up. Shortly after that she took to her bed.

Once it was decided to leave Bath I was given the choice between changing schools yet again or boarding at the Convent and there was no contest: I boarded. I had no objections to change as such, but I was too happy at school to want to leave. The fast stream did O levels in four years instead of five and I was about to enter the pre-exam year, I liked the teachers in the subjects I was good at and I had an idea of boarding schools based on Enid Blyton's Mallory Towers.

When I came home at half-term Gran Plum only just recognised me. She gave me threepence with which to return to school and called me her 'dear soul'. I never saw her again.

My brother came over from Bristol to break the news of her death. I was called out of class and told that Malcolm was in the parlour.

The parlour was a lounge immediately beside the big, wooden front door of the Convent. All visitors were put there. When we were being collected at the end of term the message would be conveyed to us: 'Your parents are in the parlour.' Once, when somebody was being expelled, we looked at each other with huge eyes and whispered, 'Her parents are in the parlour.'

Why Malcolm should now be in the parlour I did not know, but a visitor from home was always welcome and I shot along to find out. Of course the nuns already knew why he was there and looked at me gravely but I emerged dry-eyed.

'And isn't it the sensible girl that you are now?' said Madam Evangelista with relief. In reality it was merely a case of postponed grief, which overwhelmed me that night when I wept copiously under the bedclothes hoping the other girls wouldn't hear. It wasn't that I was afraid of disturbing them but of being myself disturbed by someone bringing misguided comfort. I wanted to be alone with my memories and sorrow.

My brother's mission was not only to tell me that Gran Plum had died but also to dissuade me from attending her funeral. My parents held the view, then quite common though by no means universal, that funerals were not the place for children. I actually wanted to go but did what I thought they wanted and my father wrote to tell me that they were relieved by my decision as Gran never did 'approve of women and children at funerals'. Presumably my mother, being her daughter, was exempt from the rule!

I wept that night and other nights and once, when I was ill in bed and alone in the dormitory, I wept by day as well, passing off my red eyes as the result of the flu which had confined me there. Soon, however, it was the end of term and my mother was in the parlour. Piling my cases into YKE, off we went, via Stonehenge and the White Horse, there being then no M4. I was always offered the choice between going home via Salisbury plain or via Andover and Devizes.

Home meant different things to the girls with whom I shared a dormitory. Some were going to grandparents and godparents and would not see their parents until the summer, others spent time with friends from school. Many of the forces children were RAF and even when their parents were in Britain, home would be a different airbase from the term before.

The girls were often at the Convent because their brothers were at Prior Park but the school also had some cachet abroad because we used to get girls from Spain and France. One family of three, Marie-José, Eugenia and Mercedes Beraza arrived speaking no English and left fluent, having already been schooled in France. They used to show us pictures of themselves and Juan Carlos, the King of Spain. Eugenia became very friendly with a girl in my form called Elizabeth Martin who then went and stayed with the family.

That was unusual because foreign holidays were then the exception not the norm. For the most part we went to Cornwall or the Lakes or Scotland. Often people went nowhere but merely had time off with outings to beaches. By the time I was leaving school in 1966 that was changing and I went to stay with a naval family in Malta. The school made the occasional pilgrimage to Rome and I went in both the first and sixth forms, and there was another to Lourdes which I elected not to join, being then uninterested in its history.

School itself was strict, even by the standards of the age, and old-fashioned. In one dormitory each bed had a coverlet which had to have a certain number of immaculate horizontal creases crossed by a specified number of equally immaculate vertical creases. To obtain this effect we folded up the entire fabric into a small rectangle, wet the edges and placed the result between two pieces of cardboard before putting that in turn under our mattresses.

In the morning everybody's coverlet had the required number of creases going in the required directions except mine, which looked as if it had spent the night being fought over by two pigs. Each day I was reprimanded, but I simply could not acquire the knack. Then, just when I was beginning to dread the return to the dormitory after breakfast, I noticed that the best-folded coverlet belonged to a girl, Linda Seale, for whom Latin was a mystery incapable of being unravelled, so from then on she folded my coverlet and I did her Latin prep and the nuns did not find out until we had moved to a different dormitory where the coverlets were of candlewick and required no creases.

Each girl was supplied with a washing-up bowl and a glass carafe. With these we queued in the mornings outside the one and only loo on the corridor and filled them up from the small wash basin. We then took them back, pulled curtains around our own allocated space, which housed a bed, dressing table and small, single wardrobe, and performed such ablutions as we could. After breakfast we came back, made our beds and emptied our bowls and carafes. Twice a week we went up to the bathroom floor for a bath and once a fortnight washed our hair at a row of basins by the bathrooms.

The carafes were cleaned at the end of each term by tearing up strips of newspapers, stuffing them into the carafes until they could take no more and leaving them to soak overnight. The mirrors over our dressing tables had to be cleaned each week but, ever impractical, all I managed to do was smear mine until I was rescued by Judy Avenell, a doctor's daughter from Truro, who was at the Convent because her brother was at Prior Park.

We went to Mass before breakfast in the school chapel, rising at 6.30 a.m. on Tuesdays and Thursdays and at 7 a.m. on Fridays when we had benediction as well. The incense at benediction always upset my stomach, especially when combined with the cold milk which accompanied Friday cereal. In the third form we had to polish our desks on Friday as well and the smell of the wax was the final straw. For that entire year I felt sick on Fridays.

On Saturday there was no Mass but we had Rosary in the evenings and on Sunday we had Mass in the morning. We prayed on being woken. One nun, Madam Ignatius, an easy-going soul whom we all liked, would insist on audible answers to the morning litany when it was her turn to call us.

'Great St Joseph ...'

Silence.

'Great St Joseph!'

A mumbled 'pray for us' from one bed.

'Great St Joseph ...'

And so it went on, until we had all answered in unison. Even now I joke that I do not need an alarm clock but merely somebody standing by the bed bellowing 'Great St Joseph'.

In the morning and at night the boarders were assembled on one of the landings opposite a picture of Mary, mother of Our Lord, to pray. We prayed again at morning assembly for the whole school and again at afternoon assembly, but once we had left the prep school there was no angelus at noon. We were too focused on lessons.

Non-Catholics, as we were called, made up a sizeable minority of the school but there were no concessions to us. Anglican boarders could not attend their own church on Sundays but must go to Mass instead. We were taught religion separately, our lessons focusing on scripture and the Catholics' on doctrine. In chapel my schoolmates asked Mary to 'intercede for our separated brethren, that with us in the one true fold . . .' regardless of the fact that the separated brethren were kneeling beside them.

In 1962 the Second Vatican Council, which was to introduce Mass in the vernacular with the priest facing the people and encourage ecumenical services, convened with a great fanfare, but none of its reforms was implemented until after I had left school. The Catholicism I knew was still largely exclusive, intolerant and encumbered with minute rules, which it was deemed mortal sin to break.

Some years after I left I went to the final vows of a fellow pupil, Helen Williams, and found a Catholic church operating entirely in the vernacular and singing hymns to modern music. That change continued until nuns no longer wore habits which touched the ground, nor veils which covered every last hair. Eventually they could even choose to be known by their own names and Madam Ignatius became Sister Pat Scammerton.

Yet even in the mid-sixties relations between the churches were thawing. I was allowed, at seventeen, to prepare for Anglican confirmation by attending outside classes and when at eighteen I was confirmed in Bath Abbey by the Bishop of Taunton it was not at all awkward to ask the nun who was headmistress, Madam Bernard Xavier, and the one who taught me Latin, Madam Evangelista, to come to the service. After much thought they declined, but there would have been a time when it would have been unthinkable even to invite them.

The strain between the Church of England and the Roman Catholic Church was not produced solely by the latter's insistence on its possession of absolute truth. I was growing up in a household where the main influence was evangelical and my brother and his fellow ordinands dismissed Catholic teaching as not only heretical but also riddled with superstition. He gave me formulae to deal with the situation of being expected to comply with a faith I did not follow.

For example when the Host (the consecrated communion bread) was being transported between the chapel and a sick nun and we happened to meet the priest on a corridor as he was carrying it we were expected to kneel down and bow our heads. My brother told me to comply (as if I had a choice!) but to pray in my head 'I thank you, Lord, for your free salvation, which doesn't depend on any nonsense like this.'

Both Churches were massively ignorant of what the other believed. At school a nun asked me if Anglicans believed in the Holy Ghost while at home I would hear my brother insist that Catholics thought Mary divine. When the Mass was finally translated into the vernacular Anglicans marvelled at how similar it was to their own service, as if somehow we had no common, pre-Reformation roots. It was a phenomenon which I found frustrating whenever it manifested itself and certainly it made me embrace the ecumenical movement. I was nonetheless convinced that Catholicism was both theologically unsound and superstitious.

I was confirmed in that view almost every year when the school flooded. Built on low-lying land next to the River Avon, it suffered most years from some degree of flooding, but occasionally the rain brought worse than the normal inch or so of river water. We would watch it creeping towards us, across the playing fields, on to the tennis courts and then into the buildings. Once, before I joined the school, boarders were evacuated over the roof of the gymnasium and when we had a brand-new building containing assembly hall and science laboratories it was built feet above the highest ever recorded flood level. That year the flood record was broken and it too was awash.

Each year the nuns placed a statue of St Joseph in the grounds, facing the river. 'Superstition,' I grumbled to a devout Catholic friend. 'Statues have no power.' Rather to my surprise, she agreed. I still hold to that view but these days accept the role of statues as reminders of the saints. At home the reaction was even more robust. 'Graven images,' snorted my mother.

As if floods were not enough, a dormitory was burnt out by fire. It was not the one in which I slept, but I remember the reaction of the girls whose belongings were consumed by the flames. They wept for the small things: family photos, childhood bears, reminders of home. Liz Martin cried for her old dressing gown which she had owned for years but, miraculously, it survived, the wardrobe in which it was housed being only partially burnt. We all cheered Liz's dressing gown.

The nuns reminded us, very gently, that if a single boarder or nun had been missing we wouldn't be so preoccupied with our possessions. They, of course, possessed nothing.

These traumas apart, our lives were regimented and each minute predictable. At four o'clock when school ended the boarders went to have tea, which was bread and butter with jam. On Tuesdays it was enlivened with a piece of cake. Sometimes a girl had a birthday and her table in the refectory would benefit from the cake her parents had sent. Mine was ordered by my mother from a bakery called The Red House and was invariably walnut and cream. Occasionally parents sent 'feasts', parcels of biscuits and other tuck which would be shared in the dormitory.

At four thirty we went to prep. This was supervised by a nun or prefect until we reached the upper sixth, after which we were considered to be able to concentrate alone. The rule was always silence but we could ask to visit the library or to consult another girl if we were stuck. At seven we had supper and then half an hour's recreation and then, regardless of age, bed. Lights went out at different times according to the average age in the dormitory but we all went upstairs together, prep school, first formers and sixth formers. That only changed in my last year there. The outside world was in the grip of the swinging sixties but at La Sainte Union Convent de Sacre Coeur eighteen-year-olds went to bed at 8 p.m.! Sometimes, when there was no recreation, we went at 7.30.

Weekends were also parcelled out for us. On Saturdays we did prep all morning, then after lunch we went to shoe cleaning, which involved cleaning indoor and outdoor shoes along with our gym shoes and hockey boots. It was the one day of the week when we could wear our own clothes. This was followed by recreation, then Rosary, supper and bed. Sundays meant

Mass before breakfast, then prep all morning and after lunch letter-writing. Only when we had reached the third form could we send off our letters without their having first been read by a nun.

We were told never to send unhappy letters or bad news as this would worry our parents and especially if they were abroad and far away from us; so we told of any small triumph such as coming first or being selected for a team and omitted failure. Of course we never told tales, but fortunately there was no real bullying.

Girls do not bully in the same way as boys and I can recall no instance of anyone being physically hurt, but friendships can be broken and cliques formed, which certainly happened, and girls are adept at hurtful comments. One in our dormitory was especially good at making unkind remarks about families, but on the whole we boarders constituted a minority of girls in the school who tended to stick together and help each other.

Our Sunday letters would be posted that evening at the sorting office near Bath station and would arrive with the first post on Monday morning and that was in the days of manual sorting and steam trains! My mother would grab her spectacles and run down the stairs in her dressing gown as soon as the post landed on the mat. Once, in the sixth form, I was simply too lazy to write the weekly missive and she rang up the school in concern.

After letter-writing we were formed into a crocodile for the Sunday walk. Our daily uniform was maroon but on Sundays we put on blue suits with fawn hats and, with nuns fore and aft, walked up the Warminster Road in descending order of age. At the point where we turned round was a small newsagent who also sold sweets and we would swoop on the goods as if we hadn't had a roast lunch.

Sweets were not regarded as bad for us and I always had a bar of chocolate or a Penguin at break. Indeed it did not seem to do us much harm as there were precious few fat children at any of the schools I attended and I still weighed only six stone twelve as I was approaching thirty. However what did suffer were teeth. We all had fillings galore.

Once we reached the fourth form we were allowed out alone for two hours on a Saturday afternoon and after letter-writing on a Sunday. I began to go to the afternoon service at Bath Abbey, as it was my only chance to attend an Anglican service, but on Saturdays we wandered round the shops and then had tea in Fortes or the Swiss café. Gradually an increasing number of girls used to go to the Salamander coffee bar with the explicit intention of meeting boys from Downside or Prior Park. They would then come back and talk about nothing else. As we thought that these rendezvous would not have met with the nuns' approval, who were, after all, *in loco parentis*, the conversation took a different turn when the dormitory nun came in.

Each dormitory had a nun attached to it who slept there, and that applied to the senior dormitory as much as to the most junior one. It was a guarantee that we would not make a noise or talk after lights-out, but it did not stop us reading under the bedclothes with torches. The lights along Pulteney Road were strong and another trick was to get between the curtain and the window and to read in such illumination as they afforded.

I often wonder how I, who came from a background of roaming free in the countryside and playing all day unsupervised, managed with such close supervision, with my every minute overseen, but somehow I seemed to cope. The handful of girls who came to board at a late stage found it well nigh impossible, and no wonder, but the rest of us just became acclimatised. There was home and there was school and they were very different.

Who were the nuns who imposed this old-fashioned regime while the sixties swamped the rest of the world with Beatlemania, mini-skirts and a new-found prosperity?

The order was French in origin, which is why we called the nuns 'Madam' rather than 'Sister'. Not long after I left that changed and the pupils found it hard to suddenly address as 'Sister' those they had for years called 'Madam'. The head of the convent was not Mother Superior but Reverend Mother and, overwhelmingly, the Sisters came from Ireland. There were still plenty of vocations and the nuns formed a large portion of the teaching staff, which was all female. Indeed the only man we saw in term time, other than visiting members of our own families, was the priest.

After Vatican Two some left and over the succeeding decades vocations have dried up. A tiny handful of nuns, living in a house on Pulteney Road, is all that now remains of Bath Convent, the school having closed in 1979 rather than become comprehensive.

For boarders, release arrived every third Saturday when we were allowed out all day in the care of an appropriate adult. Malcolm would come over from Bristol and take me to the cinema or to visit people we had known in Batheaston. If he could not manage it then Mrs Mitchell, the lady who had lived opposite The Mead and who had lost her husband to cancer, would fulfil the role. On one occasion Malcolm arrived to take me out for the day to find that I had been grounded.

A group of us in the third-form dormitory had decided that we would dress up as ghosts and go down to the common room to play the piano on the feast of St Cecilia but when the moment arrived Judy Avenell and Linda Seale backed out, leaving Liz Martin and me as the only participants.

It was not the easiest of tasks to pull the sheets from our beds without disturbing Madam Agnes Patricia and to drape them over ourselves in the dark, but we managed to accomplish both that and creeping out of the dormitory undetected. We then made our way down the stairs, along a short corridor until we reached the common room, where Liz played the piano in honour of the patron saint of music. Unfortunately as we returned Madam Agnes Patricia was waiting for us round a corner and jumped several feet at the appearance of two ghostly figures.

Unbeknown to us, a nun was dying in the convent that very night and various members of the community were moving about when normally all would have been in bed. One can understand that in the heightened state that preparing for a death usually produces, our antics could have produced severe shock. We did not know about the death until the next morning, but that cut no ice with Madam Bernard Xavier, the headmistress, who kept us in for the whole of our precious third Saturday.

Our antics produced a curious postscript. Both Liz and I were questioned about whether we had been on the 'black corridor', so called because of the colour of its linoleum tiles, during our prank. We had not but we were asked several times over the course of the next week, with forced casualness, the same question. To this day I do not know what happened on the black corridor that night.

The fast stream took O levels in the fourth form and then went straight into the sixth form, bypassing the fifth altogether. I chose to take Latin, Ancient History and English at A level with the first also at Scholarship level. At this time I thought, as I had for some while, that I should like to teach Latin but, inspired by Cicero, I was also inclining towards law. I therefore hovered between History and Greek for my fourth subject, beginning with the latter but eventually switching to history. It was then normal practice for students aiming at Oxford or additional A levels to return for a third year in the sixth form and it was from this group that the head girl and house captains were chosen. I became head of St Winifred's House. I was also busy with extra-mural activities: debating for the school, competing in the Mid Somerset Festival public-speaking competition, entering short-story competitions and running the classical society which I had founded in the first year sixth. A group of schools got together to put on a concert for old folks and then came the school dance.

The dance caused an enormous ripple because such a bold venture had never happened before, but the senior half of the school plus senior boys from Prior Park and Downside came together for the frivolity in the Assembly Rooms, much loved by Jane Austen. We drank sherry and teachers sat along a row of chairs keeping a very beady eye on proceedings. I danced half the night with a chap called Nicholas Moore whom I never saw again.

Dancing was largely ballroom, although there were modern records to which we did the twist and the jive. Once when we did the twist during recreation Madam Evangelista described the spectacle as the closest approach to savages she had ever seen. Many decades later Anton du Beke was to lament the advent of the twist and the success of Chubby Checker, but for rather different reasons.

He told me that until that moment the man had always had contact with the woman while dancing but the invention of the twist meant that everybody danced alone. He regarded this as severely retrograde.

Until the dance the highlight of the school year had been St Patrick's Day on 17 March when half the school sported shamrock, we all sang 'For God and St Patrick' at assembly and there was no prep. Once, driving past the Convent at about 10 p.m., my mother glimpsed through a window nuns dancing an Irish jig.

In those strict days the nuns from Ireland were never certain if they would ever see their homeland again, being sent wherever their Order decided and bound by their vow of obedience to go. I understand better now the importance to them of St Patrick's Day than I did at the time.

My interest in politics and a possible political career was growing. I enjoyed debating, and Mrs Rhymes, who ran both the debating society and the literary society, told me to do away with notes as much as possible and to concentrate on answering the points made by the other side rather than to produce a set piece. I was often to be asked by selection committees in later years if I had learned my speeches by heart or if they were really off the cuff. It never failed to impress them that there were no notes. Thanks, Mrs Rhymes.

Meanwhile my brother became ordained and then engaged. Shortly after the former event he brought me back from a third Saturday and the parlour filled with nuns wanting to congratulate him. 'The adoration of the Magi had nothing on it,' he later remarked to my parents.

The news of his engagement was received with less enthusiasm by a community which believed firmly in the celibacy of the clergy. I was both excited and uncertain, wondering whether my brother might be preoccupied with other matters now on third Saturdays.

It was Malcolm who responded to the one and only emergency of my life at the Convent. In the autumn term of 1963 I was taken ill with appendicitis and rushed to the Royal United Hospital. I lay on the common room sofa in agony while the nuns sent for Doctor Tierney, who said he thought it was an appendix problem but he could not be sure. As we waited for the ambulance Madam Mary Celine and Madam Ignatius, both of whom taught biology, began recounting to each other tales of people who had their appendices removed unnecessarily and who had either suffered badly or died. It was not the most reassuring conversation to which I have listened.

Half the boarders were peering out of the dormitory windows as the ambulance, bell ringing, took me away. I had been supposed to sell poppies in the city centre the next day but instead lay recuperating in hospital after an operation which, far from being unnecessary, had been only just in time. My parents, alerted by the headmistress, were on their way from Guildford but they had already rung up Malcolm and told him to go at once to his little sister.

My father took the call from my mother in the middle of a golf match which he conceded on the spot. I wonder how they might have reacted had they been in Singapore instead of Surrey.

Hospitals were regimented places in 1963. We were woken at 5.30 a.m. with weak tea. The nurses fussed over the exact position of the portion of sheet which was turned over the blanket. The consultant's rounds were like a visitation from the Pope and Matron was regarded with the awe normally reserved for the Deity. Visiting hours were twice daily between specific times and the numbers and ages of visitors subject to fixed rules.

I was there for nearly a fortnight – that being then the norm – after which I was sent home to recuperate with a list of what I could not do. Madam Ignatius was disappointed that I did not bring my appendix with me, as she had wished to display it in a jar in the biology room. The girl next to me in the dormitory,

Stephanie Molyneux, had packed up my suitcases which I was forbidden to lift.

I was at home, reading by a crackling fire while my mother was collecting my father from the station, when I heard of the assassination of President Kennedy.

I left in 1966 and took a great deal with me that was useful in later life: as one of a religious minority when these differences mattered I had learned to stand up for my beliefs; Mrs Rhymes had given me confidence through debating; Madam Evangelista had left me with what was to be a lifelong love of Latin; Madam Bernard Xavier had ingrained the values of self-discipline and hard work; boarding had exposed me to the constant give and take which was necessary in living in a large group and the ethos of the school had left me deeply competitive.

On the debit side, children were taught always to bow to authority without any possibility of challenge, no matter how respectful, and were constantly put down in front of their peers. A child would frequently hear herself torn to pieces in front of the whole class. The prefects had too much power to punish and humiliate. Those who were wanting academically were rebuked for low marks. House meetings were all about competition and who had failed as well as who had succeeded. True, it was so normal that few were affected by such discipline, but it should not have been like that.

I was reasonably able and reasonably well behaved so I survived unscathed. Others were less fortunate. Certainly in the midst of the 1960s we had been sheltered and I doubt if many among us were what we would now call streetwise. Innocent, ambitious, optimistic and full of dreams in 1966 I set forth to make my mark on the world.

Chapter Five

REDBRICK

Birmingham was my university of fifth choice. My first was Oxford and in the autumn term of my final year at Bath Convent I sat the entrance exam with three other girls before enduring the tense wait to see if any of us would qualify for an interview. We were to be notified by telegram and one dark winter's morning, as we made our way from the chapel to breakfast, I heard the bell of the front door peal.

'That's my telegram,' I joked to Judy Avenell.

A few minutes later the portress, a nun of advanced years, panted into the refectory and put the much-coveted missive in my hands. The excitement was massive, with everyone crowding round me to see the offer of an interview from St Anne's. Throughout breakfast nun after nun came in to congratulate me and I was woefully late returning upstairs to make my bed.

When the day girls arrived I found that two of my fellow applicants had no news but another, Angela Madigan, was also summoned for interview. I rang home with the news, decided on the appropriate clothes and thought of nothing else. Oxford!

I wanted to go to Oxford or Cambridge for no reason other than that they were the best. I had covered all my options by applying to four universities for Law, one for Latin and to Birmingham for Ancient History and Archaeology. To Oxford it had been for Law but I could not understand why I was persistently asked in the course of the interviews if I had any relations at the bar. Only afterwards did I realise that the dons, not observing the slight difference in spelling, were wondering if I were related to David Widdicombe, a QC of some renown.

The letter of rejection was very flattering. My work was of a high standard, I had done well at interview but too many applicants ... It was small consolation that Angela, who was cleverer than I, also failed at the final hurdle.

Later I wondered if I should not have simply taken what is now called a gap year and tried again with intense cramming, which was a not unusual route, but I had already stayed on for an extra year in the sixth form and the outcome was too uncertain to risk. St Andrews, my second choice, and Birmingham made me offers and as the latter was unconditional and St Andrews meant four years instead of three, I chose Birmingham. It was a good decision and one I never had a moment's cause to regret.

That summer I took my first holiday job, wanting extra money to add to the generous parental allowance. My grant, being based on parental income, was the minimum £50 but our tuition was free and graduate debt virtually non-existent.

The job was with the Admiralty as an administrative assistant and was meant to last six weeks but as the fourth week was approaching I had an urgent call from Madam Bernard Xavier. A teacher was off sick and another had unexpectedly left. Could I go back to tide them over the first few weeks of term?

Thus, a couple of months after I thought the Convent had disappeared from my life, I was back as a temporary member of staff teaching history. I enjoyed the experience tremendously and knew that I could be happy teaching. Of course a great many of my lessons were on periods I had not studied, so I kept ahead of the forms by reading a chapter of the textbook in advance but still children went home and told their parents they 'had never learned so much history'!

My biggest error was in referring to the Bloody Assize. The form just giggled helplessly.

'Oh, there are worse traps than that,' my fellow history teacher assured me. 'Avoid at all costs some of the Latin imperatives.' At eighteen I was too innocent to understand. Nowadays I would probably know the word at six. Indeed I was in the second form (year eight in modern parlance) when the Chatterley trial was in full throttle and Mrs Rhymes told us that we were too young to know the details.

I was a few months short of my sixteenth birthday when the

Profumo affair shook the country and that was the first time I learned what a prostitute does. Such matters were never discussed at school but at home there was a more relaxed attitude and my father asked me why Christine Keeler had been expelled from the Labour Party. The answer was that she was becoming too liberal with the Tories. That was our notion of rude humour in the early sixties.

When I finished my short teaching stint I felt as if I were leaving the Convent all over again. At the end of the previous term the leavers had signed each other's boaters, thrown their felt hats in the Avon and taken their Box Brownies to Cyril Howe's to have the snaps of the occasion developed. This time I simply caught a train from Bath station, but a few weeks later was back again to collect my certificates on Speech Day. The girls roared when I went up to the stage and as I was never a particularly popular prefect I could take it only as a tribute to my teaching.

My parents were as ever there for the event and asked me how Birmingham was going. I replied that I was loving it, and I was. It was however not all plain sailing.

Upon arrival I decided to switch from Ancient History and Archaeology to Latin, with Greek supplementary, knowing that I could still specialise in Roman History in my special options. Everybody was very helpful but the negotiations were nonetheless stressful for someone straight out of convent school who had been taught never to challenge authority except when ordered to sin. Then there was the compulsory sport.

It may seem quaint now but at Birmingham we all had to participate in a sport for the first year. I had been terrible at sport at school and eschewed the obvious hockey, netball and tennis. Instead, having sailed in Malta during a holiday and having enjoyed it, I signed up for sailing lessons.

There is a difference between sailing on the Mediterranean and sailing on a Birmingham reservoir and, oh, what a dashed difference! The reservoir was freezing cold. We sailed in biting winds and pulled on wet ropes. In Malta a capsize would have been fun, in Birmingham it would have been undiluted misery. I came to dread Wednesdays.

'I like it after I have done it,' said Chantâle Lyons, who had been in the same form at Bath Convent and had also chosen sailing at Birmingham, where she was reading French. It was an admirable summary as there was undeniably a sense of achievement when one had landed safely but no enjoyment while actually out on the water. As winter deepened, I gave up and switched to riding.

That decision was as good as sailing had been bad. I kept up the sport into my second and third years and thereafter until I entered Parliament, falling in love with a series of horses, taking trekking holidays on Dartmoor, learning some modest jumping. Alas, a decade after becoming an MP I got on a horse for the first time since being elected and found my nerve had gone.

There are skills you never forget, such as riding a bicycle, and skills which need continual practice if they are to remain at any given level and I do so wish I had appreciated that more when I was younger. I came back from Singapore with my swimming, especially my crawl, at competitive standard but today I simply move up and down a pool in a gentle breaststroke. I could not dive to save my life and can reach the bottom of the pool only at depths of five or six feet.

That was not entirely my fault as England then had few swimming facilities and the nearest pool, a lido, was eight miles away and there was very little swimming at the Convent. It was however my fault that I made no time to maintain my riding skills as it was also entirely my own decision not to maintain the piano playing.

My mother learned as a child until she reached grade seven and could always play, even after years of not doing so, but I gave up too soon when the piano went to the garage and from being then able to read a score containing sharps and flats I now cannot so much as make my hands play different sets of notes from each other.

My biggest loss is my fluency in Latin. I now struggle to translate it and when retirement settles down into peace and quiet that is one skill I fully intend to renew. Had I ridden and swum hard once a month, played just one piano score a week and translated no more than a page of Latin each fortnight I would have kept all of those abilities.

At Birmingham riding became a serious recreation. Weighing six stone twelve pounds and standing five feet and one inch high, I was known to the Umberslade Riding School in Dark Horse Lane as 'the small student' and was always mounted on small horses, which gave me confidence. It took two buses to get there and sometimes I travelled back covered in mud from the gallops. I tried to interest other girls from the hall of residence but nobody fell in love with riding as I did.

Everybody remembers his or her first car and everybody remembers the first horse. He was called Popcorn and had a black-and-white mane which used to wave in the air when I cantered. I then graduated to a larger horse, Suntan. At home I rode Jigsaw and Puzzle at a stables in Liphook and then a series of horses belonging to somebody in the same road.

Another shock arriving at Birmingham was the intensity of the work, for which I was ill prepared. Madam Evangelista had always insisted that we read works in the original and use translations only as an aid. Now, faced with reading a book of *The Aeneid* every week, Tacitus's histories and Euripides in Greek I could not keep up until I realised that everyone else was managing by reading these works in translation and simply doing sections only in the original. As fluency increased so did the amount read in the original until translations were indeed just an aid. I had effectively been trying to run before I could walk.

I did, however excel at Ancient History, taught by Doctor Wilkes, and Roman history has remained a passion throughout my life.

My hall of residence was Mason Hall, which was part of a collection of halls known as the Vale Site and clustered around an artificial lake on which floated ducks. Mixed halls were not then the norm as the age of majority was still twenty-one and the university was *in loco parentis*. Mason was divided into a male wing and female wing and initially there was not even mixed dining, while rules governed the times at which we could visit each other's wings.

In my first year I shared a room with Anne Jenkins, who was reading German. Anne was a very sensible girl but it amused my mother hugely that when we arrived her parents were still with her and had obviously remained only to see whether the room-mate was suitable because they left shortly afterwards. Who shared with whom was decided arbitrarily by the authorities but Anne and I got on well, although we did not become lifelong friends and indeed did not see each other much after that first year when Anne went off to a flat-share and I was allocated my own room in Mason.

Anne smoked fairly copiously. It is impossible now to imagine a university placing a smoker and non-smoker in the same room but we knew little then about passive smoking. Indeed many of the girls in Mason smoked and some would even argue that it was not addictive. We understood the connection with lung cancer but the role of tobacco in other cancers, heart disease and stroke was simply unknown to the public at large. My reasons for not joining in were not based on health at all but on my hating the smell of stale cigarette smoke.

Mason Hall was a good transition for me. I had come from an all-girls school so an all-girls hall of residence was not so strange and it was from there rather than the Latin department that I made lasting friendships. The university had a flourishing Christian Union and every Saturday night we met at the campus chapel to hear a preacher deliver a fire-and-brimstone-style sermon. By then Malcolm was building a big reputation for himself, revitalising a church hitherto marked for closure, and I always hoped he might be invited to preach but there was a rule that nobody came unless a member of the committee had heard him so my brother preached at Christian Unions in universities up and down the country but never at Birmingham.

At Mason Hall we had a Bible study and prayer group which in my last year used to meet in my room. The Pentecostal movement was beginning to undergo a revival and then came Billy Graham's mission during which the Hall was assigned a missionary, Rosemary Aldis. The campus was plastered with posters urging people to 'Consider Jesus Christ' and members of the Christian Union acted as counsellors during the huge rallies which were being addressed by Graham in person or relayed from other venues.

It is a matter of great sorrow to me that the tele-evangelists who have followed Billy Graham have proved so venal and grasping. I have urged several TV companies to consider letting me go to the States to record a programme on them and their influence, because I doubt if many of them have considered the lilies of the field for a very long time indeed but so far no media have accepted the idea.

Little did I know then that in a few years' time I would go through a prolonged stage of agnosticism, but it was not only Christians who were promoting their cause in as vigorous a manner as possible. This was the age of socialism, of student unrest and of sit-ins and it was against this background that my political views and ambitions were crystallising.

The world was then divided into two great conflicting political philosophies: capitalism and communism, and there was a battle for the future of the globe manifested by the Cold War and the Berlin Wall. In the West that battle was between capitalism and socialism but it was fundamentalist socialism and about as far removed from the New Labour movement of Tony Blair as Kinnock from Thatcher.

Harold Wilson was in power, the unions were at the peak of their might and the country was bedevilled by strikes both official and unofficial. The so-called permissive society had taken off with the abolition of the death penalty, legalisation of abortion and of homosexual acts between consenting adults. Easier divorce was to follow. Grammar schools were being abolished and replaced by comprehensives. State monopolies controlled all the essential services including the Post Office (which also took in the telephone system), railways, gas, electricity and water. Labour was against private medicine and private schooling. It believed in the power of the State and wanted to increase it.

Nevertheless Wilson lost patience with the strikes which crippled the economy and made citizens' lives a misery and he was to make a doomed attempt to change their legal basis, but the country had to wait for Thatcher before the unions were reined in.

Meanwhile the Vietnam War was being waged and most students were hotly opposed to it. Unrest in the universities was rife. Tariq Ali was elected president of the Oxford Union in 1965 and at Liverpool and Birmingham universities there were sit-ins and occupations. In 1968 Paris exploded with students being joined by 10,000 workers and the future of De Gaulle himself was in doubt as pictures of the barricades dominated the world's press.

The result of this tension was that very few young people displayed the apathy which our current politicians find so frustrating. We knew which side of that enormous divide we were on and people believed that the outcome of a general election really would make a significant difference to the way the country was run. They also believed that it could make a difference to world affairs.

I have always believed in a small state, in choice, in being able to opt out of a state system if it is unsatisfactory. Occasionally I have questioned all the big principles on which my life is founded but I have never yet found that one wanting.

I used to send my parents the university magazine, *Redbrick,* which they thought should merely have been called Red, so left wing did it appear to them. By the standards of the time it was not particularly extreme in tone and I would make cameo appearances in it as a result of inter-hall debating. For two years in succession I won the University Debating Ladies Cup, the McKee Trophy, and I belonged to the Conservative Association, attending its meetings and dinners. Sadly the debating society at Birmingham was silly and childish, dirty jokes and innuendo dominating even the most serious of debates, and I never did much therefore in the Student Union.

I did however play a full part in the running of Mason Hall and my first ever electoral success was to be voted internal affairs representative, a post which largely involved getting the hair dryers and irons to each floor at the beginning of term, but it meant a place on the committee and being involved in negotiations with the senior common room over rules and in organising the annual ball.

Helping with the ball was fun but I never attended one, instead taking coats, some of which I noticed with admiration were made of real fur. Having not yet developed moral objections to the fur trade or how it operated, I was enthusiastic to be left several fur items when Auntie Dora died. Ironically one was a large fox fur with head and legs dangling. Today it languishes in the bottom of the camphorwood chest my parents brought home from Singapore, a horrible relic of a bygone age.

The reason I did not attend the ball was simple: I had no boyfriend throughout my entire time at Birmingham. The men in the Latin department were pleasant and friendly and I met equally nice chaps in the Conservative Association and in the Christian Union but none drew me to want more than friendship. Indeed social life revolved around Mason Hall and was amazingly tame for the mid-sixties.

At the end of the day's lectures and a stint in the library we returned to hall for supper and then worked in our rooms. After that we brewed up coffee in the communal kitchen and talked for hours, sometimes crowding into each other's rooms or into the small lounge that was provided on each floor. In my second year I developed a habit of going to the tiny bar on a Friday evening and drinking a glass of Dubonnet or sometimes two. Oxford was to prove somewhat different!

There is a myth today that it was impossible to be young in the sixties and not encounter drugs. I can say with my hand on my heart, or for that matter on the Good Book, that I was never offered drugs nor was I aware of anyone I knew taking them at Birmingham.

Christine Colville and I ended up in adjacent rooms for our final year and many was the translation which was worked out between us. We also measured our progress against each other when we were revising for finals and on one occasion, before the Roman Antiquities exam, we were still up when the first shades of dawn were lighting the lake.

'Those ducks have a damn good life,' I grumbled, 'gliding

about all day without a worry in the world.' Somehow the reflection, to which I have returned often in various guises, has never been enough to deter me from the competitive life.

I am still in touch with Christine (Holmes) today as I am with Pat Sagajllo (now Potts), who was a participant in our Bible study groups, Edwina Raison (Nicol) and Jill Dixon (Edge), a chemist who sadly lost her father during our time there. Pat and Jill came to spend a weekend with me in Haslemere during which we rode and took a long walk in the Devil's Punchbowl, near Hindhead.

My parents' last move was from Normandy to Haslemere in 1968. We had lived in the village for seven years, which was a record for us, but my mother wanted a bungalow for retirement and a smaller garden. It meant a longer commute for my father, but with retirement then only a few years away that did not deter him. We took the Keng Hua sign with us and called the new house by the same name. They were still there when my father died in 1999, after which my mother came to live with me.

Pat and Jill's visit came while my father was away. They had hitchhiked all the way from Birmingham but my parents had always been opposed to this method of transport, even in the company of other girls, so I went by train. Pat often hitchhiked alone and had numerous tales to tell. Once she was invited home by a male driver to meet his family and they all had a lively discussion about religion over supper. She told me she was careful and, on the advice of another lone male driver, always made sure she knew how to open the car door. Perhaps it was just safer then, but my parents did not think so. My mother, however, would give lifts even if she was alone but now that would seem pretty risky too. In particular we never ignored the hopeful thumb of a serviceman in uniform.

When it came to our return my mother insisted on driving us all back. As usual the route took us through Oxford and as usual I felt a pang. The road then was right through the city itself and I would see the sun mellow on the stone of the colleges and the occasional figure in a gown. I began to wish that I could try again.

In my first-year exams I was graded an upper second, in my

second year an equivalent of a first and in my finals I won an upper second, but the whole outcome was nearly wrecked the night before my last exam, which was Greek.

There was a bookcase on the wall above my bed of the sort which involved loose shelves being hooked into slots. I was lying there looking up and noticed that one hook was coming loose. Dangerous, I thought, and, fool that I was, I reached up to push it in while still lying there. The next thing I knew Christine had dashed in to see what the bang was. I am here today because that shelf was full of Loeb classical texts. Had it contained my Liddell and Scott or Lewis and Short dictionaries ... But it is better not to think about it. As it was, I was concussed badly.

This revealed itself not in lying dramatically unconscious but in confusion of thought. I wanted to think there was nothing to worry about: that either I would be well enough to take the exam or not, but I couldn't form the thought properly. When a couple of years later a fellow student at Lady Margaret Hall fell down some steps, got up and carried on but then announced at breakfast next day that she had taken nearly an hour to get dressed, I knew exactly what was wrong!

In the event I was taken to the health centre next day and observed, my pulse and temperature being taken every hour. All was well but I missed both the exam (they graded me on the year's work instead) and the Trooping of the Colour, to which I was due to go with my father the next day.

A great many of my friends went into teaching and a few stayed on to take higher degrees. There had been a time when I thought that I might like to do a PhD in some study of Roman history but the political bug had bitten deeply and I decided that, instead of spending the next three years with my nose in the battle of Cannae or Trasimene, I would read politics. At least I would if I could do so at Oxford or Cambridge.

I could not have done so anywhere if my father had not been prepared to pay for it as, naturally enough, local authorities did not fund second undergraduate courses but my parents regarded it as the 'equaliser'.

I have already noted that it was something of a mystery to

my father that the girl in the family was more ambitious than the boy – in worldly terms at least, there being none more ambitious than Malcolm when it came to spreading the word of the Lord – and that in keeping with the times it was Malcolm whose education my parents had always put first. Oxford would 'make us equal'.

So in the autumn of my last year I once more sat the entrance exam, this time at King Edward VI School for Girls, opposite the university. Sitting with the sixth formers who were taking it and listening to their conversation I recalled vividly that earlier, failed attempt and I was by no means confident this time. I knew I could walk the exam in terms of what might be expected for a sixth-form applicant but I did not know how high they would set the bar for a graduate.

When I was called for interview I was excited but tense, knowing this to be my very last shot at Oxford. I was in London for my father's investiture with the CB at Buckingham Palace the day before and travelled down that evening to stay at Lady Margaret Hall overnight as once I had stayed at St Anne's. Everything I saw made me determined to succeed but pessimism set in as once again I waited for the telegram.

On the day it was due I was at home in Haslemere. By noon I had given up and went out shopping, certain it was all over and that I must now decide between a PhD, a certificate of education or a job. When I returned it was to find the telegram in the kitchen on top of a present from my mother which she had purchased weeks earlier.

'I was so sure,' she said.

I looked at the missive again. 'Lady Margaret Hall offers vacancy.'

I was off to the gleaming spires.

Chapter Six

GLEAMING SPIRES

Oxford was the beginning of what was to become a relentless drive to forge a future in politics. My advice to the young today, when they ask me how to do it, is to take the opposite course. I tell them to forget politics for a while, go away, make themselves financially secure, start a family and then try for selection. If I were able to go back and utter any warnings to me at twenty-one, the one at the top of my list would be not to be in such a hurry to arrive at Westminster, that forty is really not the threshold of old age.

Sometimes it seemed that everybody at Oxford was in a hurry. The single most striking difference between Birmingham and Oxford came not from the ancient surroundings, the quads, gardens, tutorial system or the backgrounds of the undergraduates but simply from the level of open aspiration. At Birmingham students would say they wished to be journalists while at Oxford nobody thought you mad if you wanted to be editor of *The Times*. At Birmingham a few of us wanted to be MPs, at Oxford people talked with perfectly straight faces about who might be Cabinet material.

The first resort of the politically ambitious at that university was the Oxford Union, the famous debating society that attracted speakers at the peak of their professions: Cabinet ministers, broadcasters, writers, scientists and the controversial. Throughout my time at Westminster there was a steady trickle of ex-officers of the Oxford Union arriving on the green benches.

There were exceptions. Tony Blair, who was there at the same time, made not the smallest ripple on the Oxford political scene. In 1951 Shirley Williams had become the first female chairman of the Oxford University Labour Club, but it was not until 1968 that the Oxford Union elected a woman president (Geraldine Jones). I was to become the tenth woman officer when I was elected secretary in 1971.

Nevertheless while my single-minded approach was undeniably what finally took me to Westminster, it was also to lead to mistakes, which could have been avoided had I adopted a more relaxed attitude. The first was in deciding at the outset that, having a good degree already, academic work did not matter as it had at Birmingham and that providing I did enough to secure an honours degree the class was irrelevant and that I could therefore spend my time on active rather than theoretical politics. That resulted in a third-class degree. It was in fact a significant academic achievement as I had to pass papers at Oxford standard, for which I had done precious little work, but on paper it now looks embarrassing. A note from my tutor, Margaret Paul, said she was sorry 'your union gamble did not quite come off' as it was clear I had 'just missed a second'.

The degree was Politics, Philosophy and Economics, and we could choose to do two or all three. Philosophy, with its rigorous thought and analysis, would have been vastly more suited to my abilities and liking than economics, which was too close to maths and science – at which I had never excelled – but I chose economics because it seemed more practically linked with politics than did philosophy.

At school I could read a piece of Latin prose or poetry and, without having to parse every word, know immediately what it was saying while others laboriously translated every verb, noun and preposition to arrive at the same conclusion. Conversely some of my friends would only have to see a piece of geometry to realise its structure but I would have to identify every angle and measurement. That plodding approach might eventually have proved sufficient for economics, given that all my special papers were in politics, but I wasn't there to plod: I was there for the politics. Ironically I occasionally attended a philosophy lecture by Sybil Wolfram while skipping the economic ones.

I had the wit to keep up my classical knowledge and indeed was to become president of the University Classical Society in the summer of 1971. I remember earnest discussions about *furor* and *pietas* with students reading Greats. My approach to politics contained a large measure of both.

In the first year, conscious of preliminary exams which decided whether one stayed at Oxford, I did at least apply myself to a measure of academic work and Margaret Paul was hugely pleased with my economics, on one occasion awarding me the accolade of 'a perfect essay' and telling me to dispense with that tutorial. As the work grew more demanding and I was obliged to rely more on innate ability this happy state of affairs went into reverse, but never to the extent of putting my survival in doubt.

Meanwhile I began to build a reputation in the Oxford Union. It was a steady, sure progress. I began by attending debates, then by making the occasional contribution from the floor, watching, listening, learning, rather than rushing in. At that stage the political climate in Oxford was beginning to change. Only a couple of years earlier it had been militant left but, during my time, shifted to a point where the annual 'no confidence in Her Majesty's Government' motion at the Oxford Union was lost when applied to Ted Heath's administration.

One of my encounters was with Christopher Hitchens, the left-wing atheist, who returned to make a speech in which he addressed his audience as comrades and brothers only to find it felt no fraternity with him at all. It was to be several decades before we debated with each other again, on that occasion about religion, and then the audience was solidly with him.

In my early days at Oxford the transition from idealistic socialism to centre-right conservatism was a very long way from complete and my views were unlikely to prove a vehicle for popularity, but I expressed them anyway and found that was what people wanted: honesty and belief. They may variously have thought I was slightly nutty or naïvely unblooded by the world or really rather old-fashioned, but members of the Oxford Union responded well to me.

On one score, however, I knew I was deficient: they also wanted wit. So I worked on my jokes until humour in debate became second nature as it had never been in my flights of rhet- oric at either school or Birmingham. Even now I can often tell if someone was a union debater simply by the rhythm of the humour, its timing of punchlines and its causticity. William Hague is an excellent example.

The Union was regarded as a nursery for Westminster and it is often said that it produces tomorrow's politicians, but that is not so. It is rather that the sort of people who want to become MPs will choose to try their strength in the Oxford Union, just as it is not Oxbridge which produces ambition but rather ambition which takes one to Oxbridge.

My first paper speech (so-called because one's name appears on the order paper to give a scheduled speech for an allotted time) was in favour of censorship, which was at odds with the permissive nature of the times, and which drew incredulity and some mockery from the audience but I sat down to loud, sus- tained applause. One could almost hear behind the applause that the members were saying, 'Well done, old thing. Load of rub- bish, but damned brave, what?' or more modern words, by no means all polite, to that effect.

Mindful of that applause, I took a risk at the end of that term and, eschewing the junior committees, stood for the Standing Committee. There were those who were amazed at my effrontery but I came top of the poll, ahead of far more established figures, and the following term I was elected secretary.

The summer of 1971 was a heady time. Oxford summers with punting and commems always are, but for me the term was memorable because, free from any major exams that year, I was an officer of the Union, dining with some of the most famous people in the land every week and I appeared in my first tele- vised debate.

That term we had the second female president: Sue Richards, later to become Sue Kramer and a Liberal Democrat MP. She is now in the Lords. Her American boyfriend was opposed to the Vietnam War and refused the draft. Sue used to say that if he returned he would face a prison sentence. Whether this was all a rather dramatic exaggeration I never knew, but they married a year later and went to live in the United States. So completely did I lose touch with Sue that when I heard a Susan Kramer was standing for Mayor of London, I did not immediately make the connection.

At Oxford Sue consistently claimed not to be ambitious and that she would be content with 'a couple of kids' but nobody becomes president of the Union by accident and her later forays into politics belie her words.

Initially she was a popular president of the Union and her biggest triumph was to secure a televised debate on the motion that excellence in education is more important than equality. Norman St John-Stevas and Professor Brian Cox were supporting the proposition, which was opposed by Richard Crossman and Shirley Williams. One of my duties as secretary was to meet the guests at the station but there was a confusion and I waited there in vain, only to find both St John-Stevas and Crossman had already arrived.

The former was so angry that he berated me in front of everybody at the pre-dinner reception. Subsequently, after I had written to thank them all for coming, Professor Cox wrote back saying that he hoped I was not too upset by Norman's 'shocking rudeness' and that one of the purposes of education was surely to promote civilised manners!

Some while later I met Norman St John-Stevas at a Federation of Conservative Students' conference and he greeted me with the words, 'Ah! We haven't met since you made that excellent speech at the Oxford Union,' and I had to bite back the retort 'And when you were so rude to me.'

Norman was witty and entertaining and, of course, both Catholic and Conservative, but that early encounter left me with a wariness of him, although we rarely met in later years as he had gone to the Lords by the time I arrived in the Commons.

Another difficult meeting with a speaker but for entirely different reasons was with Ted Heath, with whom I found myself briefly alone at the president's reception after a debate on Europe in 1975. By then I had, of course, left Oxford, but occasionally returned to attend a party or to vote for a friend who was still there and standing in some student election. I observed that it had been a lively debate.

'Ye-es,' drawled Heath.

And, I continued brightly, there was an atmosphere of a great occasion.

'Ye-es.'

And hadn't he got a warm reception?

'Ye-es.'

Ted never did have much of a reputation for small talk. Later, when others had joined us, he remarked that the debate was civilised and somebody commented that was the essence of the Union style. I reminded the speaker that it was not that long since Michael Stewart, the Labour Foreign Secretary had been shouted down in a demonstration and disturbance led by Chris Hitchens. Heath was delighted to have his point so well made and beamed at me.

'Ye-ess!'

The televised debate was an enormous success and I found that failure can sometimes be turned to advantage when I referred to my own lack of success at 11-plus as proof that it was not inevitable that the exam could ruin academic prospects. That exchange prompted a letter from a viewer in the *Radio Times* to the effect that I was living proof that the system provided neither for excellence nor equality.

Letters also arrived for me at the Union. Many were complimentary but most concentrated on Shirley Williams' having attributed to St Paul a quote of Christ Himself. It was an early foretaste of the generosity, eccentricity and pedantry of the British public which was to pile itself upon my desk in years to come.

That debate is in the BBC archives and a few years ago I obtained a copy. It is an odd experience, watching and listening to my twenty-three-year-old self. It was a confident, competent performance, but then we were all so dashed confident. Tomorrow was ours. I look at the Standing Committee photos from that era and laugh at the self-belief in our faces. Did we really think it would be so easy?

The press prefers photographs of those privileged young men

from the Bullingdon Club, staring arrogantly out at the world. They were fuelled by wealth and a sense of entitlement, by a belief that their destinies were assured. We were fuelled by ambition and a will to carve out success for ourselves.

Officers and speakers wear evening dress for the debates and my choice that night was gold lurex to catch the television lights teamed with a gold-and-green choker, an item then much in fashion and featuring in many of my photographs of the time.

The dress may have been carefully chosen for the cameras but it was home-made, as were many of those in which I appeared on Thursday nights for the weekly debates. This was quite a feat as I couldn't sew to save my life. At Bath Convent the fast stream gave up needlework, as it was then called, at the end of the first form – and very glad I was too.

In the exams at the end of the first term I scored 11 per cent for a hot-water-bottle cover and that was for embroidering God Bless on it in very uneven letters. Actually I think the entire 11 per cent was for the capital G which my mother had done to show me the method. The following term we learned to use a sewing machine, or rather the rest of the class did. I guided the wretched device through a whole seam of neat stitches only to find I had none at all because I had failed to thread the bobbin properly.

Now, however, dress-making suddenly became a matter of necessity because there was no possible way in which I could afford to buy a dress a week for the eight weeks of term. A girl at LMH, Wendy Barclay, took time out of her mathematical studies to show me how to make a skirt. I loved the finished product but declared it too short. No, no, my friends said, it was just right.

Looking at it in the mirror I agreed and wore it. My mother made no comment when the next one was shorter still and the third continued the upward trend until one day I innocently mentioned a stiffness in my arm.

'Well, what do you expect?' she demanded. 'Your skirts are so short you have caught a cold in your arm!' She must have been glad when the mini craze gave way to first the maxi and then the midi.

Mother was little better than I at cutting out patterns and putting together the results. Her own sewing was confined to the post-war 'make do and mend' ethic. She patched sheets and turned my father's cuffs as well as darning his socks, none of which is a skill much in demand now.

Nevertheless she rallied magnificently and the kitchen table was covered with our often comic efforts. When I ceased to be an officer of the Union I fancied I heard the old Singer sewing machine, the same as that on which I had stitched up the afore-mentioned hot-water-bottle cover, give a long-drawn-out sigh of relief.

In the normal course of events I might have moved from being secretary to treasurer and thence to librarian before throwing my hat into the ring for the presidency, those being the four offices of the Union, but that term a controversy exploded from which I learned a great deal about both politics and human nature.

The Union's finances were in a parlous state. It was being run on lines which owed more to custom and tradition than to economic sense and the bank, at which that institution had great standing and a greater overdraft, was raising unwelcome questions. The previous term an emergency meeting of the Standing Committee was convened. My father had by then retired from the MoD, which the family still referred to as the Admiralty, despite its having been absorbed along with the War and Air Ministries into the Ministry of Defence in 1964, but he was acting as a consultant to that Department. He offered to take a look at the books and the practices, and the Standing Committee, which had been facing the prospect of getting in a consultancy firm at ruinous expense, accepted.

The resulting report, which was presented in the summer term when I was secretary, was deeply critical of the management of the place and that called into question both the position of the steward, Leslie Crawte, and the senior treasurer (an academic who played an ex-officio role on the committee), Maurice Shock.

Sue Richards, in tears, wanted to take no action against the steward, who had been with the Union for decades. The other three officers, Julian Priestley, Peter Haywood and I, believed we had no choice and that the senior treasurer should go as well. The debate in the committee was fierce and emotional but a majority voted to dispense with the services of the steward. Nobody was happy but a decision had been taken and collective responsibility, which was as de rigueur there as it was on the front benches of the House of Commons, was expected to prevail.

Some chance. Two members of the committee resigned and one of them had friends in the university press, the newspaper *Cherwell* and the magazine *Isis*. They whipped up a frenzy, which reached the national press, and the following Thursday's debate was taken over entirely by the issue. The Standing Committee was instructed to rescind or resign and Sue, who had never been in favour of the move, was in the unfortunate position of having to defend it.

At that term's elections the pair of rebels stood for office and defeated two of the incumbents, of whom I was one. The steward, understandably upset by all the controversy, resigned anyway and Maurice Shock came up with a plan for a building in the garden in conjunction with a financial partner, but no financial partner emerged and the building never happened. For a while the Union lurched on until rescued by the age of sponsorship and the Japanese.

I alone on the committee had voted against rescinding and against a grovelling statement but I knew the pass was well and truly sold. I also knew that the common wisdom that we could have handled it better was nonsense because whenever we had taken the decision the same consequences would have flowed. A week's delay here or there would not have altered the outcome. The rebels would still have rebelled. They would have still had friends in the press. They would still have whipped up a frenzy. Everybody would still have believed in any alternative that did not involve getting rid of the steward and Sue's calm analysis of the options would still have been shouted down.

So I returned for my final year without the trappings of Union office but with a series of other excitements in store. That summer I had obtained my first car, an ancient Morris Minor made in 1958, which had been owned and cosseted by my god-father, Commander Pickerill, whom I called Uncle Pick. Auntie Pick had for some time been convinced that he was getting too old to drive and finally persuaded him to sell it to me for £50.

The only disadvantage was that I could not drive, or at least had not yet passed my test. I was learning on an ancient Mini, complete with starting button on the floor, under the guidance of an ageing instructor, Mr Hadleigh. The test was in the small town of Chichester and my mother would accompany me in the Morris, which I had named Methuselah, while I drove the test routes, practising hill starts and three-point turns. To my chagrin I failed so took the test again within a month and passed.

I have often wondered if my second test was unlawful, because the examiner did not carry out an eyesight check at the outset when he was supposed to ask me to read a number plate at twenty-five yards. Perhaps he decided that as I could read it less than four weeks earlier it was unnecessary, or perhaps he just forgot.

Whatever the reason I left the test centre clutching the precious bit of pink paper, took the L plates off Methuselah and drove myself to Oxford for my final year.

My first car was followed rapidly by my first love. Colin Maltby was reading Physics at Christ Church, was an officer in the Oxford Union and on the committee of the Conservative Association. Outstandingly bright, he won a double first and stayed on to read for a DPhil which he later converted to a master's degree in order to become chairman of the Federation of Conservative Students.

The romance lasted nearly three years and kept me coming back to Oxford and retaining an interest in the Union long after I had graduated until he too joined the real world and we drifted apart.

It is probably impossible not to fall in love at Oxford with its dreamy gardens, punting on the river, quaint traditions and glittering balls, but the greater inevitability arose from most of my friendships now being with men. At Birmingham my life had centred around the all-women hall of residence and my lasting friendships from that university are exclusively with women, but at Oxford my social life revolved around the Union and general political scene which was then still heavily dominated by men and hence my lasting friendships from there are nearly all male.

I always get into trouble from the feminists for saying so, but I prefer male company because it is so much more relaxing. Men are less prone to focus on their emotional state or latest grievance, their conversation is less introspective and, although I can hear the screech of the sisterhood as I write this, they are sharper, wittier and more entertaining. Oh, dear, sorry, girls.

I am, needless to say, talking very generally. There are plenty of women whose wit would flatten an army and I have mopped up enough tears of emoting males – anyone who was at Westminster during the fall of Thatcher could scarcely avoid doing so – but by and large I find men less demanding. That is probably just as well, given that I have operated in male-dominated environments for most of my life.

I therefore much appreciate the more relaxed rules governing social contact between men and women, which my generation was probably the first to take for granted. I can remember the shocked reaction of my elderly godmother, Auntie Pick – who was by then in her eighties and with whom I was staying during my campaign in Devonport – when at the end of a long day's electioneering I gave my agent dinner at a local restaurant.

'But whatever will his wife say?' she asked, scandalised.

'She will say "Thank heaven I don't have to get a meal at this hour of the night."'

My mother expressed similar doubt when I casually told her, months after we were no longer going out together, that I had just had lunch with Colin.

'Whatever will the other girl say?'

'She will say "And how was Ann?"'

Platonic friendships between the sexes are perhaps the most rewarding of all friendships. Everybody I know has them and nobody should let prurient speculation destroy them.

At Oxford the women's colleges were heavily focused on

academic work but the men's were just as pleased if their students found success in rowing, acting or student politics. When Colin won office in the Oxford Union it was written up in the Christ Church magazine and the dons took a close interest. By contrast the dons at LMH could not have been less interested when I began succeeding in the Union.

The only time I remember anyone taking an iota of notice was when I was standing in front of a long mirror in the corridor dressed in sparkling gold before the great televised debate and the vice-principal Kathleen Lea was passing by. She had a large yellow cat, Willow, who occasionally slept on my bed.

'Ah, the heavenly calm of the well dressed,' she murmured as she floated past.

It was not only among the dons but among the students too that this distancing from events was noticeable. The men's colleges closed ranks and voted for their own when an election was in progress. Exeter versus Balliol. Who would get out the most votes? The women's colleges were doing well if a dozen came out to take part in the ballot.

Perhaps it was that the men's colleges were more central geographically and did not necessitate a bike ride or long walk, or maybe the women's colleges still had something to prove in those early days of women's liberation and still needed academic success to show the girls to be as good as the boys. Whatever the reason, the Norrington Tables (the academic league statistics of Oxford colleges) were all that mattered.

As I neared the end of my time at Oxford I took stock and was more than grateful for those three years. I had played a varied role in student life – president of the Classical Society, vice-president of the JCR, secretary of the Oxford Union, member of the University Conservative Association Committee – had met and talked to a wide range of politicians, broadcasters and academics, had blossomed socially and had met the man that, at that stage, I thought I might marry.

As Colin and I danced to a South American steel band in the early hours of a summer's morning before watching the dawn come up at the Worcester College Commem, the world seemed my oyster. We floated through Oxford clad in black and white as we sat finals. Colin and I bought each other flowers from the market to pin on our academic gowns, we drifted down the river in punts and in my case at any rate prepared to meet the real world – but not just yet.

Colin was staying on and for the next couple of years I was to keep an active interest in Oxford while building a life away from it.

Chapter Seven

THE SOAPMAKERS

From the moment I knew I had been accepted for Oxford I had known also that I was cutting off at least one of my favoured career options and possibly two. Unless I wanted to be a perpetual student it would be necessary to go from Oxford into gainful employment, which meant abandoning any thought of a career as a barrister with its lengthy training and, although I could teach without a certificate of education, it would mean that I would be on a lower pay scale if I did so.

So I joined the 'milk round', the interviews which were conducted by the big banks and businesses as they sought graduate trainees. Before doing so however I wasted a great deal of my final year trying to work for the Conservative Party and putting my trust in getting a job as an agent, researcher or PR official at Conservative Central Office, which then occupied its imposing buildings in Smith Square, a stone's throw from Labour's Transport House.

In the early 1970s Central Office was a large, thriving organisation and the party needed so much space that the research department was housed in a separate building in Old Queen Street. Its recruitment literature was glossy and its output prodigious, pamphlets which explained the history and purpose of policies appearing every month. This, I thought, was where I could begin so I wrote to the chairman of the party and waited. And waited. Then I wrote to the head of the research department and waited. Then I tried the agents' department and waited.

Eventually the interviews happened but the research department decided to wait until the summer to decide. I was offered agent's training, and I was sorely tempted but when they sent me details of the pay I made the sound decision that it was too little both to buy a house on and to support the expenses of being a parliamentary candidate. Indeed it seemed to me too little to do either.

By then I was too late for that year's milk round and I embarked upon it in the autumn after actually graduating. It was a busy time, for that term I was again holding office in the Union, this time as treasurer, and earning a living by working for Oxfam. The latter was a disaster. The charity's headquarters were in nearby Banbury and a big raffle was being set up. The organisers wanted someone to sell thousands of tickets to the student population and to organise promotions in local workplaces. I took the job confidently enough but then discovered the tickets were priced at 25p each, which most of us still thought of as five shillings.

To put that in context, it cost me a pound to drive from Oxford to Surrey each term and my grant at Birmingham had been fifty pounds for the year. My car insurance for Methuselah was £19 annually. Only the richer end of the student population could have shelled out five shillings for a single raffle ticket. Depressed, I returned bucketloads of unsold ones, knowing that I had certainly not covered the costs of my employment, basic though they had been. It did however lead to my having lifelong goodwill towards Oxfam, even when its unacknowledged politics crossed with mine.

Meanwhile I was progressing with the round of applications and interviews. I tried merchant banking with an interview at Morgan Guaranty followed by a visit to the bank. Hill Samuel offered an interview, which was cancelled at the last minute due to 'internal reorganisation', which made sense when headlines screamed that it was about to merge with Slater Walker. Chase Manhattan also put me through my paces, yet it was not banking but industry which eventually produced a definitive offer and I joined Unilever to work in marketing for Lever Brothers.

The interview board, having seen my televised debate, was seduced into thinking I was a good catch while I was seduced by the company's size and reputation. We were to prove utterly unsuited to each other. Three decades later I wrote in a newspaper that my first job had been a poor choice and I received a hurt letter, written in an elderly hand, from one of those who had interviewed and selected me. Unilever was full of hard-headed, ruthless types and my comments had taken up very little space. I did not for one moment consider that anyone who had been selecting thirty years earlier would remember me or would care if they did, but I was wrong.

The offices of Lever Brothers were then in New Fetter Lane in London. I joined some months in advance of the other trainees as I had finished university and was living with my parents in Haslemere and commuting each day. Thus I began to endure at first hand that which regularly filled the newspapers: the antics of the trade unions. I am fairly certain that had I not already been a Conservative I would most certainly have become so after those years of commuting misery. Official strikes, wild-cat strikes, go-slows and disputes added themselves to the usual reasons for trains to be late or not to run at all.

In the winter of 1973–4 the miners were out and so were the nation's lights. I was doing a period of sales training at the time and clambered around warehouses counting boxes of Unilever products by torchlight. Once the wretched device failed and I spent what felt like hours locating the door.

The sales attachment was in Hounslow, where I was accommodated in a hotel whose clients were nearly all sales reps. For some attachments the whole trainee corps was kept together, but we went on our sales training individually and scattered throughout the country. I did not however miss having anybody to chat to or with whom to compare notes because all my efforts were focused on finding a flat to rent so that I could put commuting behind me and begin to assemble a home of my own.

Some landlords refused to let property to women, which was perfectly legal then. Others gave preference to married couples. Furthermore I wanted an unfurnished flat and soon found that was a major obstacle.

First there were far fewer of them because tenants of unfurnished properties enjoyed security of tenure while tenants of furnished properties did not. When they did become available they were almost invariably accompanied by a charge for 'fixtures and fittings' which was quite disproportionate to a few lightbulbs and a cooker and was effectively just key money. If I had that sort of money, I told one agent, I would put it down on a property of my own.

I persisted and was rewarded when I saw an advertisement for co-ownership flats. One paid rent and if one stayed for five years then enough was returned to form a decent deposit on another property. The longer I stayed the greater that sum would be. It seemed ideal: I would not be putting money only into the landlord's pockets but also into my own.

The property was 36 Moat Court, Ottershaw, in Surrey's commuter belt. A second blessing followed as my moving in coincided with my brother's moving from a huge, old vicarage to a more modern, smaller one. I thus inherited his furniture. As a garage came with the flat Methuselah was also comfortably housed. The move was perfect for another reason. Lever Brothers moved from London to Kingston and I could drive to work.

However all that was at the end of 1974. The intense efforts I made while in Hounslow came to nothing, but I still went to Oxford fairly regularly to see Colin, staying at the Galaxie Guest House in Banbury Road. Once when I did not appear there for several weeks the owner asked me if I had had a row with my boyfriend!

At the end of that term, in the autumn of 1972, both Colin and I considered standing for the presidency of the Union. In my case there was pressure of time because at any moment I could be successful on the milk round and leave Oxford for the real world. In Colin's case there was a little more breathing room as the rules allowed us to stand for office until twelve terms after matriculation (i.e. arriving) and he was still a student. For a while it looked as if both of us might stand but I had already had one very unsuccessful attempt and Colin was in a stronger position to win.

Eventually I decided not to throw my hat in the ring but the reaction of our contemporaries while I still contemplated doing so was divided, some believing it perfectly healthy but others

saying that I should give way to him. Nobody ever suggested
he should give way to me, and that had nothing to do with his
greater prospects of success. Women's lib had a long way to go.

'But you're Colin's bird,' protested Philip van Der Elst, the
Union Secretary. 'You can't stand against him.'

'If Ann and Colin don't mind, I can't see what it has to do
with anyone else,' argued David Thomas, a formidable classics
scholar who had revised all the Union's rules.

Colin stood and lost but went on to win the following term
having organised a very successful launch of the Union's 150th
Anniversary Appeal. His words on doing so were memorable:
'Thank God, no bloody women officers!' I suspected it was only
half a jest, but there wasn't a law against that sort of sentiment
then. I repeated it in a speech to the Union on a later visit and
the members roared with laughter. Today they would probably
walk out or sue. RIP humour and free speech.

Inevitably once I started working full time in London my
ties with Oxford loosened. Colin came more often to Haslemere
and I occasionally went to his parental home in Solihull, while
the demands of Unilever training sometimes took me away for
weeks. Additionally I had replaced the fire and fury of Oxford
politics with European youth politics.

That was something of an irony as I had never been particularly
convinced about what was then called the EEC. I was marginally
but not virulently against joining. Friends from the Federation of
Conservative Students urged me towards Young European Democrats to 'spread the Conservative message in Europe' and I did
at least buy into the argument that if this was the way the future
was taking us then we should try to influence the direction in
which Europe would be going. For this group therefore I had
some enthusiasm, but at first I dug my toes in when asked to sign
up with Young European Federalists. But the same arguments
were forcefully put: the Left was taking over and we all needed
to sign up to change direction and indeed some very right-wing
students were doing just that. So for a few years I travelled from
convention to convention where we all talked of building a
new future, but that burst of youthful idealism was soon to be

replaced by a deepening scepticism as tariff agreements proved the path to political intervention. As ever the main excitement in both these movements was provided by the annual elections and the intrigue which preceded them.

Meanwhile there was the soap. When I first joined Lever Brothers I was appointed to the Liril office run by John Stowell and his assistant Chris Carver. Liril was a brand-new soap and we were getting ready for its launch. It was stripy green and strong smelling. The same office handled Lifebuoy, which was pink and smelled like carbolic. Samples were everywhere and my most vivid memories of Unilever are of the combined smell of those two soaps which used to hit me as soon as I walked in each morning.

Liril was top secret as it was essential that Procter and Gamble should be taken by surprise, the soap market then being an effective duopoly of those giant companies. On the day of its launch each member of the sales force received an onyx ashtray wrapped up in green striped paper which I had been sent out to find. Onyx was then all the rage and Hatton Garden was full of it.

The advertising had been agonised over by Norman Strauss, a clever but playful character who stood out from the bland clones the company tended to produce. We would fill in sheets called 'Straussits' which detailed our aims for the advertisements and our reactions to them. We held meeting after meeting with advertising agencies and package designers. Everybody was hugely excited – except me. To me it was just another soap in a market already furnished with adequate choice.

When I came to write this chapter in my life I wondered what had happened to Liril, not having seen it for years. It was a big success in India.

Chris Carver smoked and so did my next boss, Richard Rivers. For years I inhaled cigarette smoke in the close confines of a small office. There were also extended lunch hours of corporate entertaining which happened almost every week. For two to three hours executives from Levers would entertain executives from the advertising agencies or vice versa. Lunch consisted of gin and tonic beforehand, several courses accompanied by wine and occasionally brandy afterwards. And then we went back to the office and worked! By some miracle I still weighed only six stone and twelve pounds when I left.

The search was always on for an original idea and one much canvassed was the concept of a floating soap. In the 1970s Britons still bathed rather than showered. One climbed into the water, rubbed soap on a flannel and washed with it. As the process continued the water grew cloudy and numerous were the occasions when the soap slid out of one's hand and sank to the bottom of the bath. Finding it was a major hassle, so the idea of having a bar which floated on the surface seemed to me both practical and appealing but instead the company decided to develop Protect, a new product based on a new idea: this soap would be the first all-over deodorant.

Why? I wondered as Norman Strauss went into overdrive with jingles and pirouettes defining the ads. Where was the proof that the bugs on your elbows smelled? Why did anyone need to deodorise all over? I mentally yawned.

Then came Knight's Castille, a pure, simple family soap which had been around as long as I could remember. I did feel enthusiasm for that one but this time it was the company which yawned. I ended by working in Persil, which washed whiter just as did every other soap powder, according to the advertisements.

Throughout all these different brand assignments we continued training. One of our attachments was to Port Sunlight, the famous village built by Billy Lever for the workers at his soap factory, where we carried out a project on tank storage. If anything seemed certain it was the permanency of the factory and the workers' employment. People would always need bars of soap. The rise of showering and shower creams was just not then foreseen.

I was settling in well at Ottershaw. I had taken too much furniture from the vicarage but discovered in the village something which has since virtually disappeared: a fifty-fifty shop. This operated on the principle of selling unwanted goods brought in by customers and splitting the proceeds equally.

Sadly, eBay has all but eliminated these useful little enterprises.

I had moved into Ottershaw towards the end of 1974 and a new chapter of my life began in more ways than one. Colin called me at work and suggested dinner at The Bear, a pub-restaurant in Esher. Well aware, from the indiscretion of friends, that he was already seeing someone else, I knew even before we met that he was about to end what was by then a failing relationship. My feelings were mixed. Naturally I was deeply upset by the end of a romance which had lasted nearly three years, but I had known well enough that it had no future and the following morning my overwhelming sensation was one of relief. Years later I was to compare the experience to the loss of the 1997 general election. I had been a minister for nearly seven years and the sudden loss of office was painful but the release from relentless pressure, red boxes and perpetually tired eyes produced something akin to euphoria.

Indeed the immediate problem was purely practical: we had accepted several invitations for the festive season as a couple and needed to spare friends the embarrassment of treating us as such. Oh, that was simple enough, proclaimed Colin, we would simply tell Barbara Margolis and everyone would know within the hour.

Barbara Margolis and Patrick Roche were friends from Oxford days. Indeed when she stood for the presidency of the Union I made an effort to return to vote for her. The pair married and so Barbara became Barbara Roche and later a minister in the Blair government. She was an inveterate but harmless gossip and took a particular interest in her friends' love life.

I therefore made sure she knew that Colin and I were no longer together, but when we arrived at the first party it was clear that absolutely nobody else had the faintest idea. 'Didn't you tell Barbara?' grumbled Colin, sotto voce. Hilariously, Barbara's explanation of her unusual discretion was 'I was so upset, I didn't tell anyone!'

Colin and I remained friends and I assumed I would meet somebody else but it was not a priority for me and, although it took some while for the recognition to become a conscious one,

I eventually realised that the reason that it was not a priority was because I was actually happy alone. At no stage did I form a resolution not to marry, but equally at no stage did I feel time was running out. If Mr Right had barged his way into my life I would have been receptive but I never felt the need to go out looking for him.

It was because I preferred to live alone that I did not join friends in flat-shares after Oxford but instead made such enormous efforts to find somewhere of my own. Since the age of thirteen, first at boarding school, then at Mason Hall and then at Oxford I had lived in close proximity to other people, sharing dormitories, rooms, kitchens and bathrooms. I wanted my own space after Oxford and I have wanted it ever since. Coming in after a busy day and shutting the door on the world is wonderful.

The desire to live solo is a minority one and the rest of the world does not understand it. Oddly if I were an outright recluse or hermit then people would understand but the concept of somebody living life to the full in the mainstream while preferring the single lifestyle is apparently beyond comprehension. It might surprise others to know that I find it rather puzzling that they should find their own company so inadequate! Similarly if I were a nun or a missionary nobody would query my unmarried state but, again, because I am circulating in normal society it is seen as odd. Yet the world is not equally divided between men and women so some are going to have to be single. That we should be quite happy that way should therefore be a source of rejoicing rather than puzzled headshaking.

Would I rather have had children than not? Yes, probably, but I have absolutely no active regrets. The *Daily Mail* and other organs of gross exaggeration have tried to suggest that I am 'sad' not to have had them, but that has never been true. Sorry, I know that it is not the expected reply but it is the honest one. After all, if I am asked would I rather have been prime minister or not, or would I rather have been a millionaire or not, then I would also say yes, probably, but nobody in his right senses could suggest that I am 'sad' not to have been!

*

The acquisition of 36 Moat Court and the break-up with Colin were not the only defining moments of my life in 1974. That year had seen two general election campaigns. In the first Ted Heath had asked a country exhausted from trade union strife and the miners' strike 'Who rules?' The reply was effectively 'nobody' and Labour came to power without a manageable working majority. Six months later Harold Wilson asked Britain to give him one and I took three weeks of my annual leave allowance of four to go up to the Scottish borders and campaign for Michael Ancram as his PA.

It was as good an introduction to political campaigning as anyone could get. Michael had won the seat six months earlier and was being vigorously fought by John Mackintosh, whom he himself had defeated by a mere 500 votes. The seat was rural and very large and we drove from village to village in cars festooned with balloons bearing the legend 'Ancram Again'. In the evenings Michael would do two or three meetings and I would go ahead of him to start the speaking and keep going until he turned up. Sometimes he was delayed and I would be haranguing the audience at length while at others I would be barely into my introductory remarks when he would appear at the door and enter to wild cheers.

One village declined to have me because I wasn't Scots, but most were friendly. During the week a large group of Michael's young friends, his secretary, his youngest sister and I stayed at the Goblin Ha' in Gifford but after the Saturday night meetings we all drove to Monteviot, the home of his parents, Lord and Lady Lothian.

It was probably the happiest family I have ever encountered. Lord Lothian played the piano while Bizza, the youngest of the six children, and Michael played the guitar and everyone sang. Lady Lothian, who wore an eye-patch having lost an eye to cancer was a formidable but friendly soul, utterly devoted to the pro-life cause. The house was large enough to get lost in and, despite a complete absence of ostentation, was well looked after by servants. On my first visit my entire suitcase was unpacked and all the clothes I had brought for three weeks were hung up, while my flannelette nightdress, made by my sister-in-law, was laid out ceremoniously on the bed. I had no small weekend bag with me and wondered how to avoid such unnecessary effort the following weekend. The suitcase itself disappeared and I found it re-packed, though rather more neatly than I had managed, when we were departing on the Monday morning.

It seemed as if half Debrett's came and went. Among them was the youngest daughter of the Duke of Norfolk, Jane Fitzalan-Howard, and the following year I attended her wedding to Michael. She stayed for a large part of the campaign and drove with terrifying speed along the country lanes while I plodded at a sedate pace in Methuselah.

Lord Lothian died in 2004. His memorial service was at Westminster Cathedral, where the tribute, given by Earl Ferrers, was less about his distinguished career than his devotion to his family. Later I congratulated the priest on the service and he said that 'the family was so nice that not one of them was nicer than another'. There can be few better epitaphs than that.

It was a lively, youthful, upbeat campaign. The music blaring out from the cars was that of 'Liberty Bell', which also happened to be the theme music for *Monty Python's Flying Circus* and which I was to adopt for my own first two campaigns. We distributed stickers urging 'Ancram Again' and we wore T-shirts with the same slogan, but most of us knew we were on a knife edge and I suspect that each of us was pessimistic about the outcome.

A huge eve-of-poll rally was full of fiery rhetoric and cheering supporters and then on the day itself I was given the task of checking on committee rooms but soon found one that was a bit overwhelmed so I spent the day in Longniddry getting out the Conservative vote.

That night we gathered at the Goblin Ha' and then went to the declaration. A group of us stood outside amidst a mixed crowd of supporters and opponents. Rumours trickled out and the suspense grew. Michael lost by 2,740 votes. The next day I went to Monteviot for the last time and then on the Saturday I made the long drive back in Methuselah to Haslemere where, as though I were a student again, I let my mother do my three weeks' worth of washing, while I slept and slept from sheer exhaustion.

Returning to Unilever I could hardly believe how slowly time seemed to move. During the campaign I had been in a perpetual rush, always short of hours in the day, always dashing hither and thither, running up to doors while canvassing, driving from meeting to meeting, hailing the populace through loudspeakers, giving out leaflets, shaking hands, writing notes when people raised issues. The old cliché about not having enough hours in the day was never far from my mind. Now time positively limped along and the pressure and excitement were gone. Marketing soap powders was never going to replace them.

Sometimes one can see clearly another's mistake and yet still commit the same error, often in the full knowledge that one is doing so. My worst argument with Colin had been when he decided to convert his research course from a doctorate to a master's degree because he preferred to spend a year as the chairman of the Federation of Conservative Students. It was, I argued, the wrong order of priorities. He was capable of achieving his DPhil and should do so. He stuck to his decision and I furiously rebuked friends who had encouraged him.

Yet from the moment I returned from the Ancram campaign my aims became entirely uni-directional and I spent the next thirteen years focused on the House of Commons. Only writing distracted me.

I knew well enough that the sensible course of action was to put job first and politics second for about ten years but I reversed the order. I was a young woman in a hurry and ten years seemed a lifetime. If I had my time all over again I regret that I would probably do exactly the same and be no more resistant to the magnetic force of politics than I was then.

I was just one of a very ambitious set of young professionals who yearned to get into Parliament and who were prepared to commit a great deal of time and rather too much income to the project. The Bow Group, the National Association of Conservative Graduates, Young European Democrats, and Young European Federalists were all organisations in which we competed with each other and strove for recognition. Others were cutting their way in the Tory Reform Group or the Young Conservatives.

The EEC, the unbridled power of the trade unions with their strikes, picket lines and closed shops, the introduction of comprehensive education, wages policy and inflation, immigration and race relations, tax and the uncompetitive nature of State monopolies were what preoccupied our conversation. We were a pretty driven bunch – driven by alarm at the condition of the country that was Britain as 1974 turned to 1975.

Chapter Eight

THE ASPIRING CARPETBAGGER

The wild decade which was the sixties had fizzled out and taken with it much of its optimism, while its legacy of permissiveness had yet to turn into moral anarchy in what remained largely a socially conservative country. Divorce was easier but still not lightly sought, abortion available but widely frowned upon, homosexual acts legal but in the closet, pre-marital sex widespread but without the wholesale promiscuity which was to come. The family unit was still regarded as the bedrock of society but children were less shielded from adult strife, class divisions were loosening but still observable. The coarseness of punk had superseded the innocent daring of rock and roll but the F word, ten years after the Lady Chatterley trial, was not yet encountered on a daily basis. Nor any longer was the N word, now largely abandoned despite growing alarm at growing racial diversity.

Britons went less to church and ate out more. They were afraid of unemployment, militant union leaders and the Iron Curtain, and they bought all their utilities from the State. Satire had driven away deference, but unthinking contempt did not yet characterise attitudes towards the clergy or the body politic.

The position of women had undergone a sea change. Despite a fierce debate about the rightness of mothers going to work while their children were very small, the practice was growing and the passing of the Sex Discrimination Act in 1975 was a recognition of the inevitable. Today, young members of the family look at me with amazement on hearing that when I was graduating employers would advertise vacancies with two different rates for men and women.

The roar of student unrest had died away as graduate

unemployment rose and reality took over but the Vietnam War raged on for the first half of the 1970s. So did the Cold War and Solzhenitsyn was expelled from the Soviet Union in 1974. He uttered dire warnings about the dangers of Soviet expansion and designs on the West. His booklet, *Warning to the Western World*, fuelled the fear of communism. His compatriot, the physicist Andrei Sakharov, remained in Russia but was perpetually regarded as being in danger.

At home the distinction between the political parties was clear despite a great deal of discussion about the 'progressive consensus'. One stood for low tax, the freedom of the individual, private enterprises and grammar schools while the other believed in high tax and high spending, nationalisation and comprehensives. The trade unions sponsored many Labour MPs while big business supported the Conservatives. Theoretically Labour was against private medicine and private education but its MPs were known to make exceptions for themselves. Few people thought that the outcome of an election would make no difference to their own lives.

My own model of a society was and still is based on the Good Samaritan. He could only help the man who had fallen among thieves because he had the beast on which to carry him, the wine and bandages with which to treat him and the money to pay the innkeeper for his care. Who pays the innkeeper? The wealth creators such as the much maligned City, which these days brings in some £55 billion in taxes and without which the economy would collapse.

Obviously wealth creation and private enterprise are essential if we want an NHS, universal education, a pension system and decent transport, to name but a little of that which we take for granted in modern Britain. People need freedom and encouragement, which means not being stifled by regulation and taxed on success. If it is the duty of the Exchequer to maximise its revenues then it should lower not raise taxation. As is now common knowledge when the Thatcher government reduced the top rate of income tax from 60 to 40 per cent the revenue from that earnings bracket rose not fell because suddenly it was worth the extra risk and not worth the hassle of offshore arrangements and complicated tax avoidance wheezes.

In this atmosphere youth politics was vibrant but now that I was settled in my own flat it was time to get involved in a constituency association and Ottershaw belonged to Chertsey and Walton, represented by the Conservative MP, Geoffrey Pattie. It had a generous headquarters called Moorcroft and a full-time agent, Dennis Arlow.

The Ottershaw branch was run by a committee to which I was speedily elected. We took it in turn to host the monthly meetings, my lounge at Moat Court being just about big enough, and immersed ourselves in jumble sales, buffet suppers, leaflet distribution and fundraising. In that first year the referendum on membership of the EEC was the most pressing issue and the consensus in favour of staying in was strong, with all three party leaders agreed.

If anyone ever urges on me the merits of consensus politics I point to that unity which was ultimately to result in such loss of control over our own affairs, but at the time the conversation was about tariff barriers and the elimination of gluts and shortages rather than about political intervention.

I covered Methuselah in stickers and posters. One of the latter depicted a war cemetery with the caption 'never again', a powerful message to a country which still had active memories of the Second World War. Then I hired a loudspeaker and urged the population to vote yes. It did. What a pity.

Meanwhile I applied to join the candidates' list at Conservative Central Office with Lord Lothian supplying one of the references. Months were to pass before I was to hear anything but by the autumn I had more pressing matters to attend to.

Despite my disenchantment with soap marketing, I had done well enough on the various training programmes, but now that phase was over and I was working full time in a brand office. I was a square peg in a round hole and knew it, and by the summer of 1975 was actively looking for another job. Initially I applied for similar posts with other companies but as soon as I decided that it was less Levers and more marketing that was the problem the offers came in. However none of the three was finalised when a fraught internal interview led to my resigning in order to avoid being forced out.

The personnel manager, Harry Barrington, told me he disagreed with the decision and others told me I could have had a case for constructive dismissal but I preferred to accept the inevitable. Levers is a large, successful, thriving company but then I had the impression it liked clones, not individuals, and two decades later, when I was talking to Unilever as an employment minister, I found the same entrenched attitude, on that occasion over ageism.

Tim Breene, the Persil brand manager, once told me that it was insufficient to offer Lever Bros one's heart: it wanted the soul too. Unfortunately neither was available: my soul belonged to God and my heart to the Conservative Party.

I refused to slink away and had a jolly retirement party. It came back to me from various quarters over the next few years that my leaving speech was regarded as one of the best ever and was remembered for quite some while. There was the usual collection and I purchased a writing case engraved with my initials. It sits in my bureau still, unused for years, as redundant as I became.

All three offers became firm but not until weeks of uncertainty had elapsed in which I wondered if the flat would have to go. As I steadily refused to contemplate signing on, my savings dwindled, so one Saturday I simply walked down Oxford Street and approached the personnel officers of every department store and then went to Knightsbridge and Harrods. They all said they had no vacancies for shop assistants, so this time I wrote to Harrods and was immediately accepted, but the offers were confirmed before I was due to start.

That experience has given me an impatience with the physically fit who sit at home living on benefits. My attitude was simply that either such work would be temporary until I found a proper job or that it might lead to rapid promotion and a career in retail. Why not?

Of the three jobs which finally materialised, the first was with the charity Help the Aged but it was poorly paid and demanded a great deal of my private time over and above the working commitment. I turned it down while praying that one of the others would come to fruition and asking myself if I was being wise in taking the risk, but I knew that, if only for my own self-respect, the next post must be successful.

The second offer was seriously interesting and might have been even more so. It was with W H Smith and the man interviewing the candidates was none other than Tim Waterstone, who later broke away to found Waterstones. I was tempted by that one and had I accepted might have subsequently been involved in the excitement that was the setting up of a new bookstore chain. The pay was also very tempting and well in excess of my Unilever package, but I fell in love with London University which was recruiting an administrator for its buildings division. The atmosphere was civilised, there was an absence of the aggression which I felt characterised Lever Brothers and the job seemed real, with a career ladder and every prospect of progress.

The leave was also generous: six weeks as opposed to the four on offer from W H Smith and additionally the university closed down for a week or more at Christmas and a week at Easter.

I worked there for the next twelve years and left only to enter Parliament.

I arrived at London University on 1 December and drew a deep breath. 1975 had been an appalling year. It had begun while I was still getting over Colin, had involved the loss of my job and the fear of losing my first independent home and had even brought the death of Mitten, the family cat. I had taken no summer holiday and the highlights had been the Ancram wedding and the referendum campaign, but bad times have one thing in common with good times – they don't last.

My ambitions for 1976 were to get on the candidates' list and to finish the book I was writing, *The Long Winter*.

I had been writing on and off for many years, always composing stories when I was a child. I was to be flattered when, many years later, an old schoolfriend got in touch and told me she still remembered one that had won a prize at the Convent and then accurately recounted the plot. My first serious attempt, a play called *The Love of Lord Douglas*, came when I was ten. This was followed by two 'novels', which were in reality a few exercise books stuck together: *Forest Trek* and *Mountain Climb*. They were pretty good, given my age, but alas, no longer survive. Inspired by Virgil, who was so dissatisfied with the *Aeneid* that he unsuccessfully decreed its destruction, I destroyed all my 'juvenilia' as I pompously put it in my mid-teens when I was commencing a much bigger work, set in Ancient Rome and called *The Fish and the Eagle,* a story of Christian persecution and full of drama and action.

Several well-wishers urged me to try to get it published when, at eighteen, I eventually finished it, but I am glad I didn't as I think the estate of *Quo Vadis* would have sued me for plagiarism!

Had politics not squeezed out *The Long Winter* I think it might have had serious potential. Indeed one day I may return to its theme if not to its exact form. Three children, from very different backgrounds but playmates because of the remoteness of the area in which they live, play a trick on an approaching car on a dark winter's day. The car crashes, killing the driver and leaving the child in the back an orphan. They are not caught but have to live with the knowledge of what they have done and the book follows each through later life until one cracks and decides to reveal all. Unfortunately, before he does so he traces the other two to warn them ...

I loved writing it and sometimes would almost resent having to go to work and not being able to stay at home with it all day but there were other demands on my spare time, demands which were soon taking up evenings, weekends and even large portions of my annual leave. *The Long Winter* began to die slowly of neglect, occasionally enjoying a brief revival, but never far from my mind. I still wrote the occasional short story but once I entered Parliament even that activity died away.

With the referendum secured, both Young European Democrats and Young European Federalists began to fade from my life and I was getting too old for the Young Conservatives, but

I needed something national, something beyond the constituency of Chertsey and Walton, beyond Ottershaw, some forum in which I could make an impact. The National Association of Conservative Graduates at first looked promising. It had an absurdly high allocation of seats to Conservative Party Conference and from 1975 onwards I went on its tickets each year, but it was a dying organisation with no reputation and I wondered if it could be revived.

The more likely to deliver long-term impact was the Bow Group, then in hugely high standing and the publications of which regularly attracted coverage in the national press. It was widely regarded as a route into politics but had a reputation of being well to the left of the party which initially had put me off. Now I was learning that actually it was neither left nor right and if anything was beginning to lean towards the latter.

For the applications process I was interviewed in the Group's tiny, cramped offices in High Holborn by Richard Barber, who was later to become my solicitor as another luminary of the Bow Group, Michael Stern, was to become my accountant.

The group was full of parliamentary candidates and those aspiring to be so and it met in the committee rooms of the House of Commons. There were some memorable gatherings. I recall David Owen, then Labour Foreign Secretary, being awarded a huge ovation after he defended his handling of the Rhodesian crisis to an initially hostile audience, and a room so packed that people were sitting on the windowsills for Enoch Powell on his birthday. After the meetings we would all go across the road to St Stephen's Tavern.

One of the principal purposes of the Bow Group was to produce research papers and, at a fairly early stage in my membership, I published 'Aids for the Deaf, a Role for the Private Sector'.

The group provided research assistance to MPs on an ad hoc basis. I had carried out an assignment for Richard Luce on the provision of deaf-aids. While the NHS provided an extremely limited range, the private sector was innovative and offered a far more sophisticated and varied choice. I interviewed suppliers, audiologists and pressure groups and concluded that NHS patients should be supplied by the private sector where their needs were not being met by the State.

Richard was delighted with the result and some while later was equally pleased when I asked him if I could publish my findings. The Bow Group had a system of vetting papers by which 'three wise men' were invited to read them and comment. My offering sailed through the process but when I was myself a 'wise man', I had my first encounter with the male prejudice which then characterised the Carlton Club.

I had been asked to vet a paper on aviation (it was not necessary to have technical knowledge, only to see if the argument was cogent and unlikely to disgrace the group) and had met with the other two wise men in the Carlton Club. We went to the drawing room but as we extracted the document and laid it on the table we were approached by a waiter who reminded us that we were not allowed to discuss business in the lounge.

Embarrassed, we fled and found a quiet corner in another part of the club before deciding to have supper in the buttery, which was located downstairs. At that point one of the wise men, Edward Leigh, who was to become an MP but who then, in 1980, was a member of the GLC, began describing how a group of councillors had been invited to see *The Romans in Britain*, a play of rather explicit nature at the National Theatre. One of the scenes had been of homosexual rape and had caused some members of the audience to leave. Edward has a voice which carries well and, as he was describing the graphic depiction he had witnessed, several old gentlemen turned puce and left the buttery without finishing their biscuits and cheese.

As we were departing I was waiting in the hall for my two colleagues to emerge from the gents. The hall has an L-shaped area which leads to the doors and as I lingered I overheard two members talking there, oblivious of my presence round the corner.

'They can talk all they like about having women in these clubs but they haven't a clue. There was one upstairs before dinner discussing business,' snorted one.

'That's nothing, old boy,' retorted the other. 'There was one downstairs during dinner discussing buggery!'

It was not until 2008 that the Carlton finally, after a prolonged controversy and several failed attempts, admitted women and I became the first of my sex to become a full member. I was subsequently also the first to serve on the General Committee but sadly had to give it up when *Strictly* took over my life.

The publication of my paper on deaf-aids also gave me my first experience of being interviewed on the *Today* programme, which was later to become such a regular feature of my life.

Other papers followed. 'A Healthier Future', 'Choosing Our Rulers' and 'Second Class Single'. The one which caused the most stir was the second of these, a study of candidate selection in the Conservative Party. It was written jointly with others under my chairmanship and proposed the replacement of the then system of twenty-minute interview with a full weekend of tests and interviews. I was again on the *Today* programme and the pamphlet was covered in some of the national press. The Conservative Party adopted the procedure and I acted as one of the guinea pigs in the first trial, but the paper and its consequences were all in the future. For my first attempt at getting on the list, in 1975, the old system still prevailed.

Nearly a year elapsed between my submitting my application and my being called for interview with Marcus Fox, the then vice-chairman of the party with responsibility for candidates. Before I saw the great man himself I was summoned to the office of John Lacey, the Central Office Area Agent for the South East.

He was not enthusiastic.

'You can't just come along and say "I want to be a candidate", you have to have a record, and there is an absence of professional information about you.'

Given my work in Ottershaw, I thought that odd and reproached Dennis Arlow. He, however, was equally baffled and said that nobody had asked him about me. Discouraged, I battled on but the interview with Marcus Fox was worse.

'You young people with your national positions and your academic backgrounds think you know everything, but it's not what we want. We want councillors and people who've got their hands dirty.'

Marcus and I were later to become friends but it was an inauspicious start. I did not get on the list but nor was I rejected: I was deferred.

Under the system then in operation there were three possible outcomes to an application. The first was that would-be candidates were approved for the list, in which case Central Office circulated them directly with all the vacancies and then circulated the constituencies with the details of anyone who indicated interest. By contrast those who were rejected were not allowed to apply for any seats nor were constituencies allowed to entertain any such application. The third category consisted of those who were deferred, which effectively meant the party could not make up its mind. We were allowed to apply for any seats we liked but would receive no help from Central Office.

My next step therefore was to find someone who was both on the list and prepared to tell me all the vacancies. Ian Clarke, who sadly passed away early from lung cancer, had been chairman of the Bow Group and was also active in the National Association of Conservative Graduates. I would ring him every month and he would read me the list of constituencies which were looking for candidates. I then wrote to the constituency chairmen, expanding my CV and list of references as my activities and contacts grew.

I made no distinction between safe, marginal and hopeless seats nor any between the easily accessible and the further flung. I just applied for any and every seat which arose.

My letters tested my creativity but I could find a good enough reason for whatever seat it was to suggest that my particular background made me suitable! For Somerset, Surrey, Sussex, Kent and Hampshire it was that I had once lived there. True, I had lived in Kent for only six months at the age of eight, but my parents had married there in 1936. For rural seats I pointed to my upbringing in the country, for industrial I spoke of my attachment to Port Sunlight. If it was the Midlands, I had spent three years in Birmingham. For all other seats I could usually summon up relatives. Was not my granny Scottish and were not all Malcolm's in-laws Welsh?

My first ever interview was for Ilkeston in Derbyshire. Over the years which were to come, for the general elections of 1979, 1983 and 1987 I clocked up more than a hundred interviews. That does not mean a hundred seats, because the norm was for three interviews in each with candidates being eliminated at each stage and the selection committees getting bigger.

The first stage of the process was for the officers of the constituency to sift the list of those applying and to decide whom to interview. Hopeless seats far from London might attract some forty or fifty applicants and seats with huge Tory majorities could get one hundred and fifty or so but the average size of the list for first interview was about twenty-five. Unsurprisingly I fell at this hurdle for most of the safe seats. In those days they were looking for experience rather than being compelled by the tyranny of the current A-list to divide up the interviews between men and women.

If one got a first interview, it was likely to be run by a small panel of the constituency officers but the second would usually be before the entire executive committee, which in rural seats with a large number of branches and two representatives from each, could be several dozen people. The final interview, by which time the list had been whittled down to three or sometimes five candidates, would normally be in front of the entire association and held in large halls.

In Ilkeston I did not get beyond the first stage, but I began to learn what was expected and made a habit of visiting the local library before each interview. Local knowledge was vital but what seemed to impress committees far more was that I always spoke without notes, something which appeared to me in no way remarkable. Often I was asked if I had learned it off by heart, but the answer was no. I merely had to decide what ground I was going to cover and the rest would flow. So I would need to memorise no more than three or four key themes e.g. law and order, health, education – or in those days more likely strikes, the closed shop, the EEC, tax and incomes policy.

Most of the applicants were men. At Sunderland a female member of the selection committee observed that I looked 'very small and frail', actually drawing a triangle in the air to illustrate her point. Was I, she asked, up to it? One of the men waiting to go in was also a bit on the slight side but I bet she didn't ask him that!

The conversation in the ante-room was always full of speculation about who might get the seat, whether the constituency particularly wanted a local person or a farmer or whatever. We discussed the most likely winner or whether Central Office favoured a particular candidate, who had fought last time and why the result was as it was. It was a harmless form of gossip but it led to my badly wounding the vanity of Steve Norris, although I did not realise this until 1990.

It was in the weeks leading up to the fall of Margaret Thatcher. I happened to be sitting next to Steve on the backbenches and I remarked that I thought it quite wrong to unseat a serving prime minister. He was furious.

Well, I didn't always get things right, did I? Did I remember when we were both trying for Oxford East? I predicted someone else would win but I was wrong, wasn't I? Oh, the satisfaction it gave him when he won.

I listened astonished. Indeed in modern parlance I listened gobsmacked, having no recollection of the conversation, which was just one of many such discussions, scarcely able to believe that anyone would take it so personally or bear the grudge for so long. Yet so much did it rankle with him that when he lost his seat and wrote his memoirs seven years later he dwelt on it yet again, throwing in for good measure that he thought I was to pulchritude what Gazza was to *University Challenge*.

'Out of order,' harrumphed the ever-gentlemanly Tam Dalyell to me in a corridor after these comments had been broadcast.

Throughout my time in Westminster I was to learn that lots of men hung on to trivial grudges and grievances. One reminded me, years later, that I had once refused an intervention from him in an abortion debate. I can truthfully say with my hand on the Good Book that I cannot for the life of me remember who refused my interventions, when or in which debates and in the only exception to that I certainly bore no grudge. Men!

In the 1970s however I was not winning interviews for seats such as Oxford East but was largely trailing up and down to the North of the country being interviewed in the backrooms of working men's clubs. London University was wonderfully flexible and my leave was taken in odd days to allow me to make the journeys to the interviews. I doubt if Levers would have been so accommodating.

Upon arrival I would book into a cheap bed and breakfast and at first was very confused because, a stranger to Northern nomenclature, I did not realise that so many 'hotels' were in fact just pubs. Once I was nearly savaged by an Alsatian when I wandered into one of these establishments in the middle of the afternoon and it was presumably guarding the shop while its owners rested.

Then I would go to the public library and read the last couple of months' worth of local newspapers, jot down a few notes, return to the B and B and change into something suitable and Tory-looking, but never anything too posh for a working men's club. I also learned to simplify my jokes from the level that had been appreciated in the Oxford Union and never refer to the Bow Group, which was regarded still as suspiciously left-wing and more intellectual than practical.

None of that means that there were not very clever people on the selection committees but rather that they were themselves looking for someone they believed would be sufficiently down to earth for that sort of seat and who could talk easily to anybody.

I did well but not well enough at Liverpool Edge Hill, which may have been a blessing as the Liberal candidate was David Alton, who was to become one of my best friends in Parliament. He was a sponsor when I was received into the Catholic Church, I am godmother to his fourth child, I regularly visit his family in Lancashire and all goes well until we talk politics. Had we stood against each other and used the rhetoric inevitable in campaigns this huge friendship might have been nipped in the bud.

I was beginning to wonder if I would ever be selected when I made the long journey in Methuselah to Anglesey, which as I recorded in my diary at the time, was all sheep and Rio Tinto

Zinc. They were being thorough. I stayed with an officer of the association so was under scrutiny the whole time and the interview was a rip-roaring success.

'They loved you,' said the Welsh area agent, Derek Laws.

I loved them and I loved the majority which, unlike most of the seats at which I was winning interviews, was marginal rather than overwhelmingly Labour. I sang to myself on the long journey back but then a problem raised its head. The final for Burnley, which was held by Labour with a 12,000 majority, was scheduled before the final for Anglesey.

I agonised and when Derek Laws rang me at home one evening to urge me to withdraw from Burnley because Anglesey really wanted me, I nearly did just that. But, of course, he could not guarantee the result. It was entirely possible, though not he thought probable, that I could be unexpectedly pipped at the post in the final, but after the last round I was miles ahead.

I sought advice from Central Office. Marcus Fox was adamant: I could not withdraw from a final. People did, of course, but then at a stage when I was not even formally on the Approved List I did not want to defy him, so I went to the Burnley final half-hoping I lost.

That attitude made me relaxed and confident and I won easily. Before I was called back to be told my good fortune, Fred Brown, who was to become a sturdy supporter, raised an objection. I was a woman (observant of him!). Was Burnley ready for a woman?

A short discussion ensued before Linda Crossley, one of the officers, ended it decisively with: 'Oh, come on! Blackburn had Barbara Castle for years!'

And with that, in October 1977, I became the prospective parliamentary candidate for Burnley.

Chapter Nine

CANDIDATE

My elation at winning Burnley was attenuated by the loss of Anglesey. I knew that probably it was for the best, that if I fought and won Anglesey I would be on a knife edge at every election while if I made a good fist of Burnley I might reasonably be expected to move on to a safe seat, but I still cursed the fate which had put the Anglesey final after the Burnley one.

I was not the only candidate to withdraw from the Anglesey final and the constituency re-ran its selection with Keith Best, who had not been in the original final, emerging as the winner. He was to take Anglesey at that election with a remarkable and much remarked upon swing, but the seat did not remain Tory.

Looking back on life and saying 'If only I had done such and such' is a pointless occupation and one in which I do not indulge but sometimes it can be fun to play a 'what if' game with a parallel universe. If Britain had taken Germany's side in the Great War would there have been any Hitler? If the Americans had reached Berlin first would there have been the Cold War? If the Conservatives had lost the 1992 election what would have happened to Tony Blair? It is a game one can play with any life: if one had chosen a different job a completely different set of friends would have brightened or blighted one's existence, if one had married A instead of B . . .

Thus I used to ponder what might have happened if I had defied Marcus Fox, been selected for Anglesey and won. I would then have been in Parliament for the first instead of the last Thatcher years.

In later years I was to be asked by someone on the Anglesey selection committee if I regretted not 'taking Anglesey'. I replied that I had no choice, that another final came first. She looked baffled and it brought home to me how little of the procedures those engaged in them actually understood.

It is a weakness of politicians that, as a breed, they assume everybody knows as much about everything as they do. It was, for example, to be a great surprise to me in later years to discover how few people knew that National Insurance is not a fund building up but rather a hand-to-mouth affair of paying today's pensioners from today's contributions. The same phenomenon is observable within Parliament where there is a general expectation that colleagues know as much as ministers about the workings of any given policy – and they certainly do not.

At the end of 1977 I had driven Anglesey, Wales, sheep and Rio Tinto Zinc from my mind and was concentrating instead on mines, back-to-back houses and the life-sapping misery of unemployment in what had once been the biggest cotton town in the North West.

I had absolutely no previous experience of the North. Even my three-year sojourn in the Midlands had taken place within the ivory tower of a university and its halls of residence. I had never lived in digs and knew Birmingham solely through its shops and its churches. Effectively I had lived only in Bath, abroad and the Home Counties. The North was an education, probably the sort of education every Conservative candidate should have.

In those days most of us did indeed have to fight an uncongenial Labour seat to start with. Today's A-list system which fast-tracks candidates, especially women, removes this blooding and thereby removes also much direct understanding of reality.

Burnley gave me my first introduction to the working men's club. There were seven Conservative working men's clubs and I would go round them by rote, one or two every Saturday night. I was made welcome and whenever I appeared in St Andrew's Club the pianist broke into 'Widecombe Fair'. I would circulate among the members, introducing myself as I wandered up to strangers. Linda Crossley, an association vice-chairman, would always come with me but often stayed at the bar chatting to others as I went round solo. Sometimes I would be invited to say a few words between the bingo sessions, and I kept them few. People had not come out on a Saturday to listen to political candidates.

It was in this milieu that I discovered the full extent of my utterly hopeless memory for faces. Names posed no problems for me. I remembered, without effort, the names of spouses, children, cats and dogs, but I was so bad with faces that I could not remember whether I had introduced myself to someone or not. I learned to memorise clothes and hairstyles but spectacles or beards were a nightmare because they all looked the same! Linda would indicate, often from a distance, if I was about to breeze up to somebody for a second time.

It is one of the occupational hazards of the public figure's life that people will regularly approach you with the words 'Do you remember me?' Please don't do this because it places the MP/ celebrity/long-lost friend in an impossible position. One is presented with the choice between lying – and hoping not to be found out – or hurting feelings.

For years I would pretend to remember while desperately searching for clues if I thought the person might be hurt, which is a way of saying that if it was a man in a pin-striped suit carrying a briefcase I would decide he was unlikely to be hurt if I said, 'Sorry, remind me?', but if it was an eager-looking, innocent old lady I would lie through my teeth and greet her with all the enthusiasm of someone who had been just longing to see her again.

I abandoned that policy in 2002 – and nowadays hurt all and sundry – after it very nearly landed me in deep embarrassment. I was back in the North West to present a prize at the Golden Bone Awards for dogs and I had only just begun circulating in a room full of cameras when a kindly, respectable-looking middle-aged lady rushed up to me and said, 'Hello, Ann, you know me!' Certainly she looked familiar. I searched my memory and came up with the usual blank.

'Hello!' I responded brightly. 'How are you?'

She nattered on for a bit and then suddenly said, 'You're a friend of Dot, aren't you?'

Dot, I thought desperately, which Dot did I know in the North

West? There was one in Maidstone ... one in Conservatives Abroad, one in my parents' circle of friends. Dot?

'You know who I mean, don't you?' she insisted.

'Of course,' I lied and was about to ask 'How is she?' when the lady said, 'I thought you were' and moved off.

There was something wrong with that answer. It implied some dispute as to whether I knew Dot. Had Dot denied it? What on earth was she talking about?

A bit later I saw the same woman across the room and pointed her out to the person with whom I was then chatting. Did he know who she was?

The answer was Cynthia Payne, the well-known madam. Clearly she was familiar from the newspapers. Oh, crumbs, I thought, who the heck was the Dot I had claimed to know? Some weirdo in her odd establishment? It was my worldly wise American secretary who enlightened me next day.

Since then I have rarely pretended to recognise anyone and have tried to make up for it by producing instead some name or detail, upon being enlightened, which might show that I had not really forgotten. But it is still difficult when someone asks you in front of others if you remember and you feel you are letting them down.

Some good did come from my attendance at the Golden Bone Awards when I met the playwright, Carla Lane, and heard about the work she was doing with her animal sanctuary. When I won £9,000 on *Fit Club* I sent her a large donation. Nevertheless the next time I was invited I declined, saying bluntly that one encounter with Cynthia Payne was enough!

If I meet somebody out of context, then even if I would instantly recognise him or her on home territory, I am hopelessly lost – as I was when I met a very familiar figure on the station at Oxford, where I had been voting in the election for vice-chancellor. The city was full of alumni returning to cast their vote for Chris Patten and I had already bumped into one or two former acquaintances.

The man in question and I chatted on while I racked my brains for clues. I asked him what he had read at Oxford but the answer took me no further forward. Eventually I gave up but enquired casually 'What are you doing now?' He broke out laughing as he answered, 'Working for you in Maidstone.' It was Keith Ferris, one of my most active branch workers and not, as I had thought, someone I knew from long ago.

As with so much, this tendency to remember names over faces has reversed with age so that now I often recognise a familiar face but mislay a name from my memory, recollecting better those from the far past than those from more immediate contexts.

Of course I quickly got to know the keenest party workers and we were blessed with a very active Young Conservatives, the eldest of whom was about twenty-one and the youngest fifteen. They were led by two young lads of sixteen or so called David Preston and Clive Dixon. Clive subsequently went to Oxford and became immersed in the Union, but neither sought a career in politics.

Their enthusiasm was infectious, along with their abundant energy and they could leaflet half the town in a morning. I have had many loyal and hard-working supporters over the years but never since so many young ones acting as a concerted band.

Nor did I have in my next two candidatures so interested and amiable a local press. The *Burnley Express* regarded my antics with a degree of wonder and rarely failed to turn up at an event, while I struck up a good working relationship with Antonia Lerse, one of their reporters. For years afterwards I kept an eye open for her name appearing in Fleet Street, but I did not see it.

The *Burnley Express* accepted most of my press releases and even used some of Linda's amateur photos as I visited every major employer and a number of very small ones too. Over time the repeated trailing round factories, peering at products, shaking hands with scores of personnel and earnestly studying graphs of progress in the managers' offices means that such visits blur into each other when recalling them, but some stand out in stark relief. One of those is the Padiham mine.

With the demise of mining the once-familiar image of the helmeted, overall-clad candidate emerging from the pit with black face and hands has likewise disappeared but then it was de rigueur, so down I went. On that occasion no aide came with me as the lads were too young and Linda Crossley pleaded claustrophobia.

I, myself, have but one active phobia and that is a severe and illogical but quite paralysing fear of heights. It is as well, therefore, that when I climbed into the cage for the descent into the mine, it was pitch black and I had absolutely no idea of the huge drop I was making. Once in the mine itself I crawled hundreds of feet along an eighteen-inch-high seam. The miners managed this at speed but for me it was laborious. There was no relief for cramped muscles and if I raised my head it hit the roof. I struggled on, guided by encouraging voices and the thin light of the lamp on my helmet which just picked out the shape of the crawling legs in front.

Once we stopped and a miner came out of an area to the side of the seam to offer me snuff! He and his colleagues stayed in that hell-hole all day, breathing coal dust, and the snuff acted as a relief. I declined it as I was afraid I would sneeze all the way back along the seam.

In those pre-Thatcherite times the miners comprised the most powerful and the most militant union. The working conditions were abominable, pneumoconiosis rife and pit disasters growing rarer but still horrendous. The miners I met in the working men's clubs often had black scars on their faces where the coal had entered a cut or they wheezed from damaged lungs. That they earned every penny of their pay I did not doubt but the experience convinced me that it would be a good day when no Briton should ever have to go down into a pit again. It was not economics but common humanity that persuaded me to support, fifteen years later, Heseltine's drastic programme of mine closures.

Of course the miners did not see matters in that light. Afraid of unemployment and of loss of identity, they fought like tigers for the right of their sons and grandsons to follow them into the same hideous life. I am unashamedly glad that they lost. Thank you Margaret Thatcher, John Major and Michael Heseltine.

The fear of unemployment was real but Burnley had made

consistent and stalwart efforts to transfer from the old economies of cotton and mining to mixed manufacturing. Over the
eighteen months I was there I visited everything from the aerospace industry to the makers of Pendelfin characters and I still
have a large Father Rabbit from the latter. I saw one of the town's
last cotton weavers in action, painstakingly doing it by hand
with the aid of nothing but a loom.

Naturally, there was precious little agriculture but I discovered a small farm and had my photograph taken with what I
joked must have been the only cow in Burnley.

All this had to be achieved at weekends. Nearly every Friday I
made the short journey from University Senate House to Euston
station and caught the train to Burnley via Preston. Sometimes
I caught the sleeper back on the Sunday but usually I arrived
home late in the evening and the logistics became manifestly
impossible. I needed the car in Burnley but I also needed it to get
about in Ottershaw, not least to get to and from the station each
morning for my commute, and I could not afford two cars. I was
staying at the Sparrow Hawk Hotel in Burnley but could not get
back in time to go home to Ottershaw and I could not afford to
overnight in London.

With enormous reluctance I decided to give up 36 Moat Court
and to move into London. I was happy and settled in Ottershaw
and eighteen months away from qualifying for the lump payment which would have been the deposit on a flat of my own.
Worse, it meant giving up my position as a local councillor.

I had been elected to Runnymede District Council as one of
the Addlestone representatives in 1976, was now vice-chairman
of the housing committee and attending three meetings a week.
I had become accustomed to getting home from London University and going immediately to council meetings.

Originally I had stood for election solely to satisfy Marcus
Fox's demands that I build a local rather than national profile,
but I had come to enjoy the work. There was an enormous Conservative majority, a much smaller Liberal contingent and a derisory Labour representation but what Labour lacked in numbers
it made up in vigour. Its leader was Ray Lowther, a firebrand but

with a sense of humour, and he was ably assisted by Ken Capper. It was Capper who first drove home to me the importance of financial allowances in making politics accessible.

We were able to claim the cost of petrol in getting to meetings, which was reasonable enough in a rural area, but also a flat-rate allowance for each meeting we attended. Conservative members felt that we should do the work entirely pro bono and that attendance allowances should be abolished. I agreed.

Then Capper spelled out the working man's reality. If he came to meetings in the evening he lost overtime, but if he came to them by day he lost wages as well. He spelled out the sums while the rest of us, secure in salaries, self-employment, professional status or flexible working arrangements listened. That speech swung enough Conservative votes for the proposal to be defeated. During the furore which erupted over MPs' expenses in my last Parliament I was often to think of Capper.

Even had I not won the Burnley nomination I do not think I would have stood for election to the council again. It was useful and enjoyable, but I did not view it as a long-term project. I was selected for Burnley in October 1977 and my term of office on Runnymede ran out in May 1978. By the time I had decided to give up the flat there were only a few months to go and both David Head, the leader of the Conservative Group, and John Shaffner, the chairman of the Addlestone branch in which my ward was situated, were relaxed and pleased at my selection.

I hated leaving Ottershaw, particularly as I now faced the reality that, in order to afford both the weekly commute to Burnley and the cost of accommodation there, I would be unable to rent a flat of my own in London. I must face flat-sharing, the option I had so resolutely avoided when leaving Oxford.

I hoped but did not expect that I might find somewhere to live at a reduced rent because I would not need to be there at weekends, and was pleasantly surprised when that happened. Gay Arnold was a computer programmer, a little older than myself, who had bought a bijou flat in Barnsbury Road, Islington just as that area was becoming fashionable. It was within walking distance of University Senate House and the freeholder who lived in the other half of the house was a Conservative MP, Mark Wolfson.

My room was so small that I had to lift up the bed against the wall in order to work at the desk. Gay also supplied a trolley on which I could stack my work and which was cramped behind the spiral staircase. When she was away I spread it out over the dining table and dictated letters on the individual problems people had raised with me in Burnley, as though I had all the status of an MP, along with my Bow Group research projects and early writing attempts.

Gay was very good at creating a tasteful home out of the space available and there was a pleasant balcony which she entered in a competition for small gardens. Nevertheless I missed my large living room, bedroom and study. My furniture was in store with most of my belongings and the rest were in my parents' loft at Haslemere.

I took a bedsit in Todmorden Road, Burnley and drove Methuselah up to Lancashire one long Saturday. Linda Crossley looked after it during the week. At first her husband was doubtful about having an extra car in the tiny parking space allotted to them but reversed his view when the winter snow immobilised their Mini and my 1958 Morris started at the first attempt!

This level of personal sacrifice, inconvenience and financial strain was by no means unique to me. It was then a common experience among candidates for whom savings dwindled and overdrafts became a way of life between selection and the poll itself. Some withdrew mid-candidature and others after the first campaign but most stayed the course and at least tried to get to Westminster.

Today that is often no longer demanded. Women candidates can be given help and A-listers can go straight into safe seats. Many candidates have never run an election committee room or dealt with the reality of working with volunteers in their local associations. Their spouses have not the smallest notion of the inroads a candidature will make into private time. Having been through every last trial in order to get there, it was rare for MPs in the 1970s and 1980s to give up their seats prematurely as the system weeded out the insufficiently committed at an earlier stage.

One candidate for a North West seat promised the selection committee that he would come up every weekend and stay in the local hotel. True to his word, he arrived on the first Friday following his selection, complete with wife and children, and they all did indeed stay in the hotel. The only problem was that the next week the association received the bill! Wiser in the ways of business than of politics, he had assumed this was an expense the party would pay and was promptly sacked at the next executive meeting.

My period with Burnley was marked by election scares every few months. The Labour government was being propped up by the Liberals in a tenuous pact but was in dire trouble in the country where it began losing by-elections on a spectacular scale. Before long solid Labour seats were voting Conservative. Workington, in 1976, went Conservative in a 13.2 per cent swing and in Ashfield the following year the swing was 20.8 per cent. As summer turned to autumn in 1978 speculation reached fever pitch that Callaghan was about to go to the country, candidates began drafting their adoption addresses and preparing election literature, journalists cancelled holidays and I began clearing my desk at Senate House.

With a mocking rendition of Marie Lloyd's 'There was I, waiting at the church' the Prime Minister announced that there would be no election and a few months later we were in the Winter of Discontent.

If I was disappointed in my hopes of a general election I found some small compensation in a successful party conference at Brighton where I proposed an amendment on the death penalty.

Britain had abolished hanging in 1965 for an 'experimental' period of five years and in 1970 Parliament had made the abolition permanent, despite the capital murder rate having risen by 125 per cent, accompanied by a large rise in the incidences of firearms being taken on robberies. The controversy was still quite fierce eight years later, especially as the public mood had been at odds with that of Parliament and the statistics remained grim.

As I am frequently asked how I, a Christian and strongly anti-abortion, can be in favour of the death penalty, I reproduce sections of the speech:

I, like any other person of civilised instincts would like a society in which there was no death penalty, no corporal punishment and fewer people in prisons.

I happen to believe that the original decision to abolish the death penalty for an experimental period – in view of the revulsion that must be felt at the State taking life – was right.

At that time there was infrequent use of the death penalty, but in 1970, when we realised that the experiment had been a failure it should have been reintroduced.

I then pointed out that in the years between 1965 and 1970, the capital murder rate had risen by 125 per cent and during the same period there was a fourfold increase in murders involving shooting and murder committed in the course of theft rose threefold. I then added:

We have to face up to our moral responsibility for the lives of the innocent. With the statistics as they are, we have to make the choice between the death penalty for the criminal and the death penalty for his victims. It is not the mark of a civilised society to tolerate evil.

I also said that if society wanted to try again in the future to do away with the death penalty, I would have no objection but that on the basis of those figures it should be restored for some years to come.

I am still convinced that the capital penalty should remain available to the courts, though not necessarily used with any great frequency, for as long as the statistics show it to save lives. I have never been impressed by the argument for retribution and if I did not believe that the evidence points to it being a deterrent then I would be opposed to its restoration.

Of course the statistics are no longer collected on the basis of a division into murder which would have attracted the death penalty and murder that would not as all murders are now lumped together, but in the immediate aftermath of abolition the message was unequivocal: hanging had been a strong deterrent.

There remains only one argument that has given me any pause for thought; that of the irreversibility of the punishment if a man or woman should later prove innocent. In the handful of cases in which such claims were made on behalf of those hanged in the second half of the last century, only one case of miscarriage of justice has been made convincingly. Hanratty was widely assumed to be innocent until DNA proved otherwise. The execution of Ruth Ellis caused an outcry but her guilt was never questioned. The Craig and Bentley case quite rightly raised concerns about the law's attitude to mental illness but Bentley was involved in the crime. The exception is that of Timothy Evans, who died for the murders carried out by Reginald Christie.

Today when we have DNA, a more enlightened law on diminished responsibility for the mentally sick and a less cavalier attitude to punishment I believe the risk of getting it wrong to be minimal and the number of innocent lives saved would be worth taking that risk.

Finally my support for the death penalty is wholly compatible with my views on abortion. I believe it right only to take life in order to save life, hence my rejection of the death penalty on retributive grounds alone. Thus the one circumstance where I believe the law should allow abortion is where the mother is likely to die if the pregnancy continues.

My amendment was carefully phrased. Several others were put down to the law and order motion demanding the return of the death penalty. Mine did not. It simply 'welcomed the commitment to a parliamentary debate on the restoration of the death penalty'. I predicted, accurately, that my offering would be more acceptable to party management.

Even so the party management was jittery. I was summoned to see the area agent, David Smith, the night before the debate.

Would I be careful not to be extreme? I said I was not in the least extreme and had no intention of ranting about murderers. I merely wanted to present the moral and statistical case for having the penalty available. He looked relieved and the next day I was congratulated by Willie Whitelaw, who had doubtless suffered the same nightmare of a conference wild enough to return to hanging, drawing and quartering.

The caricature of the Tory Party Conference as a hall full of xenophobic hangers and floggers bears no resemblance to the reality. My biggest cheer at Conference came when, as Shadow Home Secretary, I proposed wiping clean the records of young offenders in all but the most serious cases so that they could enter adult life with a clean sheet if they had stayed out of trouble for two years. My second biggest cheer came when I pointed out that the mess which was – and still is – our asylum system made life hell for the genuine refugee.

Speaking at Conference made the time and expense worth it, but the real incentive was to impress the party agents and the officers of the associations which would one day be looking for candidates. Taking a week's annual leave, travelling to either Brighton or Blackpool, staying in a hotel for four nights and entertaining one's delegation to drinks or dinner was not a negligible undertaking and if one was not called to speak there was an inevitable sense of anti-climax.

Yet, even on those occasions when I was not called to speak, Conference was fun. A group of us would go together, sharing twin rooms in the same bed and breakfast or small hotel. I either drove Methuselah or caught the 'Conference Special' as we dubbed the train which took us to the venue's station. At Brighton we stayed in the Regency Tavern, where there was a fierce Alsatian called Bacchus of whom Linda Crossley alone was not afraid. The rest of us cowered at the top of the staircase, unwilling to venture down if he was about.

I went to the conference ball each year, often with members of the Bow Group or Conservative Graduates or the Federation of Conservative Students. Bob Kerr's Whoopee Band was a hot favourite and we danced half the night away before repairing to the bar at the headquarters hotel where we carried on the revelry and deep political discussion till nearly dawn. I escaped the Brighton bomb by twenty minutes in 1984 because I wanted to go to bed 'early' at 3 a.m.!

In 1978 I returned very upbeat from Conference and immersed myself in the run-up to a campaign which must now take place the following year. I was happy, hopeful and not averse to believing there might be a small miracle. My hour might have come but even if it hadn't Mrs Thatcher's certainly had.

In that assessment I was not mistaken. We were about to embark on eighteen years of Conservative rule as the unions brought the country to a standstill and even the gravediggers went on strike while rubbish piled high in the streets. The Winter of Discontent had arrived.

Chapter Ten

A CAMPAIGN AND AN INTERLUDE

You could not be buried because the gravediggers were on strike and that was unfortunate because so were the doctors who might have kept you alive despite the disease which might easily come from the stinking rubbish uncollected by the striking dustmen. If you still had a job you could consider yourself fortunate but the chances of doing it efficiently were hampered by union rules which stated that after 10 a.m. you could not be moved to a different work station. If you preferred not to join a union that was bad luck as many trades operated closed shops which meant you could not work unless you were a member of a trade union. And, of course, if you were a member and defied a picket line you were a 'blackleg' and your life could be made difficult.

No wonder that in Britain, in the winter of 1978–79, so many people regarded the unions with all the hatred and frustration with which their ancestors had regarded the feudal barons. The disagreements were always about pay or hours but rarely about serious issues such as pneumoconiosis among miners. The family structure was still likely to be that of the man working and the woman bringing up the family so many wives were at their wits' end trying to live on strike pay.

Commuters never knew if their transport was going to run on time or even at all and Britain was known as the sick man of Europe. People hate inconvenience, which is why they ditched the Heath administration five years earlier. In theory they wanted the PM to stand up to the miners, but not at the price of a three-day week, darkness and disruption to ordinary routines. If life is orderly and predictable the governed will forgive the government anything. That explains much of the complacency which now characterises British attitudes towards elections.

The nation which had given the West its liberty was now a joke, and so was the government which presided over it. The general wisdom was that, to misquote *1066 and All That*, Labour was wrong but wromantic while the Tories were right but repulsive.

Britain liked a soft heart but wanted a hard head in control. We entered that election as certain as one can ever be of victory, despite the still rampant doubt about having a woman in charge.

The ground had been well prepared for the Burnley campaign. As I have already stated, during the course of the previous eighteen months I had visited virtually every factory and enterprise from newsagents at dawn to British Aerospace. I had been in most of the schools, the principal churches and the hospital. There could not have been a house in Burnley which had not received a leaflet or two or three, Roneo-ed on the ancient Gestetner, the back-to-back housing which filled road after road making delivery an easy and speedy undertaking. Conservative MPs such as Geoffrey Pattie from the Surrey constituency in which I had lived at Ottershaw and Richard Luce for whom I had produced my research on deaf-aids had visited and received much publicity. We had also held 'noisy mornings' when we set up in the town centre with a loudspeaker.

It was a relief when the election was finally declared and all this effort could be brought to a conclusion. I ironed the ribbons on my rosette, washed down Methuselah and prepared for action.

London University gave me three weeks' leave and my parents proposed to visit to help with the campaign, but at the last minute my father was taken ill and Mother came alone for a few days. She valiantly addressed envelopes but as there was no washing machine in my bedsit and no time to go to the laundrette she soon decided that domestic rather than political help might be what I most needed. Mother also struck up a wonderful rapport with Linda Crossley's small son, Sam, who thought it hilarious that this dear old granny could not understand his strong Lancashire accent, thus releasing his mother for duty by babysitting.

I have dwelt heavily on the unions but their antics were by no means the only sources of discontent. All Burnley was in a ferment about immigration and the issue played a major part in my campaign. Anxieties ranged from serious prejudice to well-placed but often ignored concerns about the impact on communities. We need to look at both ends of the spectrum to make sense of the climate of the times.

Nigger for your neighbour, vote Labour. That slogan, now so unthinkable, was frequently bandied about among a still large section of the population which simply did not want large-scale immigration. It did not matter that the Conservatives had admitted the Ugandan Asians in 1972 while Labour had refused the Kenyan Asians in 1968. The overwhelming view was that Labour was soft and the Tories hard on immigration. *Powell was right*. If I had a penny for every time I heard that sentiment expressed in Burnley, I would have become a millionaire.

''Eee, Melvin, you're the only white man in the street,' were the words with which my constituency chairman, Maurice Tate, hailed one of our canvassers while the rest of us winced. Tate was a perfectly kind man but he hated what he saw as the take-over of large sections of the town by an immigrant community. Polite to individuals of ethnic origin, he was callous towards them as a mass and in that he was by means alone.

I, who had come from cosmopolitan London, had to try to understand the concerns and to disentangle the prejudice from the real fears. I understood the latter well enough. In the Stoney-holme area of Burnley whites were in the minority and it had all happened very quickly. As I pointed out at the time, colour was not the issue. If it had been a French immigration the reaction would have been the same.

First there was the sudden, huge impact on schools, where in a short space of time children who spoke English as a first language became a minority. In some primary schools the English-speaking children amounted to no more than 20 per cent of the pupils. Of course the parents worried about how teachers were supposed to handle classes where most children did not speak English. They feared, justly, that it could hold their children back.

Then there was the sudden turning of a recognisable neighbourhood into what looked like a different country. The grocery shops began to sell different food, the clothes shops different dress, the conversation was in a different language. The young were intrigued, but those who had grown up in a seemingly unchanging country felt threatened. They rarely talked to me about immigrants taking their jobs or their houses: what they talked about was being 'taken over', indicating a general unease rather than specific resentments.

I tackled the issue in that election by calling for firmer control of the scale of immigration but also suggested that much of the problem was the entirely natural and understandable tendency of immigrants to concentrate in certain areas. If only 10 per cent of children in a class spoke no English I doubt if the indigenous parents would have been half as worried. Britain is a free country in which people may live where they please so any attempted breaking up of these large concentrations would have to be via incentives not force. It was a tricky tightrope.

Less tricky were law and order, income tax and the defence of free enterprise. Britain was still accustomed to huge State monopolies but it liked the small trader and the Iron Curtain acted as a visible reminder of the dangers of too much State control.

Another growing anxiety was social security abuse. Being on the dole was no longer regarded as shameful but there was a dawning recognition that it was becoming a bit too easy not to work and, again, the strong impression was that the Conservatives would tackle scrounging. Mrs Thatcher, who achieved so much and tore down barriers which once had seemed insuperable, nevertheless failed on that one. Welfare dependency grew fast and furiously during her eleven years in power.

For those who think there is anything new about ageism I recommend looking at the Burnley campaign in 1979. Dan Jones, the sitting Labour MP, was seventy and we had no hesitation in saying that he should hand over to someone younger. Once that took off we didn't have to say much about it at all and Dan's age was discussed everywhere. He was a fit man, a vegetarian, who exercised each morning and poked good-natured fun at Maurice Tate's vast girth and was almost certainly physically and mentally more capable than many half his age. Despite this he died in 1985, but then he had been a miner.

Burnley was regarded rightly as a Labour stronghold and we received little outside help, which naturally enough was directed towards the marginal seats. What we lacked in numbers was made up by the enthusiasm of the Young Conservatives and as there were local elections on the same day all the council candidates were working their individual areas. We were finding a quite discernible swing on the doorsteps and began to talk about winning without the usual irony.

I had my election address translated into Urdu but at public meetings the Liberal candidate, Michael Steed, made a big play for the immigrant vote and was largely successful in Stoneyholme.

People wanted a government which would control its own purse strings and spend less. Home ownership was now an aspiration across socio-economic groups. The successful bitterly resented the levels of taxation which saw higher rate taxpayers parting with four-fifths of their salaries in tax and National Insurance. Moderate earners were losing more than a third to what they saw as a profligate, incompetent Exchequer and lower earners lived in perpetual fear of losing their jobs. We had won on the economy before we started.

Yet I was scarcely aware of the national campaign. Jeremy Thorpe's pending trial for conspiracy to murder, the Common Agricultural Policy, Scottish Devolution, the rise of the National Front and even the IRA which had so recently assassinated Airey Neave floated away in the background as my vision shrank to Burnley. It was not what Jim Callaghan was saying that mattered but what Dan Jones was saying. Hugely popular on a personal basis, he was confronting a constituency which voted Labour from habit and the loyalty of generations but which was badly disillusioned with its government. The Young Conservatives went along to all his meetings and at a church meeting Clive Dixon managed to rattle him.

Referring to the industrial action within the NHS, he asked Dan what the Christian basis of abandoning the sick in favour of a pay rise was and was told his question was 'blasphemous impudence'! The phrase became a catchphrase within our small HQ where the Gestetner broke down under the strain of our leaflet production and thousands of envelopes, painstakingly addressed at home by the elderly stalwarts, began to fill what little space was left by the posters, stickers and balloons.

I had insisted on the stickers and balloons after seeing how effective they had been in the Ancram campaign, which I emulated as closely as I could. Methuselah was kitted out with a loudspeaker and we played 'Liberty Bell' all day as we drove through the town.

The Young Conservatives vied to address the slightly bemused populace through the loudspeaker and stood in groups outside all the big employers, handing out leaflets when the hooters signalled the end of the working day and the workers rushed out through the gates. We also handed out the very popular balloons and stickers at primary schools.

Indeed we gave them to any passing child from the campaign car, as had the Ancram electioneers, but by the time I was fighting Maidstone, eight years later, we did not give them direct to children at all but only via adults. The world had suddenly become or was certainly perceived to have suddenly become a more dangerous place in which 'Don't take sweets from strangers' applied also to balloons from highly visible, noisy, music-blaring campaign vehicles.

The campaign slogan on the balloons and stickers was 'I'm An Ann's Man'. The posters were more sober and simply bore my name.

At the end of the election Mrs Thatcher was swept to power with a majority of 44 and in Burnley Dan Jones saw his majority halved from 12,000 to 6,110. I drove Methuselah back to Haslemere in a state of euphoria which was not even much dented by the Anglesey result. I had achieved the second highest swing in the North West and felt sure that next time I would be in a safe seat.

Meanwhile it was time to pick up the pieces of my personal life. Eighteen months of travelling almost weekly to Burnley and renting both a bedsit there and a flat-share in London had left me too poor to contemplate buying immediately and I reluctantly decided that I must put up with renting for a while longer, but Gay was getting married and selling her flat so I went back to flat-share agencies and ended up first in a rather well-modernised house in Islington and then, when the owner emigrated, to lodgings in St John's Wood where my landlady, Barbara Bowles, had been a Conservative mayor.

In late 1980 I embarked upon my first quest for a place of my own and in 1981 bought a pleasant garden flat in Fulham where the owner was going to Spain. It had been two and a half years since I had last lived completely alone but now that I was blessedly free of other people I had the company of two cats.

It was while I was looking round the flat that I had spotted a large, white cat with piebald markings sitting in a windowsill. Did he come with the flat? I asked the question in jest but found that as the owner was emigrating she was indeed looking for someone to take the cat. I at once said I would gladly have it but it was a while before she summoned up the courage to tell me there were two!

They were called Blackie and Pie, but considering the first politically incorrect and the second twee I renamed them Sooty and Sweep. It was because I was so pleased to take them with the flat that the owner, Carol Roderiguez, was prepared to wait while the problems identified by search and survey were resolved.

I reclaimed my furniture from store and my possessions from Haslemere and revelled in the first home, garden and pets of my own. Shortly before I moved in I sold Methuselah and replaced the elderly Morris with a one-year-old Renault 4. When I acquired Methuselah the car was already thirteen years old and I had owned it for ten years. It had never let me down but it was getting a bit rusty and had clocked up 100,000 miles. It had been a godsend in my student days and had ferried round numerous famous people at Oxford, as well as seeing me through both the Ancram and my own campaigns. It had motored through the Isle of Skye and other holiday destinations in Scotland with a reliability which many a modern car would not have matched but I knew that sentiment could not prevail over sense.

I sold Methuselah for three hundred pounds, which was six times the price I had paid Uncle Pick. Had it been a year older with the split windscreen I could have made a bigger profit still. I had several enquiries from Morris Minor enthusiasts but they wanted the car to cannibalise for their own and I refused illogically but firmly. In the end it went to a young student called Gaynor Redvers-Mutton, whose father bought it for her, and I believed it had gone to a good home. Years later, when being shown the latest police technology, I established that Methuselah was still in existence although data protection legislation prevented their giving me any details about the owner, but if anyone has a blue Morris Minor registration number CCV 533, he or she has Methuselah!

So the move to Woodlawn Road, Fulham, heralded a new phase in my life which seemed stable enough at the time. The work at London University was growing more interesting as I moved through promotions and pay increases. The big challenge then came from the incipient mergers of several big London teaching hospitals such as Guys with St Thomas's or University College with Middlesex. The associated medical schools also had to merge, very often involving new buildings and equipment. I was working for the university's court department, which looked after the finance for all these projects.

Having never been able to understand why my parents should enjoy spending so much time digging, weeding and pruning, I now began to take an interest in my new garden. Meanwhile there was still the politics absorbing much of my spare time.

The period between the 1979 election and that of 1983 was unusual in that, there being a boundaries review, Central Office put most selections on hold with the result that when it became obvious that the Parliament was going to be dissolved a year early there was a sudden mad scramble for seats in the immediate run-up to the election. Candidates for selection were travelling from one end of the country to the next and then criss-crossing from east to west as they crammed half a dozen interviews into a weekend, frequently swapping times with other candidates in order to make it possible. Constituency agents took to issuing lists of those who were to be interviewed so that we could contact each other for that purpose.

Thus the intervening years produced only sporadic interviews. My principal activity in addition to Bow Group research papers was to become vice-chairman of a new group set up to counter the activities of CND.

CND had of course been very active when I was in my early years at Bath Covent but its cause had been badly discredited by the Cuba crisis when Kennedy stood up to Russia. The episode had seemed to confirm both the threat posed by the Soviets and the value of a nuclear deterrent in countering it.

The stepping up of the arms race, the replacement of Polaris by Trident and the siting of American cruise missiles on British soil had reactivated the seemingly settled argument and in his manifesto of 1983 Michael Foot was effectively to propose unilateral nuclear disarmament.

The CND campaigners were now led by Monsignor Bruce Kent and Joan Ruddock. Where once women marched to Aldermaston they now set up camp at Greenham Common, the proposed site of the Cruise Missiles. Michael Lingens, a Bow Group officer who was to become chairman, rang me up to say that he was engaged in setting up a political initiative to counter the rather blatant attempt to portray those in favour of Trident and Cruise as warmongers. We needed our own band of determined women making an even bigger noise than the Greenham women.

Thus was born Women and Families for Defence, run by the energetic Lady Olga Maitland, then gossip columnist for the *Sunday Express* newspaper. Of the vice-chairmen, Angela Rumbold was already an MP. The others, Virginia Bottomley, Rosemary Brown, Helen Gardener and I had been candidates. We launched to a fair amount of publicity and my own task was to produce a *Layman's Guide to Defence*, which was published in 1984.

The preparations for the launch in 1982 were carried out in secrecy and whenever I asked for time off from the university I referred to what I was doing as simply 'the initiative'. Peter Holwell, the principal, was keenly interested in my political activity and a sympathiser.

Olga was a gem of a campaigner and we even managed to book Trafalgar Square on the date normally used by CND. We were egged on by Julian Lewis, who is now a New Forest MP and with whom I had been at Oxford. He actually managed to string pro-defence banners across Whitehall under which the CND had to march on its route to Trafalgar Square a few years later. He has retained a strong interest in defence and in 1987 helped me with my maiden speech, the subject of which was Trident.

More than twenty years after the fall of the Berlin Wall, that battle now seems remote. I watched on black-and-white television images of the wall being built in 1961 and it seemed symbolic that when I watched its destruction the pictures were in vivid colour, as if the world had emerged from darkness, but from 1945 till 1989, as I have previously noted, the world was divided into two great conflicting political ideologies: capitalism and communism. The arms race was growing not merely faster but with ever more sophisticated weaponry and Soviet Russia was ruthless in its suppression of dissent. The savage repression of the Hungarian uprising, the building of the Berlin Wall, the regular shootings of those foolhardy enough to attempt to escape across it, the Russian tanks rolling into Prague, the persecution of dissidents such Solzhenitsyn and Sakharov, the intermittent spy scandals and the occasional seizure of a businessman who would then be ransomed for a spy all added up to a picture of the enemy which we rightly feared.

The case for deterrence is well borne out by history. Indeed one does not have to look much further than the Second World War. Appeasement failed. Hitler then overran Europe but did not invade Britain because he believed that we were better prepared than we were. At the end of the war America dropped the

A-bomb on first Hiroshima and then Nagasaki. Why? Because it had a weapon which its enemy did not. Does anybody seriously believe that, if Japan had also had the bomb and the USA had known that it would have received retaliatory attacks on New York and Washington, the terrible weapon would have been used?

Let him who desires peace prepare for war.

One war we were certainly ill prepared for was that of the Falklands and it was with a mixture of anger and incredulity that Britain reached out a sleepy arm for its radios on the morning of 3 April 1982 and heard that one small remnant of its imperial past had been rudely invaded by Argentina. I suspect Galtieri had calculated that we would not fight back, and one can hardly blame him as we had been divesting ourselves of overseas possessions for some time, were economically hard pressed at home and generally presented to the world the image of a nation in decline.

He got a nasty shock, but so did we when our screens were filled with battle and death. I saw statistics recently produced by Ian MacCleod, a noted military historian, showing that British soldiers have died in the course of duty somewhere in the world in each year since 1945, but that is not how it was perceived. The Falklands War seemed instead to interrupt years of undiluted peace in which only Northern Ireland proved the exception.

My interest in defence stood me in good stead when I applied to Plymouth, Devonport, the seat occupied by David Owen, as did my family's West Country history and my father's connections with the dockyard. Devonport had secured an interesting collection of MPs and candidates in the past, including Michael Foot in 1945 and Dame Joan Vickers in 1955. The neighbouring Plymouth seats of Drake and Sutton boasted Miss Janet Fookes (later Dame Janet) and the redoubtable Alan Clark.

When the election came it was certain that all eyes would be on Devonport. David Owen, Roy Jenkins, Shirley Williams and Bill Rodgers had left Michael Foot's increasingly left-wing Labour Party to set up the Social Democratic Party (SDP) and were fighting the election in alliance with David Steel's Liberal Party. There was much talk of a sea change in British politics.

Owen had held Devonport as a Labour MP and nobody could predict whether he had enough of a personal vote to hold it still or whether the Labour candidate would triumph in a seat where dockworkers made up a significant section of the electorate or whether the two might so split the vote that the Conservative candidate could come through the middle. The seat was regarded as a three-way marginal, especially as Owen's lead had always been respectable rather than huge. After reducing a 12,000 majority in Burnley to 6,000, Owen's 1,001 looked vastly more conquerable.

I reached the final and was hopeful. My local connections were genuine and strong. My mother had been born in Plymouth, my father had been educated at Devonport High School and, of course, being in naval armaments had worked at the dockyard in his early years and had visited the base in increasingly senior capacities ever since. The nuclear issue was huge and, thanks to my work with Women and Families for Defence, my knowledge was probably better than that of most candidates. It was a naval town and I had grown up on naval bases.

I sat in the ante-room with the other candidates and awaited the result with my heart pounding. I wanted Devonport with a longing I had accorded no seat since Anglesey. Surely, surely, I thought, I must have won this one. But when the door opened to admit the constituency officer I felt sure I had lost.

I had neither won nor lost. The constituency could not make up its mind and was inviting two of us from the line-up to return for a run-off. The final was effectively yet to happen.

My opponent, Tony Patterson, had been just ahead of me and, confident of victory, he had invited a TV news team to cover the final, with the result that parts of my selection were broadcast on national television, including my joke, when asked about the alliance, that two half-wits do not make a wit. He lost gracefully and helped in my campaign.

The local press and media soon found another source of curiosity – the Labour candidate was Julian Priestley, who had been a fellow officer of the Oxford Union. We had been allies and principal movers in the effort to dismiss the steward but there was enmity between him and Colin Maltby and we had fallen out badly over some subsequent Oxford politics.

He was unlikely to have been ecstatic at my selection as his term of office as president of the Union ended in controversy. His candidate had won the presidency for the following term but a vote fiddle was alleged and a recount overturned the result. As the presiding officer, Julian was at the centre of the maelstrom.

Our contemporaries expected me to brief the press but I could not see that dockyard workers would give a damn about what had happened in the Oxford Union. Both my agent and I agreed that we wanted a grown-up campaign. We took the same line when news reached us that one of the minor candidates had allegedly bounced a cheque on the printers of his literature. We would fight on issues, not personalities.

Julian had a great many advantages. He was local, having grown up in Plymouth, and had been active in local politics for a long time. It was likely to be a genuine three-way contest and was also likely to happen very soon. With Burnley I had eighteen months to prepare the ground for my campaign. With Devonport I had but two months from my selection on 6 April to the election on 9 June.

It seemed to me that defence was the key and never more so than when Michael Foot decided to propose doing away with our nuclear deterrent. His manifesto has been called the longest suicide note in history, and in a country which was still basking in the Falklands victory, it certainly injected life into the Thatcher campaign.

Once more I emblazoned an election slogan on balloons, stickers and posters. This time it was *Defend Devonport*.

Chapter Eleven

DEVONPORT

The interest in Owen guaranteed a huge media turnout and the cameras and commentators appeared on an almost daily basis. In short, it was as though I were fighting a by-election.

The Burnley campaign, while naturally serious and fought to the last inch, was also youthful, bustling and fun, but the one I now commenced in Devonport was clothed in the responsibility of winning from the start. No national newspaper would have cared tuppence what the obscure university administrator had said in Burnley, but with widespread predictions that Devonport might be winnable I found myself in press conferences where every word counted.

Three weeks before the campaign I was allocated an agent. Keith Griffiths's previous post had been in North Cornwall and he knew the West Country but he had no more detailed knowledge of Plymouth than had I. We travelled the constituency trying to conceal our maps under the dashboards of our cars, occasionally straying over its edge, acutely aware that the only other serious challenger to Owen had been born and bred in the city and knew its every inch.

On one occasion we took a visiting minister, Cranley Onslow, to address a school and followed the map only to find that the school had moved! Fortunately we were assisted by long-serving Conservative councillors and officers of the association who knew rather more local geography.

Ivor Turner, the chairman, ran a bed and breakfast while Mike Gibson and Ian Clifton had lived in Plymouth for years. A very elderly Edie Brock ran teams of pensioners addressing envelopes at the association's HQ in Alma Road.

Conservative Central Office, however, had no intention of

leaving so strategically important a seat to only the locals. The western area agent, Peter Gower, and his deputy Greta Houghton, were in daily touch, a high flyer in the shape of Greg Johnson from nearby Ivybrige was assigned to help oversee the campaign and a plethora of visitors from the Conservative heights flooded into Devonport.

These included Ted Heath, who was walking about the city centre when a man whose hand he had earlier shaken came up to my agent with a carrier bag containing five hundred pounds to add to the campaign fund.

The press, especially a journalist called Will Stewart, was more interested in persuading Ted to enter the local betting shop and pose against a board giving me more favourable odds than David Owen. I made the suggestion tentatively and received the 'ye-es' drawl with which he had rebuffed my attempts at conversation at the Oxford Union twelve years earlier.

I was therefore surprised when he obliged a delighted Will. 'There goes the nonconformist vote,' muttered the great man as we emerged, confounding those who assert that he had no sense of humour.

Another visitor was the soft-spoken Geoffrey Howe, then the Chancellor. He followed the usual tradition of playing bowls on The Hoe after the fashion of Sir Francis Drake. Alan Clark, Janet Fookes and I entered the green shoeless in deference to its maintenance. The press showed us watching Sir Geoffrey perform but fortunately did not record his unintentional double entendre when he made a bad move.

Then came Dame Joan Vickers, a seventy-six-year-old veteran of Devonport campaigns and who, indeed, had won the seat from Michael Foot in 1955. Owen had taken it from her in 1974 and she was now in the Lords. Leaning on a stick, she canvassed with enthusiasm and recalled that women had always done well in Plymouth, beginning with Nancy Astor herself, the first woman to take her seat in the Commons.

Less welcome was the arrival on the scene of an independent Conservative candidate, Jim the Fish. He was a Cornish fishmonger and although he could never have been a serious challenge any votes in that close a battle could be vital. My agent spoke to him and reported back that he was in deadly earnest and deluded that he could beat Owen. Jim the Fish in turn claimed to the local press that we had asked him not to stand.

There was a fiasco over Jim the Fish's deposit, which was originally going to be paid by a Liskeard hotelier who changed his mind when he was cold-shouldered at the local Conservative Club. The money was then raised instead by a friend, who lost it when his man polled 292 votes.

Much to everybody's disappointment, Maggie herself did not come to Plymouth but to nearby Wadebridge. Nevertheless she sent me a personal message near to polling day.

It was not only the generals but the foot soldiers who came, from far and wide. The Bow Group sent a team for the day and one of their number, Ian Donaldson, stayed on for the rest of the campaign. My brother brought down a team from his Bristol church, including my teenage nephews, and they leafleted two whole wards in a day. My mother arrived and, as in Burnley, brought the post and did the washing before going off to London to look after my flat and its cats. My father joined the campaign for a week and exploited his local name.

Once he pointed out to some canvassers a particular house and told them that it took exactly such and such a number of minutes from there to the station. It was where my mother had lived when they were courting and he had to catch the train back to Saltash.

Particularly heroic was Auntie Pick, who in her eighties not only had the candidate quartered upon her for the duration of the election, but whose house was turned into a regular watering hole for hungry and thirsty campaigners.

'Are you paying your mess bills?' my father asked me and, amused that he still felt as able to ask that as when I had been a student, I assured him that I was but that Auntie Pick felt quite incapable of letting anybody come and go without tea and rock cake.

My secretary from the university, Veronica, also came for most of the campaign and more than once stayed up all night preparing canvass returns and answering letters. Indeed for all of us the hours were exhausting, there being no computers, and the printer thumped away by night as much as by day.

Veronica was staying with Keith Griffiths and his family, and said she often feared he would fall asleep at the wheel when they drove in the early hours to his home in Tregadillett, North Cornwall.

Defence fulfilled its promise as one of my strongest assets in the campaign, both in terms of my father's connections with the dockyard and my activities with Women and Families for Defence. With Michael Foot having committed Labour to unilateral nuclear disarmament, in a naval town such as Plymouth the issue had a massive impact, given that our nuclear deterrent was based in submarines, first Polaris then Trident.

It was hardly rocket science to add that fear on to the pride in the naval role played in the Falklands and to make defence the centrepiece of our campaign.

Keith and I drove out to Haytor and, in the quiet of Dartmoor, devised the slogan *Defend Devonport*. It proved a happy inspiration, enabling us to apply the phrase beyond its obvious link to military matters. We would *Defend Devonport* against unemployment, against crime, against whatever was in the forefront of voters' concerns. The slogan also lent itself to a variety of different graphic presentations including:

```
W  I  D  D  E  C  O  M  B  E
      E  E
      F  V
      E  O
      N  N
      D  P
         O
         R
         T
```

I had always known Dartmoor as a result of visits to my wider family throughout my childhood. I loved its barren beauty and told Keith as we drove back from our brainstorming at Haytor that this was where I would eventually retire. He laughed and told me that I was still living in a schoolgirl dream and that I would change my mind in the years between then and drawing my old-age pension! Twenty-five years later I rang him as I was driving to the house I had bought on Dartmoor and reminded him of his words.

My work with WFFD meant that nobody could claim I was just cashing in on the controversy. Clearly I had a well-established interest in the subject and so many people told me they knew my father that I joked I was going to call him Lloyd George.

We were further helped by the announcement of the Labour defence spokesman, Patrick Duffy, that the plans to transfer work from Portsmouth to Devonport would be under review. That could have had serious implications for Devonport Dockyard and I wrote to Duffy to tell him so and challenged him to a public debate. It was standard political fare but it made the front page of the local press.

Julian Priestley struggled with the conflict between his party's stance on defence and the interests of the constituency he aspired to represent and this was augmented by his obvious embarrassment over Europe. Foot wanted to withdraw from the European Community altogether but Priestley was making a career in Brussels as a eurocrat and the two were impossible to reconcile. By contrast Owen was deeply committed to Europe and could play a very straightforward bat. Only the split between himself and Labour could have prevented his victory.

For me there was the additional strain – and challenge – of uncharacteristic illness. I became drenched one day out canvassing and, being busy, defied advice to go home and change. 'You'll get the dickens of a cold,' predicted Ian Clifton, who never swore in front of women.

I did and carried on while it turned to laryngitis and pleurisy and finally began to edge into pneumonia, a process mercifully halted when Keith fairly dragged me to the doctor, who prescribed antibiotics. He also told me to take four or so days out of the campaign, pointing out that I had no voice anyway. I refused, pointing out in turn that campaigns, like time and tide, waited for no man.

What followed was the fiercest struggle of mind over matter that I have so far had to face. I carried out a public meeting with virtually no voice, but if nothing else it guaranteed silence as everyone strained to hear what I was saying on a microphone as crackly as my own throat.

I stood at the dockyard gates at dawn, shivering, and every time I ran my breathing was painful. I watched the young running effortlessly up and down garden paths and glimpsed some distant future in which my fate would be forever to watch effortless physical activity and know that I would never again participate. I was glad to accompany Dame Joan Vickers as she leant upon her stick as it was the only time duty demanded that I did not hurry.

Cranley Onslow was so worried that he went to a chemist's and bought me a bottle of cough mixture. The pain had a hilarious consequence. I could not bear tightness around my lungs so I loosened my undergarments as much as possible and Greta Houghton criticised me for my slack appearance. She even offered to take me shopping for 'foundation garments'! It was the first of many such remarks which were to follow me throughout my career.

The antibiotics killed the pain towards the end of the campaign but the cough took weeks to fade and for a few years would always return with any common cold.

The tension mounted with a poll putting Owen in third place. Those who watched from afar were later to tell me that they never thought Owen in any danger of losing, given the high hopes then vested in the SDP Liberal Alliance to break the mould of British politics and the hugely successful performances of Owen on television. Within the hothouse of Devonport itself the view was less detached and the atmosphere grew feverish.

'Shock Poll Puts Owen in Third Place' screamed the *Western Evening Herald*, 'Owen Faces Fight for Survival' chorused the

Western Morning News. On the Tuesday before the poll, Winston Grant-Evans, the political correspondent of the *Western Morning News* predicted I would win. Owen himself was not immune from doubt and I heard him tell a local interviewer that, no, he would not be available for interview on the Friday morning if he was 'a private citizen'.

It was a dispiriting experience to find on nearly every doorstep that Owen was already in the lounge, his face looking at me from television screens, his voice rumbling beneath my own patter. When in the 2001 general election I was touring the country by helicopter and campaigning in my own seat once a week if lucky, I remembered Devonport and cheered up my supporters with the reflection that I would be in everyone's home almost every evening.

Our battlewagon was rolling and we stormed ahead of Julian Priestley, who had earlier enjoyed predictions of victory. I began to half-believe my own propaganda and to wonder what it would be like to find myself in Parliament instead of London University.

Yet I have always had a strong pessimistic streak, generally predicting missed grades at school, losses in student elections at university and failed applications for promotions at work. Such an approach has its compensations as I have travelled through life often being pleasantly surprised but rarely disappointed.

Thus when Owen scored a convincing win at Devonport with a majority of 4,934 I was but mildly downcast, particularly as I was in turn more than 6,000 votes ahead of Priestley, and I had the same consolation as when I had been obliged to put Burnley ahead of Anglesey: it would never have been a safe seat and now I was free to look for one.

Devonport had been a heady election and in the country at large, where the Falklands factor dwarfed the unemployment queues and Britain shuddered at the Foot agenda, Maggie returned triumphant with a majority of 144.

Nevertheless I was thirty-five. I had high hopes that after Devonport I would be asked to fight a by-election and that I would find it much easier to get a safe seat but, despite my enthusiasm for Westminster, I acknowledged that persistence needed to be more than its own reward, that I had been driving all my efforts towards a single aim from the moment I was accepted at Oxford and that I did not want to arrive in middle age with nothing but aspiration to my account and so I resolved that I would go on trying until I was forty but that if I had no safe seat by then I would give up, work abroad and pay a bit more attention to amassing money instead of spending it on travel, bed and break-fasts, conferences, subscriptions, functions, raffle tickets and campaigns as I strove in the Tory Party's *cursus honorum*.

Whether I would have held to the resolution I do not know because it was not put to the test: I entered the House of Commons at thirty-nine and a half.

Chapter Twelve

SILLY BURGHERS

T he huge victory in the 1983 election made the Tories bold and there began to unfold over the next fourteen years but especially over the next nine a radical agenda which completely altered the face of Britain. The big State monopolies were simply sold off, the waitress in the boardroom was as likely to own shares as the directors upon whom she was waiting, council houses began blossoming with bay windows, hanging baskets and fresh paint as tenants became owners, the children of cash-strapped households were admitted to public schools under the assisted places schemes and everyone was encouraged to think of himself as an entrepreneur as Britain began to boom.

Indeed it was the attitude to work which was the most marked of the social changes of the 1980s. Until then there had been a division between the professional and managerial class and the rest. Managers came to work at 10 a.m. as did senior civil servants and lawyers while the workers began at six. Top brass took long lunches while workers had strictly timed breaks. Nobody who had left Oxbridge with a good degree would have set up a window-cleaning business.

Suddenly everything became competitive and everyone could dream of being a millionaire by thirty. Managers began at six, senior civil servants were spotted on commuter trains at ungodly hours, business lunches became sandwiches and mineral water on the job, to run his own business was the dream of the chap spouting Latin at Oxbridge degree ceremonies although optimism led to more individual borrowing than was wise. Hope boomed along with the economy.

That, of course, applied to those who saw work as the way to success. What the Thatcher years never achieved was the reduction of dependence on welfare or, rather more importantly, a change in attitude on the part of claimants. Blair was no more successful and it remains to be seen whether the coalition, which promises much on this score, will make any real inroads with the benefits cap and other measures.

Welfare dependency has crept along to reach catastrophic proportions, not just for the economy but for the fibre of the nation. In the 1950s it was a matter of pride not to draw what was then called National Assistance and there was a loss of face involved in being 'on the dole'. Self-sufficiency was inextricably linked with self-respect.

That however was tough on people who quite genuinely found themselves out of work and unable to find other employment immediately. By the 1960s there was some easing in this attitude. Social security was a practical prop in time of urgent need and should not bear a stigma. Most would find that wise and sensitive but the proverbial pendulum carried on its proverbial swinging.

By the 1970s people were *choosing* not to leave the welfare system if the job on offer was not to their liking or they would be no better off in work. Abuse was rife in the shape of working and claiming, co-habiting and the healthy being 'on the sick'. The scale was growing and so was resentment among the taxpayers whose efforts were subsidising the work-shy, but the worst aspect was the growth in those who had never worked, embracing dependency as a way of life, with no aspiration to change.

Governments stared glumly at the pendulum but any attempts to halt its progress would be met with howls of outrage from the Opposition, who would immediately champion the cause of the unemployed and ill without any distinction between the genuine and the false.

Now sick notes are distributed like confetti, often without exhaustive examination, and the hunt for work becomes a ritual of applying for jobs or poring over job ads in accordance with the rules but with no real spirit of determination. Indeed the man who distributes hundreds of leaflets advertising his self-employed services is deemed not to have looked for work while the one who has applied for two jobs with no intention of following them up is deemed to have done so.

My own solution has, for many years, been workfare. In the world as run by Widdecombe everyone would have a set amount of time to look for work, with those who had a steady record of employment being allowed longer. Once the period had elapsed the claimant would have to do unpaid work in return for benefit. It has worked well in some areas of the US. Most people confronted with a choice of finding a job and enjoying a regular wage or working at whatever may be set in return for benefit will prefer the former and, of course, it makes working and claiming pretty difficult.

In the early 1990s I found myself taking the legislation for the Jobseeker's Allowance through the House of Commons. The theory was fine but the practice too easy to thwart, but of that more later. For now let us stay with the 1980s.

The Cold War showed no sign of abating and in 1983 anyone who predicted the fall of the Berlin Wall by the end of the decade would have been laughed to scorn. By contrast the arms race was intensifying and there was now much talk of 'star wars'. This referred to what was actually a defensive rather than offensive system, as the idea was to throw up a shield in space over the US which could not be penetrated by nuclear weapons. However one did not have to be a genius to work out that whichever superpower was the first to put up such a shield would then be in a position to launch an attack without fear of retaliation. There was therefore much international debate as to whether such a measure should be included in arms reductions talks. So they all prattled on at Geneva while Russia and America increased their nuclear capacities year on year.

There was not much active fear on the part of the general population, it being generally accepted that neither the Americans nor Soviets would begin Armageddon. Of course CND disagreed and there was considerable debate about our own involvement, but in practice people were more likely to fear the IRA – and with reason.

It is nearly twenty years since we suffered concerted terrorism on the mainland and the daily risk run by those whose lives took them into city centres is now a distant memory, but in the eighties that risk was ever-present. I missed the Harrods bomb by three-quarters of an hour, having been on my way there from my flat in Fulham when I turned back for something I had forgotten. Innocent shoppers were maimed and killed.

As already recorded, I missed the Brighton bomb in 1984 by less than half an hour.

In 1991 I sat in my Whitehall office chairing a meeting at the DHSS and heard the IRA mortar Downing Street. Although all government offices in the area were equipped with curtains designed to stop broken window glass blowing into the room, upon hearing the attack and knowing there was a Cabinet meeting in progress, we raced to the windows, pulled aside the curtains and peered out. It was just as well another mortar didn't shatter the glass.

The IRA failed to assassinate the Prime Minister and her Cabinet at Brighton, despite the sophistication of the device, and they failed to assassinate John Major and his Cabinet when they launched mortars at 10 Downing Street, but over the years they killed not only the occasional politician but civilians, indiscriminately including women, children and old folk. Animals were not immune either.

When they were not actually bombing random victims they were claiming to be about to or, more often, hoaxers made such claims and public buildings were regularly evacuated. Wastepaper bins disappeared from stations, left luggage closed down and party conferences put on ostentatious but futile security checks in which every old lady had her handbag searched.

The 1980s saw no advance whatever towards peace in Northern Ireland, with the government and IRA both obdurate. It was to take the courage and vision of John Major to begin the process which eventually led to peace – at any rate on the mainland. Yet there was spectacular success internationally with the fall of communism.

Ann's parents:
Rita and Murray
Widdecombe,
c. 1930

Rita Widdecombe, 1940

Captain Murray Widdecombe, 1940

Right: Rita with her son Malcolm and
daughter Ann, 1947

Ann and her mother,
Hill Head, 1951

Ann with her
father and brother
at Ordnance House,
Gosport, c. 1953

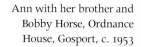

Ann with her brother and
Bobby Horse, Ordnance
House, Gosport, c. 1953

300 Kloof
Road,
Singapore,
1953

Chew
Soon Moi,
Singapore

Rita, Ann
and Moi,
Singapore,
c. 1954

Ann, Meng and Anda Panda,
c. 1954

Amah,
Singapore,
1955

Brownie in the
6th Singapore
Pack, c. 1955

Pupils at The Royal Naval School, Singapore, 1955 (Ann seated fourth from right in front row)

THE BRITISH BROADCASTING CORPORATION

HEAD OFFICE: BROADCASTING HOUSE, LONDON, W.1

TELEVISION CENTRE: WOOD LANE, LONDON, W.12

TELEGRAMS & CABLES: BROADCASTS, LONDON, TELEX   *   INTERNATIONAL TELEX 2-2182

TELEPHONE: SHEPHERDS BUSH 8030

Ref:04/R/EF   18th September,1957.

Dear Ann Widdecombe,

       Thank you very much for sending me your photograph.

       I am returning it, together with an enlargement which we used in the programme on Sunday.

       I hope my answer to your question was of some help to you.

               Yours sincerely,

              John Elphinstone-Fyffe

          (The Rev.J.M.Elphinstone-Fyffe)
            Producer "Sunday Special".

Miss Ann Widdecombe,
Quell Cottage,
Blackdown,
Haslemere,
Surrey.

CML.

First television appearance: Ann on *Sunday Special,* 1957

Bath Convent, 1960

Sixth Former, 1964

Ann with her parents and brother outside Buckingham Palace after Murray's award of the CB

Oxford Union Society ~ Standing Committee

Standing Committee of the Oxford Union, 1971. (Ann back row, second right; Colin Maltby third right) (Gilman & Soame)

The acquiring of Methuselah, summer 1971

Punting on the river with Colin Maltby, 1971

Ann at Oxford, 1972

Ann and Colin at Ann's graduation,
Oxford, 1972

Towards the end of that decade there were three huge players on the world stage who dared to imagine an end to the Cold War: Reagan, Gorbachev and Thatcher. The key name there is Gorbachev, the Russian President. Had he taken the same line as his predecessors the outcome might have been different and would certainly have been delayed.

No peace process can ever be effective unless both sides are fully committed to it. One of the most startling acts of peace in my lifetime was when President Anwar Sadat of Egypt addressed the Knesset. He and Menachem Begin, his Israeli counterpart, wanted an end to the destructive war that was raging between their countries. It was an effective peace process only because of equal commitment and there will be no similar success between Israel and Palestine until there is an equal and bilateral determination to end the conflict, so most Western intervention is doomed at the outset.

Successful peace negotiations always include the unpalatable and, if one is wise, the best reaction is to hold one's nose when long-held principles are surrendered. The IRA must have choked on the need for the Republic to give up its territorial claim to the North and Britain had a similar reaction to the release of those who had murdered the innocent. It was a measure I was to vote against, less because I denied its place in effecting peace than because at that stage there was not an ounce of semtex given up in return.

Emotionally I have never come to terms with those releases even though rationally I accept them as necessary to prevent the loss of more innocent life. Encountering Patrick Magee, the Brighton bomber, in the reception area of a TV studio, I refused the efforts of Wendy Bailey, an agent who has handled a lot of my work and a good Christian, to persuade me to meet him. He had directly killed one of my friends. I wish him no ill but I have not the slightest desire to be friendly with him or with any of those who willingly and knowingly did what they did.

The crucial words there are 'wish him no ill'. Today, promoted by some sections of the tabloid press, there is an attitude that some people are 'evil' and that there is no redemption. Those who leave prison are hounded by press photos and news of their lives, unless they are specifically protected by the courts. The view is the debt is never paid and that they should be thwarted rather than aided in their attempts to build new lives. My own view is that unless they themselves raise issues – such as demanding new identities or are still protesting innocence or commenting, usually justifiably, on prison conditions – then the rest of us should leave them in peace. If they win the lottery or set up a successful business or marry and have children then that is as much their own business as it would be of any other private citizen.

In my childhood and youth I often heard the expression *the only good German is a dead one*. My father himself used it more than once. Yet both my brother and I had Germans to stay in the house with his blessing and he expressed admiration for those of the enemy who had tried to fight a 'clean' war and, indeed, he was horrified by the Berlin Wall. But he, like others, had lost family in not one but two wars with Germany and, I suspect, that if he had ever met any of those directly responsible he would have turned away.

So did I turn away from Patrick Magee, the memories of that night still horribly vivid.

It was 02.54 in the early hours of 12 October. I had left some friends still in the bar at the Grand and was back at my hotel already half asleep when I heard the bomb. It sounded like a very loud crack rather than the boom of the mortar I was to hear many years later, and that was what misled me. I did not recognise the noise which jolted me fully awake for what it was and went back to sleep. Others were to tell me that it was not the bomb but the emergency sirens, which wailed all night, that had woken them.

Next morning Keith Griffiths, who had left Devonport to become agent for a Scottish seat and was staying in the same hotel, banged on my door before 7 a.m. I opened it still blinking away sleep, vaguely baffled by the earliness of the hour.

'Phone your parents,' he told me. 'And tell them you are all right. There's been a bomb. The Grand is destroyed.'

There were no mobile phones in those days and I had to dress at speed and, still unwashed, seek out a public telephone in the hall of the hotel. There was a queue. When I finally made my way to its head I listened for a long time as the phone rang in Haslemere. Eventually my father, finally roused from the sleep of the retired, answered.

'I'm OK. I wasn't there,' I told him as the phone bleeped and went dead. I glared at it in disbelief but at any rate he and my mother wouldn't worry. I didn't bother to seek out more coins and rejoin the queue.

Of course they worried. They had not the faintest idea what I was talking about and the phone had gone dead. My father roused my mother with the words, 'Ann is in some sort of trouble.' Then the telephone started to ring again. It was a neighbour asking, 'Is Ann all right?' Alerted to the real situation, they switched on the radio and all became clear.

At the conference centre it was total confusion, where everybody was asking after everybody else. We had not the smallest idea who was alive, who dead and who was still under the rubble. The PM was unharmed, the conference would carry on, most of the Cabinet were also unharmed, Norman Tebbit had been trapped ...

Yes, it was easy enough to find out what had happened to the bigwigs, but the fate of more obscure mortals was difficult to ascertain and that included friends. With relief I spotted Nirj Deva, a Bow Group chum who had been among those I left at the bar. He told me some of them had suffered dust inhalation but none of them had been detained in hospital for long.

Marks and Spencer opened up with the dawn to sell clothes to those who had escaped in their nightwear. Emma Nicholson appeared from her shopping trip dressed entirely in black.

I could not trace Lillian Ashdown, an elderly friend, and it was twenty-four hours before I knew she had been safely evacuated. 'I heard a big noise and thought it was the fire escape falling down,' she told me later. Meanwhile the grimmer news percolated out. It was a while before I learned that Margaret Tebbit was paralysed for life but there were five deaths:

an MP, Anthony Berry; Roberta, the wife of Cabinet minister John Wakeham; the wife of the president of the Scottish Conservatives, Muriel Maclean; the North West area chairman, Eric Taylor; and Jeanne Shattock.

Jeanne was the wife of Gordon Shattock, a vet, who was the area chairman of the Conservatives in the West Country. The bomb blew Gordon through five floors. In a subsequent letter he described his injuries to me as 'a nuisance'.

As he could then neither see straight, hear properly nor walk properly that was an understatement, but Jeanne had been blown to pieces. The night before she had been chatting to me at a reception, speculating on what she would do with the free time when Gordon had finished his term of office, and that was what I remembered when refusing to shake hands with Patrick Magee.

Meanwhile back on the candidates' round, I was eager to find a constituency in the West Country. My parental background and the massive publicity engendered by the Devonport campaign should have given me an advantage but my applications were in vain. Torridge and West Devon did not even interview me.

'Oh, they just don't want a woman,' muttered Peter Gower, the area agent, consolingly, but they chose Emma Nicholson only to be rewarded with a defection a decade later when I was a minister. I had no more success with other Western seats and when Torbay turned me down and a tactless friend remarked 'Oh, no! If you haven't got Torbay, you won't get anything,' I was tempted to believe her.

Then interviews began to come thick and fast elsewhere and I found myself on shortlists and then several times in second place. 'I knew you were going to get there when you started coming second,' said the area agent who had watched as I narrowly missed Hemel Hempstead, but to me it felt like always being the bridesmaid but never the bride.

Conservative Central Office did not then exercise quite the minutely prescriptive grip over selection procedures as it does now and some seats had introduced their own tests. I remember the agent for Chertsey and Walton, Dennis Arlow, telling me how he had made candidates on the final shortlist invite himself and the chairman for dinner to see them in their own homes. In Hemel Hempstead, a scattered rural seat, we were told to make contact with every single branch chairman and visit the branch, effectively creating a system of primaries.

Living in central London, I was trying to manage without a car and I found myself arriving at small stations looking in vain for taxis. As I stood in a public phone box on one such occasion, trying a series of taxi firms in pouring rain, I wondered if any seat could be worth the effort.

I had the same sort of reaction when I made the journey to the Isle of Wight. Then I did have a car and drove from London to Portsmouth and thence to a ferry. Did I really want to make this trek every week? A long train journey allows one to work but an hour's drive, then the ferry, then another drive would mean a lot of unusable time.

That particular selection became memorable for quite another reason. I was staying in a hotel, in a room on the ground floor where, upon arrival, I had drawn the curtains. Returning after the interview I was in the bathroom when I heard a noise in my bedroom and, emerging, found a man standing by my bed looking somewhat befuddled.

'Can I help you?' I asked, thus I suppose providing him with a defence. ('Well, M'lud, she said could she help me?') He asked where reception was and I suggested he go back out the way he had come in and walk round to the front entrance, for I could now see that what I had taken for a window was in fact a glass door. Fortunately he took my advice and I sped over to the door to lock it.

To my consternation I found this to be impossible so I went in search of the hotel management but the desk was deserted. I did however see David Roberts, the Wessex area agent, sitting in the lounge chatting to the constituency chairman. I told them something 'a bit irregular' was going on and David returned with me to my bedroom but could no more find a means of securing the door than had I.

After another fruitless search for management and unwilling to leave a lady in a room with an unlockable outside door, David suggested we move the wardrobe across it, so between us we set about manoeuvring the furniture. As we dragged the wardrobe from its place David dived to scoop up a magazine which had obviously been lying on top of it but had now become dislodged by our efforts and had fallen to the floor. I just caught a glimpse of a near-naked woman before he thrust it in his inside pocket and I giggled helplessly at the scene now unfolding: an area agent and candidate moving the furniture in the middle of the night and finding pornography.

The door was successfully barricaded and David returned to the constituency chairman, a member of the rather posh Cowes sailing set. He told me next day that every time he leant forward to make a point the offending material began to jut out of his pocket! When he finally got a chance to divest himself of it he discovered that what he had taken such pains to protect me from was merely a health and fitness magazine.

In quick succession I found myself in the final for Cheadle and then Maidstone, a constituency which had turned down Margaret Thatcher in 1959 in favour of John Wells, who had represented the seat ever since.

There is an entertaining diary column in the *Sunday Express* called Crossbencher. The weekend before the selection it ran a piece under the heading 'Silly Burghers', which described how Maidstone had turned down the future Prime Minister and then suggested that I should not therefore be too disappointed if I, a woman, were to suffer a similar fate. I have often wondered how great a part that delightfully wicked little piece may have played in my ultimate success in that final!

I bore it in mind when the selectors asked me how far I expected to get at Westminster. I replied that Maidstone had Disraeli but not as prime minister and had almost had Margaret Thatcher so perhaps it would be third time lucky! Later I looked up the account of the 1959 selection and found her referred to as 'Mrs Denis Thatcher', a custom probably dying out with Princess Anne, who for a while styled herself as Mrs Mark Phillips.

My quip must have worked because in December 1985 my quest finally came to an end when, in the hall of the boys' grammar school, I defeated two other candidates, including Michael Fabricant, now the MP for Lichfield, in the first ballot to become the prospective Conservative candidate for Maidstone, a seat that had returned long-serving Conservative MPs since 1906.

The hunt for a safe seat had lasted ten years and spanned the selection rounds of three general elections. I had applied to seats the length and breadth of the country and everywhere I went seemed to run into people who said, 'I remember you well. I voted for you.' It reminded me of Charles II, who remarked not long after his restoration that 'It must have been my fault I was absent for so long; for I saw no body that did not protest; he had ever wished for my return.'

My friends all told me that now I had a safe seat and would be able to stay in Parliament as long as I wanted, but for a while the future looked a great deal less certain. The majority in 1983 had dropped to 7,500 and the local press made much of that being the lowest majority in Kent. That may have been true but, as I pointed out, losing the seat would still have required a much larger swing than normally achieved in general elections, nearly 7 per cent, and saying that Maidstone was marginal just because it had a lower majority than other Kent seats was like saying that a man who earned £50,000 was poor just because he lived in a street where the norm was £100,000.

It was also unhelpful that the Liberal Democrats regularly turned in a strong performance in the local elections and the council was either hung or very marginally held by either the Conservatives or the Liberals. The *Kent Messenger* declared that my Lib Dem opponent had the edge and got very excited at the prospect of Maidstone changing hands.

I was also finding out that nursing Maidstone presented difficulties which nursing Burnley (I discount Devonport because of the extreme shortness of the pre-campaign period) did not. In Burnley I had been expected only at weekends but, Maidstone being so close to London, I was now expected to appear during the week as well and having had a serving MP for twenty-six years, the association appeared to have little grasp of fitting activities around someone who was still earning a living. It needed only a hold-up in London traffic and a missed commuting train to have the workers grumbling.

The *Burnley Express* and the *Evening Star* had been only too delighted to report my activities, but the attitude of the *Kent Messenger* was that its job was to report the activities of the sitting MP, so getting coverage was difficult. Again, the position being unfamiliar to them, those who were working so hard in the branches began to mutter that the candidate was not trying hard enough.

Additionally there was ill-feeling on the part of some locals who had tried for the selection and been rejected, so it was by no means an easy eighteen months. Then, just as the election was looming, what was to become a running sore manifested itself. I was anti-hunting.

I had never made any secret of the fact and it bothered most people who disagreed with me not a whit but there was a hard core of hunters who seriously believed that my views would cost the Conservatives the seat. Despite a record of rising majorities this view still held sway among this group twenty years later. They talked about 'alienating the rural vote', still oblivious to the fact that plenty of countryside dwellers, including some farmers, were not on their side or were indifferent to the issue.

I have dealt with few more arrogant minorities than the hunters, too many of whom believe that those who oppose them have no right to be heard. A good example of their arrogance was when I was invited, some years ago, to open a fête at Widecombe-in-the-Moor. They told the vicar that if I came they would come along to demonstrate at the event with their hounds, so the invitation was withdrawn. They have obviously mellowed a bit because recently I was invited along to present prizes at Widecombe Fair and nobody objected. Clearly *Strictly Come Dancing* is mightier than the hunting horn.

In 1992 some members of the association tried to have me de-selected on account of my opposition to hunting. I did not think they were likely to succeed but when David Alton heard of it he told me I must have a letter of support from a prominent

hunter and approached none other than the then Duke of Norfolk, who supplied a letter which contained the wonderful sentiment that he wished I had been at his side when he was fighting
the Mau-Mau!

I gave this to the agent and told him to use it if things got
sticky. I fully expected a gale of laughter to follow and, sitting
outside in an ante-room while the discussions raged, I waited
for that moment, but no sounds of mirth were emitted and I was
duly called in to be told I had been re-selected by an overwhelming majority.

I assumed the letter had not been needed but later learned that
it had been read out in full and absorbed in respectful silence!

In 1987 a very different letter from a prominent hunter within
the constituency contained the rather less delightful line: 'I realise it is now too late to find a more generally acceptable candidate', another sad demonstration of how the more fanatical
hunters just assume everybody else shares their views. Fortunately John Wells, himself pro-hunting, calmed the diehards
down.

The campaign itself was easy enough in terms of policies. Kent
still had grammar schools and Maidstone Grammar was one of its
flagships. There was no appetite for the Liberal Democrat policy
of abolition. Similarly with the Cold War still in place my stand
on the nuclear deterrent was popular.

The Liberal Democrats, however, made Maidstone their
number one target seat in Kent, covered the area with orange
posters and poured in front-line help. It created an illusion of
progress which in reality they were not making but which caused
much speculation in press and media. Their candidate and I held
a public meeting in every single village, sometimes clocking up
three in an evening. Labour, hampered by the pronouncements
of Neil Kinnock, had no chance and the Green candidate was an
amiable eccentric.

The Liberals swallowed their own propaganda and arrived
at the count in confident mood, but as the evening wore on
they watched in disbelief as my bundles of votes piled up. I
also watched in disbelief, scarcely daring to hope that it was

happening at last, but in the early hours of 12 June I stood beside the returning officer and heard myself pronounced elected with a majority of more than 10,000.

'Ann Widdecombe MP!' said my mother as we cracked open the champagne and fairly danced with victory. Around us my supporters whooped and cheered in both triumph and relief.

As for me, I merely observed that life began at thirty-nine and a half.

Chapter Thirteen

ARRIVING (2)

The Mother of Parliaments is a chaotic place for new entrants even today, but in 1987 it was still in the transition between an amateur business for part-timers, who wrote their letters by hand in the library during the afternoons, and a workplace for full-time professional politicians. Now each MP has his own office but then we were crammed in four to a room, with an allocation of two filing cabinets each and an office allowance that would not stretch to more than one and a half members of staff but desk space for only one.

It took weeks, yes *weeks,* to be allocated a permanent desk. If the incoming MP were to strike lucky he could find an unoccupied desk on which to 'squat' until allotted one in his own right. The unlucky dictated their constituency correspondence in the corridors and Mike Stern, a fellow Bow Grouper and later my accountant who entered in 1983, regaled us with stories of how he had worked on the floor of the gents' loo!

My major blessing was that I had immediate access to a hugely experienced House of Commons secretary in the shape of Sheila Kerr, whom I had met when campaigning for Michael Ancram in 1974. Michael had subsequently won another marginal seat, Edinburgh South, but had lost it in 1987. Sheila therefore nobly stepped into the gap until my own secretary could work out her notice and join me. She opened and drafted answers to all my post and I learned a great deal about procedures from her.

I found an empty desk in College Gardens, near Westminster Abbey, sharing a room with Michael Clark, the MP for Rochford, who had been stationed there in the previous Parliament and who tipped me off that there was a spare desk. It was a pleasant office with a view over gardens and I was sorry to leave it when my permanent allocation sent me to a much less lovely spot.

The confusion over desks was matched by a confusion over procedure. Everything was communicated in Chinese whispers and there was no formal induction process. It was all trial and error, and that included not only parliamentary processes but basic conventions. Gillian Shephard had an awkward moment when she sat down at an empty table in the dining room and was promptly moved on by a colleague who told her it was the Chief Whip's table and one sat there by invitation only. The different parties occupy different parts of the members' dining room and tea room, with the Liberals and Irish stationed in No Man's Land in the middle.

In the Chamber itself it was still the age of strict formality. I had to learn pretty quickly who was referred to as honourable and who as right honourable, who was learned (QCs) and who gallant (decorated for war service). It was – and still is – necessary not only to recognise the person speaking but to know also which constituency he or she represented. Thus one never spoke of 'Mr Howard' but of 'My Right Honourable and learned friend, the member for Folkestone'. If one erred, Hansard recorded the correct mode of address.

Those in the same party are 'friends'. When there is a free vote and consequently a mixture of parties on both sides, in the ensuing committee one has 'usual' friends on the other side and 'temporary' friends on one's own.

At the time of the huge influx of new MPs in the wake of Blair's 1997 victory, some objected but the traditions have largely survived. One which did not was that of the top hat. In the House those who wish to speak must stand and, if called, must carry on standing but the exception is if someone wishes to raise a point of order during a division. Obviously as everybody is moving about between Chamber and voting lobbies, standing up would not make one visible to Mr Speaker, so one stays seated. However other members are also seated, having already voted or having not yet moved off to do so. So to become visible the member wishing to raise the point of order must don a hat.

Hansard refers to this as being 'seated and covered'. And what more visible hat than a top hat? If several members were vying for the hat or the member wishing to speak was too far from it, then, while it was being passed along, he would hold an order paper over his head in order to fulfil the requirement to be 'covered'. Dennis Skinner once produced a cloth cap. It is perhaps unsurprising that this quaint tradition did not survive the age of television.

Being the age of the all-night sitting, it was utterly routine to be in the House till 3 a.m. and, from time to time, the whole night. If we escaped at midnight we would talk about the merits of an 'early' night! After about 1 a.m. it became impossible to concentrate, so members followed their noses to the hot bacon sandwiches in the tea room or gathered in the bars (Tories mainly in the Pugin, Labour usually in the Kremlin and others nomadically between the two).

This somewhat eccentric way of doing business had three advantages. The first was that, from a party point of view, it made for camaraderie or, as they say these days, bonding. Once it got to the point where we were too tired for desk work and we were gathering in the tea room and bars we all got to know each other well, we talked both politics and families, plotted and planned strategies, tried to interest each other in various issues, and everyone from the oldest member to the newest recruit chatted to ministers about policies.

The second advantage was less obvious. People did not think of us as idle. If you went to bed hearing on the news that MPs were still discussing such and such a bill and you woke to hear 'MPs have been voting all night on the such and such bill' then you might have thought – and you would have been right – that it was a darn silly way to run a country, but what you would not have thought was 'lazy blighters!' Certainly we were still teased about the length of summer recess but there was not, as there regrettably is now, a general dissatisfaction with our input of hours. That view of MPs as part-time and slack contributed to the terrible lynch-mob mentality which was the public response to the expenses scandal in 2009.

The third advantage was by far the most important and is too little appreciated: Parliament could carry out vastly more effectively its job of scrutinising legislation because we had the time to do so and we had some bargaining powers to get law changed if we were unhappy with it. Now there are arbitrary time limits and backbench bargaining power is but a fraction of that which I took for granted in those early years.

Guillotines, or the cutting off of further discussion, were regarded as undesirable and were only imposed when a genuine need arose for emergency legislation or where there was a discernible and protracted filibuster. They were certainly not routine. This meant that a particularly contentious clause could be debated at length without prejudicing discussion of vast chunks of the rest of the bill.

In 1997 Blair decided, most would say sensibly, that we should cut our hours but that begged the question of how we were supposed to get through all the legislation. Well, I suppose we could simply have had less of it, but that was hardly an attractive proposition to ministers who had been out of office for eighteen years and who believed they could now change half the world. That left but one solution: regular and routine guillotines which Blair euphemistically termed timetable motions.

In short, no matter how much or how little scrutiny a bill had received there would be automatic cut-offs at every stage, including the detailed committee consideration. It was this mockery of the legislative process that led me to organise a 'sit-in' when I was Shadow Home Secretary.

The bill in question was the Police and Criminal Justice Bill and the cut-off of the committee stage arrived without the Police half of the bill having been even reached, let alone discussed or voted upon. Patrick McLoughlin, the Opposition Deputy Chief Whip, James Cran, also a whip and I went and sat in the committee, to which we had not been appointed, thus bringing its proceedings to a standstill. The purpose was to make it impossible for the committee to wind up as planned and we believed it would therefore have to meet again the next day when there might be an attempt to discuss the Police section of the bill.

What happened next demonstrated the complete impotence of Parliament under a truly arrogant government.

The highly respected and experienced chairman, Roger Gale, asked us several times to leave. We refused. Unable to proceed with the business, he had no choice but to suspend the committee and name us. Naming is the process under which unruly members are reported to the House. From that not much followed as Labour hardly wanted to make martyrs of us but the government put down an unprecedented motion that the committee was deemed to have completed its business, i.e. it did not have to reconvene.

That to the lay reader will sound all a bit technical but it may be distilled thus: the Blair government decided it would pass a whole tranche of legislation which had not been scrutinised. When MPs used a means of trying to obtain extra time for such scrutiny it simply decided the committee had finished anyway. And thus is our law made: undiscussed and without vote. And the average Briton does not care tuppence.

The other way that government coped with trying to do the same amount of work in hours which grew ever shorter was simply to sideline much backbench activity by having it removed from the Chamber to a room called 'Westminster Hall'.

In 1987 all that was still ten years away and backbenchers could table business motions demanding extra time even for private members' bills and there were no time limits on backbench speeches, which could go on for hours if members were trying to bargain with a reluctant minister.

I was supposed to be working notice at London University but in the end we agreed it was an impossible combination and I brought forward my date of departure.

My twelve years there had been happy and successful but now, at last, I had achieved my life's ambition and had arrived, full time and hungry for a different sort of success.

With still some weeks of session to go before the summer recess I did not join the wild scramble for maiden speeches. I had a very clear notion of the topic I wanted, which was Trident, and the debates on the defence estimates were scheduled for October. I was prepared to wait. It is a cliché but nonetheless true that a parliamentary career is a marathon rather than a sprint. When the day came the speech went well. My father was in the public gallery and was particularly impressed when David Owen arrived in the Chamber to hear what I had to say, an example of parliamentary courtesy to a former opponent.

For the next three years, until I became a minister in John Major's first administration, my life was dominated by abortion, the Channel Tunnel rail link and ten-minute rule bills.

David Alton, then a Liberal Democrat MP for a Liverpool seat, had come sufficiently high in the ballot for private members' bills to be guaranteed a second reading and had tabled a bill to reduce the number of weeks at which late abortions could be carried out. In reality any controversial private member's bill can be talked out at later stages because, unlike in the case of government business, no matter how long a filibuster is mounted there is no procedural means of bringing all matters to a conclusion. It just keeps being sent back for more discussion until the end of the parliamentary year when all unfinished business falls.

There was therefore little prospect of success for that bill, but the view was that if Parliament demonstrated a will to change the law and was thwarted only by the employment of procedural devices then, given the head of steam which we had in the country, we might oblige government to give the matter time in a bill of its own.

I dropped David a note saying I was 100 per cent behind his bill and asking what I could do to help. The reply was frosty: I should speak to Bernard Braine, who was coordinating the Conservative effort. As far as David was concerned I was one of those right-wing Thatcherites and, grateful as he was for my support, he did not particularly want to be pally.

As the bill had every prospect of passing its second reading the campaign in the country was huge. Support was cross-party and from every religion and none. Rallies and church services were interrupted and picketed by women screaming 'Not the Church, not the State, a woman's right to choose her fate'. The Society for the Protection of Unborn Children, run by the formidable

Phyllis Bowman, flooded Parliament with postcards showing a picture of an eighteen-week baby in the womb, taken from a medical textbook. Sympathetic gynaecologists gave descriptions of the processes involved in late abortion and at the time there was massive controversy about one notorious method which involved dismembering the child in the womb.

Parliament was packed out on the morning of Friday, 22 January 1988, and there was no room left in the public gallery. Dale Campbell-Savours led the Labour support for the Alton Bill and Jo Richardson the opposition, Bernard Braine the Conservative support and Andrew MacKay the opposition. Only the Irish parties were united in support and MPs, on a free vote, spoke with passion. It was a tremendous debate but I thought I had little chance of being called as senior backbenchers were queuing to catch the Speaker's eye. Then I saw Bernard wander up to the Speaker's chair and the occupant look briefly in my direction. A short while later he called me.

I spoke briefly, aware that so many wanted to join the debate that a long contribution would alienate colleagues. David Alton listened, nodded and thawed half a centimetre, but when the division came he asked me to be a teller. This was because he had worked out that we would win (as it happened by a comfortable majority of 296 to 251) and he wanted a woman's voice reading out the results. In those days there was no televising of parliamentary proceedings and the moment of triumph was heard only on radio.

Having spoken in the debate, I was then asked to serve on the committee which would examine the bill in depth and report back to the House. The next few months were to be a steep learning curve in procedures and tactics, compromises and strange alliances but underlying it all was a fight based on a simple question: when does life begin? At birth? At conception? At some point in between? If so, what is that point?

At that time the 1967 Abortion Act was still coupled with the Infant Life (Preservation) Act 1929 which makes it an offence to destroy a child capable of being born alive. The presumptive line was twenty-eight weeks. In the exceptionally rare instances of any abortion after that date it would have been incumbent on doctors to prove that the child was not capable of life, but before that point the burden of proof rested in the other direction and any prosecution would have to prove conclusively that the child could have lived.

Guidance issued to the medical profession stated that doctors should not normally end pregnancies once they had reached the twenty-four-week point, as babies had survived that young. Abortions between the twenty-fourth and twenty-eighth week amounted to 36. If the limit were to be reduced from twenty-eight to twenty-two weeks it would save 1,046 unborn lives, at twenty weeks 2,481 and at eighteen weeks 5,929.

If a mother was in danger after the twenty-eighth week from a continuation of her pregnancy then every effort had to be made to deliver the child alive and in clinics where late abortions were carried out (i.e. after twenty weeks) it was law that resuscitation equipment had to be on hand and used where a child survived the termination. This was to be a salient issue in the case of the Carlisle Baby, of which heart-rending incident more later.

So in 1987 we had an absolute limit of twenty-eight weeks and a widely observed one of twenty-four weeks. Thus one might have two children of exactly the same age, one of whom was lying in an incubator with all the resources of medical science being poured into saving his or her life and the other being wilfully destroyed in the womb, put in a black sack and consigned to the flames. Moral? Civilised?

It is one thing to suggest a woman should have control over her own fate but the fate of the child has also to be considered and that child has no voice but Parliament's. So when is a child a child?

That was the impossible question confronting MPs in 1987. If an arbitrary line is to be set somewhere between conception and birth then reasons for the decision have to be given. Should it be when a child is capable of being born alive, when a child is fully developed in terms of organs, lungs and limbs and has only growth left to achieve, when it quickens in the womb, when it is capable of feeling pain? The undecided peered at pictures in medical textbooks and stayed undecided.

The debate and especially the public debate began to crystal-lise around the issue of handicap, which presented the pro-life side with a difficult dilemma. Many MPs had made it clear in the second reading debate that they were effectively 'lending' us their votes and that they would support us through further stages only if we exempted unborn disabled children from the eighteen-week limit. None of the bill's sponsors believed in denying rights to a disabled baby which we would accord to its able-bodied counterpart and a voluble group both in the country and in the parliamentary pro-life group argued that it would be so immoral that we should make no compromise and we must lose the bill if necessary.

I was among those who argued otherwise. The statistics were clear and 92 per cent of abortions after the eighteenth week were not performed on grounds of handicap. If we were standing on a shore watching a shipwreck and we knew from the outset that out of the hundred people on board the vessel we could save only 92 would we do that or would we simply stand back and watch the whole ship go down and save nobody? Eighteen weeks was itself a compromise, as none of us believed in abortion so late, but we were trying to save as many unborn lives as we could.

My view and of those who shared it prevailed and we agreed to exempt the severely disabled unborn children, but we then made a serious tactical error. It was going to be difficult explain-ing to the disabled section of the pro-life movement in the country why we were selling them out, why people like them uniquely would receive no protection in the womb and would not be allowed to be born. So we promised not to sell them out in debate, that we would never desert them in our arguments and that while making the exemption in the bill we would continue to stand up for the right of disabled babies in the womb to have equal treatment.

The media and public do not follow such subtle distinctions and if they hear you arguing a case then they deduce that is what you are trying to do. So even if you begin the argument by saying that you have exempted all disabled babies from the proposed limits, as soon as you argue vigorously against that exemption they lose track of its existence and the concession you have made.

We should have been ruthless and simply said every time the handicap argument was raised 'but our bill will not apply to those unborn children'. The public would have understood that. Right up to the evening of the vote I was receiving requests from mainstream, respected TV programmes and newscasters to go on to debate with parents of disabled children. When I pointed out the exemption, made long ago, they appeared never to have heard of it. Nor had Mrs Thatcher, as we found out when a group of Conservative women MPs went to solicit her support for the bill.

The law of the political jungle is keep the message simple or die.

A small band of MPs began to tour the country addressing increasingly rowdy public meetings. Once, when I was obliged to remain at Westminster on some piece of parliamentary business, David Alton addressed a big rally in my brother's church. He came back to tell me he hoped the church was still standing as people in a noisy demonstration outside were throwing things at the windows and the police were trying to hold them back from storming the doors.

He thawed another half a centimetre when I told him that my enthusiastic vicar-brother had enjoyed every minute of it.

As was predictable and predicted, we were talked out. We did manage to complete report stage (that is when the House considers all amendments) but we could not achieve a third reading. If even a couple of MPs are determined enough they can kill off a bill at report stage simply by tabling enough amendments and debating them for long enough, and when there is a sizeable number of such MPs no controversial bill can succeed unless it is then given government time. We would simply have to try again in the next session.

On the afternoon of 8 December I returned to Westminster from a visit to the 36th Engineer Regiment in my constituency to find a raft of pink slips. These are telephone messages taken by the switchboard which are handed to the Member when a messenger spots him. The messengers wear white ties and tails. I had wandered into the members' lobby and was ambling in the direction of the tea room when one of them called out to me that there were some urgent telephone messages. This was before the age of the ubiquitous mobile phone and very few of us even had pagers. Instead of texts and emails and voicemails we just had bits of paper.

I looked at the small clutch and felt excitement rise in my stomach. It was the day of the ballot for private members' bills and all the pink slips were from the press gallery. Was it possible my number had come up in the annual lottery? It had and I immediately announced that I would simply revive the Alton Bill, but I was seventh and then only the first six bills were guaranteed a second reading.

There followed a long series of parliamentary ruses and antics on Friday after Friday when we used every procedure available to choke off other bills, drive bargains, object to summarily presented bills and talk out anything that might threaten the second reading of my abortion bill. The breakthrough appeared to have arrived when I came up in the ballot for a private member's motion and I tabled a business motion to the effect that when my second reading took place it should continue to any hour, thereby preventing its being talked out.

It was arguable whether that motion would ever have been passed. MPs do not like being at Westminster on Fridays, let alone after the usual hour of the close of business, but my opponents were not prepared to take a chance. Only two things could take precedence over a motion on the order paper on a Friday morning and those were petitions and the moving of a by-election writ. It would have been theoretically possible for the opponents of my bill to present enough petitions to delay my being heard but the easier option was to debate a by-election writ and as luck would have it there was one pending in Richmond (Yorkshire), which was destined to bring William Hague into Parliament.

On 20 January 1989, Dennis Skinner moved the writ and

then spoke for three hours, dwelling at length on the Yorkshire weather. He had a little help from his friends who mounted intervention after intervention. When my own allies tried to bring the proceedings to a halt, Mr Speaker put the following motion to the vote: 'The Question is, That the Question, That the Question be not now put, be now put.' If at this point the lay reader is puzzled, so were most of us! My motion could not be debated. The morning ended with a furious eruption of points of order. I observed that the antics had brought Parliament and the democratic workings of the place into disrepute, but then added defiantly, 'I have only one thing to say as a message to all those who have held up this motion today – we shall be back, and back and back.'

Sir Bernard Braine commented, 'It is clear from today's experience ... that procedures which are firmly rooted in the nineteenth century are totally incapable of permitting bills that have passed through several stages in the House with a substantial majority to make any further process.' He went on to say that the reputation of Parliament was seriously at stake and that there would be a public backlash. However, the overwhelming feeling both on the floor of the House and in the very bemused public gallery was that the whole procedure had been a farce.

Eventually the incident led to rule changes which denied backbenchers the right to move both such motions and by-election writs, two of many changes which have reduced the power of Parliament over the Executive.

Yet, though we had never put the motion and my bill was doomed to lack of time, we had won the more important battle: when told of my motion Mrs Thatcher had said to the Chief Whip and to the Leader of the House 'Oh, sort it out. It won't go away.' The upshot of that, Tristan Garel-Jones, the Deputy Chief Whip told me, was that more than twenty years after the passing of the 1967 Abortion Act and after a series of doomed attempts to reform it, the issue was at last to be given government time, meaning that Parliament would be allowed to reach a conclusion.

For two years I had been steeped in parliamentary machinations, devices and procedures so at least I knew how to get my own back on Dennis Skinner, when I was told that he had an adjournment debate.

Adjournment debates take place at the end of the parliamentary day, which back then could mean halfway through the night or even at breakfast. They are limited to half an hour and allow one member to raise a constituency or other particular interest which will be answered by a minister. Generally the MP talks for fifteen minutes and then the minister takes the remaining fifteen minutes. There are no votes and no other member may speak or make any intervention without the consent of the one who has initiated the debate. In effect it allows the member to put the minister on the spot.

At the beginning of adjournment debates MPs flock out of the Chamber, often noisily, and hasten to the taxi rank. The benches are empty and usually, unless the matter is of pressing interest to other members, there are only four people left: the Speaker, the minister, the MP and the clerk. Outside the Chamber, the Palace of Westminster would be winding down.

It was a very different picture on the night of 16 February 1989 when Dennis Skinner stood up to raise the Rate Support Grant for Derbyshire. Word had gone round that the pro-life MPs were planning to do to his debate what he had done to ours: stop it altogether. The Chamber was packed with members wanting to witness the mischief, the press gallery was not its usual end-of-day empty self and the place was buzzing with expectation. The Deputy Speaker, Sir Paul Dean, was in the chair.

We let Skinner utter a sentence and then began to raise points of order. After a brief period the Deputy Speaker said he would take no more. We had been expecting that and had already planned to call a division, which would eat up a full fifteen minutes and if we were slow in the lobbies perhaps a couple more minutes on top of that. So we used the old device of 'I spy strangers!'

This is an arcane way of asking for the public gallery to be cleared, but of course if it is already empty the call would be meaningless and it seemed very unlikely indeed that anybody would be watching our proceedings at 12.15 a.m., so we put two people there in the shape of a couple of researchers who were utterly delighted when we stood up and pointed at them, shouting 'Strangers!'

This incident also led to a later rule change whereby we could no longer move 'I spy strangers' during adjournment debates, but it achieved its primary purpose which was to signal to the wreckers that we were no longer going to tolerate their antics. As I said on the radio next morning, 'It's war on the wreckers.'

Heaven knows what the public would have made of it if they could have watched all these antics, but they couldn't because Parliament was not then televised. There were many both inside and outside the House who thought it should be and that battle now loomed.

Chapter Fourteen

WHAT DO WE PAY THEM FOR?

The televising of the House of Commons has been a mixed blessing. On 12 June 1989, I voted in favour of it because I could not see why what was available to those sitting in the public gallery should not also be available to those at home. No very great harm had come from its being broadcast by radio and it seemed archaic to insist on only that medium when the world was taking its news and current affairs coverage from television.

Many concerns were voiced, especially about the intrusiveness of cameras and also the potential mischief of a lens focusing on a member who was nodding or shaking his head not at what was being said but at a chance comment from a colleague sitting next to him. In the event the cameras have not been intrusive and although the early very tight rules about their being only on the MP speaking have relaxed a little, there is no mischief.

What has rebounded on Parliament is that the public simply does not understand how it works. Viewers watch Prime Minister's Questions and think that is the norm for how business is conducted in the Mother of Parliaments (God forbid! You wouldn't get anybody standing for election!) or they see yards of empty benches and think MPs are idling.

Probably the best coverage of Parliament's proceedings is that given by *Today in Parliament* and *Yesterday in Parliament* on Radio Four as they deal with backbench speeches as well as the front bench ones and thus impart the real flavour of the debate, but when the Chamber is presented visually, it works only for those who are devotees of the Parliament Channel and who watch enough to understand what must necessarily elude those who see only edited excerpts.

To this day, twenty-three years after the House was first

televised, I am asked by audience after audience why there are so few MPs in the Chamber. 'What do we pay the beggars for?' is often the undertone of grievance beneath 'Where are they?'

The explanation is simple enough. All other parliamentary activities happen simultaneously with the Chamber. For example all the Standing and Select Committees are sitting while the Chamber is engaged in the debates of the day and MPs cannot practise bilocation. Given that between 100 and 200 MPs can be sitting in committee and obliged to be there for the duration of deliberations it means a sizeable proportion of the House is simply unable to be in the Chamber for large chunks of time and, of course, since Tony Blair introduced the innovation, Westminster Hall is also often sitting simultaneously with the Chamber.

That is only part of the picture. Parliamentary groups such as cross-party groups on anything from railways to animal welfare have to meet, members have to see ministers or meet pressure groups or receive individual constituents, and crucially they have to deal with what are now mountains of letters and emails and absorb documents and reports. Many will contribute a column to a local newspaper or issue regular updates in the form of newsletters to constituents.

Yet when I was first elected there would be more MPs in the Chamber on average than now and a major reason for that is television, for in those days the only way you could know what was going on in the Chamber was to be there. Indeed it was one of the measurements of how well an MP was doing whether the Chamber filled up or emptied when he rose to speak. But now there is a live feed in every office so that any MP can follow proceedings from his desk, putting his pen down or picking it up as his interest waxes and wanes.

When this first started happening I found it disconcerting. 'That was a great speech, Ann,' a colleague would say and I would stare bemusedly and reply, 'But I didn't see you there.'

The huge growth in the correspondence and casework function has also played a significant role in the diminution of attendance in the Chamber and so have the changes to the hours. When the Chamber was sitting half the night MPs could go into debates during the day knowing they had plenty of time ahead.

Do we want MPs to be spending more time in the Chamber, applying their minds to the direction of a nation and its affairs, or do we want increasing tranches of their time deployed in the solution of individual housing, benefit and medical problems? It is a highly important distinction which is raised often and resolved never. The gradual evolution of an MP's role to that of glorified social worker is one of many contributing factors to the quality of MP who is now attracted to Parliament. Serious, high achievers do not necessarily want to spend their lives upon such problems.

Yet it is undeniably true that it is the constituency work which provides high levels of satisfaction and often, when I had sorted out a situation which had at first looked unlikely to be susceptible to resolution, I knew why it was that I had become an MP and many of my former colleagues who were appointed to the Lords have been heard to bewail the loss of the constituency function. It is sad that people have so much contempt for parliamentarians when on both sides of the House and in all parties most MPs can point to moments when, because they did what they did, however quirky it might have seemed to others, they made not a drop of difference to the nation, not a trickle of difference to their constituencies but made a tidal wave of difference to an individual family. In coming chapters I shall touch upon some of my own ventures on behalf of constituents.

Naturally the work is not always about an individual's particular problems but is quite often about an issue which affects large numbers of constituents, for example a hospital closure or schools amalgamation, both of which confronted me during my time as an MP, but one of the most difficult I had to deal with was the construction of the high-speed rail link between the Channel Tunnel and the capital. It was not just Maidstone and its surrounding areas but all Kent which was in a ferment.

Some of my supporters were still not reconciled to the construction of the tunnel itself, although most were to change their minds when they began using it! However, once plans were put forward for a high-speed link between Folkestone and London, the good folk of Kent, to use a rather inelegant expression, went ape. Ladies in tweed skirts marched, waving banners. Farmers who normally worried only about prices, the supremacy of the supermarkets and European regulations, downed their plough-shares and took up campaigning.

It did not help that the government produced a consultation on not one but four options, which between them would have affected most of the constituencies in the county. The proposals for compensation for those affected were cautious and unimaginative, the picture painted by opponents of noise levels alarmist and only too imaginative. As far as the men and women of Kent were concerned, the trains would rattle their windows day and night, the construction would cause havoc on the roads, their properties would become worthless and, above all, the Garden of England would be reduced to a glorified transport corridor as the new railway was added to the M2 and M20.

The view of most of the public and of most Kent MPs was that they did not want a high-speed link at all but, somewhat unpopularly, that was not my view. It seemed to me obvious that the last thing we needed was for people travelling from the Continent to join what were already hard-pressed and inadequate commuter services to London or filling the Kentish roads with ever more traffic. I was therefore happy enough to accept the link but I wanted the train to stop at Maidstone so that we got some benefit from the inconvenience and I wanted a route which caused minimum destruction and despoliation of the rolling countryside of the Weald.

Routes 3 and 4 ran straight across my patch but 4 was dropped at an earlyish stage which left me fighting only Route 3, a horror designed to run across the Weald of Kent. I decided to support Route 2 and endured much opprobrium in the process, to say nothing of cries of 'nimbyism'. Of course the principal characteristic of nimbyism is that your constituents think you are bang on target and everybody else thinks you are a cynic.

I acknowledge some truth in that but, even twenty years later, I still think that on any practical analysis Route 2 was the best choice. Amidst all the fire and fury I remember John Stanley saying to me one day, 'Wherever they put this route, it will not be as bad as people fear.' He was 100 per cent right.

That was not however possible to say at the time and the battle raged for many months. Thus it was I realised the truth of the old cliché that if we were starting from scratch now, we would never have built the railways, let alone laid gas pipes. What? Route a poisonous substance into every home and encourage people to light it so it explodes and then they cook on the resulting fire? Are the politicians crazy?

Yet from talking to my European counterparts I found that in some other countries there is less resistance to construction and large-scale development from their citizens. Why? One of the reasons is that other countries just announce what is going to happen and then pay up rather more generously than we do to those affected.

On Friday, 2 December 1988 I moved an adjournment debate which was carried live on Radio Kent. In it I pointed out that as we had not built any railways since the turn of that century and as the compensation laws which applied to motorways did not apply to railways, Kentish residents were hopelessly unprotected. If trains now ran throughout the night where once they had run only by day there would be no compensation for the noise nuisance; there would be no compensation for anything at all until the final route was announced, which left hundreds of houses subject to planning blight and therefore unsellable; some people who had begun the process of selling before any of the routes were announced had found their buyers now withdrawing but they were still committed to contracts with the vendors whose properties they were buying. There was no statutory provision in place to cover these situations.

It was not even clear how any compensation would be calculated. Would it just be the sale value of the house or, as in some European countries, was there also to be a disturbance allowance? Would the sale value be based on the worth of the property before or after the announcement of the route? Would farmers be paid just for the loss of land or also for the loss of income arising from the land? Would the land be assessed at agricultural or developmental values?

On and on went my questions. In his reply the Minister for Public Transport, Michael Portillo, acknowledged that it was the first chance for Parliament to consider the impact of the proposed high-speed link, but, constrained by the Treasury, he did not hold out a great deal of hope of generous compensation.

In Kent Sandy Bruce-Lockhart set up Save the Heart of Kent (SHOK). Sandy was to be my constituency chairman and president, a distinguished leader of Kent County Council and a peer and died prematurely of cancer in 2008, but for which I have no doubt he would have become a minister in Cameron's government. This and the abortion campaign were both happening together and I remember vividly travelling along Kentish roads in SHOK's campaign wagon listening to an account of the Skinner filibuster.

Nor was there a shortage of other local issues: the 1987 windstorm had left many farms and woods devastated. When I first arrived in Maidstone the surrounding countryside was a sea of hops but most of the wires had been blown down and farmers, who were already finding them not particularly profitable, simply did not reinstate their hopfields.

Maidstone Hospital, then still very new and a flagship, was suffering an acute cash crisis and I was locked in seemingly endless discussions with the Health Authority Chairman, Anne-Marie Nelson, the hospital management, the doctors and nurses and the minister, Tony Newton. As the cash crisis bit, numerous constituents came to my Saturday 'surgeries' and I began trying to get them operations in areas under less pressure. I was, I told my local press, running an 'op shop'!

Obviously I sought every opportunity to raise these issues in Parliament: through questions, interventions, adjournment debates and ten-minute rule bills. This last device is an especially good one as, although no such bill is likely to become law save in the very rare cases of a wholly uncontroversial bill supported by government, the MP moving it has ten minutes in prime time, that is to say immediately after questions and before the main debates of the day begin. The member cannot be interrupted but a single opponent can put the opposite case also in ten minutes. The House then votes.

In 1987 the method by which a ten-minute rule bill was obtained – there were only two allowed each week – was to queue up outside the clerk's office on the third floor and present the bill to him when Big Ben was chiming ten o'clock. If when you arrived there was another member there, you simply went away. Those determined to get a bill arrived often at 5 a.m. to be sure of being first in the queue. Thus I presented ten-minute rule bills on abolishing Regional Health Authorities, changing the limitations on school bus passes, making stop notices applicable to caravans and other subjects that I wanted to rehearse in a slot which was early enough to catch the next day's press.

Then a government whip, Tony Durrant, told me that too many Labour MPs were getting ten-minute rule bills and we needed to raise the number of Conservative ones. Would I take on the task of making this happen?

So we began always queuing at 5 a.m. on Tuesday morning, then Labour realised what we were doing and began to queue at midnight on Monday. So we started after the seven o'clock vote on Monday. And so it went on with members organising others to stand in for them to allow them to take lavatory breaks as the queue stretched back into Sunday and finally Saturday night. I would come back from the constituency and go straight to the tiny office on the third floor with my thermos and sleeping bag. Throughout Monday a member would charge through the lobbies at high speed to vote, rush up to the office and the queuing member would rush down to vote while his place in the line was thus saved. Barmy.

In the end sense prevailed and we instead organised a turn and turn about with Labour so we got roughly equal numbers of bills. This sort of exercise also explains why Prime Minister's Questions is such a bear garden. Back in the mists of time there would be one or two questions for the PM, raised by genuinely concerned members but, of course, while government backbenchers raised helpful issues opposition members used the opportunity to embarrass the government, so the whips began trying to outdo each other in getting their own party to dominate the order paper until now we have every member chivvied to put in a question and serious concerns often lost in the lottery which determines who is called in the limited time available.

On one occasion a Conservative member arrived to find Labour already there. He complained to me and I took it up with Frank Cook, the Labour member organising his side of ten-minute rule bills. It was, he told me, an error, confusion, muddle. It was nothing of the sort but rather a ploy whereby Robin Cook, an Opposition spokesman, could take advantage of televised proceedings to move a bill on ambulancemen's pay. The government retaliated by producing a long statement to push the bill's hearing out of prime time. Party games! What fun! Just as well we were not trying to run a country or something serious like that ...

In the summer of 1989 I took my first holiday since 1984 when I had spent a long weekend with my cousin, Kate Hack, in Paris. Now I went somewhat further afield to Kenya where a friend from Oxford Union days, David Warren, was a diplomat at the embassy in Nairobi. It was a memorable safari that I embarked upon in the Masai Mara, but chief among my memories was arriving back in Nairobi to find David handling press queries because George Adamson, of *Born Free* fame, had been killed by Somali bandits. Indeed, I had a narrow escape myself when the truck which went out about three in advance of my own was ambushed.

I was a bit worried about getting to the flight on time as the Social Services Select Committee, on which I was serving, had produced a report sufficiently critical of the government's plans for the Health Service to cause a split between the Conservatives on the Committee. Nick Winterton and Sir David Price voted against an alternative report put forward by Marion Roe, and supported by Jerry Hayes and me. I was badly delayed by lengthy press interviews on the day I left but did indeed board on time and then watched the whole interview on the plane's screen. I had not had time to change but nobody recognised me as the politician earnestly defending Mrs Thatcher as they drank their cocktails.

Thanks to being so busy, this holiday in Kenya was my first in five years, but from this point on I tried to keep August free whether I was travelling or not. With the exceptions of spells of duty in government or Shadow Cabinet and the odd big charitable event or constituency emergency, I took the month off. When parliamentary hours shortened it became less of a necessity but during those first ten years of seven-day weeks and late-night sittings the annual break was less a choice than an imperative.

The only other break was between Boxing Day and New Year. Christmas Eve and Christmas Day were spent visiting hospitals, police, fire, ambulance and the homeless centre, the hospice, the Leonard Cheshire Home and similar institutions. I took humbugs and fudge (well, what else, I used to ask, would you expect from the House of Commons?), together with House of Commons chocolates, pencils, rulers and rubbers (all great men make mistakes, proclaimed the last of these). These days I dish them out to the children playing the dwarves and babes in *Snow White*.

I was growing rounder. This was not because I ate humbugs and fudge but because I was forever being taken out to lunch by journalists. There are two types of journalists with whom politicians largely deal: the specialist commentators whose work is generally serious and rarely sensational and the lobby journalists who always hope for a good story. The latter have the highest standards of confidentiality in all newsdom. If they did not, they would soon find all their sources had dried up. I always recommend to new MPs that if they are lunching with a journalist, they should first work out what they are prepared to discuss freely and so far as anything else is concerned keep a trappist vow. One small word can start a hare which can end up embarrassing a prime minister. Lobby correspondents rarely take notes during lunch: they have the memories of elephants and elephants can kill with a single stamp.

Some people find cooperation between MPs and the press distasteful and believe that they should stay at arm's length, but if politicians are to explain their policies to those who will comment on them and if journalists are to form accurate impressions of the people upon whom they report to the nation then distance for distance's sake is counter-productive and not in the public interest.

There is one batch of journalists whom politicians either love or hate but generally love and that is the group of sketch writers and cartoonists. Matthew Parris, Simon Hoggart, Michael Brown, Quentin Letts and others have an irreverent wit which even their victims cherish. Matthew called me a militant duvet and Simon Hoggart said sketch writers would offer up two whole oxen to the gods to have me to mock. He spoke at my sixtieth birthday party and brought the house down. Years later when one of the *Strictly* judges described me as 'a dalek in drag' some viewers expected me to be offended. Instead I wondered how many oxen Simon might have offered to have thought up that phrase.

It is, however, the work of the cartoonists which gave me the loudest laughs and I have a fine collection of their originals in the hall of my home on Dartmoor. Some, over time, remain intelligible only to those who experienced or closely remember the events, but all are brilliant in their caricatures, even when cruel.

'Tee, hee,' I giggled, unable to contain my mirth as I asked Steve Bell for an original which had appeared in that day's *Guardian*. 'I can't stop laughing.'

'Well, you weren't supposed to like it,' he responded crossly, before agreeing terms of sale.

It surprises me that cartoonists seriously expect their caricatures to hurt or annoy those so portrayed. If you had no sense of humour against yourself you would not survive five minutes at Westminster and the same arguments apply to the endless inaccuracies, petty libels and fanciful interpretations which so regularly appear in the press. It is not worth getting steamed up. Major libels of course are different, but of those more later.

There was but one cartoon which caused me to complain in all my time at Westminster. When I was Shadow Home Secretary I introduced a pledge that a future Conservative government would detain all new asylum seekers until their claims had been determined. I shall address the rationale for this in a later chapter but the *Independent* carried a cartoon of a train arriving at what was unmistakably Auschwitz.

That was a step considerably too far and I complained in saddened rather than outraged tones. The *Independent* responded by conducting a full and fair interview with me and everyone was happy.

All that was many years away as 1989 turned to 1990 and nobody appeared happy. In particular my constituents were perturbed by both the so-called Poll Tax and by the proposals for care in the community. The first played a major part in the fall of Mrs Thatcher in November 1990 and the second led to my leading a rebellion which actually resulted in a government defeat on the floor of the House.

I was and still am a supporter of the basic principle of the Poll Tax: every grown-up should pay something towards the local services which he or she receives. Unfortunately that meant eighteen-year-olds and students paying something, and people on benefit. We promised to upgrade benefit to take the average liability into account but people in areas of high rates roared in protest.

Above all the Poll Tax was supposed to make local authorities accountable. Some of those with the highest rates were in areas where a large percentage of the population paid nothing so local councillors never had to pay the political price of their rates hikes. Additionally there were poor rates of collection and the rates took into account the costs of non-collection which were absorbed by those who did pay.

Constituents came to my 'surgery' with their bills demanding to know why they should pay for others' defaults. I tried to point out that they always had – every year of their rate-paying lives. What was different now was that the council was legally obliged to specify the amount they were paying because others had not. Yet still they thought it something new, some fresh charge associated with the Poll Tax (I gave up trying to call it the Community Charge).

Rich single-person households benefited and the less well-off thought that unfair too. In vain did I point out that four people produced more rubbish for collection than one person and that the community charge was about services not land values. They did not expect a rich person to pay more for a pound of butter than a poorer one, so why more for a pound of services?

Reason flew out of the window and in March 1990 public discontent exploded in riots. Kennington, where my London flat was situated, was the scene of disturbances and as the protest began to flare violently in cities up and down the country I drove along streets of boarded-up shopfronts.

Yet it was not the riots which finally killed off the Poll Tax and the Prime Minister. Any government worth its salt could deal with riots: it was the simple expedient of non-payment, advocated by opponents including Labour MPs but not by the Labour Opposition itself. If one or two people had failed to pay the courts could have dealt with them, but not when non-payment was being practised by up to 30 per cent of former rate-payers, who could variously not register, contest the level of the charge, appeal against enforcement etc., thereby clogging up the courts and bringing the system to a virtual standstill.

I was to remember that when the debate arose, under Michael Howard at the Home Office but most notably under the Blair government, about national identity cards. It was a measure I favoured and still do but I also felt strongly that they should first be introduced on a voluntary basis and then their use made so attractive and convenient that people would want them. By the time most people had them it would be safe to attempt compulsion.

I had three reasons for this approach. The first was my memory of the great Poll Tax revolt and the civil disobedience which defeated the proposals. It seemed to me that if we required people to have national identity cards and they simply refused then the law would be all but stillborn. Secondly, I was old enough to remember the introduction of cheque guarantee cards.

When the banks first issued cards which would guarantee the payment of cheques up to the value of £50, some customers were insulted and proclaimed that their names on their cheques were good enough. The banks just shrugged: nobody was obliged to have such a card. Shops and businesses however took a different view and began to refuse cheques unless accompanied by a banker's card. The upshot was that eventually the overwhelming majority of those who paid by cheque chose to have a card for no other reason than pure convenience.

Thus did I reason that if a national identity card could expedite some transactions it would become convenient to have one. But there was a third consideration: CCTV.

CCTV was also hugely controversial when it was introduced. It was the spy in the sky. It was State prying. It was an invasion of the privacy of ordinary citizens going about their lawful occasions. Some councils, persuaded by these arguments and the concomitant public resistance, simply refused to install the devices. Then came the horrendous abduction and murder of Jamie Bulger and suddenly people understood the value of the cameras on the street corners and in the shopping malls.

Thus did I believe it would be with national identity cards: the first major crime foiled or solved by them would sell them to a grudging public. Softly, softly, catchee public consent, but rush in and compel and the result will often be wholesale resistance at worst or bitter resentment at best.

Bitter resentment and some resistance were now what characterised the public reaction to the introduction of care in the community. Some councils were dragging their feet in making the necessary preparations for implementing a law which was about to be passed but by which many members of the public were alarmed.

Parents with adult children did not believe that any other care for them than in large institutions was appropriate. Church workers feared a huge influx of non-copers on the streets, Social Services feared a surge in homelessness and, better placed, was a concern for public safety if the wrong sort of mentally ill patient were to be discharged.

I was fortunate in that Kent was very enthusiastic about the scheme, put good, individual provision in place and was justifiably angry when the measure was postponed due to the rather less preparedness of other local authorities. Indeed I blessed the day that the big Victorian mental hospitals were opened up and emptied as people who had nothing more wrong with them than deafness or having given birth to an illegitimate child had their first taste of normal life for decades. Their incarceration was a scandal. Others were more than capable of functioning in warden-assisted accommodation. All needed skilling in everything from crossing roads to handling money.

I came away from Oak Apple House, one of the small units in Maidstone which was receiving the discharged patients, close to tears. Here was a normal house with normal, cheerfully decorated bedrooms and kitchen in which people learned to live normal lives.

It was a common fallacy that the motive for the community care initiative was cost but anyone with an abacus could work out in five minutes that caring for someone individually was always going to cost more than locking him up in a vast institution.

I remember a particularly difficult meeting with the local Council for Social Responsibility of the churches in Maidstone. Nobody was willing to believe a word I said, there could not have been more hostility in the room if the Devil himself had popped in for a visit and the plight of those who were incarcerated and who need not have been was dismissed as easily solvable.

The success or otherwise of the new law was largely dependent on how enthusiastically local councils embraced it. But we got it wrong with the schizophrenics who could function well enough while taking medication but who often chose not to. The naïve supposition that they would take their medicine because it kept them stable underlay more than one tragedy.

For me in 1990 the big issue was not the mental health side of the new arrangements but the other part of the bill which was designed to address the care of the elderly. There had been a sharp rise in residential and nursing homes as the numbers of elderly increased and the number of families willing and able to look after them decreased. Places in these homes had to be paid for and State help was inadequate. Care-home owners could hardly just turn people out when the funding fell short. The new bill, it seemed to me, made things worse rather than better.

One of my constituents in this trap was Florence Smith. Her case was to make parliamentary history when the Thatcher government lost the vote. As a result of the role I played I was told that my own parliamentary career was also history. Many said the same after my 'something of the night' speech about Michael Howard. They were wrong on both occasions.

Chapter Fifteen
FROM REBEL TO MINISTER

Florence Smith was ninety-three years old and until the previous year had been happy in a residential home where she
could afford the charges because her income support more or less
matched them. Unfortunately she then developed specific needs
which could not be met by a residential home and transferred to
a locally well-respected nursing home, where the charges were
reasonable but by no means able to be covered by her income
support. At first her daughter could make up the gap but then it
became impossible.

'The Florence Smiths of this world remain in their nursing
homes only because the homes subsidise them,' I said in the
debate, pointing out that such cases could go on for years. What
if the person entered such a home at seventy instead of ninety-
three? What would the gap amount to, especially with her needs
increasing rather than decreasing with age?

I then drew on another case where a wife developed Parkinson's and became so ill she could not be cared for at home. There
were no children to help and the husband, a well-off professional, ran down his capital until there was nothing left. Then
how was he to pay?

Other MPs, from both sides of the House, quoted their own
cases. Who was to pay? The debate raged on but then about a
minute before we came to vote on a new clause that the government should make up the difference if a charge was deemed reasonable by an adjudication officer, one of my colleagues, Barry
Porter, stood and asked, in bewildered tones, if he had got it
right that under the government's proposals there could be a
danger, if not a probability, that some old folk could be turned
out of their residential or nursing homes.

Yes, we bellowed, and suddenly I knew that we could win. The government's majority at the election had been 102 but we had since lost two by-elections to Labour and another was pending. Thirty Conservative MPs had signed the new clause so when the debate opened it had looked as if the amendment was doomed but as we yelled 'yes' to that simple question there was a susurration on the Conservative benches. Who could support the present position?

We won by three votes.

The whips were wild. Tristan Garel-Jones, the Deputy Chief Whip, who had become a friend through Friday debates and the abortion saga, told me angrily that I had knocked 3 per cent off sterling, added £3 billion to the deficit and lost the Mid-Staffs by-election. Humph, said Michael Colvin, a co-signatory to the clause, when I told him next day. Sterling had gone up.

We did lose the Mid-Staffs by-election nine days later, but I doubt very much if my successful rebellion was too much of a factor. A little thing called the Poll Tax may have just played a greater part.

Tristan also told me that I could kiss goodbye to promotion for at least five years. Eight months later he made me his PPS at the Foreign Office and a fortnight after that I became a minister.

Meanwhile abortion was back on the agenda, or rather still on the agenda.

As Tristan had told me after the antics with the Skinner fili-buster, the pro-life group had won the fight to get government time but at the last moment there was a change of heart as Ken Clarke resisted his Human Fertilisation and Embryology Bill being, as he saw it, hijacked by the abortion issue. Had anybody given us any undertakings?

It must have taken some courage but Tristan said that yes, he had. After that the die was cast because, contrary to popular belief, ministers do not rat on deals save in completely unavoid-able circumstances.

And so it all started again: the campaign in the country, the mil-lion postcards, the public meetings, the counter-demonstrations and the parliamentary tactics. Only this time both sides knew it was for real: there would be a decisive vote and nothing could be talked out. That came as a relief to both pro-lifers and pro-abortionists and to ministers and backbenchers alike.

Knowing that most MPs just wanted the issue over and done with I said as loudly as I could that if we got a reduction in the upper time limits below twenty-four weeks we would go away for a while. It seemed to me a sensible reassurance to give waverers who might be willing to trade a couple of weeks for a period of peace but at the last minute I was contradicted by Ann Winterton, a sturdy pro-life supporter and later chairman of the all-party group, who said we would fight on. My heart sank as I read the Press Association feed in the corridor outside the library. It was a brave declaration of principle but a long way from helpful in the circumstances.

Because the issue was to be resolved through amendments to the Human Fertilisation and Embryology Bill we found ourselves fighting on many fronts with different allies on different issues. There was the issue of whether experiments on embryos should be allowed at all; whether it was moral to create spare embryos which would not be implanted but destroyed; whether fourteen days was the right limit to set for the growth of embryos outside the womb; whether it was right that they could be used for chemical or biological research by commercial companies; whether it was right deliberately to create a fatherless child. That is only a selection of the issues and all that was on top of the old arguments about upper time limits, grounds for abortion, disability in the womb, etc.

A room on the ground floor of the Palace of Westminster overlooking the terrace was nicknamed the Damery, because it was occupied by Dames Jill Knight, Elaine Kellett-Bowman and Peggy Fenner. All three formidable ladies were on our side of the argument and sometimes when I was working through the night I took refuge there. The place was out of bounds to anyone except female Conservative MPs and Elaine guarded it with all the ferocity of Cerberus at the gates of hell. This led to its becoming a source of huge curiosity to one of my colleagues, Hugo Summerson. He asked me to sneak him in there one day when nobody was about so we crept in one Friday when the Dames had departed for their constituencies. I was at a loss to understand why a few desks and piles of paper should be of such interest but he left looking like the cat that has found the cream. I think he must have won some bet.

As part of the campaign to persuade MPs to face up to what late abortion really meant, SPUC sent each and every one of them a plastic replica of an eighteen-week-old foetus. The move caused outrage but I have never seen anything wrong with people being obliged to face the consequences of their actions. Nadine Dorries, a former nurse turned MP, has spoken of the moment when she carried a still breathing aborted child out of the ward. Alas, her experience was not unique as the case of the Carlisle Baby showed.

In 1987, a young woman entered Carlisle City General Hospital for an abortion because her unborn child had been diagnosed with Ehlers-Danlos syndrome, a condition which can vary from very mild to life threatening. Gestation was estimated at twenty-one weeks but the child was born alive and lay gasping for breath on a kidney dish in a sideward for three hours while doctors and nurses rang their superiors in distress asking what to do. The law says that resuscitation equipment must be available where late abortions are being carried out in case of just such an instance but none could be located. Before the child died nurses carried out a rudimentary baptism and the coroner recommended an inquest which the Home Office turned down.

I tabled a question asking in how many cases of a death of a patient on National Health Service premises in the past three years has an inquest been refused when it has been recommended by a coroner. Douglas Hogg, the Home Office Minister, identified only the case of the Carlisle Baby.

I rehearse this case because it demonstrates how completely the NHS was in the grip of the abortion culture. If the child had been wanted but miscarried every last effort would have been made to save her and, had those efforts failed, she would have died in a warm cot in an incubator. Because she was aborted she was allowed to die on a kidney dish, after three hours of fighting, unaided, for life in a city general hospital.

When the Health Select Committee took evidence on the workings of the conscience clause in the 1967 Act, which supposedly allows NHS staff to opt out of abortions, one consultant told us that when she had left England to work in Australia the culture was that you had to justify carrying out an abortion but that by the time she returned you had to justify being unwilling to do so. Yet the law had not changed.

That observation demonstrates the difference between the impact of law and culture. Let us look briefly at a much less emotive example. England had laws against Sunday trading but shops were still opening on Sundays, whereas Scotland had no laws against Sunday trading but so strong a Sabbatarian culture that the shops stayed closed.

That is one of the reasons I fear any change to the law in respect of assisted dying. Whatever safeguards the law may have to begin with, if a culture of 'it doesn't matter' begins to prevail then the practice of that same law will change.

The 1990 bill produced an intriguing parliamentary problem. The pro-lifers put down amendments to reduce abortion to 22, 20 or 18 weeks and the pro-abortionists tried to shift the effective 24 week line by tabling 26 and 28. It presented both sides with a dilemma, because effectively one had to guess where the majority was likely to be. Supposing, for example the votes were taken in this order: 28, 26, 24, 22, etc. If you wanted the lowest possible result you could not risk holding out for 18 and voting against all the others because there might be no majority for 18 but there might have been one for 20 if you had given it your vote.

Tristan Garel-Jones found a novel way of dealing with this and introduced pendulum voting so that the default position was 24 weeks. The outside votes were taken first so we decided on both 18 and 28 before 20 and 26 and finally 22 and 24.

The majority decided on 24, which was disappointing but not as disturbing as a successful vote to decouple the Infant Life (Preservation) Act from the Abortion Act, which gave us for the first time abortion up to birth for handicapped unborn children.

The evening's voting was complicated by our advisor misreading one of the government amendments. We had drawn up voting instructions for our supporters and had sent a copy to the department two days earlier. They knew we had misinterpreted one amendment but chose not to tell us, an action for which Virginia Bottomley, the Health Minister, was to give conflicting explanations at the time, at first telling me that she had thought it none of her business and then that she had told civil servants to tell me until finally, many years later, trying to claim that she had told us after all. A likely story! Would we really have ignored something as drastic as wrong voting instructions to our own side?

As it was we found out only on the night when we had to reverse the directions at the doors of the voting lobbies, irritating and demoralising our supporters, who then began to distrust the subsequent, wholly accurate, interpretations. Troops in disarray do not fight well.

In another wretched moment there was a tied vote on the proposal that a child's handicap should be stated on the form authorising abortion. This was an attempt to prevent late abortions for trivial disabilities. In such circumstances, the Speaker tears up the tellers' slips and casts his vote for the bill as it stands. One of our best supporters, thinking the important votes over, had set off for his constituency and, hearing this on the radio, nearly crashed his car!

I also had a niggling problem in that the heel of one of my shoes had broken and I limped through the lobbies in the latter stages of the evening. It had been a rotten night. We all knew that it would be a long time before we got that chance again and indeed it has never come along since.

What with that, the Social Services Select Committee, Florence Smith, the continuing row over the Channel Tunnel rail link, the NHS reforms and the Poll Tax, life was full to capacity but as we broke up for the summer recess in 1990 few predicted the storm which would engulf the party when we returned for the autumn.

Meanwhile I took stock. I was deriving immense satisfaction from my work as an MP but whereas most of my intake were already PPSs to ministers and a few actually ministers, I had been left behind. Frank Field, the Labour MP for Birkenhead and the very talented chairman of the Social Services Select Committee supplied a possible explanation after he had bumped into Mrs Thatcher one day.

He had mentioned me and the Great Lady had responded by saying that she knew of my voting record (I had come top, beating even Dennis Skinner), from which Frank deduced that she thought of me as mere lobby fodder and hastened to tell her that I performed well on his Committee and had absorbed all the paper beforehand. Others thought it was because of my fight for changes to the abortion law and that I was regarded as a one-issue politician – although it had not been abortion on which I had defeated the government – and Gillian Shephard went to see the Chief Whip, Tim Renton, to protest. As she was on the opposing side of the argument, that was rather splendid of her. My own view was that they all thought me odd.

Whatever the reason, the absence of any sign of promotion was beginning to grate and something else was happening in my life which caused me far more anxiety: my financial situation was parlous. The flat in Fulham which I had bought in the early 1980s had proved a disaster with dry rot, mushrooms in the bathroom and a split boiler, to name just a few of the woes. Although I sold at a profit I had spent what I did not have on its modernisation and maintenance and I was left with little enough except huge relief at having finally got rid of it.

The flat I then bought in Kennington in the mid-eighties was to prove a solid investment but I had succumbed to pressure to buy in the constituency before I was ready and although that also turned an excellent profit seventeen years later I had bought at the top of the market and property prices were falling into negative equity as mortgages were high and the economy began collapsing. Creditors were pressing and the banks were tightening up.

I lurched from crisis to crisis and wondered whether to ask

my parents for help but it seemed daft that a forty-three-year-old should not be able to sort out her own money problems.

My constituents were suffering the same strain. Normally I would not have got a repossession case in a year at my 'surgery' but now I was getting a couple a month. I accompanied constituents to see bank managers, argued with their creditors, delayed repossessions and hammered out deals, sometimes with success and sometimes not. I thought wryly that I should like somebody to do the same for me. Shops began to close and businesses to fail and Labour kept on promising to spend ever more. The public was angry with the government and scornful of the Opposition.

In other areas of my personal life there was great happiness. My parents, aged seventy-nine and eighty were enjoying a healthy and prosperous retirement in Haslemere, my nephews and niece had grown up and my brother was still enthusing his Bristol church and raising large sums for missions. I had, for some years, been spiritually content and my prolonged flirtation with agnosticism had been left firmly behind, even though my disillusionment with the Anglican Church was growing. I was healthy despite discernible weight gain.

Yet the financial worries took their toll and when I sat in an evangelical church and looked at a banner proclaiming 'The best is yet to come' I was unconvinced that it was likely to come this side of eternal life.

Then I forgot my own preoccupations as I returned to Westminster and a party which was seething with plots to overthrow the Prime Minister. The new session began well enough as I was at last made a PPS – to Tristan Garel-Jones, then a Foreign Office Minister, but it wasn't to last long as events overtook us all.

We were trailing Labour badly in the opinion polls and had been doing so for more than a year. We were then anything from 14 to 16 per cent behind and if Labour had been a bit more prudent about tax and spend, I suspect we would never have recovered. The Poll Tax controversy still raged on and Mrs Thatcher had a low personal approval rating in the polls. Sure of both her position and her policies and ill-advised by her PPS, Peter

Morrison, the Iron Lady just carried on regardless and made no attempt to woo or to compromise.

That makes her sound hopelessly arrogant but one has to look at the scene from her own perspective. She had been a phenomenally successful PM, turning the country round from being the sick man of Europe to a hive of enterprise; she had tamed the unions, created property owners out of council tenants, shareholders out of shop assistants and entrepreneurs out of school rejects; with Reagan and Gorbachev, she had brought about the end of Soviet communism and fought a successful war; she had taken the Conservatives to power with a healthy majority not once but three times. She felt she was justified by her record and the rest of us could just get on with it.

This was understandable but it made her remote. One of the ways I illustrate this to audiences today is to recall the enormous difference between the way she and John Major came through the voting lobbies in the House of Commons. Mrs Thatcher would come in with her PPS and it would be like the parting of the Red Sea as she powered her way through to vote. John by contrast always came through affably, stopping to talk to colleagues about a recent speech or their wives' and children's operations or anything else and he never did otherwise, even at the height of all the pressure on that beleaguered premiership, when any PM might have been glad to have hurried away.

The muttering grew. In 1989 a stalking horse in the shape of Sir Anthony Meyer had challenged Thatcher in the annual leadership election with little success but now Heseltine, the former Secretary of State for Defence who had resigned over the Westland affair in 1986, was to do so. First, however, we had the spectacle of Geoffrey Howe attacking Mrs Thatcher on 13 November in a memorable speech from the backbenches, having resigned some two weeks earlier over her refusal to set a date for entry into the ERM and suggesting that she was like a captain who sent out a cricket team, having first broken their bats.

Afterwards we all teemed out into the members' lobby to be assailed by the gathered ranks of the correspondents from just about every newspaper. There was a popular view abroad at the time that the speech had been the result of the ire of his impressive wife, Elspeth, so when asked what I thought, I said to one journalist from a major Sunday tabloid, 'Glamis thou art and Cawdor.' He looked at me blankly before muttering 'I don't speak Latin.' Years later, when I had used the word in a speech, Anthony Howard said that my use of 'prestidigitation' had confused the press gallery as journalists looked at each other and said 'prestiwhat?' He commented that it was not an erudite gallery, which is an entertaining assessment although not wholly fair to the likes of Matthew Parris and his ilk.

Heseltine felt it safe to challenge the very next day but was defeated by Mrs Thatcher in the first ballot. Nevertheless he had attracted enough votes to persist. At first it looked like a fight to the death but on 22 November I was woken by a call from Tristan at 7 a.m. The Prime Minister was resigning, he told me, and both John Major and Douglas Hurd would be standing against Heseltine. I asked him what was the point of fielding two candidates, saying surely we would end up splitting the vote? He responded that those who did not wish to support Heseltine needed somewhere to go and it might help if they had a choice. He then said he was supporting Hurd and, as Tristan's PPS and therefore part of Hurd's department, I followed suit, but I thought it right anyway.

We were brewing up to yet another war, this time in the Gulf, and I thought Douglas had a greater experience of the world stage than John. Also John was still very young for the role of PM. Perceptions of prime ministers and the age they ought to be change with each political generation and whereas mine felt PMs should not be so young, a succeeding generation, used to both Major and Blair, considered Ken Clarke too old when he contested the leadership in 2001.

At about 9 a.m. the *Kent Messenger* rang to ask whether I was still supporting Thatcher. The information Tristan had given me was confidential, but this was a Thursday and the *KM* was put to bed by lunchtime. I did not want to mislead a local reporter. So I said that he should be careful, that I could say nothing but if he phoned me back at lunchtime I might have some news for him. As soon as the conversation ended he rang Chris Moncrieff, the redoubtable Press Association political reporter, and told him, 'Ann Widdecombe says anything we say about the Tories will be old hat by lunchtime,' which was a free but very canny interpretation of what I had actually said.

Moncrieff tore along to Downing Street and afterwards commented to me that I was well informed. What else was one who worked for Tristan, that master of plots, plans and conspiracies, supposed to be?

So I reported for duty to the Hurd camp. Most of the work was carried out either in his rooms at Westminster or in a nearby house belonging to the MP Giles Shaw but never, of course, at the Foreign Office, where it was business as usual. Andrew MacKay, my old opponent on abortion, was running much of the campaign, organising MPs to come and see Douglas and coordinating the press and media.

Given different circumstances I would probably have aligned myself with Heseltine, who was both highly competent and highly charismatic, but I could not forgive him for the disloyalty he had shown in knifing the Prime Minister, although undeniably he did the party a favour if by that one means being able to surge ahead in the polls and win the 1992 election, which in retrospect most of us wish we had not. He was strongly supported by Emma Nicholson, also a member of the 1987 intake, who believed she had found the winner.

I had been badly shocked by the revolution that could oust a sitting prime minister but I noted quietly the twin failings which had made her unable to survive it: complacency (why on earth did she go to Paris for a European summit in the middle of it all?) and bad advice (Morrison). Be there and sniff with your own nose is one of the fundamental laws of the political jungle. More than a decade later it was how I knew that, despite the media hype, I was never going to have a chance of the leadership myself. I sniffed hard and the message on the air was clear and consistent. There were so few votes in it that she might have survived.

I admired John Major and not least for his down-to-earthness.

Near my Kennington flat was a Greek kebab house which also served fish and chips. I had made friends with the family who ran it and was taking a particular interest in the children, Theodora and Nikos Louridas. One day I was there reading a novel by Douglas Hurd, for whom I was not then working, when in came John and sat opposite me. He glanced at the title.

'Ah,' he said. 'The moral of that one is "Don't sleep with your Private Secretary".' He then ordered kebab and chips and I had to pinch myself to remember that this was the Chancellor of the Exchequer.

So I suppose that I would not have found it difficult to be reconciled to the outcome, whichever of the three won. It was the last leadership campaign in my time there which was run on very gentlemanlike lines with none of the three candidates rubbishing one another. Future campaigns were variously fraught, bitter or malice-strewn, culminating in my hearing one of the cruellest rumours of all, which I still regard as unrepeatable, in the 2005 leadership campaign. If the man who told me over a cup of coffee in Portcullis House expected me to repeat such a horror, he was doomed to disappointment. I remember it only to his, not his opponent's, discredit.

Fifteen years earlier it was all very different. The many supporters of Thatcher would have no truck with Heseltine and emotions were still running high. I mopped up enough tears and calmed enough temper tantrums while the struggle to oust her was on that I later remarked to Alastair Goodlad in the whips' office that I never again wanted to hear anyone say that men were not as emotional as women. Yet, despite that, personal attacks were taboo. We fought on issues as well as personalities and that fight was a close one.

It became clear at an early stage that we were not going to win but Douglas said he was glad he had tried. His would have been a steady hand on the tiller but he lacked the charisma of Heseltine and Major had the advantage of the Prime Minister's endorsement. When the latter won Tristan circulated a note to the Hurd camp saying, 'Sometimes when we lose, we win.' He was a close friend of Major.

I remember him also saying quietly when the TV screen filled with a picture of John and Norma arriving at Downing Street, 'Poor Norma.' She was not ambitious for Number Ten in the same way Anne Heseltine had seemed but she filled the role with a charm and dignity which should have provided a role model for Cherie Blair but sadly did not.

Uproar broke out when John Major appointed his new Cabinet without a single woman in the team. Perhaps, I reasoned, that would make him look more closely at the women lower down the pecking order. Emma Nicholson was overtly hopeful and had good reason: she had been prominent in the Heseltine campaign and John would be looking to include colleagues from all the teams. Then Bob Hughes, now a whip and a supporter of Major, whispered to me that another name was in the frame and hope hammered through me.

On the day the lower echelons of government were appointed, I refused to detach myself from a telephone, though I kept my hopes to myself, so when I had to leave my office and go over to the palace of Westminster I kept ringing my secretary on any excuse, dearly wanting to hear her say, 'Number Ten has rung.'

The day wore on and I schooled myself to stop hoping but still could not resist ringing and became highly frustrated when my secretary suddenly did not answer. I tried again, telling myself I was daft and that I should go and have a cup of tea, calm down and carry on.

When I emerged from the tea room a messenger handed me a pink slip. It was a message from my secretary, Emma, telling me that she had been hunting high and low for me. Downing Street had rung.

Chapter Sixteen

PUSS, PUSS

My initials now changed. I was no longer a PPS but a PUSS, which seemingly feline initials stand for Parliamentary Under Secretary of State, the lowest form of ministerial life.

The Department of Social Security as it was then known, was, John Major told me, an excellent place to cut one's teeth. He was one of many who had begun successful ministerial careers there. I was succeeding the newly promoted Gillian Shephard and the Secretary of State was Tony Newton.

Tony Newton was one of a rare breed of politicians who are seriously able but not overly ambitious. They like the work for the work's sake, are content to be as little in the public eye as possible, adore the constituency work and never deliberately do down another MP whether on their own side or not. Tony was a sturdy workhorse and was one of those few ministers with whom I have worked who knew more about their subject than the civil servants advising them.

By and large ministers come and go, rarely staying more than a couple of years, and civil servants regard themselves as the permanent fixtures, experts in their field, whose job it is quietly to control their ministers. They will never overtly defy but if they can covertly frustrate they will. Sir Humphrey exists at all levels.

First, they flood their political masters with work in the shape of red boxes full of submissions, questions, letters and copies of the work of other departments which may impinge on one's own. When a minister goes to his constituency the boxes follow, securely locked in sacks and specially delivered by the local post office. If he remains in the constituency for any reason he puts the completed work back in the boxes, locks them once more in the sacks and takes them to the post office for special delivery back to the department.

For security reasons a red box must never be taken on a train so then the minister travels with a brown box, from which he must not take any classified document if anybody is around to see. Documents have various classifications from confidential all the way up to top secret, the latter a highly rare occurrence on the desk or in the box of a junior minister.

MPs also handle confidential material on trains, from constituents' private problems to Select Committee papers to sensitive replies from ministers. It is one of many reasons why the current vengeful attitude that they should always travel standard class is silly and vindictive. The majority of MPs have substantial journeys to get to their constituencies and it is a minority within commuting distance. It is a waste of time not to work. Therefore they need sockets for computers, relative quiet, an uncrowded carriage and a trolley service which saves them having to pack everything up every time they so much as want a cup of coffee. That is exactly how businessmen travel and the real problem is with the silly title 'first class' with its archaic implications of snobbery and privilege. Were it called 'business class' there would be less resentment. A few hours' concentrated work is money well spent on behalf of the taxpayer.

The more normal mode of travel for members of Her Majesty's Government is the ministerial car. In those days each minister had an assigned car and driver and I inherited John Major's Chas, who did not want the hassle of Downing Street, but alas not his car. My rank had to make do with a Mondeo. The car took one everywhere: to votes in the House, when it would drive down Whitehall with its headlights flashing, to the TV studios at Millbank which were less than half a mile away, to the Isle of Skye if necessary. The driver moves departments with the minister, picks the minister up in the morning and delivers him home at night.

The drivers are the fount of all knowledge. They know before ministers when the reshuffles are coming because the arrangements for moves are beginning to be made; they know who is having an affair with whom; they hear and overhear conversations; they know when you have toothache because they take you to the dentist while you crunch the red box in the back of the car; they know what breed of cat you have because it meets you when they are carrying the boxes to the front door.

There is however one type of journey they never make: it is absolutely out of the question for a minister to be driven in a ministerial car to his constituency or to a purely political engagement, with the exception of those few who are allocated a personal protection team in the interests of security. Many was the time that I combined a ministerial visit to a social security office or a prison in another part of the country with a visit to the local Conservatives and where this happened there was strict demarcation between my transport to the Conservative event and the rest of the visit.

As my father was a civil servant I had grown up absorbing the ethos that it was the duty of such a person to protect the minister of whatever party, because if something went wrong the minister took the flak and the civil servant remained anonymous. That was now changing.

In the past, when civil servants had been named, it was considered historic and worthy of pages of agonised commentary in the public prints. At Oxford I wrote an essay about the Crichel Down affair, a controversy which supposedly established the principle that a minister is responsible for the failings of his department, and while I was still there another controversy exploded about the naming of Christopher Jardine, a civil servant, in the wake of the collapse of a big insurance company.

By the time I joined government all that had changed dramatically and, seven years later, that change was central to my very public row with Michael Howard as detailed in chapter twenty.

Now we had Next Steps Agencies, which delivered large parts of departmental responsibilities, under contract and subject to targets, both financial and performance-based. The heads of these agencies were accountable and began to appear on television after the fashion of ministers. Inevitably, although ministers alone could answer to Parliament, these very senior civil servants developed a public role. It was very much a national role in the way that, say, chief constables of police did not operate. If there was a bank robbery in Preston then the Chief Constable of Lancashire was the one to whose door the press and media beat a path, but if there was a prison escape from deepest Dartmoor it was to the Head of the Prison Service in London that they came.

The overlap of responsibilities was confusing. Michael Howard made an ill-judged attempt to distinguish between 'policy' and 'operations' which compounded rather than removed the problem.

Whereas in the past senior civil servants tended to have progressed up the civil service ladder, some heads of agencies were being drafted in from the private sector and other parts of the public sector, which was beneficial in many ways but did mean that some of them had no feel for the political dimension, which could cause problems for ministers at all levels.

I found myself dealing now principally with two of these organisations: the Benefits Agency run by Michael Bichard, who had been drafted in from local government where he had been chief executive at both district and county level, and the Resettlement Agency run by Tony Ward, who was an internal appointment. There was also the Contributions Agency responsible for National Insurance and contributions-related benefits, but that appeared to run smoothly enough.

The Resettlement Agency's job was to remove the reason for its own existence. Until then the Department of Social Security had run its own resettlement centres which looked after the long-term homeless and unemployed, providing shelter and assistance with re-training and help with moving on to permanent accommodation. It was becoming increasingly obvious that there were other organisations, for example the excellent Foyer Project, which were doing the same work and often doing it more successfully. Furthermore the department's role had become focused almost entirely on the assessment and delivery of benefit. The direct provision of other services duplicated the role of local councils, charities and of course the Department of Health, which in 1988 had been separated from Social Security.

There were now seven remaining resettlement centres, largely run down and dilapidated sometimes to the point where demolition was the only option, and the plan was to close them all and provide new, substitute accommodation to a high standard which would then be handed over to other organisations to run. The difference between the old and the new accommodation was wonderful but I remember one charity worker saying to me as we stood in the light, airy, sparklingly clean reception area of a new building, decked out with armchairs and pot plants: 'I am not so sure. Our smelly old tramps won't come in here.'

It may have been a politically incorrect observation but it was nonetheless an astute one. I was to think of it often when passing vagrants in the street.

The resettlement programme gave me one of my earliest tastes of media manipulation, when I was rung up one day while on leave. Radio Four's *Face the Facts* wanted to do a programme on Bridge House, a London resettlement centre being closed in favour of more modern accommodation. We had 'such a good story to tell' that officials were keen for me to break my holiday and give an interview. As I was only at home, little more than a mile away, it seemed an easy enough request to grant. How I wish I had been in Timbuctoo or Vladivostok.

The programme had supplied a list of questions and the press department was enthusiastic. Grotty old Bridge House was a disaster and we could use it as a demonstration that we were putting money and effort into helping the homeless by supplying better and more respectful premises.

I glanced down the list of questions and foresaw no difficulty, which, in retrospect and after decades of dealing with a wily, often unpleasant press and media, should have rung alarm bells in itself.

What I was up against was the time-honoured resistance to change. I had met it in my constituency where parents solemnly defended a manifestly failing school just because it was there. I had only been in it five minutes before knowing that County was right to close the school but that the parents would not accept that better existed until their children were actually settled elsewhere. I had met the same attitude with the community care programme when parents of adult children were afraid of exchanging an impersonal institution for small, tailored units. I had met it with care homes where peeling wallpaper and the elderly sitting round looking blankly into mid-distance somehow seemed safer than a bright, hopeful home close by. And now I was meeting it on *Face the Facts*.

The questions began reasonably and then they bowled one about a report that suggested Bridge House could be repaired, renovated and brought up to standard so why were we closing it? I had no knowledge of any such report, the detailed work on the choices between demolition, closure and sale or renovation having been mainly done and dusted within the agency and most of it before I arrived. However given that it was the building we were closing not the service, I was impatient. We were upgrading the provision so why be attached to a particular heap of dilapidated bricks and mortar?

Would I publish the report? No. Why not? It was an internal document. Would I show it to them in confidence? No. Why not? Because they had no locus. And so it went on.

When the programme went out, there was a heart-rending contribution from a man who regarded Bridge House as 'home' but by definition Resettlement Centres are not home, merely a place of refuge until a permanent home can be found.

As if that were not enough, somehow my voice was different. I do not know why, as the microphone was in the usual place in my office and the civil servants' recording of the interview sounded normal, but as soon as I heard it on the airwaves I winced.

The hate mail was huge. There was a cover-up. I was hiding some secret report. I was doing the homeless out of a chance to survive. My voice was dreadful.

Immediately the BBC team had departed, there was a post-mortem. What was this report and why didn't I know about it? Please could I now see it yesterday? Why wasn't I alerted? Had it ever crossed my desk, even if only in a bundle of background papers? The responses were all reasonable: it was a report on just one option. Had they known the interview was going to be about that option of course I would have been briefed but all the indications they had received pointed to a general interview about the closure programme.

The reader may well ask at this stage why I did not simply say to *Face the Facts*: 'I haven't a clue what you are talking about.' However, even a very junior minister under immediate media pressure could work out that the row from that would have been twice as large and vastly more damaging and could have been used to cast doubt on the validity of the decision itself, which, even after I had read the report, I never had cause to doubt. I could not simply say, 'That is a matter for the Resettlement Agency.'

It was, of course, one of the hazards of agencies. Their chief executives did the sums and read the reports of experts, crunched the results and presented résumés to ministers. As long as they were operating efficiently within policy and within budget and reported to us regularly, the work was effectively devolved.

I was to have two more serious run-ins with the media while in that department, both in the shape of the BBC's *Today* programme, but my quarrel was not with those formidable interviewers but instead with the reporting which followed the interview. Indeed it is a very common experience in politics to have no issue with an interview but then to endure vast distortion in the subsequent reporting. 'Did you actually *hear* the interview?' is an oft-heard cry of disbelief.

As the *Today* programme often sets the agenda for the rest of the day it is particularly susceptible to this and headlines are often derived from it. By elevenses one's alleged views are unrecognisable, by lunchtime every local radio station is playing carefully chosen excerpts and inviting comment on phone-ins, by teatime experts from charities, pressure groups and universities are commenting on what one has not said and at bedtime the phone is still ringing. Our press is blessedly free and long may it ever be so, but it certainly is not accountable and accuracy is a long-discarded habit.

In the first instance a charity, the National Children's Homes, produced a report in June 1991 claiming that 25 per cent of those on benefits could not manage and did not have enough to eat. In the course of the interview I said that clearly as 75 per cent could manage it was not the system as a whole that was at fault. Then I observed that the report covered people on a vast range of different benefits: from income support to in-work benefits, from those who had 100 per cent of their rent paid to those who had to meet their mortgage repayments, from those on short-term benefits to those on long-term. It was not possible, I argued, to deduce from that where the system was failing so we needed to ask which category of benefit-receiver, within that vast melting pot, was not getting enough to live on. 'Who are *they* and why can't they manage?'

It was a highly pertinent question in context, but that one line, taken on its own with no explanation, laid me open to any journalist with a malicious or sensational agenda. For, shorn of the reasoning which preceded it and of the emphasis which I have rendered in italics, it can be read as snobbish, unsympathetic and out of touch. For a long time afterwards I carried a transcript of the interview in my briefcase to wave under the nose of anyone who claimed I had dismissed the plight of the poor.

In a later interview I also enlarged upon my view that there were things which people could do to ease the strain, such as buy food from markets rather than supermarkets. At this point the sky fell on my head.

The *Daily Mirror* went to the aforementioned Greek kebab house to quiz the owners about what I ate. A neighbour found two people at the back of the block poking around in the rubbish sacks. When challenged, they claimed to be journalists and departed swiftly. I had a choice between defending myself or refusing all interviews and chose, as I was often to do, the first, because the more people who heard me, the more would hear my true views.

The second occasion came much later in my time at the DSS, in the next Parliament when Peter Lilley had succeeded Tony Newton. The Chancellor, Norman Lamont, announced in March

1993 that VAT would be applied to fuel and a debate broke out about how pensioners and those on benefits would cope. In an interview with the *Today* programme on 18 March I was arguing against a blanket exemption but stating that we would cope with the issue by raising pensions and benefits.

But, asserted John Humphrys, this was a pretty special rise in costs. My response was, 'Why is it special? ... I don't mean that the rise isn't out of the ordinary, but I don't think that something has happened which is so out of the ordinary that we in Social Security do not have the ordinary means of addressing it.' Needless to say, the piece which was quoted was 'Why is it special?' and usually without the rest of the answer. That was another transcript which spent years in my briefcase.

Meanwhile there was the day-to-day work of being a minister: policy development, legislation, red boxes and visits. I was inheriting Gillian Shephard's private office, but I did not realise that was supposed to mean only the people who worked there rather than the office itself.

The Department of Social Security was housed in a very grand building on Whitehall called Richmond House. Some of its meeting rooms, especially the Versailles Room, were extremely ornate and imposing. Once when Dennis Skinner was bringing a delegation to talk about some aspect of miners' welfare, we decided to squash the numbers into my office rather than expose such grandeur to that left-wing firebrand but were thwarted when, passing the Versailles Room, he opened the door and peered in!

My office was large and comfortable, with a small sitting room en suite. It had been intended that when Gillian left it would be assigned to a senior civil servant but I was so keen to get started that I arrived as Gillian was leaving and innocently installed myself, after which nobody quite dared to oust me.

The function of the private office is to support the minister and organise his or her life. A favourite question to those applying for such jobs is 'Do you think you will be working for the department or for the minister?' The answer is the latter. It is the minister's interests they protect. One of my future staff, Adrian

Jones, found that out in a fairly dramatic way when I fell out with Michael Howard.

My office, despite the hours it worked, was staffed by commuters. My Private Secretary came from Reading, my Assistant Private Secretary from Southampton and the Diary Secretary from Kettering. If I had an adjournment in the middle of the night one of the first two stayed and sat in the civil servants' box in the Chamber. They read every document before I saw it and highlighted the most important passages, acted as gatekeepers and everywhere I went one of them went too.

It was a shock to realise that I was not allowed out alone. The first time I had a TV interview I absorbed the briefing and then announced, 'Right, I'm off.'

'Oh, no, you're not,' replied Claire, the Private Secretary, and I discovered that these words meant that I was to be escorted by both her and a press officer and that we would travel the few hundred yards to the studio by car. Months later, when Whitehall was clogged up and she had to suggest we walked, I looked under the desk and announced triumphantly: 'Feet! I've still got feet!'

I told my private office to call me by my Christian name, which was a departure from the norm. Every department has a member of the House of Lords on its ministerial team and ours was Lord Henley, a jovial chap with a freezing cold castle and a charming family. He came to see me, looking uncharacteristically solemn.

It was, he told me, a bad idea. My private office should do as all the other civil servants did and call me Minister. I replied that everyone I had ever worked with had called me Ann. After he had pursued the issue a little more, I delivered myself of my final argument: 'Look, God calls me Ann and what is good enough for God is good enough for everybody else.'

He looked surprised. 'God calls me Lord Henley.'

PUSSes are the dogsbodies of ministerial life. They handle the late-night debates and they sign boxes of letters every day. Social Security, the NHS and immigration provide the biggest workload in terms of correspondence. If there is a particular issue then it becomes a mechanical exercise as the replies are standard. Mostly such issues are serious but sometimes there is a wave of concern based upon a complete misconception. One such phenomenon was the baffling case of dogs' benefit.

There arose a widespread and enduring belief, which had no foundation whatever, that the reason so many homeless persons had dogs was because we paid benefit for the animals. Indeed some even quoted the exact amount of this fictitious payment as £7.50.

My wrist ached with signing letters reassuring an outraged public that there was no benefit for dogs, but in one public meeting when I, the responsible minister, categorically denied the existence of the benefit one woman in the audience was so utterly convinced of its validity that she argued with me. 'There is!' she asserted and nothing could shake her.

We never found the source of the rumour. Perhaps there had been some spoof but if so we didn't track it down, or it may just have been word of mouth. It lasted not months but years, still appearing in the boxes of my successor, William Hague.

The reason that so many homeless persons on the streets have dogs is the obvious one: it arouses sympathy and makes their begging more effective.

In other cases people worry unnecessarily simply because they have misunderstood a piece of news or commentary. When I was the Pensions Minister, Paul Lewis of *The Money Programme* discussed in one edition the measures the government could take in order to save money. On the list was means testing the pension or means testing one of the major benefits associated with it – automatic free prescriptions.

My first reaction when the letters began to arrive was anger with Lewis for what I believed was irresponsible scaremongering, but fortunately I asked to see a copy of the programme before I expressed the sentiment to him. He had at no stage suggested that the government was considering such measures but had merely looked at areas where it was possible to save money. One imagines that viewers of such programmes are quite bright but the public do not analyse statements with the minute attention of somebody taking a comprehension test, a basic fact of public and journalistic life which frustrates me even now and makes sensible commentary a minefield.

Ministerial boxes would be much lighter if MPs' letters were genuine requests for help or information instead of exercises in public relations. When I was dealing with constituents' correspondence and knew the answer because I had already raised the issue on behalf of another constituent I replied quoting the original ministerial response. Many MPs however simply send on the letter to the minister because they want to assure the constituent that the minister is personally aware of his or her views or plight. So I would get shoals of letters raising an identical issue from the same MPs week after week and their offices would go on getting the same answer. What a waste of time and public money.

One or two MPs were so brazen about the process that they did not even bother with a covering letter but just sent a form saying they had received the attached letter and would be grateful for a reply. When I suggested sending out a standard letter saying 'I refer you to the reply I sent last week/month/year' the reaction was one of horror, but had I ever risen to the dizzy heights of Secretary of State that is exactly what I would have implemented.

I can only hope that my replies or decisions were not as puzzling as some I received when I was on the other end of this process. Recently I came upon this note which caused me to smile. It was written by Lesley Polley, my caseworker:

> Do you recall Mrs C? Lady with husband who entered illegally on back of lorry three years ago, then lied about his name, then denied he was Mrs C's husband? Guess what? They granted him settlement papers! Funny life, isn't it?

Then there was the reply from a Labour Education Minister, who assured me that yes, a Latin A-level paper could be marked by somebody without a degree in the subject.

Letters might be supportive, argumentative or abusive, but if

About to go down Padiham mine,
Burnley, 1978

Methuselah campaigning, Burnley, 1979

Learning to train hops,
Maidstone, Kent, 1986

Ann, Lady Olga Maitland and Mrs Thatcher at the launch of 'A Layman's Guide to Defence', 1984 (PA)

The Popemobile, Maidstone, Kent, 1987

Minister at the Department of Employment, 1993

John Major's women Ministers, 1993 (Ann, back row, first left) (Solo)

ANN WIDDECOMBE

WIDDECOMBE

Ann at her home in Sutton Valence

CONSERVATIVE.

Ann at Kloof Cottage, Sutton Valence, 1997

Shadow Health Secretary. Ann celebrates her triumph at Party Conference with William Hague, Bournemouth, 2000 (PA)

David Willetts

Shadow Cabinet, September 2000 (Conservative Central Office)

Campaigning for Jacques Arnold, Gravesham, 2001

'Arise, take up thy mat and fly' – Ann's helicopter campaign, 2001

I had to nominate the most unpleasant I ever received it was in 1998 when the Shadow Cabinet was considering Clause 28. Had it been in green ink from an illiterate ignoramus, it would have merited nothing more than a grimace but instead it came from a Cambridge student, written from his college, and I had to dissuade my secretary from ringing up the Master.

Dear Miss Widdecombe,

I am a highly intelligent and articulate, First Class student of Medical Sciences at Cambridge University. I have just read about your loathesome views on homosexuality and my reasoning capacity deserts me.

You are a filthy, evil whore. I genuinely hope that you die lonely and in great pain. You are a stupid, barren, pointless witch.

You are wrong. History will judge you and your ilk as misinformed, ridiculous anachronisms and laugh in scorn, as I do now.

I look forward to hearing that you have developed cancer.

He had the guts to sign it but it would be cruel for me to give his name here when maturity may have made him kinder. The only consideration which made me pause to consider whether my secretary's reaction was the right one was that this man might one day be a doctor and yet could wish cancer on somebody. How would he react to a patient needing his help of whose views he disapproved? I decided that he would grow up and dearly hope I was right.

Overwhelmingly however the public is kind. When I wrote in the *Express* that I had once had a piece of the Berlin Wall but that the cleaner had thrown it away, thinking it rubbish, a reader sent me his piece of the wall. On another occasion a lady sent me her grandfather's rosary in a First World War tobacco tin.

I also learned that there was quite a complicated etiquette attached to ministerial letters. Letters received direct from the public were answered by civil servants. Letters from the public

sent on by MPs were answered by ministers and always personally signed. Industrious ministers added a handwritten PS
even if it was only 'Thank you for the opportunity to comment'.
Replies to letters from members of the Cabinet, eminent privy
counsellors and senior members of the Shadow Cabinet were
generally signed by the Secretary of State.

There was a great deal of grumbling when heads of agencies
began to assume responsibility for answering MPs' letters, especially as the letters were often signed by personnel below that
rank, but it was a relief to ministers.

A minister must know not only what is happening in Whitehall but what is happening in the department round the country
so I began a programme of visits to Social Security offices, sometimes in city centres, sometimes in small towns and sometimes
in remote locations such as Skye. It was a time of considerable
change and there was the usual unease which is so often atten-
dant upon the abandonment of the familiar. The new technology
had arrived.

When a mere three years earlier I had become an MP, secretaries were still using electric typewriters. One of my older
ones, Charlotte Wallis, resisted even the self-correction device.
Now computers were taking over and everybody loved them,
especially Charlotte, who eventually became an advocate for a
paperless office, a feat we never did manage.

I had, of course, visited the local Social Security office in Maidstone. Then a supervisor sat at the head of a table around which
the staff were performing calculations. The proposal now was to
computerise all the calculations and assessments as well as the
correspondence.

To understand the uncertainty it is necessary to put the initiative in the context of the times. The fax machine was regarded
as a remarkable invention. I was issued with two as a minister,
one for my London flat and one for my constituency cottage,
and they were still of the kind which issued long reels of paper
rather than individual sheets, so that I felt like an ancient Roman
reading a scroll. Mobile phones were brick-like and unreliable.
I had a pager at an early stage of my parliamentary career but

it was not until the arrival of Tony Blair that, in an age which preceded the ubiquity of small mobile phones, their use became widespread.

Computers were nothing new. I had one in my office during the latter stages of my time at London University, where we were actively encouraged to play a detective game called 'Mansion' in order to get used to handling the device! What was new was the concept of the desktop as the norm.

The change was handled sensibly by the Benefits Agency, which rolled out the programme gradually with staff from offices that already had it mentoring those in offices where it was just coming in. Some employees left but they were a very small minority and I doubt if they managed to remain technology-free! The rest, young and old alike, learned the new system, which was then refined and adapted. Whenever I visited an office where the new system had been running for a few months there was unanimity of opinion that nobody wanted to return to the old ways.

In addition to the new technology the Agency was upgrading its buildings, which sometimes meant decanting but always involved a high level of inconvenience. When I saw the bright, newly refurbished offices where claimants were received in decent surroundings, I was hugely proud but inevitably some grumbled that it was a waste of money.

More controversial were the issues of screens, corporate dress and name badges. Civil servants did not wear uniform and there was some worry that if they left the office in corporate dress they could become targets for dissatisfied claimants and that if they wore name badges they might even be traceable at home. Again the Agency was sensible, introducing name badges with Christian names alone, allowing pseudonyms in special cases and insisting on corporate dress only for those dealing with the public. Gradually the changes were accepted but screens remained a major anxiety.

As part of having a more personal approach to claimants it was proposed to remove the bank-like screens between claimants and officials, but with some customers becoming very agitated if refused benefit, staff were justifiably nervous. In the end managers took decisions about where such protection was necessary so in the same office it was possible to have screens in one section but not in another.

Walking round the offices, speaking to staff and claimants and meeting management and unions, meant I became extremely familiar with the system but others who needed to know what was going on were Opposition spokesmen. They required permission to visit. It was traditional that this was always granted unless there was an obvious propaganda element involved or in the rare instances where a visiting politician had caused serious concern to staff, which I had to deal with only once when as a Home Office Minister I was in the regrettable position of having to ban Emma Nicholson from Asylum Reception Centres after staff reported a disturbance following one of her visits. There was no suggestion that she had meant to be provocative but some tactless questions to some of the residents were profoundly resented and staff requested a ban.

One of the most exciting aspects of a minister's life is legislating. The process of getting a bill on to the statute book is long and hard but those involved are changing law, making a difference, perhaps righting an injustice. At least that is true of good laws, proportionately made and after much thought and analysis; a description which could never have been applied to the law on ownership of handguns which I had the misfortune to take through the House of Commons after the Dunblane disaster, but I shall return to that unhappy experience in chapter twenty-one.

My first experience of legislation as a minister was the bill that introduced Disability Living Allowance (DLA) and Disability Working Allowance (DWA). I was assisting Nick Scott, the Minister of State at the Home Office. I was especially glad to serve on this particular bill as it addressed an issue on which I had always had strong views and on which, in the years between the Devonport campaign and winning the Maidstone selection, I had carried out some research. This was the question of partial allowance for partial inability to work.

Until 1992 it was a question of all or nothing. If you were too disabled to work you were entitled to benefit, but if your disability was such that you could do some work then you got no benefit at all. So if you were still able and willing to undertake at least some paid employment the message from the State was effectively, 'Give it up or we won't help.' That was wrong both from the point of view of the public purse and the dignity of the individual.

A similar feature also existed in the allocation of Mobility Allowance and Attendance Allowance whereby people who had significant difficulties but not severe ones got no help at all and those who had really serious needs got too little. Disability Living Allowance would replace these benefits but would be graded so that the seriously disabled got more help and those with minor needs would be brought into the system but at a lower rate of benefit.

The committee stage was good-natured as Nick Scott, a left-leaning Tory of the Heath mould who had served Thatcher well when he was a minister in Northern Ireland, was well liked on both sides of the House and the changes were generally welcome.

Most of the arguments revolved around age, with the Opposition questioning why children under five and the elderly could not be within the bill's scope. The answer that children under five were not expected to do things for themselves was convincing enough but the issue of the upper age limit was rather more complex.

Of course pensioners were not expected to work even if some chose to and of course infirmities and declining vigour are naturally part and parcel of the business of growing old, but whatever line was set for DLA had to be arbitrary and therefore open to challenge. It was different for DWA as it was an income replacement benefit and therefore duplicated in task the state pension. The volume and nature of the forms, the questions that would determine the existence and extent of disability and the role of doctors were all examined and debated in depth.

Nick and I divided up the amendments between us, the civil servants passed us notes and Tuesdays and Thursdays were devoted to the committee and its proceedings. Those were also the days of Prime Minister's Questions so the committee would break at 1 p.m. for lunch, then we would go into the Chamber for PMQs, then a quick dash to our desks, then more briefing from civil servants then back into committee at 4.30 for the rest of the day until the House itself rose in the early hours of the morning, after which there were the red boxes with which to deal.

There was still the constituency work. This was the era when ministers lost a proportion of their parliamentary pay because it was considered they did less as an MP once they had been promoted to office. This rule was rightly dropped in 1996. Constituents do not write fewer letters or seek fewer 'surgery' appointments because their member is a minister – indeed, the reverse is true.

However there must of necessity be a much greater degree of delegation. My secretaries would come over to the department several times a week to resolve any outstanding issues but by and large they handled matters themselves. I saw copies of every letter sent out in my name if I had not signed them in person and only occasionally did I have to ask for a different approach. An MP's reputation in the constituency can be massively in a secretary's hands.

Most of my secretaries were utterly reliable and stayed with me for years but I lost three of them to full-time motherhood. In the third case a very bright lady, Carolyn, had been trying for years to have a child but at last gave up and was expecting to work in the House of Commons for a long time to come. Within a year she was pregnant and other staff joked that whoever sat in my secretary's chair could expect a baby to follow. It did not go down well with her successor who already had a ten-year-old.

Such was my respect for Nick Scott that I would not be writing what follows at all if his problems with drink had not entered the public domain and eventually brought about his downfall, but it must have been around this time that he started drinking unwisely or perhaps he had already been doing so but had managed to keep it hidden from the rest of the world.

One night I was sitting on the front bench while he answered an adjournment debate and I realised that he was seriously drunk. Mercifully the Opposition did not call attention to it because they liked him, but from then on the problem grew worse and all of us, from Tony Newton down to the loyal driver, handled it in the worst possible way – by covering up.

I began to understudy for every adjournment debate he was due to handle. Bob Hughes, the department's whip, covered for him when he fell into a stupor and missed a vital Maastricht vote. His driver got him from his office to the car each night despite the bad temper directed at him from a swaying Nick.

He was obviously deeply unhappy. Nothing had quite worked out for him. His first marriage had ended in divorce and he, who had once been a shining star widely talked of as a future prime minister, was drudging away in middle-ranking office. Deeply committed to the disabled, he was later to be badly vilified when he destroyed a well-intentioned but impractical private member's bill to outlaw discrimination against disabled people, an action publicly attacked by his own daughter.

Perhaps if we had covered up less and left him to the consequences of his own actions he might have got help. Our approach was born of friendship but we might have been better friends to him had we not adopted it.

I was to remember this many years later when a popular radio presenter was alleged to have been drunk during one show. Immediately everyone seemed to rally round saying that rumours of excessive drinking were untrue. Yet I knew that was not so. At a naval dinner I was once addressing I was told that she had been a previous guest but became too drunk to give her speech and on another occasion at a bookshop the owner told me that presenter had been so drunk when doing her own signing that she had been glad to get rid of her.

'You are not her friends,' I murmured sadly when reading her colleagues' denials in the papers.

In March 1991 I needed friends myself and the problem came not from a bottle but from a bank, as my financial situation finally imploded. I was now earning more and gradually repaying debt but not fast enough for some of my creditors, one of whom was the HFC bank.

I returned from a service for the International Women's Day of Prayer on a Friday morning to find a message on my answering machine from a Fred Madel at HFC bank. They had received an enquiry from 'a major Sunday newspaper'. I rang back, surprised at how calm I felt. The paper was the *News of the World* and the enquiry was about the bankruptcy petition submitted by HFC.

What bankruptcy petition? Incredibly they had given me no notice of it and had the grace to admit it subsequently to the press. There could be no question of bankruptcy and family and friends came to my aid with great speed, but today I doubt that I would have survived so easily. Both the House itself and the media are much less forgiving.

There was one financial mistake that I never made: I did not fool myself that the increase in income from being a minister was anything more than just an interlude between a backbencher's pay and a backbencher's pay and did not allow myself to live up to the salary I was receiving. Instead I began to pay off the mortgage faster on the cottage. When, six years later, I came close to resigning from the Home Office, the one aspect that did not therefore feature in my deliberations was the sudden drop in pay, nor did I feel any financial impact from the loss of the 1997 general election, even though the rules had by then changed and ministers were no longer deprived of their full parliamentary salary.

When I was appointed a minister I was told that the rules required that I live in London and that if I was claiming the second home allowance on my London home I must switch to doing so on my constituency cottage. No such switch was necessary because I had always regarded London as my main home, having been living there before I entered the House, but it was a fact of ministerial life that had I a mansion in my constituency and a rabbit hutch in London the rules would have required me to declare the rabbit hutch as my main home, an aspect of the expenses scandal that was never properly explained to an angry public.

As London was always my main home it meant that I had to declare it, rather than the cottage, as my address on my nomination forms in general elections. Once I arrived at a polling station to hear a man observe to a woman, as he turned away from the notice, 'Oh. Ann Widdecombe doesn't live in the constituency.'

'Oh, yes, I do,' I said in pantomime tones.

It never seemed to make any difference. I was still returned with large majorities and the largest of all, 16,286 was in the election of 1992 after which I was once more a PUSS but with a different role and a different Secretary of State.

It was not the outcome I expected, being convinced that Labour would win, but it was certainly an election to remember.

Chapter Seventeen

PENSIONS MINISTER

Now I do so dearly wish we had lost the 1992 Election. If we had, Labour would have endured the collapse of the ERM and the subsequent impact on the economy, which would have confirmed the general wisdom that they had no idea how to run the nation's finances and would have put us back in power for another long run. The country would have been Blairless and I would probably have been in the Cabinet, the first of these being much the greater blessing.

Naturally I saw it very differently at the time. I was so convinced that we were going to lose that I took all my pot plants home from my office at Social Security and gave the civil servants a farewell drink. Three weeks later I brought all the pot plants back, put them down in the same positions and gave the civil servants a 'hello again' drink. I could scarcely credit the return to normalcy.

It had been a momentous election both nationally and locally and was the one in which I discovered the difference between being an ordinary candidate and being a member of the government. MPs cease to be MPs the moment Parliament is dissolved for the election, but as the country has to be governed one remains a minister until the election itself so, albeit at a much-reduced rate, the red boxes still come.

No minister can take policy decisions during an election. Indeed when I was later to be signing off a long-agreed policy relating to the prison ship HMP *Weare* at the gates of the 1997 election I was obliged to ring Jack Straw, my Labour opposite number and successor, for his agreement. All the standard work and correspondence however goes on as normal, especially as civil servants take the opportunity of a prolonged period without the nuisance of ministers to clear their own desks thoroughly.

Ministers fight a national campaign in addition to that in their own constituencies. For very senior personnel that is something of an advantage because the chances are that you are beamed into your constituents' sitting rooms almost every day. As I have observed, if I found it demoralising to see Owen in the background when voters opened their doors to me in Devonport, I knew throughout the 2001 election that my local opponents were encountering the same irritation.

For junior ministers it is much less of a blessing, for it takes one out of the constituency and into the marginal seats but does not confer the benefit of national coverage. In 1992 I was still sufficiently junior to be able to limit my national role to once or twice a week, but friends who were fighting seats in difficult conditions asked me to speak for them and, remembering how speakers had come to both Burnley and Devonport, I was anxious to oblige.

In Maidstone there were four women candidates, three for the main parties and one for the Greens, and it looked as if it would be an all-female contest until the Natural Law Party put up a male candidate. His candidature brought a wonderful dimension of light relief as his very seriously argued answer to everything was yogic flying. The electorate stayed polite and smiled rather than sniggered but it was no great surprise that all 310 Natural Law candidates lost their deposits.

Meanwhile I was much assisted in Maidstone by a series of scandals and fiascos which had struck the Liberal Democrats, who were the principal challengers. When their candidate was first selected I expected a tough ride because it was the leader of the Liberal Democrat Group on the local council, Paula Yates. Then came the Boro'line pension scandal.

Pensions were much in the news as the previous year Robert Maxwell had disappeared from a boat and died at sea after revelations that the *Daily Mirror* pension fund had been plundered. Until then the widespread assumption had always been that pensions were as safe as houses, unassailable and unstealable.

Indeed, according to OECD, Britain had the only sustainable pensions system in Europe.

I was the minister at Social Security who was dealing with the aftermath of Maxwell, trying to steer a course between helping the Mirror pensioners and preserving the interests of the Treasury, which could not be seen as willing to underwrite what was effectively a massive theft. I was therefore better placed than most to appreciate the implications when it was revealed that the Liberal Democrat-run council in Maidstone had not been paying the workers' contributions into the pension fund. The local headlines were huge, the population, which had absorbed the acres of coverage about Maxwell, was stunned and the Liberal Democrat candidates were annihilated at the local elections which followed the general one.

Meanwhile Paula was being taken to task at every turn by a very effective Catriona Titchener, who was the leader of the Conservative group on the council. The crowning misfortune for the Lib Dems came when a children's entertainment turned out to be an obscene theatrical performance.

So at a time when the Conservative majority in Parliament was reduced from 102 to 21 my own rocketed from 10,364 to 16,286.

John Major took, literally, a soapbox around the country. Undeniably the electorate was fairly fed up with its government after three terms and ready for change but John presented himself as the change after eleven years of a different Prime Minister and Neil Kinnock scared the country with a programme of tax rises and old-fashioned socialism, promising vast new expenditure.

'How are they going to pay for it?' was the consistent reaction of every London cabbie I encountered.

On the doorsteps it was less friendly. People had gone through enormous personal anxiety as a result of the recession, the Poll Tax still rankled even though it had been comprehensively abandoned and electors were increasingly worried about the NHS's capacity to deliver. In such an atmosphere it might have been easy enough for the country to sleepwalk into voting Labour.

Then came the Sheffield rally, Labour's single biggest mistake.

Screeds of analysis have been produced attempting to demonstrate why this one event had such a decisively negative impact.
Some likened it to the Nuremberg rallies of the 1930s, seeing a
comparison not with the evil therein but with the sheer triumphalism. Others took exception to Kinnock shouting, 'We're all
right,' as if the election were already won. Others still merely
sniffed that it was all too American and un-British.

My own view is a simpler one: at the point where the Shadow
Cabinet was paraded individually as 'the next Home Secretary',
'the next Chancellor' and left-winger after left-winger basked in
the roars of the crowd, the country suddenly faced the fact that
this could happen. We really could have a Labour government
and in those days that meant a socialist one.

Some commentators still claim that the Sheffield rally had no
real effect but they are wrong. In the weeks before Sheffield
angry voters were saying 'never again' when I canvassed them.
In the days which followed Sheffield, worried voters were crossing the street to say, 'You won't let them in, will you?' There had
been a sea change.

The *Sun* encapsulated those worries with its headline: 'If
Labour wins tomorrow, will the last person to leave Britain
switch off the lights.'

The atmosphere among returning Conservative MPs was one
of euphoria. Even level-headed senior members were saying
that they did not see how Labour would ever win again if they
could not do so in those electoral conditions. We had just won
a record fourth term and there was a boundaries revision due
which everybody expected to be favourable to us.

This is a good example of how so many, whether it be commentators, practitioners or voters, regularly make the mistake
of assuming that the political conditions of today will prevail
tomorrow. If polls are bad three years away from an election
people will predict disaster as if nothing can possibly happen in
between to change the landscape. The old cliché that a week is
a long time in politics is often glibly quoted but rarely informs
opinion.

Labour's single biggest handicap was true socialism but the

man who was to recognise that what the electorate now yearned for was a Tory agenda without the Tories was not yet leading that party.

I stayed where I was in the reshuffle that followed the Election but Tony Newton moved on to become Leader of the House and assumed an even bigger workload. He was replaced by Peter Lilley, a clever and politically astute right-winger. The first change he made was to separate political advisors from civil servants in the daily morning meeting, having strong views on not mixing the two. His own advisor was vastly more vocal than Tony's had been and the meetings changed in tone as well as in personnel.

My own brief now moved from general benefits to being heavily concentrated on pensions, and there was certainly enough to do. The Maxwell fallout was still enormous; a ruling from the EU had left us with little choice but to equalise state pension age; a report, under the chairmanship of Professor Goode, was commissioned into the safeguarding of workers' pensions schemes; the first hard evidence of mis-selling of personal pensions was beginning to emerge and the time was approaching when the mathematics were suggesting that those who had opted out of SERPS might have maximised the advantage and could be advised to re-enter the system. Then there was the perennial problem of financing the care of the elderly in residential homes, with much analysis of insurance options and whether they might be made affordable for the population at large.

When the Maxwell pensions scandal had broken the previous year there were those in the parliamentary party who believed that the State should not intervene at all, that it was a civil matter between the pensioners and the Mirror Group with of course any illegalities the sole concern of the police. Given that some £450 million was missing and thousands of people dependent on their pensions, that was not such a bright view of the world. Not only was common humanity missing from it but it exhibited a complete absence of any appreciation as to the damage that would be inflicted on confidence in the occupational pension system, which was one of Britain's strongest economic and social assets.

Equally it would have been quite wrong for the Exchequer simply to have opened up its coffers and compensated the pensioners in full as that would have sent a message that the State was underwriting theft and would always pick up the bill of any irresponsibly run scheme.

The first task therefore was to try to trace the assets. Where had Maxwell spent the money? How much was lying around in institutions in the City? How much had been used to make risky money purchases and how much was recoverable? Asset tracing was a painstaking process but by mid-1992 it was all too obvious that there would be a huge shortfall between what was taken and what could be located and reclaimed.

Peter therefore appointed the then Sir John Cuckney, a former M15 officer and astute businessman who had played a major role in the Westland affair, to trace the assets and also to set up a trust and solicit contributions from City institutions. It proved to be the right response led by the right man.

The face of the Maxwell pensioners was Ivy Needham, a lady in her mid-sixties who regularly appeared on television to complain that we were doing too little. She led delegations to see Peter and always embraced me enthusiastically. 'Eeh, Ann's luverlee,' she told Peter on one such occasion. He kept a straight face.

Ivy was more than clever enough to know that we were doing all we could and that we were not going to write a blank cheque but rightly recognised her own role as being to keep up the pressure so that we were not tempted to think the problem would quietly die down. Therefore the press always knew when she was coming to see us and were always present when she emerged to rant on the doorstep of Richmond House that government was letting the pensioners down.

The press and media, as they so often do, took Ivy's ragings at face value. It is, after all, more interesting to report confrontation and dissatisfaction than quiet, steady progress. So the *Mirror* itself thought it had a coup when its journalists arranged for Ivy to 'confront me' at the next Conservative Party Conference. Tipped off by Sheree Dodd, one of the *Mirror*'s better journalists, there were media with rolling cameras as well as the *Mirror* snappers present as Ivy came towards me.

'Ann!' she cried and threw her arms round me.

'Ivy!' I cried, returning the hug.

Over the top of Ivy's head I glanced mischievously at the cameras. Sheree was laughing ruefully and the 'confrontation' was accorded no space at all in either press or media.

It was not simply a case of a nice old pensioner being naïvely friendly. She knew exactly what the press was up to and knew also that attacking and embarrassing ministers on a personal level would be counter-productive. In 2011, by now eighty-six and a great-grandmother registered both blind and deaf, Ivy was on the warpath again, this time over her council having sent along a male carer to put her to bed.

Ivy Needham was justly awarded an MBE and became well known for supporting Help for Heroes and the Royal British Legion, accompanied by her guide dog as she went about her fund-raising. She was ten times as effective as any trade union leader because she spoke from the heart without losing her head.

If I was doubtful about the way our membership of the EEC, then in the process of becoming the EU, had developed since I had campaigned for Britain to belong in the 1970s, then my first experience of ministerial life confirmed my worst fears. I spent a great deal of time in all three departments but especially in Social Security and in Employment, where EU law bit deep, negotiating and arguing with my European counterparts. There were regular proposals to place demands on our social security system or on small employers which were costly, undesirable and bureaucratic to the last degree.

Our occupational pensions schemes were funded. It seemed to me a fairly simple idea to grasp, with its three-way partnership between workers, employers and State. Workers and employers paid in monthly contributions at set rates and the government granted tax relief on both contributions and gains earned by the funds which built up the money to pay the pensions. Yet the obvious implications of this seemed lost on a Europe which by and large relied instead on taxpayer funding of pensions.

Holland had similar arrangements and Germany a book reserve scheme, but to the rest funded schemes were a minority interest. So they would demand extra provisions without understanding the impact on actuarial calculations.

We had managed to rebuff a proposal for almost overnight equalisation of male and female provision in the occupational pensions sector but that sector was working towards full equalisation and several large schemes already operated on that basis. We were allowed to continue with different retirement ages in the State sector but clearly that was not going to be sustainable in the long term and so the question which now preoccupied us was: at which age should we equalise?

We issued a consultation document which proposed four options: 60, 63, 65 and a flexible decade whereby people could elect a retirement age of any year between 60 and 70. Each had its advantages and drawbacks, and over the weeks that followed I received representations not just from individuals but from many groups with particular agendas. In each instance I conducted the meeting by inviting them to state their case and then arguing in detail the opposite case and listening carefully to any rebuttals they offered. Occasionally that produced new considerations and it was a worthwhile and genuine consultation exercise. I spoke the simple truth when I assured each of these groups that government had an open mind. Too many consultations, the obvious being the recent example on redefining marriage, begin with the view that ministers already know the course they intend to adopt and are merely going through the motions of listening to public opinion.

Indeed there had been a sizeable argument the previous year about whether we should issue the document before the election. I, anxious to get on with it, said we should, urging that the public was not daft, that all sane people knew we had a rapidly growing elderly population and that providing the timescale was long enough they would accept changes. The more politically motivated said no, the instant we mentioned 65 the voters would just assume that's where we were going, however open-minded we were, and we would end up having to disown the option and would thereby prejudice the discussion before it started.

It was, I think, wise counsel but now the same approach was being taken towards 67, which I had wanted to throw into the melting pot as some other countries were already moving or had moved in that direction. Peter was adamant we should not offer it just because, being the one option that was not already familiar within the system, people would assume that was what we preferred. I countered that we had an entire Parliament to get over any such obstacle and that if people really believed we were heading that way and we did not then they might be relieved even if we went as far as 65, but he insisted that the debate would get bogged down around 67 so we never did consult on it. It is a measure of how far the thinking has developed that Britain is now willing to encompass 68.

So we stuck to four options. Of these, 60 was clearly attractive politically as it meant giving advantage to all the men while disadvantaging nobody. Unfortunately it was also vastly expensive, meaning extra costs of some £4 billion each year and an increase in the dependency ratio as there would be more pensioners to pay and fewer workers supporting them.

To understand the full implications of that last point it is necessary to understand the workings of the National Insurance Scheme, which is a pay-as-you-go scheme whereby there is no fund building up but instead the government takes in this week's contributions and pays them out to this week's pensioners. If the pot falls below the minimum prescribed by the government actuary then it is from general taxation that a subvention is taken.

I have already commented that many correspondents assumed the NI fund to work as an occupational fund. Indeed when I wrote back to one lady that it was instead a pay-as-you-go scheme she riposted, 'I know very well that National Insurance is a pay-as-you-go scheme and if the government has not had the sense to invest the money that is not my fault!'

The situation is a long way from that envisaged by the founding fathers of the welfare state whereby we would insure our health, pensions and right to assistance by paying our weekly stamp. Indeed right up until the time I retired in 2010 I was still receiving indignant letters from people let down by the NHS who protested '... and I paid my stamp all my life'. I would then have to explain that it was decades since National Insurance had been enough to cover health, that these days it just about covered pensions and contributory benefits.

Nevertheless we are locked into the wretched system, for if we suddenly decided to let people opt out altogether into private schemes or decided to put the money in an investment fund we would not have the wherewithal to pay the pensions today. When, after the fall of communism, we were advising former Warsaw Pact countries how to set up welfare systems, our strongest counsel was never to base any major system on the pay-as-you-go principle for government.

I had initially been in favour of the flexible decade but changed my mind when research showed that the overwhelming majority of people would choose 60 as the preferred age bringing with it all the baggage already described.

I was attracted to 63 but it had all the disadvantages without many of the advantages. It would cost the exchequer extra pension payments and two years' lost contributions from the men but still anger the women, who would have to work another three years. If we were going down that route then perhaps we should look well into the future, take a deep breath and announce 65, which would save money and be sustainable in a changing world where the pensioner population was growing year on year.

Of course the women would complain but we had enjoyed a grossly unfair advantage for many years, living on average five years longer but retiring five years earlier than the men. Again, I argued, phase the changes in over a long enough timescale so that nobody in their late forties or fifties was facing a full five years extra work and they would be accepted. Begin the phasing in, say, 2010 and complete the whole process by 2020 and people would calm down.

The final decision had yet to be made when I left the department in 2003 but that was what was eventually decided and became the basis for the 1995 Pensions Act.

I have made the options and their arguments sound easy but in reality they were not. It would be tedious to list all the ifs and buts here but, just as an example, there was the difficulty of calculating the impact on the working population of reducing male pension age to 60. Already large swathes of workers and especially professionals and public service employees with salary-related schemes, retired anyway at 60 and lived on their occupational pensions alone until they became eligible for the state pension.

Sixty-six per cent of the population had some income, large or small, over and above the state pension and the value of the average occupational pension was then roughly equal to the state pension. It was a growing trend and pensioner incomes had increased on average by 30 per cent in the Thatcher decade. In other words the state pension was playing a decreasing role in pensioner income. Yet it was still all some retired persons had in the world and there was much discussion about targeting help where it was actually needed.

Whenever I think back to those discussions and to our healthy pension funds I rage against Gordon Brown and his robbery. The difference between what he and Maxwell did was that the Chancellor used legal and fiscal means and the newspaper tycoon illegal ones but the effect was the same: the wreckage of a once-strong pension system to which I will return when I come to the advent of Blair.

If the actuarial calculations were difficult and sometimes I plotted graphs in my sleep, the politics of pension change were hardly easy. Media assumed we were preferring 65 at a time when we had simply come to no conclusion at all and interviewers tried hard to persuade me to defend that option. I knew that however much I qualified my replies anything I said in favour of 65 would be taken in isolation.

The correspondence was huge. People were in a panic – and that is not too strong a word – because they assumed that any change we made would directly affect them when they were of an age well outside any net we might cast. One man wrote to ask if the already retired would have to return to work and one lady described how she wept after hearing about the change on the news because she was looking forward to her sixtieth birthday in a few weeks' time and now she couldn't retire after all.

I argued with Peter about the standard letter we should send out in reply. I wanted to reassure people by pointing out that any scheme would be phased in over a decade and would not even start for years. I proposed pointing out that other countries, e.g. Italy and Germany, were raising their pension ages and were phasing in with 2016 and 2017 as the aim. Peter disagreed. He thought the relief would be greater and therefore also the acceptance if we revealed that when the final decisions were made.

I suppose it was only an extension of the argument that I had made when I had pressed for 67 to be included, but I had not wanted to consult on it for that reason alone and I strongly resisted prolonging mental anguish and anxiety. As I was not allowed to add such reassurances to the text of the letter, I simply wrote them in postscripts in my own hand.

> *If Mrs Smith is fifty-six next August she could not possibly be affected by any changes we might decide to make. Italy and Germany are raising state pension age and neither is expecting the process to be complete before 2016. There are many considerations which dictate such a timescale ...*

It added hours to my correspondence work but I considered it well worth the effort, especially when some worried persons then replied in delighted relief.

It must have been about this time, although I have no precise note, that I instituted a challenge within the correspondence division over grammar. David Higlett was by then my Private Secretary and I told him that if I saw one more mixed singular and plural I should go mad with frustration.

We all have our bêtes noires when it comes to grammar. The split infinitive enrages John Humphrys, the misplaced apostrophe Lynne Truss and the mixed singular and plural Ann Widdecombe.

A pensioner collects their benefit is, I proclaimed, rot. A pensioner collects his or her benefit. Ah, but the letters are standard, Minister, and might refer to a man or woman. Then simply say his benefit. Masculine takes precedence over feminine. Not politically correct, Minister. Then write his or her each time. Too clumsy, Minister. Then make the pensioner plural too and write pensioners. A possessive pronoun must reflect the number of the noun. Eh, Minister?

It does not take a grammarian to recognise the lack of inverted commas in the above exchange and that is because I have now given up the battle against informal grammar, having comprehensively lost it in the course of working in three government departments and for editors of a tabloid newspaper. Indeed this work exhibits offences against the language which I would never have countenanced in any of my four novels.

I remember with affection and admiration Bernard Levin's pieces in *The Times* wherein he could make a single sentence the length of a paragraph without once losing control of grammar, subordinate clauses, participles or punctuation. It was positively Ciceronian.

The Times now produces some terrible grammar and I presume its readers have also given up because one no longer sees letters of the nature of one I have always cherished and which appeared during the Cold War, when *The Times* had run a headline 'Russians Tell Reagan We Can Beat You At Arms'.

Lamenting the absence of inverted commas, the reader asked: *Are you, Sir, really in a position of worrying nuclear superiority over your readers? If so, how did the Russians find out and why did they tell the President?*

Today, as I have observed, I have lost the battle. Language has always changed with the passage of time or forsooth we would still be speaking as Shakespeare did or possibly even Chaucer but it still sets my teeth on edge to hear decimated substituted for devastated or the transitive lays for the intransitive lies, as does the confusion between I and me. All London must have heard when some hapless editor changed one of my sentences and actually wrote 'a minutiae'. She might, I raged impotently for the article had already gone out under my name, just as well refer to 'a cattle'.

Did Labour ever do anything good? Yes. It introduced the literacy hour.

Then, however, I was still fighting a rearguard action and so I promised the correspondence division a bottle of wine if it produced a straight run of fifty letters without a mixed singular and plural. It took some weeks for it to win a bottle of House of Commons red wine.

Meanwhile however busy I was with Maxwell and equalisation of pension age, the ordinary work of a pensions minister had to continue and I was pleased to see from comments in specialist journals that I was beginning to impress the industry. I dared to hope that promotion would beckon at the next reshuffle but soon it was not my political but my spiritual welfare which preoccupied me for as the autumn leaves blew across my Kentish constituency the Church of England took itself and most of Christendom by surprise as its Synod voted to ordain women as priests.

Chapter Eighteen

POPE OR PENSIONERS?

Most people outside the Church of England had no idea what all the fuss was about as it tore itself apart. Those inside understood only too well but found the apostolic succession and the notion of the priest standing *in persona Christi* at the point of consecration a trifle difficult to explain to a secular world. It did not help that nobody had expected the vote to go through for another five years and both Canterbury and Rome were wholly unprepared for the inevitable consequences. The first had made no proper plans about how to deal with dissenting clergy and the second had no formula for receiving them if they decided to cross the Tiber. It also did not help that the vote which took place on 11 November 1992 was carried by only the narrowest margin. The majority was two. There was fury towards opponents who did not vote and even greater anger towards the then Archbishop of Canterbury, George Carey, who had the indiscretion to brand those who opposed the move as heretics.

I had told the Bishop of Maidstone, then David Smith, that if the Anglican Church ever voted to ordain women I would leave but like everybody else I complacently thought that day was still some distance away. When Chris Moncrieff of the Press Association rang me that evening to tell me that seventeen minutes earlier the Church of England had voted to ordain women my response was immediate. I had, I told him, ceased to be a member of the Church of England seventeen minutes ago.

I did not expect much public interest nor did I seek it. I was a very junior minister and unlike John Gummer, who had opposed the measure vigorously, I was not on the Synod and had not hitherto been publicly asked for my stance on the issue but within minutes of the conversation with Moncrieff there was an avalanche of telephone calls. If I assumed anything from this it was that all the spokesmen were tied up in Synod and were holding fire until an agreed statement had been produced. I agreed to appear on the nine o'clock news, feeling fairly certain that I would be stood down in favour of some bishop.

In the members' lobby of the House of Commons I rang Gavin Reid, who had taken over from David Smith as Bishop of Maidstone, and my brother who, as a vicar also opposed to the measure, was certain to be approached if my own stand were to become well known. Looking back now, that assumption of not much interest seems hopelessly naïve but hindsight is a wonderful gift and I still cannot fault my reasoning at the time. Who was I compared to bishops, clergymen, academics and members of the Synod?

Gavin asked me to wait a little but I said no, the die was cast.

Before examining the tidal wave of publicity which was to engulf me five months later when I elected to become a Roman Catholic, it is necessary to ask how I had arrived at this point in my spiritual life.

The family's Anglican roots were strong. As I have previously observed, my father's brother was a vicar. My brother was also a vicar in Bristol, and in later years his son, Roger, was to become a vicar, currently in Cheltenham. There had also been lay readers in the family and whichever branch of the family I looked at I saw churchgoers. It was true that there were influences other than Anglican at work. My mother's mother was a Baptist and her father a Catholic, my father's sister was a Methodist, my mother's cousin a Baptist but at home we were all Anglicans.

I have already described how I went to church each Sunday and also to Sunday school and then to a convent boarding school. After that came the University Christian Unions and the Billy Graham missions. When I moved to London I began to try out different churches but always Anglican and then came a period of agnosticism, before a return to Christianity.

Throughout it all, I despaired of the Church into which I had been baptised, brought up and confirmed and the mistake I made was in returning to the Anglican Church instead of looking more closely at Rome for which my admiration was growing but the roots were just too strong at that stage to be tugged up and discarded.

I despaired because it seemed that the Church of England was always ready to sacrifice faith to fashion and creed to compromise. In 1963 the then Bishop of Woolwich, John Robinson, published *Honest to God,* a book criticising traditional Christian theology. It was enough for Hugh Montefiore to suggest that Christ might have been a homosexual for him to have been made a bishop before the rest of us had finished gasping. Then there was the then Bishop of Durham, Jenkins, who actually questioned articles of creed. The point in each case is that this was not some ordinary clergyman going off-message but the very hierarchy of the Church itself. If a bishop is going to question the resurrection and stay a bishop then the Church has no purpose.

It was not until some months after my conversion to Catholicism that Pope John Paul II published the encyclical *Veritatis Splendor* but it sums up the essence of the Catholic Church's approach to modern controversies, which is simply that you cannot determine what is good and what is bad merely by reference to its popularity. A view may be widely held but still false or something very unpopular but still true. Truth is not put to the vote.

By contrast the C of E's approach was to follow not to lead. Whatever the world did must be a guiding star and so it came about that when the controversy over women priests broke, the debate was heavily centred not on the theology of the question but upon the Church's acceptability to the world. If the early apostles had taken that line we would all still be worshipping Zeus.

When George Carey wrote to me shortly after I left, asking how I could be a woman MP but deny women the right to be priests, I knew I had taken absolutely the right decision. Neither I nor any MP, whether male or female, stood *in persona Christi* nor conferred any sacraments and if I had to explain that to the Archbishop of Canterbury, of all people, then I was glad I was no longer among his flock.

I am pleased to record that he and I eventually reached a rapprochement but at the time I was livid as his letter suggested that he could see the priesthood simply in career terms comparable with politics.

However angry and upset I may have been, I was not going to fall into the trap of disowning the Church which had formed my faith and when I did decide upon Rome I was careful to say in interviews that I regarded myself as crossing a bridge, not jumping across a vast abyss but added, rather sadly, that even when crossing a bridge you had your back to one side.

Did I ever turn and look back across the bridge? Yes, but if I sometimes had attacks of nostalgia, brought about by the sound of church bells pealing over the Kentish countryside or the smell of pews and polish as I entered an Anglican church, I never once had regrets. At first I felt like an Anglican who had been driven by storms into harbour at Rome but it was not long before I found it difficult to remember that I had ever been anything but Catholic.

Theology can be difficult to crunch down for consumption by a society which no longer comes into daily contact with the gospels but as that change in the Church of England was sufficiently important to drive out thousands of laity, hundreds of priests and a handful of bishops, I am going to make some attempt to explain the issues and the thinking of the various groups which left. The best explanation of all, from the Catholic view, if the reader is already versed in basic Church teaching, is 'A Letter to Marianne' by Maureen Mullins, published by Scepter Booklets.

Opposition to the priesting of women came from the two opposite ends of the Church of England, the Anglo-Catholic wing and the evangelical wing and was based on very different reasoning. The middle-of-the-road Anglicans did what they always did and muddled along in a Church so regularly at sixes and sevens.

For the evangelicals, who take scripture literally and seek answers there, the issue was 'headship'. St Paul writes in his epistle to the Corinthians: *I want you to realise that the head of every man is Christ and the head of the woman is man and the head of Christ is God*. They take the view that this establishes a clear line of authority in the Church and that a woman cannot exert headship over a man.

The Anglo-Catholic wing had different grounds for objection and although I was not Anglo-Catholic by background I shared them. First of all there was the position vis-à-vis the Catholic Church. The C of E was a breakaway church formed by Henry VIII when the Pope would not allow him to rid himself of his lawful wife for Anne Boleyn.

It still regarded itself as a part of the Catholic Church, however, albeit a reformed one. *I believe in one holy, catholic and apostolic church* is as much an article of Anglican creed as of Catholic creed, said solemnly by Anglicans across the land each week. The position of many, including John Gummer, was that if we were to take a decision on the nature of the apostolic succession in isolation from Rome then we would no longer be a part of the Catholic Church but would effectively become a sect.

So what is the apostolic succession? The frequency with which I was asked that question showed me just how far the ties had loosened between the Church and society as a whole. So, with apologies to those who are well versed in the history of the Church, I will give a brief and, of necessity, simple explanation here of a concept which could take an entire book to explore in depth.

Christ appointed twelve apostles whose responsibility was to establish His church on earth after His ascension into Heaven. After Judas fell from grace and died, the early Church appointed someone to take his place (Matthias). This simple act is the apostolic succession, whereby the teaching and authority within the Church is passed on and covers bishops and priests who are regarded as being part of the apostolic succession and sets the example for St Peter to be directly succeeded in generation after generation (the popes).

There is plenty of evidence that Christ regarded women highly. His first miracle was carried out upon the request of His mother, Mary, and women were chosen to be the first witnesses of His resurrection but He did not appoint a single female apostle.

Sometimes it is argued that well, of course, He wouldn't because it would have gone so much against the conventions of His time but the evidence shrieks the opposite for this was the man Who broke the Sabbath, scandalised all Jerusalem by feasting with publicans and sinners, was called a glutton and a winebibber, tore through the temple upsetting merchandise and merchants, challenged authority and defied all censure. And er ... He would not have dared appoint a woman?

So why did He not choose a woman to be an apostle? This is where it gets complicated and involves the differentiation between priests and ministers. A priest has a sacramental role and is not just a teacher of the faith. At the point where the communion is consecrated he stands *in persona Christi* representing both priest and victim. Can a woman do this? The best way to demonstrate the difficulty of that is to ask if a man could stand in the person of the Virgin Mary. This is, as I have said, a serious simplification of a complex subject.

In my view both the Roman and Anglican Churches missed the more vital debate, which was over the role of the laity. It is a nonsense to argue that a woman cannot play a full role in the life of the Church just because she cannot be a priest. Mother Teresa? Indeed if one goes back sufficiently far then we find mitred abbesses before whom any mere priest would have quailed. A huge number of the saints are women. They have never been regarded as inferior but rather as having a non-apostolic role.

I was already carrying a very large bundle of straw as far as the Anglican Church was concerned but perhaps the priesting of women would not have been the last straw had the debate been more theological and less secular. Would I have still been in the C of E had there been no priesting of women, if the vote had always gone the other way? I suspect not. The bundle was simply too large.

Between leaving Bath Convent and entering the House of Commons, my contact with Catholicism had been extremely limited but the first three years of my parliamentary life were heavily dominated by the anti-abortion campaigns and I spent a great deal of time at meetings convened by both evangelicals and

Catholics. Many of my comrades-in-arms were Catholics including David Alton, David Amess, Ken Hargreaves and Julian Brazier and many was the religious debate we had in the Pugin Room during late-night sittings.

Many people assume I am pro-life because I am a Catholic but the opposite is probably true: I am a Catholic because I am pro-life. It was the Catholic Church which provided the statements and the public stance which helped us. By contrast the Archbishop of York claimed in the House of Lords in the embryology debate that all life was a 'process'.

Oh, I scoffed, at many a public meeting, so we had better rewrite scripture. 'And it came to pass that when Elizabeth heard the salutation of Mary the process leaped in her womb', 'And Mary brought forth a process and laid Him in a manger'.

I began occasionally to attend Masses at Westminster Cathedral and to notice, somewhat disconcertedly, that I felt quite at home but in the Pugin Room I still argued my increasingly wobbly Anglican position. Despite that, however, I remained sufficiently unconvinced of some Catholic doctrine to refrain from immediately seeking communion with the Catholic Church in November 1992. It was, I told Tim Wood, then a whip but previously a friend in youth politics, just all too superstitious.

The correspondence following my departure from the Church of England was vast. Some wrote to agree or disagree with my position on the priesting of women, others to say the Anglicans were well rid of me but many, including some who belonged to the Greek Orthodox Church, to urge me to join them. I took no decision until the following March and press enquiries began to wither away leaving me to come to a decision in peace.

My own path to Rome was not easy. I distrusted the sacrificial nature of the Mass, was not convinced about transubstantiation, hated the Marian emphasis and, above all, was unreconciled to the existence of purgatory. I needed to discuss all these matters and remembered a priest whom I had met when he was producing a book about people's visions of Heaven and I had contributed a piece for him. Ken Hargreaves had introduced us but had lost his seat in that year's election so I rang him up.

'Oh,' he said. 'You mean Michael Seed. He's at Westminster Cathedral.'

Michael was then a virtually unknown priest, who was eventually to become as famous as the high-profile figures he led over the Tiber. He is often perceived now as a frivolous individual who has crossed the line between being a priest to the celebrities and being a celebrity himself, who has feasted with sinners so often that his own feasts are now tainted. That is, however, an incomplete picture of someone who can argue persuasively and who is more adept than most at persuading the rich to part with their money in good causes.

Over the next four months Michael became a regular visitor to the House of Commons, as my own portfolio was too heavy for me to leave to visit him. And we argued and argued and argued over teas and dinners, in intervals between divisions and late at night in the Pugin Room, where our discussions attracted other participants, until only purgatory remained as a stumbling block.

Some may find this preoccupation with the minutiae of doctrine strange and wonder why, given that I was broadly in sympathy with the Pope, I did not simply become a Catholic with reservations as for years I had been an Anglican despite immense disillusionment. The answer lies in the solemn statement which each person who is received into the Church must, individually, say: *I believe and profess all that the holy Catholic Church teaches, believes and proclaims to be revealed by God*. Unless therefore one is prepared to commit an act of perjury at the point of reception one does have to accept all Church teaching.

Indeed, as I subsequently observed to Cardinal Hume, the convert faces a much higher bar than the cradle Catholic, who may develop doubts about half the canon but still stay a Catholic. Years later when Tony Blair became a Catholic I wondered if that meant he had changed his views on abortion and other such issues or whether the Church had made a unique exception and allowed him to be received without having to say those words, as the only other possibility was the unthinkable one that both he and the priest had shrugged off perjury. I never did get an answer.

I was far from alone in the path over the bridge I was now crossing. As already observed Rome had made no preparations for the situation it faced with thousands of Anglicans seeking reception and in particular it had not the slightest idea how to handle the problem of hundreds of clergy. The result was that in a diocese such as Westminster they were welcomed with open arms, while in places like Salford they met with resistance. There was simply no set formula. One priest went to France and found himself concelebrating Mass almost immediately while in this country others were told they faced an extensive period of re-training.

There was, of course, nothing new about Anglican priests being ordained as Catholic ones but if they were married then they were not appointed to parishes but instead served as chaplains to hospitals, prisons or the armed services. The decline in vocations and the need for more parish priests fuelled speculation that this rule would be relaxed, as indeed it has been over time, but it is not hard to understand the resentment that could cause when Catholic priests who wished to marry were forced to choose between that and the priesthood.

Meanwhile thousands of defecting Anglican laity were encountering similar chaos and unpredictability and the position of Graham Leonard, a well-respected and married Anglican bishop, was the subject of deep discussion in the Vatican.

Some of the laity were told they would have to undergo the full RCIA course, an insult if ever there was one as it stands for the Rite of Christian Initiation of Adults and includes the most basic Christian instruction. 'Do they think we have just put our totem poles in the dustbin?' fumed one irate correspondent to the *Catholic Times*. Others were, more reasonably, given an adapted version. In my own case Michael Seed said bluntly that none of that would be appropriate and our conversations over the last few months would suffice.

The normally sure-footed Cardinal Hume caused a furore when he commented that perhaps this was the beginning of the re-conversion of England for which Catholics had so long prayed. Certainly it was the moment when Catholicism at last began to come out of the closet in which it had for so long hidden in Britain.

I was to be asked on *Woman's Hour* when I announced my own decision to become a Catholic if I felt any discomfort at having joined a religion of 'Irish navvies and Italian waiters'. Today such sentiments would be outlawed under racial hatred laws but then it was a permissible question on a mainstream programme. It is an important one because it illustrates a view of Catholicism which was prevalent at the time: Catholicism was foreign.

Cardinal Hume changed that perception almost single-handedly, for he was of solid English stock and from a family which had served the establishment with some distinction. Today a statue of him stands opposite the central railway station in Newcastle. His father was a knight and eminent surgeon, his family pillars of society. Slowly but surely he worked on putting Catholicism at the heart of English Christendom and his efforts culminated in a visit from the Queen to Westminster Cathedral in 1995, an event which would have been unthinkable only a few years earlier.

During those months when I remained undecided about the direction my spiritual life was to take I received hundreds of letters from those facing the same problem and I sought a meeting with Cardinal Hume to try and clarify the way ahead for laity but especially clergy now seeking communion with Rome. At the end of the inconclusive discussion he asked about my own position and I responded that purgatory remained a problem, pointing out that more was required of converts than of cradle Catholics.

However there was a possible way forward, I suggested. The statement *I believe all the Church teaches to be revealed by God* is immediately followed by the creed. Suppose we were to insert a colon between the two instead of a full stop? He smiled and said, 'Let us call it a smudgemark.'

Thereafter 'smudgemark' became a code word that Michael Seed and I used in the period between my deciding to be received and the public announcement as I was still getting press queries from time to time and did not want to find that journalists had revealed my intentions before I was both fully decided and ready. I knew there would be a flurry of interest but again hopelessly underestimated its extent.

Only David Alton foresaw the media frenzy. The rest of us took my line that a junior minister changing from one Christian denomination to another would be worth no more than a few paragraphs.

At first it was intended that my reception into the Church would take place in the crypt of the House of the Commons. Some religious correspondents asked if they could cover it but Black Rod said no and if our plans had gone ahead the ceremony would have taken place in a press-free zone but Paul Goodman, later deputy editor of the *Daily Telegraph* who was to become a Conservative MP nine years later, caused a sudden upheaval.

I was to be received during the course of the weekly Mass which takes place in the crypt at 5.30 p.m. on Wednesdays. The date selected was 21 April by which time Parliament would be back from the Easter break. The invitations were sent out. My brother, in a gesture of solidarity, was to attend and participate at the altar. My mother, family members and Catholic friends would also be present. Enquiring journalists had been told that I would give interviews on the Green, that grass square with the Houses of Parliament in the background so familiar to watchers of television news. My sponsors were David Alton, John Patten and Ken Hargreaves. The hymns had been chosen and printed.

'It's all sorted,' I told my parents when I was visiting them the weekend before the ceremony, joking that the 'press was squared and the middle class was quite prepared'. Then Goodman lobbed a hand grenade into the midst of these neat and orderly arrangements.

That Sunday, with only three days to spare before the event, he wrote an explosive article in the *Sunday Telegraph* entitled 'The Commons Crypto-Papist' in which he portrayed the ceremony as an exhibition of triumphalism. We had, according to Goodman, chosen the date because it was the Queen's birthday and had selected a hymn 'Faith of Our Fathers' which contained the line 'Mary's prayers shall bring our country back to Thee', it would be the first reception of a Member of Parliament into the Church to be held in the crypt and the first High Mass since the reformation. The smell of incense would reach Paisley's office.

As my parents took the *Sunday Telegraph*, I had read the article and was amused rather than irritated. I think that was the first moment that I had realised it was the Queen's birthday as I had been too preoccupied with my own arrangements to pay attention to the monarch's. However when I returned late that evening it was to find a series of frantic messages on my answerphone from Michael Seed who had been trying to contact me all day. He did not know I was in Haslemere and we were still not in the age of mobiles in pockets and handbags.

The Cardinal, he said when I returned his calls after midnight, was having kittens over the Goodman article. The ceremony could not go ahead in the crypt. Relations with the Anglicans were strained to breaking point and any suggestion of triumphalism was out of the question. The Cardinal had been appalled by the arrangements and even though he accepted that they were not intended as portrayed there must be no room for even the smallest doubt and that could be achieved only by moving the ceremony.

It was my turn to be appalled. It effectively left us with forty-eight hours to cancel everything and put in hand an alternative venue. It was, I said, impossible. We must simply cancel my reception and give ourselves a sensible timescale in which to re-think. Michael, however, had spent the day re-thinking. We would still go ahead with the service in the House of Commons crypt exactly as planned and that would be my first communion as a Catholic but it would be to celebrate a reception which had already taken place that morning. He had established that the crypt at Westminster Cathedral was free at that time and had already booked it.

It was a good solution and there were few arrangements to change. John Patten could not be present at the revised time and venue so Julian Brazier, a Catholic MP who had done so much to convince me over transubstantiation, stood proxy. 'Don't remind the Cardinal that he is the MP for Canterbury,' I mut-tered to Michael, suddenly searching for Goodmanesque sym-bolism in everything we did.

The change of venue, however, unleashed press and media in what was to prove a tidal wave of publicity. Christopher Graffius, who was David Alton's invaluable assistant on pro-life matters, took responsibility for notifying the press that there would no longer be interviews on the Green on Wednesday evening but instead outside Westminster Cathedral early that morning. Instead of circulating only those who had asked ini-tially, he simply sent a round robin to the entire press gallery.

What we had all overlooked was that whereas the Commons crypt was off-limits to the press, Westminster Cathedral was not. So Father Norman Brown, a blind and elderly priest who had volunteered to direct people to the cathedral crypt, found himself ushering scores of journalists and cameramen down the stairs but being unable to see much did not realise.

Michael did. We had expected none but the sponsors and possibly a few eager friends and representatives of the Catholic press to turn up as we had left everyone else to come to the Mass as planned and had sent out no general notice of the revised arrangements. As for the media, we naïvely expected such as were interested to be outside as Christopher had indicated. When I arrived I asked cheerfully if there was any press 'creep-ing about the crypt' and Michael fairly choked.

He lectured the assembly sternly before starting the reception. This was a holy event and they must not be intrusive. To be fair, they behaved immaculately, as quiet as mice, until the moment when Michael was making the sign of the cross on my forehead and then I closed my eyes against what seemed like thousands of flashbulbs lighting up the crypt.

The next day that picture appeared across the national press, on the front pages of broadsheets and the inner pages of tab-loids. 'Eyes closed in prayer' read a caption in the *Daily Express*. No. They were closed against the blinding camera flashes. I was interviewed by every major television station and some print journalists appeared at the Mass that afternoon, though with their notebooks nowhere in evidence. Throughout the following week I was deluged with enquiries not just from British media but from numerous foreign papers as well, which, it is safe to say, could never before have heard of me. And to this very day I do not understand the reason for all the fuss.

When I had left the Church of England the previous November I had made an effort to mention my period of agnosticism in as many interviews as possible because I knew the way the press worked. *The Times* had carried a photograph accompanied by a caption stating I was leaving the C of E after twenty-seven years. It was quite true that it was twenty-seven years since I had been confirmed in Bath Abbey but I had not been continuously a Christian throughout and I knew that if I did not make a pre-emptive strike this would suddenly be all over the press as a 'revelation' with the unspoken suggestion that my claim to membership of the Church was somehow misleading.

Now, five months later, I pointed out as often as I could that it was the change in venue which had led to the ceremony being open to the press as some commentators were suggesting the event had been publicity-driven. Paul Goodman dropped me a line to say he was sorry that his article had led to so drastic a change in the arrangements, but I could not see that there was any need for an apology.

Even the most serious events in one's life can produce funny moments and mine came with my choice of confirmation name. Determined not to deny the role the Anglican Church had played in my life and to maintain the metaphor of a bridge rather than an abyss between the two communions, I chose the name Hugh after Hugh Latimer, one of the Anglicans' most notable martyrs. It was he who, burned alive at the stake, comforted his co-martyr Ridley as they faced the terrible fate together with the words, 'Be of good comfort, Master Ridley, and play the man; we shall this day light such a candle, by God's grace in England, as I trust shall never be put out.' Michael Seed, with his customary ingenuity, therefore set about finding an appropriate Catholic saint named Hugh and selected Hugh of Lincoln.

A week or so after the ceremony I was chatting over tea in

a packed Pugin Room. 'I seem to have upset everyone,' I said cheerfully. 'I've had letters from Anglicans complaining that I dared to use Latimer's name to celebrate leaving the Church for which he died and letters from Catholics to complain that I have dared to adopt a confirmation name after a protestant martyr. The only people I haven't upset are the Jews.'

A few days later I received a complaint that Hugh of Lincoln had been anti-Semitic!

There were also some sad moments; being out of communion for Easter and realising that my brother would never be able to give me communion again were two of them.

The publicity brought with it a tsunami of letters. Many came from people who were following the same path and who wanted my view on doctrine, others from Catholics welcoming me and others still from Anglicans wishing I had stayed in their Church to carry on the fight. But there was no fight. The battle had been lost when the decision was taken.

Many letters were abusive or antagonistic to what I had done. The bigots on both sides wrote in shoals: my soul was in danger from Romish doctrines; the Pope was the anti-Christ; I should never had been admitted without the RCIA course; I had done it only for the publicity; it was a disgrace that the Church had received me; what would I do when the Catholic Church admitted women? I answered each and every one individually.

Addressing a rally of Forward in Faith at Methodist Central Hall, I urged the seriously unhappy to consider the path to Rome adding: 'The gates of Rome are open.' I then asked what was preventing them entering and joked '... or are you afraid that Rome will ordain women and we shall all have to sign up with the Patriarch?'

The audience laughed but a mischief-making journalist decided to report it as if I had really meant that if Rome ordained women I would apply to the Greek Orthodox Church, with the result that I received a pompous letter from one of that Church's spokesmen telling me that was not the basis on which they admitted souls. Jocularity or sarcasm rarely survives translation from speech to print as I found out years later when, asked yet again about global warming, I wearily said, 'Look outside, it's snow-ing.' The journalist laughed but in print it looked as if I meant it.

I had gone straight from my reception at Westminster Cathe-dral to the Department of Social Security's morning meeting and then from my desk to the crypt for the afternoon's service. I took calls from journalists about religion in gaps between meetings on pensions and calls about pensions in gaps between discussions about religion. I wrote articles and made speeches about both subjects and took to asking journalists who arrived in my office, 'Is it Pope or Pensions?'

Over the next two years the Anglican Church lost thousands of laity, some three hundred priests, five bishops, four MPs and a member of the Royal Family to Rome but it calmed down again until shortly after I wrote this chapter when, nearly twenty years later, it narrowly voted against consecrating women bishops. It has always seemed to me an illogicality to say that women are part of the apostolic succession but cannot be bishops and the situation will not be sustainable in the longer term but at least this time any resulting exit will be orderly. Rome has offered the ordinariat and over the twenty intervening years many existing dissenters have left or retired while new ones would have been unlikely to seek ordination in any great numbers but, at the time of writing, the Anglican Church has still no detailed code of practice for accommodating dissenters who wish to remain.

My own decision was the best I have ever made. Just before Christmas 2012 I received a letter telling me that I had been made a papal dame for 'my forthright and devoted adherence to the Catholic social and moral teaching in the public forum'. That was hardly difficult given that it was exactly that teaching which had led me to begin my journey to Rome.

On two issues only have I been silent. The first is contracep-tion. I have disputed vigorously and angrily the silly charge that the Church's teaching on contraception is responsible for the tendency of women in the Third World to have more chil-dren than they can afford, for I know well enough from my own travels that the driving consideration is the combination of the terrible mortality rate with the fear of being old with no children to support them. In the West, where we take it for granted that our children will still be around when we are pensioners, we have lost sight of just how great that fear can be. Mrs African living in a shanty compound in Lusaka can hardly apply to the Abbeyfield.

Similarly I have no patience with attempts to link Church teaching on contraception to the prevalence of AIDS. The idea that somebody who defied the Church's teaching on adultery or promiscuity would solemnly observe its teaching on contraception is, to put it mildly, far-fetched. The best cure for HIV and AIDS is chastity before and fidelity within marriage, which is the teaching of the Church and if people want to reject that, as of course they indeed do and always will on a very large scale, then it is hardly fair to blame the Church for the results, particularly as that same Church runs more AIDS clinics in poorer countries than any other nation.

Yet I do not volunteer comment unless challenged for it seems to me that someone who is unmarried and never going to have children and has therefore never had her faith tested upon the subject is not best placed to judge the millions of her fellow Catholics who choose not to observe the Church's guidance.

The other issue is that of married clergy. Celibacy for the clergy has never been a doctrine of the Church and indeed for the first millennium of its life its priests did marry. It is merely a rule which I think will probably change again at some point in the future and I rather hope, though by no means believe, that will happen in my lifetime.

Chapter Nineteen

FROM PUSS TO MOS

A s I have observed my work on pensions was attracting a great deal of favourable comment and by 1993 I had begun to swallow the speculation that I would be promoted in the next reshuffle. I should have known better after seeing what had happened to Gillian Shephard while she had been in Social Security and the press had been full of predictions that she was due for promotion. When it didn't happen that year she warned me against 'believing one's friends' propaganda'. I nodded wisely, then fell into the same trap.

I was not expecting a reshuffle until the summer, there being two very good reasons why prime ministers tend to reshuffle immediately before the summer recess – to allow the wounded time to recover away from the Westminster glare and the newly shuffled time to get on top of their briefs. However while I was preoccupied with Maxwell, state pension age, the Goode Report, personal pensions mis-selling, SERPS and bad-weather payments, great financial cataclysms were shaking Britain to the core and the Conservative Party's fault lines on Europe meant that in some votes on the Maastricht Treaty we could never be entirely certain of a majority.

Indeed the period since our surprise victory in the general election and the spring of 1993 had been one of political misery. In February 1992 Britain had signed the Maastricht Treaty, which now had to be ratified by individual member states. The policy represented a significant shift in that it turned the EEC into the EC which later became the EU, thus formally recognising what had long been obvious – that the agreement was more than economic and it was not only Britain which was unhappy. France, often regarded along with Germany as being the very heart of the EEC, returned a yes vote in a referendum on ratification of the treaty with 51.05 per cent in favour. The Danes went further and their referendum simply failed to produce enough votes for ratification. After that there were some hasty exceptions drawn up and Denmark agreed.

At Christmas in 1992 I amused the family with the following pastiche on the well-known Christmas carol 'Oh, Little Town of Bethlehem':

Oh, little town in Holland,
How still we see thee lie,
Above thy deep and dreamless sleep,
The referenda fly.
The French oui'd by a whisker,
The Irish by a mile,
The Danes said no,
The Brits went slow,
It cramped Delors's style.

The Brits went slow. We did not have a referendum but instead Britain was among those states which left ratification to Parliament and months of painful debate, uncertain votes and party infighting ensued. John Major had negotiated significant opt-outs for Britain, the most important of which was that of non-compliance with the Social Chapter but this was bitterly opposed by Labour, now led by John Smith.

The Social Chapter was that part of the Maastricht Treaty which covered such matters as Health and Safety and workers' rights. Eleven of the then twelve states had signed up to it but John Major adamantly refused.

That opt-out was crucial for Britain's well-being and during the period that we retained it we were receiving 40 per cent of all the investment by the USA and Japan into the EU. Wales benefited particularly. It was an irresistible combination which we offered the world: we were in the EU with all the trading advantages but, because we were not in the Social Chapter, we had by far the most flexible labour market.

Our own rebels, whose strength occasionally exceeded our majority, were simply opposed to any further European integration with expanded opportunities for interference from Brussels. Fortunately because the Labour opposition and their own were from entirely different standpoints, the chances of their getting together to defeat any of the opt-outs and render the Treaty unacceptable to government were very slim but never entirely absent. Fortunately also, from the government's point of view, some who might have been determined and serious Euro-rebels such as Michael Forsyth were actually ministers and were therefore shackled by collective responsibility.

Meanwhile there had also been the debacle of the ERM, which we had been forced to leave in September 1992 at a cost to the Treasury of £3.3 billion and a much greater one in terms of government credibility. Worse, the government spent £27 billion of its reserves in propping up the pound to prevent a devaluation and in the frantic bid to keep Britain in, interest rates had shot up to 15 per cent. It was a short-term measure but terrified millions of mortgage-payers.

That had cost the Tories their strongest electoral appeal: that they were the economically competent party. Britain had never really wanted to give us that historic fourth term but had been terrified by Neil Kinnock into doing so. Now it felt free to hate us.

Then in October 1992 Michael Heseltine announced a huge programme of mine closures which proposed the shutting down of as many as 31 of the existing 50 deep-shaft mines. It was not an easy decision and he had made a great deal of preparation, touring the country and talking in depth to miners' representatives but the miners were still very heavily unionised and their demonstrations were joined or supported by people still reeling from the ERM fiasco's impact on their own security, looking for a conduit through which to vent their fury with their government.

The miners believed all Britain was with them and that they could force the government to abandon the project. 'We shall never desert the miners,' wrote one of many constituents to raise the matter with me.

'Yes, you will,' I thought. 'As soon as your interest rates drop and your property values rise.'

And so it came to pass. The scale of the closures was drastically cut following the protests but quietly revived over time and today there is only a small handful of deep-shaft mines left and the public never uttered another squeak.

With the Maastricht Treaty, the ERM and the mines, we could have done without the sleaze. In July 1992, David Mellor had to resign from the government after revelations of an affair. It was the beginning of a long series of sexual and financial indiscretions to blight the party's image which would include a disastrous attempt by John Major to promote a 'back to basics campaign' which was promptly portrayed by press and Opposition as a morality campaign and was used to legitimise revelations about personal conduct going back years.

As we returned from the Christmas recess in 1993 I wished John Major a happy new year. 'It can't be any worse than last year,' was his response, to which I in turn said, 'Oh, come on! We won the Election and nobody expected us to.'

'One good day in the whole year,' snorted the Prime Minister.

It is one of the ironies of public life that a politician can survive enormous difficulties and then come to grief over trivia and thus it was with Norman Lamont. He had survived the terrible turmoil of the collapse of the ERM and was putting in place a fiscal programme which had already sharply reduced interest rates with further falls not far off. In the first part of 1993 it was obvious that a badly shaken Britain was beginning to recover with inflation dropping rapidly. He should have been secure despite his attack on borrowing which gave rise to some tax increases.

Then came the storm in a teacup which can upset ships of state. At the Newbury by-election Lamont was asked for his regrets and he replied, '*Je ne regrette rien*.' It was a joke which played badly with people who had suffered in the recession and in the aftermath of the ERM. The government lost the by-election and Lamont his job. In his resignation speech he accused the government of giving the impression of being 'in office but not in power'.

So the reshuffle came in May rather than July and I nervously awaited the call from Downing Street. In addition to my belief that I had been a good Pensions Minister and that neither Tony Newton nor Peter Lilley would say anything to my detriment I had made a political calculation that there was a gap at minister of state level as far as women were concerned and that the powers that be would be wanting to address it. Both Virginia Bottomley and Gillian Shephard were in the Cabinet and Edwina Currie was uninterested in a return to the front bench. I had no interest in being promoted simply for being a woman but only a fool could have missed the obvious gap that existed and I knew that what I dismissed as tokenism was still a big factor in the calculations of those who delivered the posts. Additionally I had been at Social Security for two and a half years and was surely due for a move. Those who had entered government with me had by and large moved on to higher pastures.

As the reshuffle got under way, there was a buzz of expectancy in my private office, where it was generally predicted I would be promoted. I told them not to expect too much while doing just that myself. When Downing Street called I noticed all the lights on my phone were switched on as each person in the office picked up an extension to hear what the PM had to say. He offered me a post in the Department of Employment.

In Latin questions expecting the answer 'no' are preceded with the word *num* and those expecting 'yes' with *nonne*. Had I been composing the next question in Latin there is no doubt I would have begun it with *num*.

'As a PUSS?'

'Yes,' said John Major. 'For now.' And every drop of happy expectation oozed out of me.

Dave Higlett told me, when he wandered disconsolately into my office a few minutes later, that my pause was so long they all thought I was about to refuse and over the next two days I arrived at the conclusion that I should have done just that and that it might make sense to phone the PM and tell him I had changed my mind.

It was not pique or disappointment which led me to this

conclusion but an assessment of the future. It was obvious, I thought glumly, that I was not rated at Westminster. Had I not been the last of my intake even to be made a PPS? Now here they were, chronically short of women, which apparently mattered so much to them even though I thought it should not, and the one on offer clearly did not measure up. Less impressive colleagues had forged ahead. Were not two of my intake already in the Cabinet with so many others ministers of state? It seemed obvious that they were keeping me at the lowest rung until someone else could be found to take my place. Well, why wait for that? If I had no future at all in government there were all too many campaigns I wanted to take up on the backbenches and I could throw off the shackles of office.

I came within a whisker of calling Downing Street but had, naturally, warned my private office and my intentions came to the ears of the Permanent Secretary, Sir Michael Partridge, who came to see me and urged me not to give up just yet. He said he had seen many ministers in the position I was now and had advised them to give it another year and none had regretted taking his advice.

I was not wholly convinced but I forced myself to consider that I was only where I was through sheer persistence and that I might be looking at the future from the wrong angle. Had I not thought Oxford written off for ever when I was first rejected? Why had I so resolutely kept going on the candidates' round despite being deferred by Central Office and rejected by so many seats? I had never taken defeat personally so why do so now? Why not just take the line that I would not let the blighters get me down? That I would prove their doubts misplaced? After all, I had been made a minister in my first parliament. Sir Michael was right; it would be premature to return to the backbenches now.

The decision taken, if with a very bad grace, I set off for a new department and a new boss. Having moved from a Secretary of State on the left of the party to one on the right when Peter Lilley had taken over from Tony Newton I was now back with one on the left in the shape of David Hunt.

I thanked Peter when I left and said, truthfully, that I had enjoyed working with him and had loved pensions. When he dropped into the conversation that he had expected me to move on promotion I guessed that Michael Partridge had spoken to him.

Pensions provided some tricky problems, real challenges and the constant awareness that one held a huge part of people's futures in one's hands. The pensions industry was run by bright financial brains with whom it was a privilege to deal. It was a highly responsible post and, at first, Employment seemed like an anti-climax. First, there was not much of a problem as unemployment was falling and second, the issues were very easy to grasp and the intellectual challenge low by comparison with pensions. I probably also underestimated the difference it made to have entered the new post with all the experience of the old. For example, I already understood the benefits system backwards.

There were other aspects of the job I did not like such as too much government intervention and an obsession with equality and, of course, targets.

Targets, like rule books, make good servants and bad masters. Suppose, for example, there is a target to answer x number of letters in y weeks. The almost inevitable result will be that all the easy letters are answered timeously while the hard ones languish in the heap. I had not been in government long before I decided that if ministers wanted real accountability they would abolish targets. It is particularly pernicious when applied to policing. By requiring the police to tick boxes for arrests we encourage them to harass innocent citizens instead of those who are tormenting them, to use forms instead of discretion, to look for the statistics rather than the solutions.

The Child Support Agency was an excellent example of a target-orientated culture. Instead of pursuing the men who had never supported the children of their one-night stands the Agency pursued responsible fathers, whose whereabouts were known, and by applying rigid formulas which took no account of informal arrangements drove some to suicide. The same attitude prevailed when the Home Office began to press for more removals of failed asylum applicants. Officials turned up on the doorsteps of those who had observed the law to the letter because they knew where they were, but eschewed the vastly harder task of tracking down those who had deliberately disappeared and were living in the black economy.

In particular I was now responsible for the delivery of the guarantee we had given young people that we would find them a job or training within a specified period. The organisations which delivered this guarantee were the Training and Enterprise Councils (TECs) and I spent a great deal of time visiting them to see what wonderful schemes they had produced. I did however notice that they seemed to employ a large number of the young people themselves, which I suppose was one way of delivering the guarantee!

All governments lament the disappearance of the old apprenticeship schemes and many have tried to come up with something to replace them, so during my time we introduced the modern apprenticeship. This followed National Vocational Qualifications (NVQs) and General National Vocational Qualifications (GNVQs) and there was much talk about parity of esteem between the vocational and the academic. Germany, I was often told, had a splendid system of vocational training but when I visited that country to see what we might learn I found that the underlying principle was to divide the academically gifted from the rest at an early stage, a process that we had ditched with the grammar schools!

There were many reasons why the original apprenticeship schemes had dried up. Unions, employers and the young themselves were all responsible. The unions wanted proper pay for apprentices instead of training wages which of course employers were not going to provide when they were not getting equal value from a qualified and unqualified worker. The employers were too often ruthless about using apprentices as sources of cheap labour and did not always follow up training with long-term job prospects and the young people themselves suddenly found they were living in prosperous times with a vast range of opportunities open to them and the idea of grinding away with more study and poor pay for several years lacked appeal.

When I was leaving school the girls who were not going to university faced a choice between being nurses or secretaries and not much else. By the time I was an Employment Minister it was a much happier world with careers fairs and choices galore. The big retailers all had their own career ladders, young people went into banks and business, catering and tourism, public relations and computer programming. Call centres and junk-food outlets were mopping up the unskilled as once had building sites and shipyards. Trying to sell a sustained period of hard work for poor pay was never going to be successful.

Then there were the results of the policy undertaken before I arrived and which I regarded as the daftest of all: upgrading polytechnics to university status and calling diplomas and certificates degrees. It did very little for parity of esteem and a great deal to turn first-class polytechnics into third-rate universities.

This was the background against which the department I had now joined was working. One of my first arguments was with David himself, a clever lawyer and wonderfully kind man whose job was now to persuade me to accept the brief of Minister for Women. The role had previously been filled by Gillian Shephard and it made sense to keep it in the Employment department where so much work needed to be done on behalf of women.

I did not believe there should be a minister for women, I told him. I was fed up with tokenism and I could not see myself trotting out all the politically correct nonsense that went with the job. We did not have a minister for men so why should women be patronised? What help had Margaret Thatcher needed to make it to the top? Did not we have women judges and Cabinet ministers and bankers and chief executives so what was this supposedly pressing problem? Glass ceilings? What glass ceilings? Why all the whingeing?

David grinned and agreed to be the Minister for Women himself but of course I often had to deputise for him and still delivered the occasional 'glass ceiling' speech through gritted teeth. As far as I was concerned the women suffering real inequalities were those who wanted to stay at home and bring up their children and who were being treated like second-class citizens. So at least I could espouse the causes of job sharing and flexible working patterns with conviction because those enabled women to combine family and home instead of having to make an exclusive choice.

There were however two issues into which I could sink my teeth and chew with vigour. The first was ageism. There was much hand-wringing over inequalities for women and some well-placed concern about the disabled but the really blatant discrimination which was both widespread and ignored was that directed at older people.

I had come from pensions and knew well enough the perils of the demographics, that a time was looming when the dependency ratio would cause serious problems and that it was in the nation's hard economic interest as well as in its social interest to tackle the problem of older workers being squeezed out of the workforce. Any person over fifty who was suddenly unemployed, trying to return to the labour market after bringing up children or just wanting to change jobs was seriously disadvantaged despite the obvious benefit of greater experience.

The reasons given would have scored delta double minus in any debating contest but went seemingly unchallenged. It was suggested that if you employed someone of fifty-five that person would only give you ten years at most, five if a woman, but that if you employed a younger person you would have a much longer term employee. That might well have been true forty years earlier when people tended to stay with one employer all their lives but now the young sought career prospects wherever they arose. Only one of the trainees who had entered Lever Brothers with me in 1973 was still there, twenty years later. Indeed because it was so difficult for older workers to change jobs they offered greater not lesser stability.

Oh well, maybe, but older people were more difficult to teach new skills. They were not technologically minded, for example. I pointed to the mass computerisation of the Social Security offices only a couple of years earlier.

The old were more likely to be ill, weren't they? The young were strong and healthy and would not be absent on sick leave so often. No, I countered, because when taking on an older person an employer had access to an entire life history of health and would know exactly what the record of the applicant was and anyway older people did not get pregnant and go on maternity leave ...

I pointed also to the stock market crash of 1987. Too many City whizz kids and not enough older heads who had seen it all before meant too many panicked reactions.

Largely my arguments fell on deaf ears and I had one particularly fierce dispute with a Unilever manager when I was visiting that company's premises on the Embankment. It made me smile when I said that at least an older person would remember how to use Sunlight Soap and he looked at me angrily, knowing I was mocking but not sure how. I came out glad I had not spent my life there.

The arguments also initially fell on deaf ears in the department itself and as I was a mere PUSS the mandarins thought it safe to ignore me, claiming that there were no funds for the campaign I wanted to launch. I went to see David Hunt who agreed we should try and after that some real effort was forthcoming.

By now I knew only too well that argument alone would persuade nobody. I had to find examples to illustrate my thesis that the older person was an under-used resource in a country with a demographic time bomb ticking inexorably away. So we launched the *Getting On* campaign and at the same time a competition to find Britain's oldest worker.

I set the criteria strictly: we were looking for somebody who was working full time and not just keeping his or her hand in a couple of days a week in retirement and we were looking for someone who was working for someone else rather than self-employed because I wished to prove that the older person could still give satisfaction to an employer and be a genuinely valued resource. I was keen to find somebody of seventy-five because then I would have a powerful message to send to employers about people who were twenty years younger.

We launched the competition on local radio stations as well as by standard announcement, as I wanted a good geographical mix of older workers. At first I was treated with the suspicion naturally accorded to any government minister, with several interviewers making the mistake of assuming that I was out to save money because if older people worked for longer they wouldn't draw their pensions. I explained that people could both draw their pensions and work at the same time but surprising as some may have found that, it was as nothing compared to their surprise at the responses which suddenly flooded in from the listeners and local radio stations began to get very excited at the stories which emerged.

Meanwhile back at the ranch we were realising that we were getting so many nominations that we would have to close the competition to anybody under eighty and eventually the oldest male worker turned out to be ninety-four and oldest female worker ninety-three.

Len Vale-Onslow worked six days a week and Hilda Ford five. He went to work on his bicycle and she sang in a local choir. By coincidence, he, a former motorcycle builder, worked in a motorcycle repair shop and she in a motorcycle spares shop. Len was from Birmingham and Hilda from Lancashire. There was some discussion about Len as he owned the repair shop he worked in whereas Hilda worked for someone else but it seemed like splitting hairs in the face of a remarkable achievement. We held a lunch in their honour and both went on to receive MBEs, with Len also being the oldest ever subject of *This is Your Life* in 1999. I attended Hilda's 100th birthday party and Len lived to be nearly 104. He was still riding motorbikes at 102.

A very small but amusing personal consequence followed my discovery of Hilda Ford. Her family kept in touch with me on and off after her death and her daughter, Heather Hudson from Todmorden, invited me to read *Peter and the Wolf* at a charity concert. I am tone deaf so thought it impossible as I would not hear the musical cues and would not read to the right number of beats but the conductor simply waved his baton at me every time I had to read and somehow we got through.

Whatever the cares of office, the constituency work does not grow less demanding and it was while I was in Employment that I had one of my greatest successes in individual casework.

John Jones was a lorry driver who was asked to go to Morocco and pick up a vehicle which a fellow-employee had left there because he had suddenly to go to Ireland to see his sick mother. Jones duly went and found the lorry which was in a public place and fully visible to anybody moving about there. However when he went to drive it back home the weighbridge showed a different result from the manifest. He was detained and the police found a specially constructed compartment in the lorry's roof containing a serious quantity of hashish.

The other employee was found to have been operating under several aliases and the story about Ireland could not be proved. It was obvious that John Jones simply had no opportunity to construct the hiding place or indeed to fill it. Morocco, urged by the West to clamp down on the amount of drugs that were getting into Europe from there, took a position towards drug smuggling akin to the one we take towards driving without insurance. It is always an offence whatever the circumstances and ignorance of the true situation is not a defence. So your friend might tell you he is insured when you borrow his car but you are still guilty if he has misled you. So a man might believe he was only transporting apples or dog food but if he is also transporting drugs, however unwittingly, then he is automatically guilty.

By the time his wife came to see me Jones had been convicted, sentenced, had lost his appeal and was facing nine years in a Moroccan jail. I thought an intervention in another country's justice system doomed to failure but began all the normal diplomatic representations which got me where I expected: nowhere. As the last throw of a dice which I considered was irretrievably loaded against me, I asked John Major if I could go to Rabat. He agreed but stressed I must not let the Moroccans think this was an official government approach.

As there was no head under which I could claim the expenses from the fees office I flew by the cheapest means and found, to my consternation, nobody waiting for me at the airport. They were all in the VIP lounge, certain that *Madame La Ministre* must be travelling first class. I explained that in this context I was not *La Ministre* but *La Députée*. They looked puzzled.

I stayed with the Ambassador, Sir Allan Ramsay, who accompanied me as translator when I saw the Interior Minister, the Justice Minister and the King's Counsellor. I visited John Jones in prison and found him in good spirits.

When I was able to ring his wife up, some months later, and tell her that her husband was out of prison and would be home in forty-eight hours, her reaction told me why I had become an MP.

I had worked closely and productively with Bob Hughes, the whip in Social Security, but the whip in Employment was Irvine Patnick and we had never got on particularly well although I do not think there was any personal dislike between us. The second issue I took up with enthusiasm in this department was Sheffield and Irvine, representing Sheffield Hallam, resented my interventions.

The government was acutely conscious that large swathes of the North had Labour councils and very little Conservative input and that there was tension between some of our largest and most important cities and national government, which played into the perception of a North–South divide. Accordingly it had adopted the practice of 'sponsor ministers', whereby a member of the government got to know a city and carried out what was effectively a diplomatic role between the city and central government. I was allocated Sheffield and Hull.

Sheffield was red in tooth and claw, having had such left-wing leaders as Clive Betts, David Blunkett and now Mike Bower, with whom I struck up a good rapport. The city had big transport issues with an initiative called Supertram having cost a fortune and the clear need for an airport. There were badly run-down areas, especially one called Kelvin Flats, and overwhelming regeneration needs but, above all, it was locked in argument with central government over its budget.

Originally wealthy as a result of steel, Sheffield still had a thriving cutlers' industry with an annual feast to rival anything produced by Buckingham Palace. Master Cutler was a person of major consequence and the charming tradition of giving a new penny to somebody who gave you a gift of a Sheffield steel knife still persisted. Simon Wood and Gill Cholerton, my private secretaries, always carried a small supply whenever we visited.

I began to take up various causes enthusiastically and to have discussions with Treasury ministers about the budget. Irvine was not impressed. He even complained to David Hunt that I had visited the city without telling him.

There is a convention in the House of Commons that if you are going to be in another MP's constituency on official business you must notify him or her of your arrival. Most of us manage to offend against this dictum at some point in our careers because it relies upon a secretary notifying the right MP in good time, and occasionally it goes wrong but, by and large, it is carefully observed and, normally, if one errs one drops the MP concerned a brief note of apology or explanation.

This, however, was different. 'He says you are raising issues on behalf of his constituency,' said David.

It was one of the few times I swore in the workplace and certainly the only time I swore at a Secretary of State – and that includes Michael Howard – for I was just becoming optimistic about getting some concessions out of the Treasury and here was one of the MPs who would benefit complaining about my efforts.

'Of course I am raising issues on behalf of Sheffield. I'm the bloody sponsor minister.' Doubtless that was what Irvine called me too.

His colleagues in the whips' office, who had plenty of bigger issues to worry about, were highly amused by the whole matter and Greg Knight, the then Deputy Chief Whip, who has a mischievous sense of humour, devised a memorandum purporting to be from me and copied to Irvine about a 'surgery' I was supposedly proposing to hold in Sheffield. In the end his nerve failed him and he didn't send it but it gave the whips' office a much-needed laugh at a difficult time.

Greg Knight was a good colleague who took his fondness

for animals to a rarely seen level when one night in the smoking room we saw a mouse and he immediately put down some cheese.

There was, as I have said, no personal animosity between Irvine and me but to my surprise tension did begin to grow between me and Michael Forsyth, whom I not only liked and had known from student days, but whom I admired as a sensible, Eurosceptic right-winger. I was pleased that he was the Minister of State in the department and had looked forward to working with him but we disagreed occasionally on minor aspects of policy and sometimes had to ask David Hunt to arbitrate.

If Michael won he would return to his office and declare loudly to his staff, 'Another great victory!' But if I won he would leave the meeting looking very put out. None of this would have mattered, had the private offices not then begun what almost amounted to a feud, with mine regularly complaining about lack of cooperation or sometimes downright obstruction from his.

That in turn might not have mattered but in the 1994 reshuffle I inherited his job which normally would have meant also his office and his staff. I told the Permanent Secretary that I would keep my own office and my own staff but he said the room was not suitable for a minister of state. So I said I would move only if my own staff came with me. The issue was solved when Michael took his to the Home Office and all was well until the next year when I again inherited his job and the same issue arose.

It is possible for ministers to take staff with them between departments because the private offices work for the minister not the department, but it is hardly encouraged and normally civil servants prefer to stay and develop their careers in one place where they will have made the contacts and the right impressions and not start again where nobody knows them. Yet in that same reshuffle Michael Portillo, who took over from David Hunt, also brought a civil servant with him, Peter Wanless.

I approached the reshuffle fairly confidently but as I had approached the last one in the same frame of mind and had been severely disappointed, I dampened my expectations. I had had the heady experience not once but twice during the past year of having my colleagues waving order papers and cheering when I finished a speech.

'I haven't seen that with a PUSS before,' commented Tony Newton as I passed him in the lobby during the vote on one of these occasions.

'Peter Tapsell says he will vote for you as leader,' laughed another colleague.

I took neither comment literally but enjoyed the plaudits. Surely this time it would be Minister of State? I would not, however, allow myself to hope too much but was very certain that if I was offered another PUSS role, I really would call it a day. As I had done a year earlier I began to go over in my mind what I would give priority to if I were to find myself once more on the backbenches.

It proved an unnecessary exercise and I was relieved rather than elated when I was made a Minister of State. Perhaps one of the reasons for that was that I was being left at Employment, that politically correct land of equality and government interference. Elation was to be deferred to the next reshuffle but meanwhile there was a new Secretary of State.

Portillo was a joy to work for: incisive, decisive, calm and humorous. The new PUSSes were Philip Oppenheim and James Paice, two very different characters. James was quiet, hard-working, and conscientious while Philip was flamboyant and prepared to give his heart only to that in which he was interested. Sometimes when I asked if he would look in to my office I was told he had gone home. He was not much interested in the tedious work of visiting jobcentres all over the country. It was true that he had a marginal constituency and could not spare weekends but that still left four days on which he could have made the effort. He was, however, intensely interested in employment statistics and made himself a master of the arguments surrounding them. As we were often quite falsely accused of massaging the figures this was a more than helpful input.

In an early encounter when we were dividing up the work of the department he refused point-blank to take on disability issues because he simply wasn't interested. He regarded a bill to prevent discrimination as interventionist and a burden on employers and he wasn't wrong, but the government had decided to bring it forward so we had a responsibility to devise a proper piece of legislation. The matter went to Portillo for decision and he decided to assign the job to me rather than Philip. I was annoyed only because I thought Michael had undermined me and guessed, correctly, that Philip would take this as a signal to ignore me in future. Philip for his part thereafter ascribed any dissatisfaction I expressed about anything at all to this incident, which was both childish and inaccurate.

I nevertheless enjoyed that second year in the department. The Disability Discrimination Bill threw up crazy discussions such as how far to apply it to the Army but William Hague had the lead in the Social Security department and the real legislative work of our own department was the Jobseeker's Allowance Bill which was a joint one between us and Social Security, with Roger Evans the responsible minister from the DSS. It was my first and only experience of a joint bill between departments and effectively working with two sets of civil servants.

I was determined from the outset that we would have a 'participation' committee when the bill reached the committee stage. It may sound a little odd to those not versed in the ways of Westminster but by and large if you sit on the government side of a bill you contribute only a very limited amount to the proceedings. The Opposition has particular clauses and amendments to which it wants to devote time and the usual channels (the whips) arrange enough time for those debates with a view to getting the bill out of committee by an agreed date. That means, in order to get through the bill, MPs on the government side turn up, vote as required and do little else except their correspondence and Christmas cards. Of course, particular MPs will have particular interests. After all they are only on the committee because they spoke at second reading and presumably have therefore some expertise but they will not be encouraged to take part in the rest of the bill as it goes through committee. Occasionally they will be told to stop intervening even with brief questions and points if time is running out.

I decided on a different approach and, although it was a headache for the whips, chose to let our side intervene and put down amendments. Ian McCartney led for the Labour side and it was a good-natured business with Gary Streeter, one of our MPs, putting down an amendment to prevent men wearing earrings at job interviews and one of my civil servants muddling an account of transferability between husband and wife so that I appeared to be saying that the dead spouse could claim the allowance. Was the government so desperate that it was promising eternal life? asked a Labour member. Only the committee chairman, David Knox, was bad-tempered.

The Jobseeker's Allowance was an attempt to address a problem that had been around a very long time: the work-shy living at the expense of the workers. Once Labour would have opposed this on the grounds that we were being oppressive and unfair but we were now in the age of Tony Blair and instead much of the argument was about efficacy.

In truth none of us saw this as the last word in the battle against abuse of the welfare state but we did see it as a start and indeed Labour was to build on it in later years. The bill's premise was simple: to qualify for benefit an applicant had to be able to demonstrate that he was making consistent and serious attempts to find work. Benefit could be refused if the applicant did not take a job which had been offered or a place in full-time training or on an environmental task force. Applicants could no longer just sign on, turn up and walk off with taxpayer-funded benefit.

The bill tried to close loopholes. Applicants must be punctual and properly dressed for interviews. If they tried to fail an interview deliberately they could lose benefit. It was a brave attempt, expanded by Labour after 1997, but still the work-shy avoid work and my own belief, as already stated, is that only an uncompromising workfare scheme will stop them.

Proposals for workfare had been put forward for some years but were always rejected by government because they were too expensive to administer. My attitude now is that the expense is worth it if it stops the corroding effects of the dependency culture.

While I was legislating, looking after Sheffield and Hull, trailing around jobcentres and worrying about whether the disability provisions should apply to those chaps who do double somersaults through windows with guns at the ready, the world was looking ever more precarious for the party to which I was devoting my life.

The Maastricht votes had culminated in a defeat and a vote of confidence, we were losing by-elections, beset by sleaze and Labour had a fresh new leader in the shape of Tony Blair. Not all was bad; the economy was growing stronger, unemployment was falling as were interest rates and inflation and a major initiative in Northern Ireland was to bear real fruit but somehow we still looked as if we were drifting.

I was out of Westminster on departmental business when I heard that John Smith had died and was given the news by Gill Cholerton. A year later I was again away and she was again accompanying me when she approached me with a serious face. 'Who's dead this time?' I asked warily.

'Nobody. The Prime Minister has resigned.'

John Major had finally had enough of his fractious party and was challenging his detractors to put up or shut up. They decided to put up in the shape of John Redwood. Never mind mid-term by-elections, we now had a mid-term leadership election.

Chapter Twenty

DREAMS AND NIGHTMARES

M ajor was right to force the hands of his critics. The alternative would have been another six months of infighting and backbiting until the annual leadership election in November. The election was being effectively fought over Europe.

Why Redwood rather than any of the other leading Eurosceptics? Michael Portillo had a collection of extra telephone lines installed but did not declare. Presumably he was waiting for the outcome of the first ballot when, if John Major had been mortally wounded, he could have stood but was not prepared to make the first move. Some called it cowardice and others caution. I called it a pity about the telephone lines, which were the equivalent of an uncertainly waved banner.

Peter Lilley stayed loyal and Michael Forsyth had neither the following nor a safe enough seat. That left Redwood, who had the courage but was the least charismatic of the prominent Eurosceptics. He was too cold and most certainly not a team player. His intellectual powers were formidable but his grasp of basic *ars politica* was revealed to be little above zero when he launched his campaign with a photograph in which he was surrounded by a bunch of hard-core Maastricht rebels and right-wingers.

'Barmy army,' sneered some. 'Divisive,' mused the more thoughtful.

I was and still am a Eurosceptic myself but had never the smallest doubt where my loyalties lay and they were firmly with Major, who had negotiated vital opt-outs to the Treaty which Labour would be certain to surrender (they did) and who was being consistently undermined by his own party, who expected him to ape Thatcher without the majority she always had enjoyed. The divisions were playing badly in the country where we were seen as an undisciplined rabble and were leading to a certain Labour victory.

In addition to all of that, the politics of this particular rebellion seemed odd as the right might well get rid of Major only to see him replaced by Clarke or Heseltine, which would have pleased the party at large at that stage but not the people who were challenging Major.

The rules were clear but there was the usual speculation that Major had a private view that if he did not get a certain number of votes then even if he won he would resign. He won sufficiently well and the leadership issue at least was settled until the next election. In the early evening news I was seen on the steps of the campaign headquarters dancing with delight.

I had not had a great deal to do in the battle itself because most of the parliamentary party had flocked to his banner but on the Sunday before the vote I rang up as usual to see if I was needed and William Hague said they were all hungry. Could I bring some refreshments for tea?

Oh, dear! I did not normally go into supermarkets on the Sabbath as a protest against the way they had begun opening on Sundays before the law allowed it, so I tried a few corner shops but could find nothing but a couple of stale croissants and packaged cupcakes. Reluctantly I pushed a trolley into Sainsbury's and arrived in Cowley Street with a fine collection of cream doughnuts, madeira cake, chocolate eclairs and some sober digestive biscuits.

As my colleagues fell on them I muttered, 'Better love hath no man than this; that he lay down his principles for his friends.'

As this pathetic challenge to John Major and most of his troubles had their roots in Europe, this may be the moment to examine my own position on the subject which can be summed up as wanting to leave but utterly unconvinced that there is any plan in place to provide for a future outside the EU. I am not prepared merely to run away; I need to know where I am going next.

If I had doubts about the direction Europe was taking before I joined government, five minutes in any of the posts I occupied would have convinced me that we were in the grip of an extravagant, regulation-bound, interventionist Leviathan of a would-be superstate, the ultimate aim of which was federalism. In Social Security we had to fend off moves which would have wrecked the pension system and in Employment Portillo and I seemed to spend acres of time resisting proposals which properly belonged under the Social Chapter but which our European counterparts were trying to slide in through other means.

We resisted for instance proposals to make firms offer employees three months paternity leave. In vain did we argue about the disproportionate impact on small employers. But, posited Teso of Italy, if the leave was unpaid there would be no impact. I talked about laying off, recruiting, training, re-employing, laying off again. We began slowly to convince him.

'Ring Teso,' Michael instructed me before one meeting.

I did, only to find that he was no longer in office. The Italian government had changed yet again.

Michael was a very competent linguist, a calm arguer and a suave diplomat but in private we despaired. They just did not understand.

Nevertheless it is too easy to blame Europe for every last pettifogging regulation which binds us when France and Germany will turn a directive into two pages of regulations and Britain into forty-two. I think there is a widespread belief that if we left the EU we would be immediately released from the officious diktats which determine the position of our rubbish bins, whether we can hold egg-and-spoon races on wet grass or whether the WI can sell cakes without a certificate. We would not, because these are the results of British preoccupations not European ones. It is not that other European countries ignore EU law but rather that they just interpret it more proportionately and sensibly.

However, even given that we are directly responsible for much that we try to blame on the EU, there is plenty of intervention that we could do without, so, yes, I would like us to be free of it but we need then to ask, 'What next?' Those who refuse to engage in this discussion are being plain irresponsible.

Consider Moses. The Israelites were crying out to him to get them out of Egypt, away from slavery and oppression. He then achieved just that but when the Promised Land did not materialise for forty years they became a little peeved and turned on him, saying they had been better off in Egypt. Regardless of where people put their own crosses on a referendum ballot paper they will blame the politicians for the results if the prevailing option goes wrong.

'Why did you bring us out of Egypt?' will simply mutate over the intervening millennia into 'Why did you bring us out of Europe?', unless we plan properly for an orderly exit.

When we were first negotiating to enter, it was a very different scene. Britain enjoyed a huge position on the world stage and was still reaping the kudos of the Second World War. We could attract inward investment just by being Britain. We had a very active Commonwealth in economic terms and the EFTA agreements with the Scandinavian countries. None of that prevails today. What impact would leaving the trading block have on inward investment? What would the trading terms be with Europe? Where would our major export markets be?

I am tired of hearing Norway quoted as a demonstration of how a withdrawal can be successful when that country has a small population and large natural resources while we have a huge and burgeoning population and limited natural resources.

Whenever I make these points, someone is sure to say I am being defeatist but I am not saying that it cannot be done, merely that I want to know what is going to be done before voting to leave. Foolish is the man who jumps ship before knowing if he will swim or sink.

Then there is the law, much of which stems from Europe. It cannot just be left to collapse like a pack of cards if we withdraw from the Treaty of Rome. We need to know what is planned: what we will keep and what the statute book will look like the day after we go it alone. Otherwise employers and workers, to name but one group, will find themselves in a state of anarchy.

These are very simple arguments: the detail is hair-raisingly complex.

For some time now I have believed that David Cameron should announce that serious work, backed by serious resources, will be put in place to examine exit strategies and then put a time-table on its completion. The results should then be published in intelligible form and there should follow a national debate. Then have the referendum on continued membership. At the time of writing the Prime Minister has promised that if he wins the next election then he will negotiate a new deal with Europe and, on the basis of that new deal, Britain will then vote in a referendum on whether to stay in or leave. This is a welcome step forward but it scarcely answers the concerns I have outlined above for it means we will enter a referendum knowing the scenario for staying in but not that for coming out.

Redwood paid the price of his challenge, being seen not so much to have lost the contest as to have lost his judgement. Cabinet ministers should either be serious challengers or loyal, not act as stalking horses. If he was serious then he badly overestimated his support and if he merely wanted to wound then he should have left that to a more lowly figure.

John Redwood is undeniably clever and talented and has contributed much to public life so it does seem a pity that, unless his fortunes suddenly change, he will be remembered best for pretending to sing the Welsh National Anthem.

The party now settled down and in the ensuing reshuffle I was, at last, given the job I had always coveted when John Major sent me to the Home Office, where I was to look after prisons and immigration. The Home Office was my dream job and it helped that my boss was a fellow Kent MP, Michael Howard, whose determined approach I admired. I was much looking forward to working with him.

Whatever it was that had caused trouble two years earlier in Employment was obviously still troubling Michael Forsyth's civil servants because his Private Secretary left virtually as I arrived, staying long enough only to give me my first boxes. Perhaps I should have asked outright what the difficulty was but I was more concerned with those I was leaving behind as the Department of Employment was being abolished altogether, its work divided between Education and the DTI.

My efforts to bring Simon Wood with me were resisted but

a very good private office was set up and, as with each of my other private offices, we all got along extremely well, which was a blessing given what was about to happen.

Michael Forsyth, now Secretary of State for Scotland, took me aside at a very early stage. There was trouble, he told me, between the Head of the Prison Service, Derek Lewis, and the Home Secretary. He had the highest possible opinion of Lewis, as had those who worked with him, and he wanted me to form my own view and not be too influenced by Michael Howard. I promised him I would assess the situation fairly without having much idea about what the situation actually was.

In my first interview with Michael Howard he told me that he would be 'interested' in my opinion of Derek Lewis but volunteered nothing beyond that. Sir Richard Wilson, the Permanent Secretary, gave me no indication of the size of the rift beyond saying that prisons were a poisoned chalice. Had I known then what I knew by the autumn I would never have gone away for the summer.

Derek Lewis had been appointed in December 1992 by Ken Clarke, who had brought him in from the private sector to run the newly created Prison Service Agency. Ken's greatest fear was that he would be badly resented by the service as an outsider, especially as the then head of the Prison Service, Joe Pilling, had effectively applied for his own job and been turned down. That Lewis very quickly built up a loyal following among the Prison Service was in itself quite a feat but it was as nothing to the way he then focused and directed a poorly performing service which was over-unionised and demoralised. His brief was to implement the Woolf Report which had been produced after the Strangeways riots in 1990, when the nation had watched television images of prisoners on the roof, rioting with apparent impunity.

Escapes were rife, assaults a daily occurrence, prisoners were still slopping out, overcrowding was normal and the order of the day in too many prisons was idleness. Three years after his appointment, Derek Lewis had reduced escapes by a staggering 77 per cent, purposeful activity had increased by hundreds of thousands of hours and overcrowding was reduced despite a sharp rise in the number of prisoners. He had also set up so successful a private finance initiative that it became a model for the rest of Whitehall. Indeed Michael Howard himself praised the achievements of the Prison Service only a few months after Lewis had left.

Above all Derek Lewis simply grasped the detail, even if that did mean a certain amount of micro-managing. One of the Prison Service press officers told me of an occasion when he accompanied Lewis on an unannounced inspection of a prison in the early hours of the morning and was surprised when the first thing the Director General did was to put his hand on top of a television set.

'It's warm,' said Lewis. 'That officer has been watching television when he should have been on duty.' Doubtless he was remembering that when some IRA prisoners broke out of Whitemoor, an officer had been playing Scrabble.

The pressure on the service was huge but not resented because morale rose in line with performance.

Before Michael Forsyth, the Prisons Minister had been Peter Lloyd, who shared his successor's admiration as did the Permanent Secretary, Richard Wilson, but the one who did not was Michael Howard and the vehicle he chose for his move to dismiss the Director General was a report into the escapes at Parkhurst in January 1995, prepared by General Learmont, a former Quartermaster-General.

Whatever may have been going well for the agency, there were two major disasters. The first was an attempted escape on the part of six high-risk prisoners, including five IRA terrorists, from the secure unit at Whitemoor Prison in September 1994. Four were recaptured almost immediately and the other two within hours. None was found further than half a mile from the prison and no member of the public was endangered but they had got out of the secure unit and had used firearms. An inquiry was bound to follow and the subsequent Woodcock Report damned everybody from ministers to prison staff.

Whitemoor was one of the first prisons I visited in my new role. Situated in the bleak, fenland area of March in Cambridgeshire, the approach to it lies through dykes and ditches into which any car veering off the road will fall. Indeed a female prison officer died in just such an accident on the day the trial of the prisoners collapsed. The number of deaths in similar circumstances raised some eyebrows and caused some mutterings about coincidence and conspiracies.

The prison was designed as a Category B which is to say a secure prison with enhancements such as dogs, but was re-categorised to a maximum-security Category A, with its own special secure unit.

Housing some of Britain's most dangerous prisoners, White-moor had a difficult history and in January 1994 was the scene of a riot which was swiftly contained. A new Governor, Brodie Clark, understandably sought to calm the dispersal wings and put in hand measures to prevent any future rioting or major disruption. The Chief Inspector of Prisons was pleased with the progress and in a report in March 1994, just six months before the break-out, described the secure unit as 'virtually impregnable'. Probably to the IRA not much was ever impregnable but the speed of reaction caused what appeared to be the pickup vehicle to retreat and disappear, a triumph for the prison officers which did not receive the credit it deserved.

In his book, *Hidden Agendas,* Derek Lewis paints a vivid picture of the confusion in which two dogs fought each other, then turned on a prison officer before finally chasing the prisoners, who were equipped with pepper to throw at the pursuing beasts. The scenes were a mixture of bravery and comedy.

Visiting the prison was a stark introduction to my job. As I walked round prisoners hurled verbal abuse in which the adjective began with F and the noun with C. I chatted amiably with one inmate in his cell, making friends with his budgie, and afterwards asked what he had done. He was a multiple child killer. Years later, when I read Sandra Gregory's book about her time in prison following her conviction for drug smuggling, *Forget You Had a Daughter*, I was struck by her description of Rose West keeping a pet bird and often wonder how people can pity and love birds but be indifferent to the suffering of the humans they attack.

In the secure unit there were cells they would not open for fear of attack from within and which officers entered only in groups and as I was talking to one officer an IRA prisoner inside his cell called out contradictions to what I was being told.

Whitemoor was settling down, having received a great deal of time, money and attention since the events of a year before and when I made a second visit, the following year, it had improved still further and the atmosphere was quite different.

The second disaster for Derek Lewis had occurred within four months of the first when some high-security prisoners broke out of Parkhurst on the Isle of Wight in January 1995. They had used their jobs in the engineering workshops to produce a replica key and parts of a ladder which could be concealed among the stock and tools without arousing suspicion. They were much assisted by the video camera having been pointed the wrong way. Neither Michael Howard nor Derek Lewis was responsible for patrolling the workshops or aiming the video cameras. One could reasonably have expected the Governor to have checked such systems but it was also true that a contributory factor to the escape had been the absence of geophones and equally true that these devices had been asked for ten years earlier. Meanwhile Richard Tilt, the competent but very recently appointed head of security, produced a damning report: security procedures had not been enforced even to the extent of the Duty Governor often being at home rather than at the prison and the corrective action on security recommended by the Chief Inspector the previous October had not been implemented despite categorical assurances from the Governor, John Marriott, that it had.

This led to a serious row between Lewis and Howard, which to this day, seems to me to have been as unnecessary as it was unproductive. It is so central to the events which followed that I must dwell on it here.

The common ground between Lewis and Howard was that Marriott should not remain in post after such a debacle and particularly in view of the false assurances. The choice was between suspending him or moving him to another role pending the outcome of a disciplinary investigation. I admit that if I had the handling of it I would have wanted to sack him on the spot but the Code of Discipline which governed such matters stated that the preference should always be to find another role until the disciplinary process was completed. Lewis therefore decided to move Marriott to a non-operational job pending the outcome of these proceedings.

Howard would have none of it. He wanted suspension and I can understand why. Had I been the Prisons Minister at the time I would have agreed but then he indicated (this is a neutral word as opposed to *threatened* which was later to become the preferred verb in Paxman's famous fourteen questions) that if Derek Lewis did not do as he wanted he would overrule him. He asked the Director General to leave the room and reconsider.

The account of what happened next as given in Lewis's book appeared corroborated by the material which I found and later deployed in my 1997 speech to Parliament. Neither his book nor the events as detailed in Nick Kochan's biography of me were challenged, and nor was the detail of my own speech in 1997, although Michael Howard in his response offered a different interpretation. Wilson told Lewis that things were getting 'white-hot' and 'in danger of going nuclear'. But he also advised Howard that he could not overrule Lewis and a call to Number Ten resulted in the advice being upheld.

A statement was drafted saying instead that Marriott was being moved from his duties that day. There was a sizeable argument about the use of the word 'today' which was to have huge ramifications later.

All this took place before I arrived at the Home Office. I was appointed in July and had already planned to be away visiting my old amah in Singapore throughout August as I was not scheduled to be on duty in Employment. It was agreed that my plans should stay in place. I can imagine Lewis's feelings when Michael Forsyth, upon whom he could rely, was moved and his replacement disappeared for four weeks. The Learmont Report was due in October and it was understood among the senior echelons at the Home Office that Howard was likely to use the report to sack him.

In September I became aware of it too. The Prison Service had some fairly impressive statistics and, naturally enough, was anxious to design a press release around them, which I innocently agreed. No, no, came the response from the Home Secretary's office. We must put nothing out that praised the Prison Service: Learmont was going to be very critical indeed and we should look fools.

I argued that if Learmont was going to lambast the Prison Service for failures at the beginning of the year then we should get our defence in first but the very last thing the Home Secretary wanted was any sort of defence. He needed a picture of unmitigated disaster to sack Lewis. Indeed this politically driven nonsense continued well after the dismissal, when I noticed that questions supplied to backbenchers to elicit favourable statistics were simply not appearing on the order paper. I asked my PPS, Bob Spink, why this should be so and was told, 'We are not saying anything good about the Prison Service yet.'

He had apparently been instructed by Rachel Whetstone, Howard's special advisor, that we would look silly if the Prison Service was seen to be performing well when we had sacked the man responsible. I confronted Rachel who backed off and said the instruction was 'an old one'. I then went to Michael who agreed we could now put down the questions. I also had words with Bob about taking orders from a political advisor instead of the minister, but I understood well enough why he had been lured into doing as Rachel had said.

There were two special advisors, the other being Patrick Rock, and I found them to be as loud and disrespectful as it is possible to be. Meetings were chaotic as Michael allowed a free-for-all at his table and they shouted down ministers with impunity, interrupting and often speaking over each other let alone the rest of us. I, unused to such disorder, simply sat with my pen raised to indicate that I wished to speak. When Michael noticed he would turn to me but I would be lucky to get out two sentences before Rachel or Patrick barged in. I nicknamed them the Shriek and the Shout.

Both Emily Blatch, the minister in the Lords, and Richard

Wilson expressed quiet displeasure behind the scenes but Michael had unlimited faith in the pair and too often showed little respect for his own ministers, the notable exception being David Maclean, the highly competent and combative Police Minister to whom he was grateful for extracting the department from a major public relations disaster with the police at an earlier stage of Michael's tenure.

Not long ago somebody told me that Patrick was now advising Number Ten, to which I responded that I might send David Cameron a pair of earmuffs. I had a great deal of faith in Rachel, whom I liked, but her blind loyalty to Michael was an asset to him rather than the department.

Meanwhile I had been using the recess after my return from Singapore to read in to my brief not only on Prisons but also Immigration, where asylum was presenting us with a major problem.

Getting into Britain lawfully in 1995 was hard. A trickle entered on work-permit schemes and the close dependants of those already here could get visas as could students for the duration of their studies but primary immigration was well controlled and anybody arriving without the right documents would be turned away. To that there was one notable exception: if the immigrant claimed political asylum, when we were obliged to determine his or her case individually against the criteria of the 1951 Geneva Convention.

That convention had been enacted to prevent any repetition of the appalling events of the 1930s when boatloads of Jews had been turned away at port after port as a result of which many perished in horrendous circumstances under the vile regime that was Nazism. International law now said that anybody fleeing persecution must be given a safe haven and nobody must be sent back to their country of origin if it would put them in danger.

This was all very noble and just but the world of 1951 was a far cry from today's. Then there was very little civilian airflight but now people can cross the globe in twenty-four hours. Then there was only limited television but now any African eking out an existence in a makeshift hut, with tarpaulin for a roof if lucky, can see daily images of the West and its splendour, where even the poorest are housed and adequately fed, where the shops are piled high with goods and the schools have roofs on. That understandably is what they want for their own families.

The reader's response at this stage might be to doubt whether the mud-hut dweller has access to television but what struck me when visiting Lusaka was the network of wires and aerials in a place where food and work were scarce. There might only be one set between twenty households but the images will be shared. So the poor parts of the world now know in a detail hitherto denied to them how the inhabitants of the richer parts live and they can get there if they can raise the money for the airfare, usually possible only for those in work who also have family in work prepared to make an effort for just one of its members.

Then, of course, in 1951 large tracts of the Third World were still colonised and run peaceably. The withdrawal of the West over succeeding years gave rise to wars, genocide and persecution and, more frequently, the collapse of economies under incompetent and corrupt regimes. The impetus to escape was huge and Britain was seen as a soft touch. We made only very limited use of detention, had a flourishing black economy, no national identity cards and an appeals system which could be long-drawn-out. There can be few other countries in which it is so easy to disappear.

If somebody who had entered the country unlawfully in the back of a lorry were detected he would simply say – and still does – 'I claim asylum', whereupon he would be able to stay in the country lawfully until the claim had been determined.

An economic migrant trying to get into Britain from an area where there is no persecution at all will simply lose his passport and travel documents in the course of the flight or in the airside loos, stay airside for hours and then present himself at the desk with claims to come from a country which does practise persecution. As we can return people only to countries which recognise them as nationals this provides a serious difficulty for immigration officials. Foreign nationals have claimed asylum and so even if the officer is certain that the claimant neither looks nor sounds like a resident of, say, Somalia, he must admit him to the country while the claim is determined. The policy I was to advocate, as Shadow Home Secretary, was for immigration officers to meet the planes.

I also persuaded William Hague to agree to a policy of universal detention so that all new asylum applicants would be held in secure reception centres until their claims were determined. That would enable us to pick out the genuine ones much quicker so that, instead of being held in a queue with tens of thousands of others from whom they were not easily distinguishable, they could be given a proper welcome package to Britain. As for those whom we were going to refuse – and that could be up to 80 per cent – we would know where they were and could return them.

Obviously there would still be difficult cases but the deterrent effect of a system which promised detention, early assessment and return would be huge. After the 2001 election Oliver Letwin became Shadow Home Secretary and made the policy even tougher by suggesting that we would detain such applicants offshore. Today such is the emphasis on the perfectly lawful but large-scale immigration from Eastern European countries, that this aspect of our much-abused immigration system is all but overlooked.

One only has to look at Sangatte, the refugee camp just on the other side of the Channel, to realise just how soft a touch we are. There are hundreds of people describing themselves as refugees who have arrived in France which is of course also a signatory to the 1951 Convention and a perfectly safe country but instead of applying to stay there, these people spend their days trying to get into Britain illegally because the message goes across the world that if you succeed in getting into Britain the chances of being removed are small.

Michael stopped short of universal detention but was proposing a package of proposals which would be my job to take through the House and I relished the work. First we would streamline procedures to tackle bogus claims more quickly, second we would put the onus on employers, backed up by criminal sanctions, to make sure that anybody they employed really did have a visa which allowed him or her to work here and third we would restrict social security rights where a claim had been refused in the hope that would persuade the applicant to leave rather than draw out a long system of appeals, challenges and new grounds. We also established what came to be known as 'The White List', which was a list of safe countries where there was no serious risk of persecution. I felt useful and engaged.

The size of the task on prisons was much less easy to crunch. The first prison I visited was Holloway and I was appalled by the inactivity within. The women were sitting about doing nothing and it did not unduly surprise me when, a few months later, the Chief Inspector of Prisons, David Ramsbotham, walked out without completing his report. Between my arrival in July 1995 and the declaration of the election in March 1997, I was to visit 135 prisons. Some like Coldingley were excellent and others like Leeds, which was the last prison to end slopping out, were depressing. Some were modern and some too old and cramped to be adapted. Others had large remand populations which changed so much that a settled routine was impossible, others like little Shepton Mallet had stable populations and excellent regimes.

The Prison Officers Association was militant in some (Reading) but quiet in others while in two cases officers whispered their real views to me when the POA rep had disappeared. I visited on both weekdays and weekends so that I could see operations in both busy and quiet times and I talked to prisoners, staff and governors. I ate prison food, visited health centres and watched visiting times. At Dartmoor the roofs leaked and in Exeter a prisoner, who should have been in a mental institution but was denied a place on the grounds that there was no room, held on to the bars of his room in the prison health centre making idiot noises, head and tongue lolling.

I was alternately encouraged and disheartened but the sheer size of the task was daunting and it needed focused and steady leadership, but instead in October 1995, Michael Howard produced uncertainty, discontent and a miserable lapse back into some ways that were beginning to be forgotten.

On 27 September 1995 I was at the Home Office strategy

conference at Chevening when the Learmont Report arrived. I read it into the early hours of the morning and, even with my limited experience, could pick holes in some of the contents. It painted a bleak picture of the Prison Service which I knew would seriously demoralise staff, ignored much that had been achieved and included hearsay but I knew that Michael would use it to do what he had long wanted to do and get rid of Lewis.

I raised with Derek himself some of the content of the report and Michael observed us in discussions and took me aside. I should not, he told me, 'get too close' to Derek Lewis as the Learmont Report had 'serious implications for his position'. That seemed to me an odd reaction to the Prisons Minister discussing a major report with her Director General and confirmed me in my view that Michael would be unlikely to look at the report objectively and that he was getting jumpy.

However we believed we could rely on Richard Wilson, Derek Lewis had the support of the prisons board and it seemed to me that we could all argue ourselves to the right conclusion. I think only another couple of months of experiencing Michael's leadership style would have told me that to be a forlorn hope but I was then too new to realise it.

What Lewis's supporters should have done was to create external pressure on Michael by trailing in the press the possibility of his using Lewis as a scapegoat and there were those who were well-positioned to do that but neither he nor I considered it. I had never briefed against a fellow minister in my entire political life and at that stage it would have been unthinkable for me while Derek was still batting straight as if the bowling would also be. In principle we were right to try and solve it from within but it played into the hands of Whetstone and Rock, who were trying to keep Michael's intentions quiet precisely so as to avoid any build-up of support for his victim.

Michael's advisors were simply not looking beyond the present and were intent only on shifting any blame away from Michael and giving him the scalp he wanted. Who would thereafter run the Prison Service, what the effects might be on the government's efforts to recruit from the private sector, what the hideous costs of accepting Learmont's Report uncritically might amount to, as well as the impact on the Prison Service's morale, the reaction of the other directors (two non-executive ones were to resign) and the likely subsequent build-up in the press of adverse reaction were just pushed to one side, if they were considered at all.

Although this was my first glimpse of the Learmont Report both Derek and Richard had already seen it under what is called Salmon procedures whereby any person to be criticised in a report has a right to see it in advance and put in comments. Richard was not criticised but for some reason had seen it anyway.

The following Sunday Derek and I met at Prison Service HQ to determine the response to the report. Derek was opposed to many of its recommendations as impractical, costly or undesirable. He proposed to say so and I realised in one of those blinding flashes, which occasionally assail members of the human race, that here was the root of all the trouble: Lewis did not think politically.

'Michael cannot go to the House and rubbish a major report. He must be seen to be responding positively. Your job is to help him do that.'

Oh, dear, he was actually surprised. He had been brought in to implement the Woolf Report which talked about 'a structured stand-off from ministers'. But, once he had grasped that his role was not as he had always thought but that he had to think as politically as Richard Wilson was obliged to do, he could hardly have been better at it and hope rose within me.

For example one of the recommendations of Learmont was that Parkhurst should be downgraded from Category A status and that a super-secure prison should be built elsewhere, the so-called Supermax. Derek's reaction was that it would be madness given the huge amount of money which had been poured into making Parkhurst more secure since the January escapes.

'Right, so we reject it and keep Category A prisoners at Parkhurst and there is another escape. Where does that leave Michael?'

It did not take him more than a few seconds' thought to

produce the compromise that in view of all the work that had been done at Parkhurst since the Learmont inspection a member of the General's team should be invited to re-visit and give an updated view, pending which the issue of Parkhurst's categorisation could languish in the long grass while all the fuss died down.

On the basis of that experience I asked to see the Home Secretary. I was honest, telling him that I was not going to try to sell him Derek Lewis as I was aware he did not want to buy him and was rewarded by a small smile. I then said that the problem was not Derek's management, which was quite exceptional, but that it was his political nous which was causing the problems. I said that was not new to me, having encountered it in other senior officials who had been brought in from outside Whitehall, especially in Michael Bichard who was now doing so magnificently well. However I had spent all Sunday with Derek drafting a response to Learmont and once I had persuaded him to look at things more politically, it had all gone well. I quoted Woolf and the basis for the misunderstanding. I said I could guarantee that I would keep an eye on the politics and believed that I would not have to do so for very long because once Derek had embraced such a way of operating he would be very good at it.

Afterwards Richard was very enthusiastic. He had never been so proud of a minister. He believed I had changed Michael to being fifty–fifty whereas before he was overwhelmingly in favour of dismissal. We could yet prevail, particularly as on one point Richard had already been successful: Derek must have the opportunity to put in a full personal defence against dismissal.

That defence, which was later published, was voluminous and Derek wanted to run it past me while I was away in Blackpool for party conference. Michael got wind of his impending visit and summoned me to say it should not go ahead. I responded that I needed to see Derek anyway about other things and that if I were to cancel the meeting he would guess the reason and assume dismissal was a certainty. The speed with which Michael then reversed his ruling should have alerted me to his obvious desire to prevent the story of impending dismissal leaking. It did not and as I was still playing by the rules I doubt if I would have acted upon the realisation even if it had occurred to me.

If, however, I was not prepared to look outside government I tried to find allies within and rang Tony Newton to express my disquiet. Michael Forsyth was already alerted and, I could only hope, active. I had no choice but to wait and see.

Michael does not hide his feelings and intentions well and is easy to read. I asked him point-blank if, having read the document and found it convincing, he would not then dismiss his Director General. He could not bring himself to lie to me but nor would he admit the truth and what came out of him was a non-committal sound which was neither yes nor no. I knew then that the exercise in asking Derek for a defence was window-dressing and that the latter was wasting his time and energy.

Farce then ensued. I had agreed with Michael that I would not look at Derek's defence document. We met in a small room, on the ground floor of my hotel. Its walls, being made of glass, caused us to feel as if we were exhibits in an aquarium. Around the outside lurked Whetstone and Rock, occasionally peering through, then looking quickly away. Quite what they were going to report to Michael, I never knew. Had I seen the document? Well they could only know if they could distinguish it from the other material we were discussing. As a matter of fact I did not see it and was faithful to my assurance that I would not, but we discussed the major points of Learmont and the concomitant rebuttals.

Later Rock and Whetstone said their being there had been coincidence. Yes, and I'm an Albanian great-grandmother.

That was not the only comic moment although the second felt anything but funny at the time. At the end of that week Derek sent the final version of his defence to Blackpool but the darn thing got lost. Anxious that the Home Secretary should not have the excuse that he had not received the document but even more anxious that it might land in the wrong hands, I ended up crawling around the conference postal room at Blackpool, among boxes and mail bundles, trying to locate it.

By now I had a fair grasp of Michael's psychology and I knew that if his conference speech went well he would be on a high and feel capable of anything but that if it was not a success he would be far less sure of himself. As the time came for him to make it, I found myself for the first time in all my years as an MP uncertain about wishing a Cabinet minister well upon a public platform. I did not want him to do badly – the party was in too parlous a state for that – but I could not wish him a great triumph. A consummate performer, he had one nevertheless.

Michael, flushed with success, began to dig in. Sir Duncan Nichol, one of the four non-executives on the prisons board wrote to Michael to ask for a meeting between him and the board under access arrangements which were part of the terms of its appointment. It was refused.

On the morning of Sunday, 15 October Michael and I met at the Home Office and he told me what he intended to do. My response was prophetic: 'You'll get away with this tomorrow but by the next day Derek's fight-back will have started and he has a lot of support. There will be resignations and by Wednesday the tide will have turned in his favour.'

Knowing argument to be in vain I still argued, becoming upset. Howard said that Learmont and Lewis painted two very different pictures of the Prison Service and he preferred Learmont's. That was what he said to Derek when he then called him into the room and demanded his resignation. Lewis refused as I had known he would. The atmosphere in the meeting was terrible with both men speaking so softly that sometimes I could hardly hear what was being said.

'He won't go quietly,' I warned Michael but Michael simply hoped what he described as 'wiser counsels' would prevail. The deadline for the resignation came and went and so did another. I sent a note over to Downing Street telling the Prime Minister I disagreed with what was being done. John Major rang back to ask what I intended to do. I had been asking myself the same question all morning.

The dream job had become a nightmare. I had little respect for the man for whom I was working. A major act of injustice was being carried out and I would, under collective responsibility,

Right: Orpington campaign, 2001

Above: The 'forgotten decent', Arden Estate, East London, 2001. Ann announces her decision not to stand for the Conservative Party Leadership. (PA)

Above: Campaigning, City of Durham, 2005

Left: Unlikely alliance? The Party's Right and Left. Ann backed Ken Clarke unsuccessfully in three leadership elections. (PA)

The Catholic Church's latest recruit, April 1993 (PA)

With Pope John Paul II, January 1996 (Foto Felici/PA)

The Preacher. St John's Church, Bath, 2011

Above: Rita, Murray, Ann and Malcolm in Haslemere

Ann and Malcolm, 2007

Ann and Rita, Chelsea Flower Show, 2005 (Edward Winstanley)

First winter at Widdecombe's Rest, 2008

Watching the latest generation grow up – the pool at Widdecombe's Rest

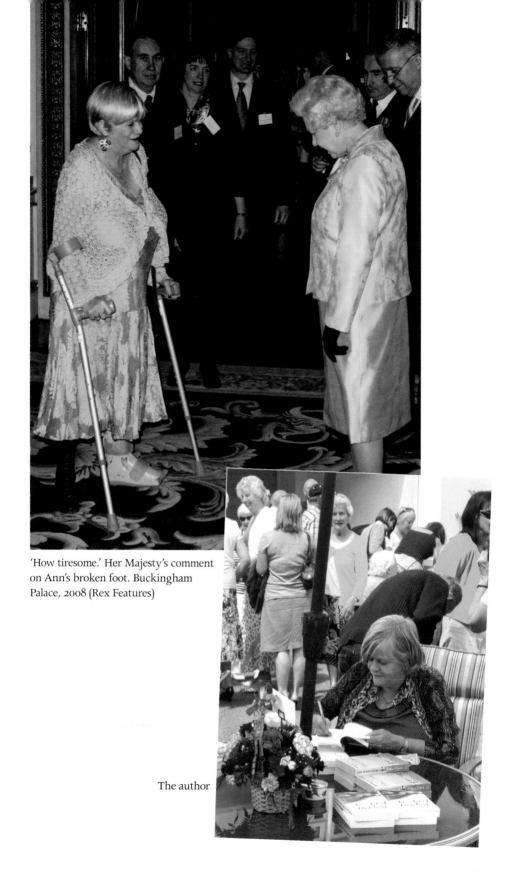

'How tiresome.' Her Majesty's comment on Ann's broken foot. Buckingham Palace, 2008 (Rex Features)

The author

Ann receives an Honorary Doctorate, Birmingham University, 2012 (Ede & Ravenscroft)

'At least you danced': an unusually kind comment from Craig Revel Horwood on Ann's Quickstep with Anton du Beke, *Strictly Come Dancing*, 2010 (BBC) have to defend it. Dismissal was a wholly disproportionate reaction but I would have to say it was reasonable.

Yet I had all the loyalty in the world towards John Major, who was besieged on all sides and I did not want to make his position any worse. At that stage, of course, I did not know so much that I was later to find out. I was merely conscious of a grave injustice and of a certain brutality. Had I resigned then my speech would have simply been about Lewis and his record. There would have been no mention of *something of the night*.

Chapter Twenty-One

ENTER DORIS KARLOFF

On Monday, 16 October, as MPs returned from the long recess and party conference season, ministers met in the Home Office. Afterwards Emily Blatch told me that she thought the decision wrong and I realised too late that she might have been an important ally as she was close to the Prime Minister but by now the opportunity had passed.

Disbelievingly I listened to the head of the press office telling Michael that the statement he made to the House that afternoon about the dismissal of Lewis had gone well and that the press was happy as a head had rolled. Both seemed to be suffering political myopia.

Two non-executive members of the prisons board resigned. Geoff Keeys was a director with the Prudential and Millie Banerjee with BT. Both understood what Lewis had achieved against enormous odds. The senior civil servants' union took up the case, irate governors flooded the Home Office faxes, the Opposition began sniffing the air and the press began to turn. Two days of mounting pressure followed, with Paxman embarrassing Howard on Monday's *Newsnight* by suggesting that he had sacked the Director General to save his own skin, me shouted at by a meeting of governors on the Tuesday, the publication of Lewis's defence to an increasingly sympathetic press on Wednesday and, Heaven help us, the issue of a writ itself by Derek Lewis alleging unfair dismissal which arrived shortly before Howard was due to defend his actions in a debate called by the Opposition.

As the pressure mounted, Tony Newton apologised to me: he had been meaning to act on my phone call but had somehow overlooked it. I assured him there was little we could have done anyway. With growing speculation that the Home Secretary might have to resign and that the Opposition had a smoking fax, I told John Major in the lobby that, quite apart from what I regarded as the injustice of the decision, Howard's action had been daft politically. If he had tried to save Lewis then all the pressure would have been on the Director General with calls to sack him instead of on the Home Secretary.

We had a good party conference and now we were in another damn mess almost before the new term had begun.

John agreed, looking sad, but thanked me for staying on. When the true extent of the disagreement in the Home Office emerged in May 1997, many speculated that if I had resigned I would have brought down Michael, but I doubt the wisdom of that analysis and, in any event, I was not then looking to do so. I wanted to save the Director General of the Prison Service, not destroy the Home Secretary with whose policies I agreed and whose determination I still admired.

From the moment the Opposition called the debate, Howard was jumpy because I was going to be winding up from our side. He had no choice but to field me as if any other than the Prisons Minister had performed the task, speculation of a rift would have been rife but he trusted me not an inch. Of course he was not afraid that I was going to denounce the decision but he was nervous that I might say something favourable about Derek Lewis.

I responded that if we were going to defend the Prison Service I would have to make favourable comment about its performance, but that as he himself had praised the Director General in the past, the two positions were not incompatible. He looked only partially relieved but on the morning of the debate I was called to his office in the Commons where I also found Simon Burns, the MP for Chelmsford, who told me that a journalist had asked him in the lobby if it was true that I had disagreed with the Home Secretary's decision.

Michael, panicky, demanded that if the question was put to me in the House I must say that his decision had my full support. As by then the Opposition was claiming that he had misled

Parliament about the amount of pressure he had put on Derek over the Marriott affair, it seemed an odd moment to ask me effectively to mislead the House nor was I so daft as to have been unprepared for such a question.

Having always feared that details of our disagreement might leak, the formula I had concocted was: 'The Home Secretary himself has praised Mr Lewis's achievements and so do I, but it is inescapable that we have had two of the most serious operational failures in the history of the Prison Service.' That combined truth with discretion. If somebody wanted to point to worse horrors in the past, my statement would still hold true.

All that week colleagues had been muttering to me that they thought Lewis to have been a good DG. Michael Stern recalled how he had managed to convince a sceptical Select Committee of the merits of the Wolds, an early experiment in prison privatisation. Simon Burns himself said he had been impressed by some dealings he had with him. A complete outsider whom I knew only from the Bow Group told me how refreshingly competent he had found him after years of dealing with civil servants.

Yet the party held together well. No rebel went down to the Green to demand Michael's resignation on camera. Those who had doubts may have told me but they did not tell the media. As far as they were concerned a decision had been taken and it was their duty to support it. A few staunch supporters of Howard, such as Ivan Lawrence, were loud in their support while Peter Lloyd made a brave speech lauding the former DG's record but not castigating Michael.

As Jack Straw launched his attack our benches howled their support for Michael. Listening later to some of the backbench speeches by people who knew next to nothing about the Prison Service, I realised it could have been I who was standing there, denigrating a man for the sake of party loyalty, careless of justice, ignorant of the case for the defence, heedless of the effect on his family, parroting a Central Office brief taken entirely on trust. We all had our areas of specialist knowledge and interests but for too much of parliamentary business we trusted others to brief us properly. I never did so again and, when I did return to the backbenches, spoke very sparingly on matters beyond my own experience.

I did not want Straw to bring down Michael solely because of the damage it would do to Major but I did very much want him to make Lewis's case well. Sadly this normally sound performer made a mess of his brief. Partially deaf, he failed to hear a killer question put to him about whether he would have sacked the Director General and he floundered trying to make a case about too much interference on the part of Michael Howard without the contemporaneous notes which would have proved it.

The general reader may well ask why it mattered if Michael had intervened but it was his own distinction between 'policy' and 'operations' which left him able to deny any responsibility for the failures of Whitemoor and Parkhurst. If he could be seen to have become involved in 'operations' then his defence fell at the first hurdle.

I knew rather too much by now of the row over Marriott and I became uneasy as Michael said unequivocally, 'There was no question of overruling the Director General.' Dear Heaven, had he not asked Derek to leave the room to reconsider his decision and then taken advice about whether he could overrule him?

I had not then seen the contemporaneous note which actually records Michael as saying, when Derek objected to the use of the word 'today' in the removal of Marriott, 'No, no, no. I want today.' I merely knew the tenor of that meeting from notes and conversations with those involved.

If Michael had never made that very precise distinction between policy and operations then he would not have needed to deny his pressure on his DG. He could simply have said, 'Yes, I did tell him to suspend Marriott and yes, I would have overruled him had I been able' – doubtless to cheers from our side. Instead he set a trap for himself that several times threatened to snare us on completely different matters. Indeed, by the end of my time in the Home Office I was applying in my private thoughts to 'policy and operations' what George V once said about Bognor. Even Rachel Whetstone once admitted to me that the distinction had been 'unhelpful', an understatement if ever there was one.

I gave a vigorous winding-up speech, vocally supported by Michael and watched with some amusement by Richard Wilson, who described me as a human windmill. The day, which had so much potential for disaster, had turned into one of triumph and Michael left the Chamber on a high.

That mood sustained him when we all met in the PM's office for a celebratory drink. Had I caused four days of anguish for the party, produced an Opposition censure debate, been served with a writ against the Home Office, endured resignations from serious players and brought about a media frenzy which over-shadowed a successful party conference, my uppermost feelings would have been of relief and gratitude that further disaster had been avoided. I would have apologised to the PM and said, 'Now let's move on and put it behind us.'

That was not Howard's way. Triumphant, gloating, vindictive, his first words when we had all sat down were, 'Now I am going to get the press cuts about when Lewis left Granada.'

Derek had left Granada amid a huge controversy because he had invested some £200 million of the company's money in BSkyB. It turned out to be a stake eventually worth several billion pounds, so his detractors got that one wrong, but the parting had been difficult and Michael must have thought he could capitalise on that to Derek's discomfort. Quite why he would wish to do that when he himself had just so triumphantly survived would not be obvious to anyone not given to kicking men when they are down.

What anybody said next, I do not know because I got up and left, outraged but also deeply upset. Women who take their careers seriously do not let male colleagues see them in tears and I knew that was where I was heading. Not content with having destroyed a loyal servant's career, put his family through hell and hearing his own side cheer it to the echo, he must now gratuitously indulge in a vengeful feud. But my tears did not flow for contempt soon replaced the pent-up feelings of the last week. I recalled Howard's earlier panicky demands that I say I supported his decision and contrasted his demeanour then with his nasty certainty now. It revealed, I thought, a dark side, *something of the night*.

The Prime Minister later sent for me and I told him that vindictiveness and triumphalism were hardly appropriate, but if that was the course Michael wanted to pursue then I would not be following him along the path. In the course of the weekend Michael rang me at home to say that I needn't worry about anybody 'being vindictive'. Clearly the Prime Minister had told him to reassure me, which probably means that he was still fearful I might resign.

From then until 1997 Michael and I worked together on all manner of projects and legislation in which we both had faith. It was often said that he left me to take the flak on television when things went wrong while being quick to appear himself and grab the credit when events turned out well, but that was not true. Michael had a hands-off policy towards his ministers and the media, leaving it to our own judgement and I found that a relief after the tortuous discussions with previous Secretaries of State, who tended to regard the media as I might have regarded an ouija board, always terrified of what they might conjure up.

While on the subject of conjuring up, let me lay to rest the silly story that I thought Michael possessed and wanted an exorcism. I can say quite categorically that I have never encountered any case of possession and do most fervently hope that record will remain as I am sure it must be a most disconcerting experience. The myth arose from a joke exchanged between Michael Seed and me when he visited my office.

As we passed the Home Secretary's quarters, he asked in jest if he should sprinkle it with holy water and I snorted that bell, book and candle might be more appropriate, whereupon Michael said he had a Bible and candle in his briefcase but no bell. I suggested the division bell and then we passed to more sensible conversation.

All would have been well if we had not repeated the joke to friends, laughing that Michael Seed had taken bell, book and candle to the Home Office. Like most good stories it must have become mangled in the re-telling because I next heard it repeated back to me seriously and then Jim Naughtie actually claimed that an eminent journalist believed I had a priest in the gallery of the House of Commons to exorcise Michael! It showed not merely an astounding credulity but a woeful ignorance of exorcism procedures in the Catholic Church.

I began to suspect Michael Seed, who can exaggerate greatly and amusingly when merry, was embellishing the story but he denied it. The denial became worthless when his own book came out and the story was included with even more fictitious circumstances. I was unlikely to sue my own priest but I demanded that he give me a written retraction, which he did. His explanation was not credible; that the ghost writer had confused exorcism with blessing. Finally he told me that there were about fifteen different drafts, the wrong one was published and that I was not the only one complaining. I can quite believe that but it still does not explain how the story got into any of the drafts and I suspected that if I sued the publishers I would be presented with a tape of a mirthful Michael leading his listeners up the garden path. Garden paths can be dangerous, O Priest.

My own media policy was to keep Richard Tilt, now the acting Director General, off the airwaves as much as possible so that we were not setting up another scapegoat and to tell it as it was.

Telling it as it is does of course rely on having the right information and within three months of Derek Lewis leaving I found out that was not quite as straightforward as one might have thought.

Before I joined the Home Office the Prison Service had carried out a survey of escapes and had found that women were proportionately more likely to escape between prison and hospital than the men. The reason was not hard to discern: men were routinely handcuffed for the duration of the journey and the restraints were, of course, removed when medical treatment began. Women, by contrast, travelled unrestrained so it was not surprising that some made the most of the opportunity afforded. It was therefore decided to introduce some gender equality and to secure women as well as men and also to take off the cuffs when medical treatment started but that left the problem of pregnant women going in to hospital to give birth. When was medical treatment deemed to have started? To have waited until labour was sufficiently far advanced to warrant medical intervention would have been barbarous and so it was decided that once labour was confirmed, at however early a stage, the handcuffs would be removed. It seemed a reasonable decision.

That then was the policy I inherited. I was but vaguely aware of it until Channel Four secretly filmed a prisoner from Holloway who was giving birth in the Whittington Hospital. That film showed her quite clearly moving around the ward, unrestrained even before she went into labour and also after the birth was over, proof positive that the policy was being proportionately rather than rigorously implemented.

However there was a moment before labour was confirmed when she wanted to smoke. In those days that was allowed in the general areas of hospitals but not on the wards so a prison officer took her into the public areas and therefore applied handcuffs. Had it been a straight wrist to wrist cuff between two females the resulting film would have been somewhat less dramatic, but the prison officer was male and therefore, for reasons of decency, space had to be kept between him and the prisoner. This was effected by means of a long chain linking the cuffs and the image which was broadcast to a scandalised nation was woman, bump, chains. The media had a field day.

The Opposition, with some cause, demanded a statement. Michael was in an aeroplane somewhere between the Indian subcontinent and Heathrow, so the job fell to me. In my opening paragraph I told the House: 'It is the policy of the Prison Service not to keep women handcuffed while in labour and childbirth. It has never been Prison Service policy to keep women handcuffed during labour and childbirth.'

That seems to me a sufficiently unequivocal statement but even now there are those who believe that it was my policy to keep women in handcuffs while giving birth. I am confronted with it when I give 'An Audience With' evenings, when being interviewed on the media and sometimes even in the street.

The *Mirror* carried a photograph of my head superimposed on a pregnant body in chains and Paul Flynn, a Labour MP, dubbed me Doris Karloff, which stuck. As cartoonists sometimes cannot understand why MPs enjoy their rude caricatures, so journalists were surprised by my lack of resentment at this nickname. After insisting with one that I had nothing to add I terminated the conversation with the words, 'That's it. Karloff has spoken.' His colleagues in the press gallery were consumed by mirth.

In the course of the debate which followed my response to Jack Straw on 9 January, he and other members continued to argue as if the prisoner had been in labour when handcuffed which made my job easy but I was more than happy to concede that it would be desirable to try and ensure the presence of female rather than male officers on such escort duties. Unfortunately I also repeated the very clear advice which I had been given by the Prison Service that we had not received any complaints from the hospital itself about our practices.

When that statement was challenged shortly afterwards, the Prison Service repeated its statement. We had received no complaints, Tilt assured me. I therefore maintained the position but on 11 January I received a letter from the Chairman of the Whittington NHS Trust telling me that she had indeed complained to the Governor of Holloway as long ago as the previous August.

I told my private office to find out where the letter was filed and it was located in the Governor's files sitting right on top of one marked 'Whittington'. The acting DG had been right when he said the Service had received no complaint if by that he meant at HQ. Nobody had thought to ask the Governor.

It was one of a number of occasions on which I sought the advice of Derek. Indeed, without telling the Home Secretary, both Richard occasionally and I frequently consulted our dismissed DG. It is an eloquent comment because we would hardly have sought his counsel if it had not been worth having.

I also kept in touch with Derek on a more personal level and he advised me about the progress of his quest for a new role but one subject was largely taboo between us: his lawsuit against the Home Office where my sympathies lay firmly with him and my duty with the department in which I was a minister.

Nevertheless I began taking risks which would once have

been unthinkable. When the subject came up with lobby journalists I told them, strictly off the record, that I strongly disagreed with the dismissal. I also consented to speak informally to anyone looking for a reference for Derek, although I drew the line at a formal letter. In short, I was no longer playing by the rules. I trusted the journalists because lobby terms were so strictly observed but also, more cynically, because I knew the story was as dead as the dodo.

Twice the dodo showed signs of resurrection. The first incident came when Derek comprehensively won his case for unfair dismissal in the High Court. In the privacy of my cottage I cheered while in public adopting a solemn mien and talking about 'respecting the decision of the court' and 'being glad the issue was now resolved'. My only regret was that the headlines, so humiliating for Michael and thus also for the government, came as the party faithful were gathering for the annual meeting of their Central Council and must have been decidedly demoralising. Those loyal workers deserved better.

The second stirring of the dodo was when Derek produced a book, *Hidden Agendas*, giving his side of the story. His account left no room for doubt that I had taken his side and was reflected in the headlines that accompanied publication.

Some months later when the election was called and I was preparing to leave the Home Office, I walked into Politicos, a Westminster bookshop, and bought copies as leaving presents for my private office to remind them of one of the more turbulent periods in their civil service careers. The owner, Iain Dale, was curious but said nothing.

He and I were later to form quite a partnership in a show called *An Audience with Ann Widdecombe*, which we took round the country for ten years under the auspices of Clive Conway Productions, playing to audiences which ranged from 30 to 500. A less successful venture was the publication of a book of my speeches. As I do most of them off the cuff there was only a limited written record and not a particularly exciting one. Seriously busy and not then a leadership contender or policy bigwig, I had no reason to produce long, philosophical theses and the collection was quite banal. Dale next commissioned a biography of me by Nick Kochan, which performed rather better.

Iain Dale is a competent, entrepreneurial, humorous individual whose attempts to enter Parliament merited success but did not attain it. In the 2005 leadership election he was to pin his colours firmly to the Davis mast.

None of this had yet happened when, bruised and angry with the Prison Service, I rang Derek Lewis about the chains and childbirth debacle.

'Always go to the Governor,' he said. 'Never mind the protocol. Ask the chap who knows. I found that out often enough.'

I resisted attempts to persuade me to correct the information via a letter placed in the library or a written question. I had accidentally misled the House and would correct it on my feet in that forum via a personal statement. Michael also amended the policy so that women were still handcuffed between prison and hospital but the restraints would be removed upon arrival. Gradually the fire and fury receded.

Despite all the name-calling, the incident included only one really painful moment for me on a personal level. The *Mirror* approached several Labour female MPs for a quote but the only one who would oblige was my friend from Oxford, Barbara Roche. Joan Ruddock refused to comment and Mo Mowlam said she had debated against me at Cambridge recently and I was b***** good. Frank Field went on the record in my support even to the extent of saying I should be in the Cabinet. But my so-called friend, Barbara, contributed the following comment: 'She has done nothing for women throughout her political career. She has shown a total lack of understanding of women and families.'

Two years later when I was in full attack mode against Michael, I was accused of anti-Semitism and Barbara, who was born Barbara Margolis and is Jewish, pointed out that I used to vote for her at Oxford which silenced some of the critics. That went some way towards healing the rift that her earlier remarks caused.

If the chains controversy was the low point of that January, a visit to Rome produced the most memorable moment of my life. I was at yet another meeting of European ministers and asked

Adrian Jones if we could fit in a papal audience between sessions. I had visions of a general audience and, at most, of lining up to shake the Pope's hand. To my utter amazement and joy I found myself in an individual audience which lasted twenty minutes, an allocation normally reserved for Heads of State. John Paul II spoke immaculate English and the conversation, led by him, ranged over the Anglican situation following the vote on the ordination of women, the numbers of women in Parliament and the role played by them and the state of Christianity in Britain. He then organised photographs with long-practised skill and presented me with a rosary that he had blessed.

It was only afterwards that I realised all the publicity surrounding my conversion, which had reached Rome, convinced Vatican officials that I was worth a full audience.

My lasting impression of John Paul was one of immense holiness, a sense of being closer to God just by being in his presence, an almost tangible link with the early Church. That is a very rare occurrence. I felt something of it with Cardinal Hume and to a lesser extent with Mother Teresa, whom I had met in 1994 when I visited her mission in Calcutta, but with the Pope it was extremely powerful.

The Prison Service did not take long to supply me with another headache, when one evening I was rung up at home, where I had been looking forward to an unusual early night. It seemed prisoners might have been released too early as a result of a miscalculation of their time spent on remand. I groaned. How many? It was not yet clear but perhaps as many as twenty.

The next day twenty would have seemed like a godsend. Throughout a tense meeting with the acting DG and responsible officials the numbers changed every few minutes, with people coming and going to get more information, until the estimate was put at 521. Michael was white-faced with anger and frustration. He tried unsuccessfully to get to the bottom of how it had happened and who had performed the calculations but he was known as a hardline sacker and everybody was busy covering himself or herself.

The farce of the distinction between policy and operations

manifested itself yet again when Michael began telling Richard Tilt what he wanted to see in the press release. This was an operational matter, intervened Richard Wilson, so it was important that the Home Secretary should be able to say that he had not interfered in any aspect, whereupon Michael desisted and then, when Tilt had gone off to prepare the release, told Wilson what should be in it. Wilson then relayed this to Tilt as 'advice'. You couldn't make it up.

A round of the media followed in which Tilt carried out interview after interview, taking the blame. 'How many more?' he sighed sotto voce at one point.

'I hope you are going to sack the chap responsible,' said a fellow MP, Michael Stephen.

'You mean the acting Director General? So what do we have then? An acting acting Director General?'

Michael had tied his hands by his previous actions and even though on this occasion the blame was firmly in Prison Service HQ rather than with the laxity of some guard looking at CCTV cameras out in the fens, he could take no action. A second dismissal would have won him no credibility at all.

He had also tied his hands with regard to finding a successor. It quickly became clear that the private sector was not interested. Michael, as ever impressed by anything military, sounded out David Ramsbotham.

'I have a very good man,' he told me, but Ramsbotham preferred the post of Chief Inspector of Prisons, from which he gave us a great deal of trouble. Some of Michael's ideas were wild such as when he suggested the brother of a minister who had 'always wanted to run the Prison Service'. Richard Wilson was more circumspect but no more successful.

It was well-nigh inevitable that we would appoint Richard Tilt.

When prisons were quiet, Michael and I were always tensed for the next disaster but there were plenty of other flashpoints and asylum seekers could always be relied upon to fill in any gaps in drama left by the Prison Service. Two in particular stand out: the hunger strikers and Al Mas'ari.

The hunger strikers stirred strong emotions. They amounted to a handful of detained asylum seekers in Rochester Prison, who in January 1997 decided to go on hunger strike in protest at their detention. The numbers involved, as I reported to the House on 29 January, fluctuated considerably but by then about seventeen were said to be refusing food.

The strike had begun on 6 January but as that month drew to a close some six detainees were also refusing fluids, or at least claiming to be so doing, a vastly more serious state of affairs as dehydration causes death a great deal quicker than starvation. They were all under observation in the prison health-care wing, where it was suspected that some took in fluids during visits to the lavatory.

The media began to get very excited about what was happening but as I pointed out none of the detainees was there simply by virtue of having asked for asylum. Some were convicted criminals awaiting deportation, others had absconded when asylum was refused and more than a third were illegal immigrants. Detention was used sparingly and at any given time only 1 per cent of asylum seekers were detained. Indeed one of the six had already served a prison sentence, had been removed and had re-entered the country unlawfully.

Behind the scenes we were working hard with the local Imam, who visited the prison, and with the psychiatrist who was known to me from Maidstone Hospital. We would not give in to blackmail and we would not force-feed but any persuasion which could be tried was gratefully received. It appeared at first unsuccessful and there came a weekend when we fully expected a death.

The private office was in sombre mood but I pointed out to the members of that loyal little band that the decision was mine, not theirs, and if a death resulted it had nothing whatever to do with them. Michael and I kept ourselves up to date almost by the hour.

No death resulted and the strike was abandoned shortly afterwards. When Labour was elected a few months later and subsequently faced a similar situation ministers adopted the same line that governments must not be blackmailed. Some very affronted local Christians told me they were surprised, as they thought 'this government would be different'. I asked them to work out what they thought would happen if government released hunger strikers? It was one of many occasions when I watched scales drop from people's eyes as they groped their way out of the fog of propaganda which had taught them that all these problems were the results of a harsh, uncaring, Tory government.

Al Mas'ari was a nuisance. He was a Saudi dissident who attacked the Saudi royal family from his base in Britain. The Saudis were running out of patience and some very big British contracts were now at risk. It would have been unthinkable to return him to Saudi Arabia but it would clearly prejudice British jobs and investment if we continued to give him refuge. The solution was a safe third country and Domenica offered to take him. I therefore proposed to deport him as soon as possible.

The uproar was predictable and the courts overruled me but at least we had demonstrated to the Saudis that we had tried to get rid of him, or as I put it rather more grandiloquently, 'we had sought a solution which combined preserving British interests with observing our treaty obligations'.

Despite regular outbreaks of drama, the ordinary work of the department went on. Part of my job was to set tariffs (the time a life-sentence prisoner must serve before he can be even considered for release), approve moves to open prisons, sanction recalls where a prisoner had broken the terms of his licence, etc. In the course of such work I came upon names which had been notorious in my youth such as police-killer Harry Roberts, the Cambridge Rapist and of course Myra Hindley.

The decision to move people to open prison prior to release was always attended by the fear that I could get it wrong in either direction. I might read in a newspaper years hence that an offender I had agreed to prepare for release had killed again or, although I would never know it, I might delay the entry back into the world of a perfectly trustworthy man. In the event it was nothing I did as a Home Office minister which came back to haunt me but a constituency situation where, because of my lack of supervision, staff inadvertently assisted a paedophile to obtain a new identity.

I did not have direct involvement with the setting of Hindley's tariff as she was subject to a whole life sentence, meaning she was one of about two dozen prisoners for whom the only release would be death. The Home Secretary dealt with such cases and Michael was unfairly pilloried for taking a 'political' decision and 'playing to the tabloids'. Rot. It would have been massively difficult to justify Hindley's release against any criterion by which we worked.

She had been complicit or directly involved in the deaths of three children and two teenagers. The deaths were premeditated and occurred over time not in a confined period. For years she had denied the killing of two of the victims, thus causing additional anxiety to the parents who throughout that period still did not know whether their young ones had or had not been murdered by her and Brady. If such a case had come to me *de novo* I would have sent it straight to Michael as meriting a whole life tariff and would have been outraged had he refused.

My attitude towards Hindley caused a fair old contretemps with Frank Longford. I met him for lunch together with his daughter, Antonia Fraser, and my priest, Michael Seed. I had very recently been in Durham where I had asked not to meet Myra Hindley or Rose West. Frank was outraged and when Antonia tried to defend me launched into a tirade about how she was no better as she had left her husband. Antonia took it all calmly and affectionately, doubtless being used to these flights of moral comparisons, but I struggled to equate adultery with the murder of five innocent children. Theologically Frank was doubtless right as all sins offend Infinite Goodness.

I also found myself locked in theological debate with Philip McDonagh, my old friend from Oxford Union days, who was now in the Irish embassy and who came to see me to protest about the incarceration of IRA prisoners. A Catholic, he waxed lyrical about forgiveness and I countered with the need for expiation. My Private Secretary, Adrian Jones, gave up and his draft minutes included the memorable line 'there was some talk of Catholic theology'.

Another depressing aspect of life at the Home Office was that of the suicide reports from the prisons and, distressingly, sometimes from young offender institutions. There were then about 65 such deaths each year, which rose in the early part of this century to 95 and now stand at about 60.

Unless we can watch every prisoner twenty-four hours a day there is simply no way to prevent self-inflicted deaths but the Prison Service has the equivalent of the Samaritans in its Listeners scheme and does try to work out who might be at risk when first entering prison. The elimination of overcrowded cells is a big step in the right direction but single cells make it easier to take one's own life. It is nevertheless possible even in dormitories.

At one of our young offenders' institutions a young man got up in the night to go to the lavatory. On his way he decided to play a joke on one of the other inmates and pulled the bedclothes off him. Underneath the covers the other young man had been trying to hack into his wrist veins with a pencil.

Most suicides occur at an early stage in prison life but bullying can occur at any time as does family break-up, both factors in the prison suicide rate.

Michael had a tough prisons policy and we were introducing laws to make a third offence of burglary subject to an automatic three-year sentence and a second serious violent or sexual offence to a life sentence. Furthermore we were proposing honesty in sentencing so that the sentence given became the sentence served.

The last was not as easy as it sounds. Let us suppose a judge awards four years in the expectation that the prisoner will serve two, then in future he would award not four but two years. There was some muddle about the calculation of time off for good behaviour, prison governors insisting, rightly, that it was a necessary tool of discipline, and at one point it looked as if the combination of lower sentencing plus time off could actually mean prisoners were serving shorter sentences.

Although none of these measures was yet law, the prison population began to rise until the point was reached where we were running out of space and the building of new prisons was lagging behind the surge. I needed new cells desperately. Labour's reaction to a similar crisis was to ask judges to stop sending so many people to prison and to step up early release on tagging. Mine was a series of emergency measures.

We brought in a prison ship from the States and stationed it at Portland. The inhabitants were unhappy but I predicted to Ian Bruce, their MP, that they would eventually resist its removal and I was right. Labour derided the plan as 'the return of the hulks' but then kept the ship in use for nine years. I also imported disused Portakabins from Norwegian oil rigs to provide extra space in Category C prisons, the lowest category in the secure as opposed to open estate. The press wanted to know if they had en suite facilities.

I looked at a disused holiday camp in the North West, which had plenty of accommodation and needed little more than a secure perimeter to make it operable but neither this nor a disused airbase was ever actually commissioned.

Two big successes were Michael's boot camps which he and Derek Lewis had put in place for young offenders, where the inmates would have a structured, demanding day from six in the morning till lights out, including physical training and education and vocational schemes. I visited Thorn Cross and tackled some of the assault course obstacles myself but the unit at the Military Correction Centre at Colchester was more formidable.

Michael did not want to call these institutions either 'Short, sharp, shocks' or 'boot camps' so we called them High Intensity Training Units which would have been fine had not someone worked out that the initials were HIT U. Labour abolished the unit at Colchester soon after taking office, which was a shame because it had not been running long enough for any proper analysis to be carried out on its effectiveness.

Given that most youngsters drift into crime because they lack order and structure, these units had serious purpose and I had faith in them.

Prisons were being made more controllable places by the introduction of incentives and privileges which probably explains why I encountered no verbal abuse on my second visit to Whitemoor.

The work was non-stop and a great deal of useful legislation and amendment to prison regulations was taking place but there was also a rather silly piece of legislation under way for which I had responsibility because in March 1996, a crazed gunman had run amok in a primary school in Dunblane and politics overrode common sense.

It was not the first time. After the Hungerford massacre in 1987 public hysteria demanded a response, despite the obvious consideration that most of the shootings in Britain are carried out with unlawfully owned firearms and that homicidal madness cannot ever be guaranteed to be ruled out. A backbencher at the time, I discovered to my bemusement that some of my constituents were armed to the teeth, as I was taken to see private arsenals housed in unpretentious semi-detached homes among fresh flowers and wood polish where Hyacinth Bucket might have felt at home. Colleagues reported the same phenomenon as pressure against a new law was mounted by the shooting lobby.

We had then just had a general election and many argued that there was no urgent political imperative, that we could afford to park any legislation in the proverbial long grass, that time and other disasters would diminish the demand for immediate action. Others took the opposing view, that a trail of innocent dead citizens could not be overlooked, that if we did nothing and a single citizen died in a shooting we would be accused of culpable complacency and that, anyway, if we did nothing the Opposition would make hay and put forward a private member's bill.

Now the same arguments raged over Dunblane but more intensely, owing to the imminence of the next election. The outcome was never in much doubt: we would make some more law knowing that the next time a gunman ran wild it would be equally tragic and unpreventable. I looked at the school photos with the dead children circled and felt heartsick. Whatever we did, there could always be a next time.

Some serious good did come out of Westminster in that school security was much improved across the nation and I wondered that it had taken a tragedy of these ghastly proportions to bring such obvious measures about, but with the gun law I had little patience. It was another Dangerous Dogs Act: window dressing to answer a political necessity which would rebound on decent competition shooters as that Act had rebounded on decent pet-owners. I hated it but accepted from the outset that at least we would leave some competition pistols in place while the Opposition wanted an outright ban on all handguns.

So I briefly became an expert on .22s and front-loading muskets and replica guns. There was even talk at one stage about licensing air guns.

'What are they illegally used for?' asked Michael at one meeting.

'Shooting cats,' said a civil servant.

'But apart from shooting cats?'

'Home Secretary, I take shooting cats seriously and there will be a major rebellion from your minister if you don't,' I said from the end of the table.

'Oh, yes. There would be from my children too. And my wife.' There was then a pause before he hastily added, 'Oh, I like cats too' amid general laughter.

By the time the Firearms Act 1997 was ready for the statute book, it was obvious that we were going to lose the general election and one day Rachel Whetstone came to see me to ask what I now thought of Michael. As the conversation progressed it became evident to me that she was sizing up whether I could be persuaded to support Michael in any post-election leadership contest. I could not and I made that clear without either of us acknowledging what we were really discussing.

I had decided that the candidate most likely to win my support was Michael Portillo but for now there was a looming election and, unless Major could once more pull a rabbit from a hat, we were all doomed to opposition. I was approached by lobby journalists to be asked how I felt about having my chances of being in the Cabinet swept away. One minister returned during the campaign to find the name of his Shadow already on his door. Both press and Whitehall were preparing for change.

For me those winds of change were about to blow up into a gale.

Chapter Twenty-Two

SOMETHING OF THE NIGHT

When, in 1995, I rang Derek Lewis to find out how he was after the week of the dismissal and censure debate he responded simply that it was not a week he would wish to repeat. I was to say the same about the week of 12–19 May 1997. And I doubt if Michael would have wished to relive it.

The election had been the predicted disaster and I had narrowly averted a personal one. One evening when I was driving from London to Maidstone, I called into a petrol station and filled up the tank. I was heavily preoccupied with a neighbour having told me there had been a television team outside the block waiting to speak to me earlier and I was searching in my mind in case I had missed an agreed interview. Ten minutes later, as I drove along the Old Kent Road, my eye fell on the credit card lying on the front seat. I had not used it. Dear Heaven, I had not paid.

Frantic, I turned the car at the next available opportunity and drove back to the garage, my heart hammering. I was greeted with mirth rather than resentment but if I had not realised and returned, John Major could have had a scandal on his hands from the most unlikely quarter. Minister steals petrol. No amount of protest would have persuaded the press that it was innocent and even if the journalists privately believed it was, they would still have written it up as dramatically as possible. Yet politicians, like everybody else, occasionally have absent-minded moments.

I had been ready for defeat but the scale of it caught me unawares. As I walked into my count, having spent most of the election on the national trail, sometimes with Michael, I was greeted with the inaccurate news from one of my supporters that John Gummer had been defeated in Suffolk Coastal, to which I responded that if that was the case we had all lost.

'No, you have won,' was the response.

I hate counts, with my pessimistic streak always telling me that I have lost. On one occasion I managed to convince my chairman that it must really be so because a whole boxful of my votes was reposing under a table and neither of us spotted it until the tellers retrieved it and tipped out the contents for counting.

A succession of constituency officers at Maidstone has contrived to keep me away from the count until supporters can greet me at the doors with news of victory and on those occasions when I am giving television commentary in London until the early hours they have breathed a collective sigh of relief.

In 1997, despite a comfortable win in Maidstone, it was all gloom and despondency as the national results dripped through. Most people remember the iconic moment when Michael Portillo lost his seat to Stephen Twigg but I was far more upset by the loss of David Hunt's seat and Tony Newton's. Given that I was hoping Michael Portillo might be a candidate for the leadership election, that may seem an odd reaction but I sensed that whereas he was young and ambitious enough to start again, the others would almost certainly call it a day. I also thought them more vulnerable, more likely to be devastated, which in view of what happened to Portillo now seems ironic. Gillian Shephard held on by a whisker and Michael Howard survived in Folkestone.

Later people were to ask me if I would still have made my speech against Michael had we won the election but that was the less difficult question, the answer being a resounding yes. The question I have never settled in my own mind is what I would have done had one of us survived the election and the other lost, for if I had held Maidstone and Michael lost Folkestone then any such attack would have appeared as kicking a man when he was down while if the reverse had happened then it would have looked like sour grapes and, unable to use the medium of Parliament where speeches are recorded in full, I would have had to rely upon the indifferent accuracy of a drama-seeking collection of papers and media programmes.

We both won and I stood upon the bank of a personal Rubicon. The defeat was overwhelming. Blair was returned with a record 179 overall majority. Forecasts were being made of our being out of office for decades and the party which limped back to Westminster was divided, fractious and utterly unfocused. Meanwhile Blair made a triumphalist entry to Downing Street and the country was in the grip of wild euphoria, such as it probably had last experienced at the end of the war. I made a more distant comparison and looked back three centuries before to the Restoration and the scenes of wild rejoicing which had greeted the returning King. Whichever comparison one chose, there was the inevitability of future disillusionment but the Conservative Party, mesmerised by the scale of the defeat, seemed unable to concentrate on preparing for that day.

In truth we had a good record. We left behind the lowest interest rates, inflation and unemployment rates for thirty years and, above all, we had won the agenda: Blair not only accepted that he would not re-nationalise that which we had privatised but he actually implemented his own programme of further privatisation. In short, he took our programme forward, along with promises not to return to the old Labour record of high tax and high spending. New Labour had turned its back on socialism and Clause Four.

There can be few triumphs more complete than to oblige your political opponents to adopt your political agenda but the party was in too great a state of panic to notice. The electorate would never come back to us unless we changed, was the common wisdom and we must ape Blair and turn everything we believed upon its head.

In vain did I point out that our position was very different from Blair's. He had been responding to a complete rejection by the electorate of the socialist agenda and addressing the problems of a party which had been out of office for four terms. By contrast we had comprehensively won the agenda and had the problems of a party which had been in office too long. They were different positions from which to plan the future. We should treat the defeat as Churchill had treated Dunkirk: hugely serious but a long way from decisive.

It was an approach which went down well in the country but

produced no response at Westminster where successive leaders urged us not to talk about the past. 'Concede and Move On' was William Hague's famous mantra. Conceding that all was failure meant naturally enough that the myth grew that the Conservative years had been a disaster, a phenomenon which baffled some very envious European politicians.

No party can afford to live in the past and tomorrow is always more important than yesterday but ignoring achievement altogether and then asking the electorate to trust you with the future is rather like applying for a job with a blank sheet where the qualifications should be listed. My own speeches were, like all Gaul, divided into three parts: what we had done, what Labour was doing, what we would do when returned to power.

Meanwhile our coffers were all but empty as a result of having to fight a general election and the result hardly augured well for attracting donations. We were demoralised, in disarray and leaderless. The last of these was the first of the problems we must address. John Major had immediately announced his resignation and the candidates who appeared to be emerging to succeed him were: Peter Lilley, John Redwood, Ken Clarke, William Hague, Stephen Dorrell and Michael Howard. Of these Ken, who had been Chancellor, Home Secretary, Health Secretary and Education Secretary had the greatest stature while William Hague, young and still more famous for his party conference address when he was sixteen than for his policies while in office, seemed to represent the future rather than the past.

It remains my view that if Ken, well-known, calm, likeable and determined had taken us through that first term in Opposition and William had come into his own later, then the history of our party might have been a vastly more reassuring one. Instead we wasted the talents of both men, either of whom could have been successful as prime minister.

I have often been asked why I so consistently seem to back the loser in leadership elections. The answer is simple enough: I back whomever I want to win rather than the person I think most likely to win and in 1997 I certainly would not have placed any bets on Peter Lilley but of the candidates available he seemed to combine ability with loyalty and to be closest to me in political thought. However I went to see him at a very early stage and told him that I intended to launch a major attack on Michael Howard. Therefore, I said I would not be joining his campaign as I expected colleagues to hate what I was doing – the tradition at Westminster is not to attack your own side – and it might damage him. I maintained the same line when later Gillian Shephard asked me to help him but that did not stop David Willetts briefing the press that I had been thrown off the Lilley team.

My decision to speak out after the election when I could no longer damage Major had been taken months before. I had used some of my time in the Home Office to trawl through documents which I would never have seen had I left in October 1995 and I had seemingly innocent conversations with those who remembered events. I confided my intentions to the same handful of people who knew the extent of my disagreement with Michael over the Lewis sacking.

Nobody calling himself my friend wanted me to do it but it was a source close to Michael who warned me what the likely defence would be. 'They will say you fell for Derek.' I laughed at the improbability of it but had the foresight to relay the conversation to David Amess, a rare example of an outspoken but still utterly discreet MP who, in all the time I have known him, has never betrayed a confidence. I asked him to remember it for future reference.

On Saturday, 10 May, I was in my constituency cottage when David Alton rang and asked me if I was still minded to speak about the matter. I said yes but had not yet decided what mechanism to use. At that stage I had in mind an open letter to John Major and had begun to compose it but he was distancing himself from leadership and it seemed likely that he would merely say it was a matter for his successor. There was a possibility of a personal statement but that is usually made only by those resigning or correcting a statement they have made to the House. I suspected the Speaker would not agree. It looked as if I would have to intervene in a debate but I would still need the Speaker's agreement that I could address matters not covered by whatever the motion was. Of the three options the open letter still seemed the course to offer me the most control over length and fullness.

Five minutes later Michael Preston of the *Sunday Times* rang me. I told him that, yes, it was true that I intended to question Michael's conduct publicly but indicated that this would probably be through a letter to John Major. In the course of our conversation I used the expression I had already tried on a few unsuspecting individuals, *something of the night,* and which had always produced the reaction that people understood just what I meant. Today people often ask me what I meant but then they did not have to.

Next day the expression took off everywhere except in the *Sunday Times* headline which said that I had called him dangerous.

A few minutes after I had put the phone down from this conversation, Rachel Whetstone rang. I was still deciding how to deal with making my concerns known and had not spoken to Michael, as I would have done had I finished the letter and decided to post it. Now he had found out from the press instead of me and that is the only aspect of the affair about which I have any regrets.

I told Rachel that no, it was not true that I had yet written to John Major but yes, I had serious concerns. The latter could hardly have provided her with any great surprise.

On Monday the first of the Dracula-style cartoons, which were to dominate that week and which now adorn my walls on Dartmoor, appeared with one in the *Express* depicting Michael and me in a graveyard, he as Dracula, I as Frankenstein. In the same edition, Sandra Howard gave an interview in her husband's defence. I deployed my line that the sacking of Lewis had been 'unjustly conceived, brutally executed and dubiously defended'. Naturally enough the media homed in on the last and began a frenzy of speculation that Michael had lied to the House although I steadfastly refused their enquirers anything more dramatic than 'unsustainable statements'.

Alastair Goodlad, the Chief Whip, called me in to say I must leave the front bench if I went ahead. I said that it was news to me that I was on the front bench, no appointments having been made pending the outcome of the leadership election. Significantly, he did not try to dissuade me from my course of action. Indeed I found that throughout that week I was being quietly supported by various senior members of the party who came up to me and sympathised. In some cases it may have been because they were hoping the attack would damage an opponent of their chosen candidate but in others they had their own experiences to relate. I found the same phenomenon at that year's party conference where, instead of being shunned or challenged, I received congratulations.

I discarded the option of the open letter and Betty Boothroyd rejected, predictably, the option of a personal statement, but she agreed I could intervene in the Home Affairs Debate set for Monday, 19 May and that she would not accept any points of order that my remarks would be too wide of the subject in hand.

Monday 12th was frantic and my secretary, Harriet Potter, did little but take calls from the media. We both expected the next day to afford some relief as I was due to go to Scotland to take part in a television programme on image. We would tell the press that I was unavailable. That calming prospect was blown apart by the Howard camp which made a miscalculation of gigantic proportions.

I arrived at Westminster with a small suitcase and time to spare before departing to the station. I flipped through the papers and saw the *Daily Mail*. Under the headline 'The Wooing that Won Widdecombe' Paul Eastham alleged that Derek Lewis had wooed me with chocolates, bouquets and private dinners and that it was one of the most 'unusual professional alliances Whitehall had ever seen'. Then he quoted 'an insider' as saying, 'I think she fell in love with him. He flattered her vanity. He sent her flowers and took her to dinner. I don't think she was used to that, poor girl.' I never did go to Scotland.

I asked David Amess if he remembered how I had told him this was to be their line all those months ago and he did. I tried unsuccessfully to contact Derek for several hours before he picked up the message. Meanwhile I set out the facts for a press that could hardly believe its luck.

I had arrived in the Home Office in July and had been absent all August. The dismissal took place in the first half of October. In the whole of that time there had been not a petal of a flower nor crumb of a dinner and no friend would ever give me chocolates because they would be too concerned for my girth. The only flowers had been from me to Mrs Lewis after her husband's dismissal, for which 'kindly Christian gesture' I had been rebuked by Michael. Indeed when he did offer me dinner as a thank you for my efforts after he had left, I was very uncertain how the occasion would turn out because I did not know Derek at all socially. Those were the facts. Many months later he and his wife sent me a bunch of flowers when he learned I was ill at home with bad flu and I had once joined his family for dinner at their home in Essex. Where was the wooing in that?

Feminist journalists, who normally hated me for my stand on abortion, women priests and the shackling incident spat fur and feathers at the sneering claim 'she wasn't used to that, poor girl'. So a disagreement always meant a woman was emotionally involved, did it? If you were overweight and unbothered with appearance, it made you a sad old spinster, did it? As Allison Pearson put it, a man may be impressed but a woman is seduced. From my point of view the hint of immorality was enough. I would never have become involved with a married man and I was insulted to the core while still seeing the funny side of what was becoming absurd.

As I put it at the time, if I was in love with Derek, then I was in love with half the world. I hated injustice, hated brutality and hated the crude exercise of power and could grow angry and upset when confronted with them. I had stood up for many a constituent with equal vigour. Was I in love with John Jones, whom I had never even met, when I went all the way to Morocco at my own expense to try to secure his release?

After that, it was mortal combat. I began to receive letters and calls accusing Michael of other misdeeds but I resolutely refused to include any such material in my attack. I would speak only of what I knew about because the smallest inaccuracy would destroy my case. I guessed Michael would be receiving similar communications from my enemies and indeed somebody did try to resurrect my financial problems but he too stuck to the issues in hand, doubtless for the same reason. Neither of us was a fool and we had, in any event, quite enough with which to deal without venturing down byways which could turn into blind alleys.

Derek rang to offer to procure secretarial help but I thought accepting it would be a hostage to fortune and Harriet competently coped with the avalanche which poured on to our desks while my caseworker Charlotte tried to keep the constituency work as normal as possible, as one journalist after another trailed into my office.

My dilemma was to be accessible to them while not giving away my entire speech before it was made. On the night of the *Mail* article Michael and I appeared on Channel Four news and on *Newsnight*. The first went well for him but the second was a huge disaster and did much to assist my case. We were in separate studios and I roared on Jeremy Paxman as fourteen times he asked Michael if he had threatened to overrule Derek and fourteen times he refused to answer. It did more than I could ever have done to persuade the media that Howard was hiding something.

So delighted was I that I put a message on my answering machine saying that for anyone tempted to vote for Michael, Tuesday's *Newsnight* should be compulsory viewing. Jeremy sent me a small box of chocolates with the message 'never mind the girth worries'. Five months later he came to my fiftieth birthday party in the House of Commons. My relations with Paul Eastham naturally turned in the opposite direction and I refused ever to deal with him again, making him unique in my dealings with the press. There are journalists of whom I am wary and to whom I would not accord specific interviews but none other than Eastham with whom I would not deal at all.

Some colleagues urged me to stop. Most of them apologised when, as leader of the party some years later, Howard went on a sacking spree which included the MP Howard Flight, whom he not only expelled from the front bench as a result of an incautious remark about public expenditure but then kicked out of the party altogether, thereby making it impossible for his victim to stand again for Parliament. My phone was hot with colleagues saying 'You were right, Ann'. Two hard-working parliamentary candidates suffered similar fates. Danny Kruger used an academic term 'creative destruction' when talking about the Health Service and Adrian Hilton was accused of anti-Catholic bias in an old article about Europe, published with the consent of the Chief Whip.

Howard just never knew when to stop, always confusing toughness with personal destruction. When I pointed out that so many Catholics had rallied to Adrian's defence he told me I was not a typical Catholic. Quite what Michael knew about Catholicism, I am not sure, given that on one occasion he tried to persuade Cardinal Hume that priests should reveal conversations about IRA activity which they had heard in the confessional!

Meanwhile both Peter Lloyd and Emily Blatch were reported as making comments supportive of my case and Charles Wardle was opening up criticism of Howard on another front as were former members of the Prison Service. Michael appealed to John Major who called me in but, as Alastair Goodlad before him, made no serious attempt to dissuade me. I saw him smile slightly as he told me, 'I will tell Michael you are of fixed purpose,' and wondered if Michael had ever used that phrase to him. He also said he thought the overnight briefing (that I had been wooed by Lewis) a disgrace and that he had told Michael so.

The pressure in the Howard camp was growing and a mole was reporting to Kim Sengupta of the *Independent*. Kim contacted me to say they were 'very scared' that I might have seen the contemporaneous minutes, which gave a rather different impression from the official minutes which Michael had released in the House. Then I met Adrian Jones by accident in the street and he said there was a 'hell of a fuss' about what I might or might not have seen. My private secretaries had been called in by Richard Wilson and interviewed separately. Was anything missing?

Adrian had noticed a handwritten note from Wilson to me

had not been returned but there were no official documents missing. Had I seen the contemporaneous notes? He said he did not know but they were not on file in my office and I had never sought them.

So now I knew the notes existed and indeed when they were eventually published they supported Lewis's case, but I had no right of access to the notes of a meeting I had not attended.

Derek of course also had documents to support his case and I went to Essex to consult his files. Louise Lewis told me with some amusement that the press, expecting that I would do just that, had been massed around the gates but had given up about half an hour before I arrived. Journalists were also very keen to film me putting notification of the matters I was raising through the Howards' letterbox but I refused, preferring to send the details via fax from the Lewis abode.

On Monday, 19 May after a week of escalating speculation, Harriet came to my flat and we printed out a seventeen-page speech on my fax, which was of the old and slow variety. I arrived in the Chamber and saw the press gallery packed to standing-room only and the green benches were themselves fairly full. My stomach was rotating and when Betty called my name I did not want to stand up.

The events of the previous week had confirmed me in my intentions but I was about to destroy a colleague and probably make an outcast of myself for a while to come. The sun shone through a window and illuminated the speech in my hand as I began at 4.41 p.m. and, once started, I forgot all but the importance of getting it right until I sat down at 5.20 p.m., exhausted but relieved.

I was heard in silence and without interruption. I paid tribute to Michael's achievements in the Home Office, then turned to the nation's perception of Parliament as being full of people concerned with their own interests and their own survival, that it was viewed as 'devoid of honour and a sense of service' claiming that there was an urgent necessity to counter that view.

When I began upon my specific analysis of the events of which I was complaining I pointed out that it was unjust to reject from

325

others defences which we regularly mounted for ourselves; that ministers who were criticised in independent reports often did not resign. 'If a party can go to the country and urge that its occasional disasters, however monumental, be overlooked on the basis of its otherwise truly magnificent achievements, it cannot in honour deny that same defence to others.'

I then set out Derek's record – which Howard had never denied but simply discounted – also stating that a report had specifically exonerated Lewis of any blame for the Whitemoor escape.

I next criticised the methodology of the Learmont Report. When appearing before the Select Committee, Learmont had revealed the embarrassing fact that he had no idea how escapes were calculated. He made a large number of recommendations relating to Prison Service HQ and then admitted that he had never visited the headquarters.

I went on to say that, having been successfully sued for unfair dismissal we had to pay £220,000 in compensation plus costs of £41,000 plus our own costs for all of which the taxpayer got nothing in return.

And did we eliminate disasters in the Prison Service? I referred to the release of 541 prisoners too early and, to laughter, said, 'They did not even have to break out.'

Having finished with querying the justice of the decision I then examined the execution of it, stating that on two occasions the DG had been refused the chance to discuss the basis upon which he was being dismissed. Despite the production of a comprehensive defence, which even Michael had described as 'persuasive and impressive', the interview lasted less than twenty minutes and a subsequent attempt lasted twelve minutes.

Next I looked at the question which was the one engaging most of the press and media. Had the House been misled? In the 1995 censure debate Michael had specifically denied 'that I personally told Mr Lewis that the governor of Parkhurst should be suspended immediately'. I then quoted the evidence I had seen and heard to the contrary but also referred to Michael's own admission on *Newsnight* that he had given Derek Lewis the 'benefit of my opinion in strong language'. I also detailed the nonsense of any claim that as Michael had assured the House 'there was no question of overruling the Director General'.

I detailed some instances where, in different matters, corrections had not been made to statements which were later seen as misleading. I condemned 'semantic prestidigitation'. My peroration said that courage and toughness were more than instant law and instant dismissal and that we demeaned our high office if we mistreated public servants.

The following day the press was overwhelmingly favourable and I knew my job had been done. Michael came last in the first ballot and I sent Lewis a pager message: *Mission Accomplished*.

The anger of eighteen months drained away from me and I began to consider what I should now do with the rest of my time in Parliament as I found myself an Opposition backbencher but there was to be a curious postscript to my speech.

That summer I picked up the Hansard report and noted that some significant pieces of my speech had been changed. I wrote in surprise to Ian Church, the editor, pointing out that I had supplied an exact transcript and that, the House being silent, the tape was very clear.

First, the words 'the minutes showed' had been inserted before something which the minutes had not shown and I was indeed complaining that the minutes were not complete. My sarcastic comment that the Home Secretary had an 'exquisite way' with words had been changed to a 'persuasive way' with words and, most important of all, the 'Home Secretary wanted suspension' had been changed to 'The Home Office wanted suspension'.

A baffled editor replied that each complaint was fully justified and that he was at a loss to explain why. However what he could promise was that the bound volume would contain the right version. I went to see him and, after some puzzled discussion, asked him a question with my eyes. No, he said, the reporter had not been 'nobbled'.

Church then sent me a proof of what would be in the bound version and I approved it as accurate. In time the bound version appeared and was correct. Two years later I discovered that there were *two* bound versions, one called 1996–7 and one 1997–8. Inevitably people would look in the latter and that contained the old and inaccurate version. What, I demanded, on earth was going on?

In his reply a beleaguered Ian Church said, 'You ask, with justification, what on earth has been happening. This disastrous sequence of events beggars belief and is unparalleled in my experience.'

The upshot was the printing of a third edition with both correct year and correct version of my speech. Humph. Fortunately I have never been much of a conspiracy theorist.

Chapter Twenty-Three

HAGUE'S LIEUTENANT

Idid not back Hague in the final leadership ballot, believing, as
I was to later say of Cameron, that it was too soon, that he had
not the experience, that he was too little known and therefore
could be portrayed in whatever light the media chose. Ken, I
thought, would be a more reassuring figure but the party was as
ever obsessed by Europe and not even a coalition of Clarke and
Redwood could persuade it otherwise.

When people ask me what I noticed most about the switch to
Opposition, I surprise them by saying that the pricking behind
my eyelids disappeared. I had endured six and a half years of
late nights, early mornings, red boxes and detailed legislation.
Suddenly I could go to bed and rise at seasonal hours. I began to
feel rested, healthier and fitter. I had time to stand and stare, as
the poet puts it.

In his recent biography, *Last Man Standing,* Jack Straw writes
that his first two opponents as Shadow Home Secretary, Norman
Fowler and Brian Mawhinney, did not have their hearts in the
job and that it showed. The reasons he adduces are that they
had both been in the Cabinet and both knew they would have
retired before the next Conservative government was elected.
He then says I was different, a terrier from the outset.

I make a slightly different analysis, which is that by virtue
of being consigned to the backbenches I lost the habits of government almost overnight. Going from office to shadow office
means you can continue thinking in the same way, which is to
say you think responsibly, understanding the difficulties posed,
considering a great deal of detail, remembering past attempts,
rehearsing arguments you would need to make to persuade the
Exchequer or the colleague in a different department.

Opposition, by contrast, is by its very nature irresponsible. One calls for what the nation wants rather than what it can reasonably expect, castigates mistakes however understandable they may be and generally gives the impression that governments can deliver wonders and miracles if only they wanted to. The longer a party is out of power the more detached it grows from the reality of day-to-day government which is why the Blair administration found itself rowing back from so many of its promises. It took Jack Straw less than five minutes to realise that abandoning private prisons was not a sensible way forward, despite his promises to the Prison Officers' Association (POA).

I left office and left the habits of government behind. I still had friends in various departments and began by finding stories and then briefing the press but the press was still in Blair mode, believing it had entered some brave new world and it was still difficult a year later when I became Shadow Health Secretary to persuade even the Press Association to accept individual stories.

There were however plenty of opportunities within Parliament itself and I could now enjoy, for the first time, attacking a smug Prime Minister from the freedom of the backbenches. He had decided, quite arbitrarily and with none of the usual courtesies, to move Prime Minister's Questions from two days a week to one day. It was a perfectly rational decision as far too much time is spent preparing for this circus but it was done in so highhanded a fashion that it gave a powerful warning of the way Blair was to sideline Parliament throughout his term of office.

In November of that year I had my most successful foray against Blair when Patrick McLoughlin told me that Planet Hollywood, which had just given a million pounds to Labour, was paying its workers £2.98 an hour, which was below Labour's much trumpeted minimum wage. As the PM was then suffering the scandal of having exempted another big donor, Formula One, from a piece of legislation I asked if he would assure the House that Planet Hollywood would not be exempt from the minimum wage.

My interventions began to draw favourable press comment and my name to appear in reshuffle speculation but I had plenty to occupy me with the Standards and Privileges Committee in the months that followed the general election.

This once powerful and highly respected body used to be composed of very senior members with long experience of the House and whose careers were behind them so that they had to please nobody. Now, at a time when it was vital to restore Parliament's reputation after a series of sleaze scandals, it was peopled by newcomers who had just been elected. That was how seriously Blair did not take the immense task in hand.

The inexperience showed from the start but that was not the main problem, which was that the committee simply lacked the power to deal with anything much more than failing to make an entry in the register. That year we were facing the complexities of the Neil Hamilton case, in which the former MP stood accused of accepting bribes from Mohamed Al Fayed, the owner of Harrods, in brown envelopes. The Commissioner for Standards had found him guilty but Neil wished to dispute some of his findings.

We were not allowed to examine witnesses, we were not allowed to question Neil himself and there was no appellate function. So we had to listen to him address us for two and a half hours without being able to ask a single question. Farce is an inadequate word to describe such proceedings.

I refused to reach any verdict. It was, it seemed, impossible to determine guilt or innocence and I would not support any report which attempted to do so. However, there is a strong tradition that such committees provide unanimous reports so Dale Campbell-Savours, one of its few senior members, worked hard to produce a neutral verdict which read: 'the committee could neither add to nor subtract from the Commissioner's earlier report'.

The Labour chairman reported this as accepting the Commissioner's report in full and I wanted no more to do with such stupidity and lack of natural justice. As I was not allowed to ask questions, I could reach no verdict and if other people thought this a reasonable way of proceeding then they could proceed without me. This time I did resign.

The Register of Interests has itself become a nonsense. It was set up with the laudable aim of transparency. MPs were required to declare any remuneration or appointments which might reasonably be expected to influence their votes or speeches. It then grew until we were having to register any payment, no matter how unlikely to influence anything at all. What was my appearing with Basil Brush likely to influence? I demanded of the then registrar Elizabeth Filkin. My stand on hunting? It then grew again until we had to register every bunch of flowers we received after giving a speech or opening a building. My entry would resemble the botanical gardens, I told the House of Commons.

The gap left by my resignation was filled by hunting. Tony Blair had promised a free vote followed by legislation if Parliament voted to abolish hunting, a promise he was to make several times before unwillingly delivering the law. Mike Foster, a Labour MP, had secured a place in the private members' ballot that year and had put forward the Wild Mammals (Hunting with Dogs) Bill. I decided to speak in the debate on second reading.

As I sat there taking notes, I did not think my speech was going to be particularly memorable but when I sat down it was to the unusual accolade of clapping (from the Labour side), quickly squashed by the Speaker. The speech went on to win me a 'Straight Talker of the Year Award' from Talk Radio and was played much in the media over the next few days.

I come from a hunting family. My mother used to walk to otter hounds and I grew up with the head of one poor beast decorating the wall, while my father rode to foxhounds in his youth as did my grandfather throughout his life. My only cheerful memories of that otter's head came from my father one day putting a cigarette in its mouth in order to frighten the vicar. My parents abandoned any defence of otter hunting after Gavin Maxwell's *Ring of Bright Water* was made into a successful film which we all went to see. I say, Spielberg, perhaps somebody needs to do the same for foxes?

I do not object to killing foxes, which can indeed be menaces to farmers, but I strongly object to the chase whereby an animal runs for its life with the hounds getting closer and closer. It is barbarous that such an activity should be regarded as a sport.

However sometimes cruelty is necessary and one might reluctantly accept it if there really was no other way but the fact is that over 90 per cent of fox destruction is *not* achieved by hunting. In other words if it is a pesticide it is a highly inefficient one.

Much was made in the debate of the impact on rural employment but as I pointed out in my speech crime keeps the police in work and ill health keeps the doctors and nurses in work but nobody would deploy that as an argument for maintaining crime and ill health. If hunting is both cruel and unnecessary then it is wrong and the fact that people make their living from unnecessary cruelty is not an argument for keeping it.

Some MPs argued that banning hunting would mean all the hounds being put down, ignoring both the inevitable growth there would be in drag hunting and the inconvenient fact that one does not tend in any event to see geriatric hounds out hunting.

There were few who agreed with me on our side but that did not worry me and I was delighted to be asked to serve on the committee. The Bill followed the path of all contentious private members' bills and ran out of time but being back as part of a campaign invigorated me.

John Major rang me up one morning upon another matter and asked me if I had seen Peter Oborne's piece in that day's *Express*. I had not. Although I did not say so I was not even out of bed. After years of early mornings and late nights the backbenches had given me the occasional lie-in. Indeed when Oliver Letwin was robbed at five in the morning the reaction of most colleagues was 'Poor Oliver!' while mine was 'Thank God I no longer have to be up at 5 a.m.!'

John told me Peter had written that if Howard was the major block to my entering the Shadow Cabinet, then Hague should ignore him. And if he threatened to resign then he should be allowed to resign. I was too good to be overlooked. I had no evidence whatever that Michael was an active obstacle to any promotion but the tone of Peter's article began to appear in other speculative pieces and I was asked informally if I would have any objection to working with Michael. I had none. After all, I had worked with him for eighteen long months. If he had any objection to my arrival at the Shadow Cabinet table he must have swallowed it and bowed to the inevitable.

William summoned me to Conservative Central Office and offered me the post of Shadow Health Secretary and thus began my three happiest years in Parliament. I had never before had so much scope to devise policy, having always been in subordinate roles. Now I had my own team and could decide the terms of attack.

My opponent was Frank Dobson, a left-wing ideologue. His next in command was Alan Milburn, a Blairite, and if he had been at the helm, Labour health policy might have taken a very different turn. Dobson hated the private sector and hated any-thing the Conservatives had done on principle. While Jack Straw entered the Home Office, took stock and quietly dropped a few promises in the light of the reality of governance, Frank entered the Health department blinkered by Labour rhetoric.

The first casualty was GP fundholding, a successful initiative at first resisted by the medical profession but which proved itself so well that by the time we left office 60 per cent of all GPs were either fundholders or had outstanding applications to become so. Effectively it put GPs in charge so they could decide where to send a patient for treatment instead of being forced to use a particular hospital. The result was to raise hospital standards and suddenly patients found they were no longer expected to wait four hours as a result of block bookings while cancellations could mean the patient went elsewhere. Some GPs spent their funds on providing minor surgery so that patients did not need to go to hospital at all.

With Labour regarding this as introducing market forces into the Health Service, Dobson put into effect the promise of aboli-tion but Blair was obliged to U-turn some years later, saving face by calling it 'GP Commissioning'.

Dobson seemed also to believe that Labour really could pro-duce a perfect Health Service and was quite affronted when I asked him why waiting lists were rising.

I began with a very different assumption: that the NHS, then celebrating fifty years of existence, had never been able and never would be able to meet every last demand that was made upon it. We had rationing from the very start but no government would face the use of the word and successive ones pretended that somehow the NHS could do everything.

The first rationing was introduced by Nye Bevan himself when he lamented the 'cascades of medicine pouring down British throats'. Thus prescription charges were born. Furthermore the NHS was conceived on the false principle that as we all got healthier demand would decline whereas the explosion of medical science over the past sixty years has sent demand soaring towards infinity. Before hip-replacement surgery was developed there was no queue for hip replacements.

Rationing is now fiercer than ever. The private sector rations by price and the public sector by queue. The National Institute for Clinical Excellence may enjoy the acronym NICE but as I said at the time of its introduction by the Blair administration it is actually rather nasty, for its role is to ration not just by efficacy but by price. I vividly remember a woman at a public meeting telling me that the only reason she could still see was because she could afford to, having bought Lucentis which NICE was still then prohibiting to NHS patients. Yet it is de rigueur to pretend that the NHS will look after you in every instance, for nothing, when calamity strikes.

Many other Western countries have fewer problems but even the most cursory examination of their health models shows that they spend vastly more and that the difference is not public but private money because they simply charge, some for visits to the doctor, others for the first week's stay in hospital, others for 'hotel' charges in hospitals etc. Only Spain has our system of automatic free prescriptions for pensioners. In yet other countries the income of children is taken into account when assessing the costs of care for the elderly. In each case the poorest get help but often have to find the money first and then claim it back.

I looked at it all carefully but did not like the idea of an extensive system of charging which would probably deter those just above the threshold for help from using an essential service and

I dismissed the idea of 'hotel' charges which would be complex to administer and probably cost as much in bureaucracy. Instead I preferred to look at expanding people's contribution to their own health via insurance and the scheme I based my ideas upon was the pension system.

In those happy days before the Gordon Brown pensions raid wrecked the system, our occupational pensions scheme was the best in the world and it was based on a partnership: the employer paid contributions as did the employee and the State then provided tax relief. The result was that growing numbers of people did not have to look to the State to fund their old age and were enjoying levels of income which the State could never have provided.

If, however, an employer wished to provide a private health scheme for employees not only would the State not help but it would classify the scheme as a benefit in kind, tax the employee as if it were cash income, levy National Insurance contributions on the same basis for both employer and employee and provide no tax relief to the schemes. In short, the State discouraged independent health provision.

I wanted to look at the possibility of doing with health what we did with pensions and I wanted to break down the Berlin Wall between the private and public sectors so that if the latter were overrun we could pay the private sector to help. Indeed, why not an NHS Nuffield Hospital with separate wings and shared facilities so that the private sector could contribute to costs?

That then was the essence of my speech to the 1998 Conservative Party Conference at Bournemouth, although it was remembered less for its content than its style of delivery. Later it was unlikely that I would have got away with either but at that early stage when we were still settling down into Opposition and had yet to devise mechanisms for collective agreement, party conference speeches were more or less down to the Shadow Secretary of State.

I tore up the guidelines which said we should not dwell on our achievements of the past and made sure that my introductory comments reminded everybody of the huge increase in operations, doctors, nurses and hospitals over which we had presided. Why concede a myth that we had been cost-cutting and uncaring?

Those were not the only guidelines I tore up but the others were not written down; they were the product of evolution and custom and I drove a coach and horses through them with all the respect of a revolutionary intent on reaching the Bastille.

Until then the major speeches were delivered by the Secretary of State or, when in Opposition, the Shadow Secretary, standing at a lectern and reading notes or more latterly an autocue. Below the stage the press and media massed in front of the lectern, cameras focused. I had watched such performances each year since 1975 and the format had never varied. I had also spent much of my youth and early adulthood watching powerful evangelists rousing audiences, never using notes, pacing the platform, declaiming uncompromising messages with passion and conviction. It was the method I preferred.

Michael Ancram, who succeeded Cecil Parkinson as Party Chairman, looked fit to lay an egg when he found out what I was intending to do. Supposing I dried up or forgot a vital announcement? Or supposing I muddled up a sentence and a policy with it? Only the technical manager was on my side, foreseeing something new and different.

As I went out on to the stage I did have a moment's doubt. Was this really such a good idea? Then I launched into my speech, alternately reasoning and haranguing, joking and accusing. As I did so I moved about causing havoc among the media who began falling over their leads and equipment as they desperately swung the cameras to follow. I began to enjoy myself too much and ran seriously over my allotted time, then, as I finished, I watched the conference come to its feet in one spontaneous movement.

That was my greatest reward, by which I do not mean that I merely liked the applause which rang to the rafters but rather that I drew such huge satisfaction from that reaction. It is difficult now to remember just how crushed and demoralised the party was in 1997. It blamed its MPs, not altogether unfairly, for ruining its electoral chances through divisions and infighting and for turning a defeat into a rout. Its workers, who were fed up with the officers brawling in the mess while the troops stood at action stations in the country, hardly approached the conference in an upbeat mood. Their expressions as they stood cheering and clapping, hopeful at last, made the effort more than its own reward.

William had been standing off stage waiting to come on with Cecil Parkinson, whose time I had stolen. He was euphoric and waved away my apology for overrunning, while Cecil was grinning from ear to ear. My team was loving every moment, especially Graeme Tennyson, who had been so instrumental in writing the speech.

It was a good team which worked well together. I had at first been uncertain about Alan Duncan, my second in command, who had flirted with legalising soft drugs and who had given William disastrous advice about being photographed whooshing down a slide in a baseball cap and appearing at the Notting Hill Carnival. It gave the leader not a modern but a trivial image. I also guessed that as he was so close to William he had been put there to keep an eye on me, the Westminster oddball who was so unaccountably popular in the country.

Alan was intellectually formidable and unafraid to challenge prevailing thought. His was an invaluable input. He called me Matron and teased me but loved the scope I gave him as I delegated freely. The third member of the team was Philip Hammond of whom I wrote that he must surely one day be Chancellor of the Exchequer, a prediction to which I still adhere.

It was he who spotted early the sleight of hand which Labour was about to produce in the budget. I did not believe him but he was right and I wished I had listened.

If one year you are spending ten thousand pounds, the next twenty thousand and the third year thirty thousand then you have achieved a rise of twenty thousand over three years. At least that was the way government spending had always been calculated until now. But, in the world of Blairite spin you have achieved a rise of forty thousand because you have to spend the extra ten thousand from year 2 again in year 3. So, if in year 4 you spend another ten you have reached not forty thousand but sixty thousand because you have spent the extra from years 2 and 3 again and so on. The dishonesty was staggering as was the claim that the NHS would have 7,000 extra doctors when it transpired that the 'extra' included every medical student from year one onwards already studying because these had not yet graduated and so would be 'extra'.

No wonder I had thought Philip misguided to consider they would do anything so blatant, but they did. The next day most of the serious commentators had rumbled them but meanwhile the headlines were taking what ministers had proclaimed at face value and by the time disillusionment set in the nation was no longer preoccupied with the detail.

The incident caused a major row between Adam Boulton, the Sky commentator, and me, when he adamantly refused to let me explain the facts on air, despite my having in my hand the Chancellor's own figures, which showed in black and white the true level of any rise, which did not even exceed some of those we had implemented.

No government could have got away with that in normal circumstances but there was nothing normal about the situation we were in. The most dishonest, lying, manipulative government in my lifetime did as it pleased and the nation lapped it up uncritically. If we tried to explain what was really happening we were treated as irritating children who should be told to go away and shut up. We had been ejected after eighteen years and nobody wanted to hear from us.

That was how Gordon Brown wrecked the pension system without so much as a squeak from the public, which went on voting Labour back into office in 2001 and 2005 and then suddenly realised that its old age was not going to be as prosperous as it had been taught to hope. No wonder Brown got away with it. ACT relief? Oh, of course, at the Pig and Whistle they talk about nothing other than Advance Corporation Tax.

Here was a stealth tax to end all stealth taxes and what should really hurt those affected is that it was all so unnecessary.

Previous governments, even under serious economic pressure, left the pension funds strictly alone. James Callaghan watched Britain's cheques bouncing and the IMF virtually taking over our affairs and left the pensions alone. John Major, faced with a bill of some £24 billion for the ERM collapse, left the pensions alone. Everybody understood the inevitable results of taking money from the funds for the nation's old age and if pensions collapsed or lost their value it would fall to government to keep people in their retirement. Elementary, Dear Gordon.

Gordon Brown did not need the money. He had inherited a golden economic legacy in which we had overcome the difficulties post ERM at the cost of some difficult decisions. It had hurt but it had also worked. Yet he still, in the full knowledge of what would happen, took tax relief away from pension funds so that there was less to invest and therefore less growth. He cared not a whit, probably because he thought he was unlikely still to be there when the results became manifest.

The Conservative Party was hardly silent. We devoted Opposition debates to the subject, raised the issue at Question Times and briefed all the editors. We were greeted with indifference and yawns. ACT relief? People drawing pensions in twenty years' time? Where was the drama? Although specialist commentators did understand and some editors gave us space, they soon moved on to other more immediate matters while we yelled in anguish from the sidelines.

'We didn't understand' has been the response when I point out to audiences that anyone who voted Labour in 2001 or 2005 voted for the demise of their own pensions. 'No,' I always counter. 'You did not listen.'

Politicians are often accused of not listening, but it is equally a charge we can level at the public who seem to think it will be all right on the night and that, if it isn't, then it is our fault. How about their own responsibility to inform themselves properly before casting their vote? How about flying pigs?

Some votes are indeed cast after much thoughtful analysis but too many are the results of prejudice, upbringing, resentment and the simple absorption of image and mantras. It is no good lamenting this as it will always be so in any democracy and politicians play the same game, but the pensions crisis never fails to bring my irritation with it to the fore. That crisis did not have to happen. Why, oh why, did nobody *listen*?

There was, however, a willingness to listen to arguments over the NHS. The electorate is a very long way from stupid and most people knew well that the NHS could never do everything, even if wanting to believe that it could. After my conference speech I was invited by Jonathan Dimbleby to appear on his Sunday lunchtime programme. It was fifty minutes long and involved an interview with just one politician, leaving plenty of time to examine the issues properly rather than in soundbite form. There was an audience of Health Service workers from whom I expected a rough ride but instead there was a genuinely thoughtful and open discussion. In 1998 they too knew that what had served us well enough in the second half of that century was unlikely to survive the next. After all, they lived daily with the strain.

It was the most sensible interview I have ever had. Dimbleby was thorough and persistent but he had time to unpeel the onion (his words) and we both had time to enlarge upon issues or to return to them with qualifications or supplementary questions on his part and information or clarification on mine. The atmosphere was exploratory rather than confrontational. The audience had time to respond as well as query. It was by no means an easy fifty minutes but I enjoyed the experience immensely.

'You played a blinder,' said a very happy Michael Ancram. No, I merely had a sensible interviewer who enabled me to discuss rather than dig in and defend a position.

'The Tories have begun to think,' observed Peter Riddell of *The Times* after my conference speech. Indeed, because at that stage thought was not rationed in favour of entrenchment.

Alas! Such interviews have now all but disappeared from mainstream TV channels. The public is accredited with the attention span of a newt and discussion is tailored accordingly. I was to try with no success whatever to counter that tendency in my own later television programmes, knowing full well that the public deserves better than such patronising infantilism.

Earlier that year I had made my first set of programmes in a series called *Nothing But the Truth*. Until then I had appeared in a number of one-off programmes and had been the subject of documentaries but now I effectively had my own programme. The format was a court-room style debate in which two real-life barristers, Michael Topolski and Jerome Lynch, debated a topic and a jury composed of members of the public voted. I was the judge, impartial and keeping order. I loved it and rather hoped for another series but sadly that did not happen.

I was also writing a regular column for the *Sunday Express*, having been rung up by the editor, Rosie Boycott, and offered a sum much higher than my parliamentary salary to produce weekly comment on subjects of my choice.

Such spare time as was left to me was employed in writing *The Clematis Tree*. I had never entirely given up my ambition to write novels but since entering Parliament had not even managed to produce a short story. That year on the backbenches had produced some of the time necessary and it was now known that I was writing. In 1998 I went to Singapore again and spent each morning with my laptop while Amah's daughter, Moi, was carrying out her nursing shift. The book was growing but so were the demands of being in the Shadow Cabinet. It was finally published in 2000 and became a *Times* bestseller.

The reviews were divided between those who wrote about the book, which were largely favourable or mixed, and those which concentrated on my having written it, which were consistently unfavourable. The subject was a family with a very seriously handicapped child against the background of a euthanasia bill going through Parliament. Despite the people in the book having mixed views, changing views and conflicting emotions, commentators trawled the text for any line which they could ascribe to me. Even Edwina Currie, who should have known better, ascribes to me a sentiment uttered by one of the characters.

Ian Hislop and Professor Jonathan Bate reviewed the book very favourably on television and by the time my fourth novel was published critics were beginning to be positive. I suppose when my next novel comes out I shall have to endure the same process, but this time the image in the critics' minds will be *Strictly Come Dancing* and they will be looking for evidence of a rather vacuous celebrity.

It never ceases to surprise me that the absence of explicit sex in my novels should be such a source of comment. If Jeffrey Archer and Ruth Rendell can sell millions of copies without it and never be asked why it is absent then it manifestly is not an issue for authors at large, but the interest in it simply reflects the preoccupation of the critics with the authorship rather than the work. Even a military historian, asked to read *An Act of Treachery* for historical accuracy, upon discovering that the heroine is pregnant, complained that he calculated when she might have conceived, went back to earlier chapters and could not find the sex! It is wonderfully naïve.

The publication of my first novel, however, was two years into the future as I took on Frank Dobson across the Commons, inveighing against waiting lists and waiting times. I visited hospitals and talked to consultants, nurses, doctors and patients. Over the year I was thus engaged, their attitudes underwent a marked change. At the beginning it was all hostility, the view still prevailing that everything which had gone wrong with the NHS was down to the mean Conservatives but when it became apparent that there was no magic wand, that if there had been then any government would have waved it, that demand would always grow and problems always persist, that the Treasury would never have unlimited resources and humans would always be fallible there was a measurable thaw and a greater willingness to seek out different ways of approaching the issues.

Sadly, I have to say that the description which I then gave of the NHS still prevails in that it is a three-tier one. On the top tier are those who get first-class NHS treatment or who choose, quite voluntarily, to use the private sector. On the next tier are those who do not receive a good NHS response, either because the treatment is not available or is available but too far away or the lists are too long or there is postcode prescribing. Those on this tier may not choose to use the private sector but they can, even if at great sacrifice. On the third tier are those who do not get their NHS treatment and if they starved themselves for six months still could not afford the private sector. They are utterly dispossessed and yet are the very people whom the system was set up to help.

It will take political courage to face up to asking those who can to begin contributing towards their own health care. I did, but that was not long after an election we had comprehensively lost and years before the next, which nobody expected us to win. Theory is easy but it takes government to deliver and the courage simply is not there.

I was discovering the limitations of help as my father began to decline in both mental and physical health. He was then eighty-eight and was moving from a man who did the *Telegraph* crossword every day to one who, suffering from cataracts he would not have treated, got up, sat in a chair and did little else before retiring to bed. My mother got rid of the car because she was terrified that he might try driving but that left her, though perfectly fit and enthusiastic, less mobile than before. He could not be left alone and so Mother became increasingly confined to the house, leaving it only when a friend could take her place.

Naturally I sought help and a carer was supplied once a week but my father simply would not cooperate with him. I knew his naval mentality well and that he would respond only to authority and asked the caring service to send someone with a white coat and stethoscope but that was outside the rules and they refused. Nor would they try to insist upon washing and eating because it was 'his right' not to. In the end the carer was doing no more than giving my mother some company.

Then one night my father had a bad fall. The telephone was out of order despite my having three times contacted British Telecom and it was the middle of the night. Mother went to the front door and called but nobody heard. Alerted by a neighbour the next day, I drove at speed to Haslemere and told the doctor bluntly he must insist on hospital. My father would listen to him just because he was the doctor and he would listen to the hospital medical staff in a way that he would not do to us or the carer. The doctor agreed but when the ambulance turned up, Dad tried refusing to go and predictably the paramedics began reciting his right to do so.

'Get a stretcher,' I demanded wearily.

'No, I can walk,' rebelled my father and that was how we got him to hospital. I would not go in the ambulance because I was aware that if I did he might be examined and sent home but that if he was there on his own they would have no choice but to admit him. It hurt leaving him to be driven off alone.

'Give it a few days,' I told Mother. 'They will bath him, make him eat and you can rest and if there is any damage from the fall they will find it.' Meanwhile we would visit each day and I took time off from Westminster.

Once back there, my mobile was never off, not even in Shadow Cabinet. My London flat would not accommodate both parents and was on the first floor with no lift so I began house-hunting. My father was transferred to a local Catholic hospital for a week while we put in hand arrangements for home nursing, in which I had no faith as I was sure that whoever came would merely recite the mantra that it was my father's right to starve, dehydrate and refuse the assistance for which we would be paying a fortune.

On Wednesday, 24 February I did not attend Shadow Cabinet but was in Haslemere. We visited my father throughout the day at Holy Cross nursing home and he was well enough to groan in protest when I told him that he was coming home the following Monday to a special chair and a full-time nurse. He did not need either, he snorted.

The doctor looked in while we were still there and gave him some antibiotics because we were all worried about his chest. Then Mother and I went off to a Chinese restaurant being too exhausted to cook. As we arrived home the phone was ringing. Come at once, urged Sister. We did and were beside him when he died.

Of all the condolences I received in the week which followed, by far and away the most memorable was Michael Howard's. Michael had lost his own father much younger than I had and recalled the 'hammer blow'. His was a letter which showed he understood and remembered the impact of death rather than merely being a formal one of commiseration. His mother was still alive and I made myself a promise that when she died I would write to him in the same vein but sadly when that happened, some years later, I missed it and wrote belatedly.

My parents had been married for sixty-two years. They had given me a happy, secure childhood and had been an unfailing support in adult life as they had also been to my brother and his family. They had come through two World Wars, a stillbirth, foreign postings and family separation in the name of Empire and were tough and uncomplaining, hard-working and loyal, loving and humorous. My father was eighty-nine when he died and until the last two years enjoyed gardening and golf, as well as the *Daily Telegraph* crossword puzzle. His memorial service was attended by an admiral representing the Ministry of Defence and we played the sailor's hornpipe but James Murray Widdecombe, CB, OBE, Director General of Supplies and Transport at the Ministry of Defence is best remembered as Dad and Granddad, grumpily rather than demonstratively affectionate, demanding as well as encouraging, proud when events were turning out well, a rock when they were not.

'Oh, you dear soul!' cried my grandmother in delight when, in the first form, I came home and announced I had come first with 92 per cent in Latin.

'Well, done, Baba!' said Mother.

'Damn good!' said Malcolm.

'What happened to the other 8 per cent?' asked my father.

I still grin when I recall that conversation in the kitchen of The Mead.

1999 had started badly but turned out well politically and, in other ways, personally. I finished *The Clematis Tree* and in that year's reshuffle was promoted to the job of my dreams when William made me Shadow Home Secretary. I knew the brief well from having so recently been in office and it put me in one of the most senior positions in the Shadow Cabinet. Told not to reveal the move, I simply said to journalists outside Central Office, 'I'm going home.' The word had a double meaning for I meant to hint not only at the Home Office but to suggest also that I was returning to my natural subject in politics.

Home in its literal sense was changing. My mother no longer wanted to live in the house she had shared with my father for thirty-one years and I had found a four-bedroomed house complete with garden and garage. It was brand new and was still being finished around us when Mother moved in three weeks after me.

I had also had an excellent summer as the member of the Shadow Cabinet on duty, blow-torching Labour but especially Tony Blair. He had gone off on holiday to Italy and lived very grandly with beach roped off and many trappings for which he had not paid. I attacked him, as did others, as a scrounger.

Tony and Cherie Blair were to use Downing Street as a springboard for wealth in a way I had not seen any other prime minister and spouse do, but that was not then fully manifest and the holiday he now took provided the first serious ammunition about personal greed. It was two years since the election and his halo was slipping.

I recalled a much earlier incident, when I was first a backbencher and an oil company had invited us to spend a weekend at Gleneagles to discuss the tax regime for the North Sea basins. It was a cross-party occasion and Blair was among those invited. He alone came with his entire family including children and a relative.

In the summer of 1999, when I was issuing comment on anything and everything, knowing the press was always receptive in the down season, I wrote a piece in my column for the *Sunday Express* lambasting Blair for scrounging. My editor, Michael Pilgrim, turned it down. I appealed to Rosie who upheld him so I wrote another piece instead.

Then Simon Walters of the *Mail on Sunday* rang me up to say it was all very quiet and did I have anything for him? I let rip about Blair and the story took off, covered by not just the *Mail* but by an equally bored media. Preoccupied with moving and also helping my mother to pack up the house in Haslemere, I thought nothing of it.

I was talking to the BT man who was fixing the lines in my new study when the phone rang. We both laughed. Clearly the installation was a success. A few seconds later I was certainly not laughing as my agent, Carol MacArthur, told me I had lost my column at the *Express*. Needless to say they did not give that as the reason but they must have been smarting from having lost the story to their main competition entirely through their own fault. Indeed it was only later that I put two and two together.

My contract was terminated forthwith. Unfortunately they had not bothered to consult their lawyers who would have pointed out that they were obliged by that same contract to give me two months' notice or pay me in lieu. A legal wrangle followed before they paid up.

I had always known, as every freelancer does, that the contract would not last for ever but its unexpected loss at that time was a financial blow as it was my major source of income. It was a long time since I had any anxieties over money and I had not been silly enough to base the new mortgage on anything other than my parliamentary salary but the loss of thousands per month was just a little inconvenient.

I had enjoyed my column with the *Sunday Express* and had only one occasion when I wished I had not written a particular piece. A young man, David Pleydell-Bouverie, had been killed by a lion in Africa and, shocked by the details given in *The Times*, which I found unduly distressing, especially as it was obvious that some journalists had been ringing up the relatives, I wrote advocating greater restraint. In doing so I naturally referred to some of the descriptions to which I objected.

I then received a letter from David's father saying that he had kept all the papers away from his wife immediately after the event but that my piece, not appearing until the weekend, had slipped through his net and she had there read the details for the first time. It did not help that some of it was inaccurate. Mrs Pleydell-Bouverie was severely distressed by my piece.

I wished I could have turned back the clock. Meeting the

father at an unrelated event, I could hardly believe the misery I had inadvertently caused. It is a daily risk in politics that some utterance or action will profoundly upset someone but that stands out as the opinion I wish I had never ventured, despite Mr Pleydell-Bouverie agreeing wholeheartedly with what I had written.

If the loss of the money was a nuisance the release of time was a blessing, for Home Affairs was busy and so was the party, which was just beginning to come out of its post-defeat stupor. Central Office was becoming more focused, the donations were returning, ideas were flowing and the shine was coming off Labour.

I was embarking upon a heady, challenging time. Then Michael Portillo came back.

Chapter Twenty-Four

CIVIL WAR

My return to Home Affairs in June 1999 began with a gift to me in the form of a deep muddle at the Passport Agency which had people queuing for hours if not days or losing their holidays altogether. I promptly went to visit the queue in the pouring rain flanked by press and covered with an umbrella.

I respected Jack Straw. He was throughout an honourable opponent and an able minister but as I well knew the Home Office could always be relied upon to keep the Opposition in drama and it did not disappoint me. I called a debate to condemn the government's handling of the passport crisis, which it was bound to win but it was a good start.

It got better. During that fateful week in 1997, when I was attacking Michael Howard, I had made friends with the lobby journalist, Andrew Pierce, who worked for *The Times*. All politicians trust some journalists more than others and we built up a rapport over the next couple of years. So when he phoned me up and began the conversation with, 'Swear you won't tell anyone yet ...' I assured him my lips were sealed and waited for what I was sure would be some revelation about prisons or immigration or some minister's dodgy dealings.

Had he given me twenty guesses I would never have chosen Russian spies. The Cold War had been over for a decade, Le Carré was looking outdated and what had once been Warsaw Pact countries were now open and friendly. Burgess and Maclean, Philby, Blunt and Blake were names from history.

Melita Norwood was then an old lady but for years she had spied for Russia, betraying secrets to the KGB. She had been mentioned in the Mitrokhin archives (Mitrokhin was a defector and former KGB officer) and *The Times* had located her and carried out an interview which was recorded. Andrew told me that he was shaken by her blatant lack of any regret.

William and I both called for her prosecution as we believed that treason should never go unpunished. Jack of course could not take a view on prosecution which was the role of the Attorney General and so he looked soft and indecisive. I had great sport, but that was all it was. There were more serious issues brewing.

My party conference speech was another huge success, although this time I was more nervous, knowing that I had a great deal to live up to. My mouth was so dry as I began that I muddled up the names of the peers, Lord Cope and Viscount Bridgeman on my team as I introduced them.

I put rehabilitation in prisons at its centre. For this reason Matthew Parris and others called the speech 'liberal' but, as I told the conference, rehabilitation in our prisons had never been 'some soft, wet, liberal, optional extra' but was a crucial tool of public protection, for unless the person who left the prison gates was more law-abiding than when he had entered them, it would mean more victims, more crime and more sentences at the taxpayers' expense. The redemption of an individual is a blessing for us all. That redemption rested upon education, work, training and behaviour management courses, upon getting away from drugs and staying away, upon full, constructive, demanding days and upon being taught to respect and value oneself.

Some 75 per cent of those who come into Her Majesty's Prisons are either illiterate and innumerate or, if they are not quite that, they are wholly without qualifications. They have been excluded from or truanted away large tranches of their secondary education and usually a mixture of the two. They come from grossly disordered backgrounds with either no dad at all or a procession of men or have been ejected from the family home by a stepdad, with whom they did not get on, even before they have reached the age of sixteen.

At sixteen they are supposedly ready for the labour market but in reality are ready for nothing, not only in terms of lacking formal qualifications but in terms of lacking the most basic workplace attitudes: getting to work on time, speaking properly to customers, getting on with colleagues, respecting superiors, overcoming boredom, taking pride in the quality of their work. It is foreign territory to them.

If we take such people and lock them up in idleness then all we do is create a revolving-door prison system and the recidivism rate suggests that is exactly what happens.

I was proposing that every single convicted prisoner (remand prisoners are not always suitable for regimes which rely on stability) should have to spend every weekday doing a full day's work either in the prison education department or the workshops or both and that the work must be real.

We have all heard of the days when prisoners sewed mailbags but that had long been abandoned and by then they were making socks – literally millions of socks. These were not for onward sale but for consumption by a prison population that in those days hovered around 65,000.

'Where are all these socks?' I used to demand to laughter until the day I did so on the Clive Anderson programme and he promptly responded that they were being knotted together and hung down over the prison walls!

I wanted prisoners to do real work, supplied by real contractors for delivery to real customers so that we could pay real wages and from them take real deductions, thus inculcating not only the habit of an orderly working day but also the habit of an orderly distribution of income.

It is simple common sense so why does it not happen? Expense is often posited as an objection but it need cost little if education relies on volunteers and workshops are allowed to keep profits and become self-financing.

It no longer surprises me but still frustrates me that commentators pigeonhole politicians into arbitrary and often meaningless categories and then react with surprise when they say anything not fitting into the caricature. Thus because he was tough on immigration Enoch Powell was always, quite illogically, expected to support capital punishment, which he did not.

One of the silliest divisions is supposed to be that you must favour either punishment or rehabilitation. One can – and I would say should – support both. They are not mutually exclusive. Who does or does not go to prison is a matter for the courts but what we do with prisoners once they arrive is down to government, yet it is never a priority. There are no votes in prisons, either literally or metaphorically.

Political parties do not consider that spending money on prisons is a vote-winner and serving convicts are not allowed to vote. Nor should they be, for if somebody's crimes are either so serious or so persistent that a judge decides to remove him from society then it is daft giving him a say in how that same society is run.

I also advocated the asylum policy of universal detention which I have earlier described and which was to have some entertaining consequences when *The Clematis Tree* came out. As I toured the country giving talks and performing signings, demonstrations gathered and at Oxford, Waterstones became the scene of custard-pie throwing. My very ladylike publicist, Katie White, was delighted, telling me the name of my book would be in all the papers next day, while the manager reported that customers were demanding copies which had been hit by the custard pies.

I had nicknamed Jack Straw *Calamity Jack* and his luck got no better. In February 2000 a hijacked plane landed at Stansted with 156 passengers on board. He had hardly invited it but now he must deal with the consequences which concerned not the real passengers, who were released unharmed, but the hijackers who promptly claimed asylum as did many of the passengers themselves who were clearly all part of a conspiracy.

'Hi! Jack,' I and many others joked as we passed him in the corridor. Of course it was easy for us, especially when Jack gave us a hostage to fortune by stating in the House that all those on the plane would be removed as soon as 'reasonably practicable'. At regular intervals I asked for a progress report. There was virtually no progress at all and many of those concerned are still here.

Asylum statistics, immigration, the state of the prisons, the abandonment of honesty in sentencing, police numbers, criminal justice, crime and youth offending were easy enough for me as I simply opposed Jack from the right but there was what I believe to be a mistaken attitude on the part of the Shadow Cabinet that we must always oppose even where we agreed and so occasionally I found myself coming from the left. That happened with both Freedom of Information and football hooligans.

The latter was particularly difficult as we had called upon the government to take action, I had assured Jack that we would be broadly supportive and then the Shadow Cabinet decided we were going to oppose the measure on grounds of liberty. As for Freedom of Information we contended that the measure did not go far enough as it was thought it would be politically unacceptable to oppose it on principle.

I never had much faith in Freedom of Information and I suspect that historians will in future come to despair of it. Civil servants and specialists expect to be able to give advice on controversial and sensitive matters without having to prepare their submissions with all the caution accorded to a press release. Ministers expect to have full and frank discussions when making law. I had already seen with Michael Howard how an official minute could be accurate and yet completely misrepresent the nature and tone of a meeting and I believed that once the Freedom of Information Act became law this type of minute would be the norm and that more would be done verbally in corridors or on the telephone or in the margins of meetings so that whatever was eventually released would tell but half the story.

It is my firm belief that it is the duty of Opposition to presume fault and then do its level best to find it and that the worst disasters have occurred when all parties have agreed, but there must also be occasions when it is appropriate to limit fault-finding to detail rather than principle.

There is however one area of the 'right to know' which I would support changing. Ministers are not allowed to comment on individual cases on the basis of confidentiality. That, of course, is quite right but it means that a social security claimant can present a hard-luck case to the press when the facts are seriously different or an illegal immigrant can make up any old story and bruit it in the public prints and ministers are too often helpless unless the case comes to court where proceedings can be reported. We knew, for example, that one failed asylum seeker whom we had deported had not 'disappeared' mysteriously but was living secretly with a woman who was not his wife.

The most ludicrous example occurred when I was Social Security Minister. One day my Private Secretary asked me if I was claiming benefit. I said I would hardly qualify so she explained that someone using my name and address had put in an application for income support! I was amused and asked to know the outcome of the case, whereupon I was told that would be possible only if it reached the courts but otherwise it was 'confidential' to the claimant. Eh? It was a fraud using my name and I was a minister of the department against which the fraud was perpetrated, but still I had no right to know any 'client details'.

My new role had given me a new prominence and the success which I was then enjoying made me a target for those who saw me as a threat, especially those who saw me as a future leadership candidate. I got an early taste of this when Peter Lilley made a speech in the spring of 1999 which was said to abandon Thatcherism but in fact merely made the entirely valid point that Conservatives had always seen a role for public sector services and there had never been any question of dropping the NHS or State education.

The press went into overdrive as a result of rather too much briefing and the Shadow Cabinet divided angrily. Michael Howard and I made common cause and I was particularly upset because a major plank of my policy was to introduce private sector money into the NHS and I did not want it compromised by a reading of the speech which suggested the old 'Berlin Wall' between the two sectors.

Unfortunately the situation was then compounded by the leak of an earlier draft of the speech which suggested Lilley might have been even more radical. One of the journalists involved was Andrew Pierce and suspicion fell on me as he was known to be someone I briefed. Peter Lilley rang me and asked for reassurance that I was not the culprit, but whether he believed my denials I do not know.

Central Office was awash with rumour and Andrew Cooper, the Director of Strategy, told Amanda Platell, who was then still the fairly new head of press and media operations, that he had spoken to *The Times* and I had been identified as the source of the leak. Amanda, not being a fool, was immediately suspicious as journalists never reveal their sources but there was a ground-swell of rumour within the party that I was responsible.

Amanda also knew Andrew Pierce well, having worked with him on the *Sunday Express*, and rang him privately. No, said Andrew, it wasn't Widdecombe. She decided simply to turn detective and a check was ordered of faxes and emails through-out Central Office. The leak had come from Michael Simmonds, head of marketing, who had sent the speech to his brother-in-law, Tim Hames, a writer with *The Times*. He was immediately required to leave and Andrew Cooper left a couple of months later.

It had been an unpleasant experience but it was to become almost routine after the return of Portillo. William had never doubted that my denials were true and when after my success-ful summer that year, leadership speculation began around me and his friends became defensive he quelled any briefing, being perfectly happy to be surrounded by tall grasses. His judgement was sound: I was utterly loyal to him personally and would never have made any move while he was still leader.

The Lilley speech was an indication of how the party's right was reacting to the enormity of the defeat and seeking some new image for the Conservatives. Neither Michael Howard, Michael Ancram nor I saw any reason to throw the baby out with the bathwater but there was a collective failure of nerve and the high priest of image change was the king across the water, Michael Portillo.

Portillo had been devastated by his defeat and had undergone a conversion of Damascene proportions. The man who had always taken a hard line on the economy was suddenly the champion of the low-paid and had carried out a stint as a hospital porter, but he had also taken on the social conservatives and was now the voice of homosexual equality, while we were still supporting and voting to retain Section 28, which has become synonymous with homophobia when it was aimed merely at protecting children.

He was hardly the only Tory to think in this fashion and there were useful debates to be had but it was not only his views which had changed. The man who returned was different from the man who had left.

Despite the press already pitting us against each other in anticipation of conflict, I was quite looking forward to Michael's return because I still thought of him as the man for whom I had worked: clever but never short of time for other people. Even when he was a Secretary of State he would stop to talk to colleagues in corridors and it was always the colleagues who broke off the conversations. He would drop everything to help if a backbencher was let down by a speaker, he was kind to subordinates.

The man who now rejoined Parliament after a successful by-election in November 1999 seemed focused only on his own ambitions. I went to his constituency on three separate occasions but he refused point-blank to come to mine. At first I thought his office had made a mistake when an invitation was turned down so I spoke to him.

'It's a bit of a waste of time going to colleagues' constituencies, isn't it?' was his reply.

Flabbergasted, I pointed out I had been to his, to which he responded that was easy because he represented Kensington and Chelsea. Maidstone, I observed tartly, was hardly Inverness. For nine years David Amess had been his loyal PPS so one day I asked him what his impressions were of the new Portillo. He did not know because Portillo had not sought him out or bought him a drink or in any way tried to renew contact.

Nevertheless, I was not wholly convinced that Michael was directly responsible for the backbiting which now ensued and intensified as time went on. That he failed to control his own supporters and those of his henchman, Francis Maude, was undeniable but that did not mean he was egging them on. He had enough experience of collective responsibility and was unlikely to abandon it wholesale, especially as it was not only me on the receiving end of their briefings but also William himself.

When, however, I watched the way they abandoned William on the night of the 2001 defeat, I decided I had been a bit too generous.

Petty jealousies are normal and no serious player can expect not to encounter them. One of the irritants in my life was John Redwood who, aided and abetted by Bernard Jenkin, seemed to try to make my job as difficult as possible when he had to submit policy proposals to a group I was chairing. He resented not being able to send them straight to William and played silly games, always holding up the meeting to complain about the times at which we gathered. It was wearing but hardly worrying. So when a fairly perceptive colleague said to me that he thought Portillo was jealous of me, I did not brush it aside.

It was feasible. Michael had known me as his junior in Employment and an admiring supporter. Now he saw me as the darling of the party in the country who dealt with him on equal terms. Yet I knew there was more to it than that, knew that he hated my views, hated my style and could hardly believe that this frumpy little woman could be considered seriously in the same breath as the suave, charismatic Portillo.

I think he also thought that I was censorious of his private life but what he had and hadn't done at Cambridge was none of my business. I believed in fidelity and marriage as the bedrock of society but, as I have pointed out elsewhere, if I made that the basis for forming friendships and political loyalties I would be leading a rather lonely life.

In any event our clash over gay rights was not as deep as the silly mods and rockers analysis suggested. I hardly wanted to make homosexuality illegal and it was Michael who, as Shadow Chancellor, devised the policy of fiscal help for married couples with families. Such nuances are not convenient to a drama-hungry press.

Michael was a fool. If he had behaved differently then, when

I assessed that I had too little support at Westminster to stand myself, I might have rallied behind him. Instead he alienated people who might have been his supporters, with an arrogant disregard for the consequences. Francis Maude, his loyal lieutenant, must have seen the danger but either did not advise a change in approach or had such advice rejected.

From 1999 until 2001 the Portillistas ran their campaign while the rest of us tried to secure an, admittedly unlikely, election victory. In reality what mattered was to win back enough seats to make victory possible the time after.

It seemed to me that was a reasonable ambition. We had lost many seats by a very small margin and it was likely that they would return to us almost by default and certainly with vigorous campaigning. Tony Blair no longer walked on water as far as the electorate was concerned although there was as yet no sign of serious disillusionment. Our huge victory in the European elections with our slogan 'In Europe but not run by Europe' had shown that people were still willing to vote for us.

I had been hoping the Common Sense Revolution would strike a chord with the electorate but it was before its time. Above all, the public hates a squabbling party and it could hardly be claimed that the Tories were a united force about to storm the enemy citadels. We were consistently ahead in the polls on crime and immigration and I battled on but we needed a broader appeal and also to take better advantage of those times when Labour had its back to the wall as it did over fuel duty and we sacrificed advantage to caution.

Maude and Portillo were as cautious as it was possible to be when it came to public spending. I had been arguing for some time that we should pledge to stick to Labour spending on health and education because it simply was not politically feasible to enter the election promising to cut spending on vital services. Given that was so, why not end the uncertainty now? It was elementary *ars politica*. Francis however was always worried about 'the aggregate expenditure level' and it wasn't until Oliver Letwin arrived on the scene that we began to get any determination to afford policies we wanted to espouse.

The tax guarantee was another bone of contention. William had pledged that an incoming Conservative administration would reduce the share tax took of the nation's income over the course of a Parliament, which would play well if people began to wake up to Labour's habit of taxing by stealth. It seemed a solid Conservative principle to me but Michael Portillo wanted us to row back. I was more sympathetic than I might have been because at that stage the nation simply didn't feel over-taxed and the guarantee would only be of interest if it did. However there was also force in William's argument that a U-turn on something so fundamental would be a U-turn too far. Portillo had already abandoned opposition to the minimum wage and independence of the Bank of England. I would have preferred to say we would withhold judgement until sufficient time had elapsed to see how both would work under a variety of different conditions but was not very bothered by the new position which seemed to me better taken now than at the gates of an election. I could see that a third retreat might be damaging.

These were essentially policy wrangles which were often portrayed as being evidence of strife within the party but I challenge any historian to produce any Cabinet or Shadow Cabinet which did not have policy arguments. It is their very *raison d'être*.

Malcolm Gooderham, Portillo's spin doctor, stood in the wings mocking my party conference speech in full sight of my own aides and knowing that they could see. That was how tribal we had become and the antics of the two factions in Central Office speak vastly louder than any policy discussion ever could. Tom Baldwin of *The Times* rang Amanda Platell to say that I was forming a camp in preparation for a leadership challenge and that he had this on good authority from 'insiders' at Central Office. I told Amanda to tell him that I denied it with my hand on the Book.

'What book?' he is alleged to have asked.

'One you have obviously never heard of,' snapped Amanda.

I was travelling the country addressing Conservative associations, something I did before Shadow Cabinet and after Shadow Cabinet and still do, though now at a reduced rate. 'Another chicken and another speech,' joked a close friend but Baldwin had decided it was evidence of drumming up support.

Even after all this time it hurts that we did not do what we should have done when a rise in fuel tax led to demonstrations and blockades in September 2000 and sent us ahead of Labour in a major opinion poll for the first time in years. All we had to do was promise a substantial cut in the cost at the pumps. It was worth it if it really was the rabbit we could pull out of an otherwise pretty empty hat and reports were suggesting that if the government had the will the money was actually available so surely we could manage it? But Michael resisted. 'Do we want to win?' I asked as the Shadow Cabinet met for its away weekend. 'Do we really want to win?'

A month later the infighting erupted in major bloodletting and the blood on the carpet was mine.

Chapter Twenty-Five

WEED AND FLYING MATS

The party had long since abandoned the policy free-for-all that had characterised my first few months in the Shadow Cabinet and decision-taking followed strict lines with the Shadow Cabinet reaching a collective view. However Shadow Cabinet did not meet regularly in recess and that was when I was refining a policy for which I had long hankered: zero tolerance for drugs.

I had been out to look at Giuliani's project in New York and was full of admiration but realistic enough to know it could never be replicated here. Giuliani had put 11,000 extra police on the streets of New York and I would have been hard put to promise such a number for the whole country, let alone one city, nor could Home Secretaries intervene directly in police operations as could he. However what we could do was apply the policy to one area which accounted for a very large percentage of overall crime: drugs.

Figures showed that drugs accounted for nearly a third of all crime and a staggering 80 per cent of acquisitive crime as people stole and burgled to pay for drugs. If we could make some impact on what had been a losing battle for years – the use of drugs – then we would make a disproportionate impact on the over-all crime statistics. Drugs produced a number of challenges for law enforcement: at the supply end police had to mount time-consuming surveillance operations in order to collect the necessary evidence and then had to repeat them several times as one dealer replaced another. As the law then stood the police could close down opium dens(!) but not crack dens. People carrying quite large amounts of soft drugs could claim they were for personal use and the police could not prove intent to supply. As for small amounts, the police often turned a blind eye rather than embark upon the cumbersome processes of arrest and caution or arrest and court procedures when the offences were so widespread.

I wanted a policy which tackled the entire chain from supply of hard drugs to possession of soft, from promising the police extra resources to tackle supply, to creating a new offence of substantial possession with penalties analogous to those for dealing and a fixed penalty of £100 for those caught in possession of lesser amounts of soft drugs. As I spelled out in my conference speech it would not be an on-the-spot fine with people expected to pay up there and then but a fixed-penalty fine such as is given for speeding. It would make the police's job far easier.

Over that summer William approved the policy and so did Andrew Lansley our drugs czar but the extra police required meant that I also needed Michael Portillo's agreement. I met him face to face. Archie Norman, the Shadow Secretary of State for Environment, Transport and the Regions, was also in the room but not involved in the meeting so he had no obligation to note what was being said. I later in vain asked him to recall, which was a pity as Michael had also opposed his plan to spend on regeneration as he now opposed mine on extra police. It was true I could give him no reliable estimate as to how much the fines would bring in but at least the plan did generate some revenue. He still refused to endorse the policy.

I appealed to William and a compromise was arrived at, whereby I would re-jig my Home Office budget to find some of the funding. John Whittingdale, William's PPS, undertook to broker this with Portillo and, after several increasingly anxious enquiries, I was told this had been done. The stage was now set.

Then I made the worst misjudgement of my entire political career. I had trialled the idea with the police as I went round the country, particularly with ordinary constables who would have to turn it into reality on the streets. They liked the plan but many of them, as did many of their superiors, pointed to one potential pitfall. The current law provided for imprisonment of up to five years for possession of soft drugs although the reality was nearly always a court fine or a caution or sometimes community service. If we substituted a £100 fixed penalty for that or merely added it on as an extra tool for the police (I was proposing the latter) then we might be seen to be decriminalising use of soft drugs.

The very last thing we needed was headlines saying the Conservatives were going to decriminalise cannabis and it was the very last message I wanted to send so we toughened the rhetoric, I in my speech and David Lidington, my second in command, in his press release and background notes. We were clamping down. The miscreants would still receive a criminal record.

The speech, on Wednesday, 4 October, got the usual enthusiastic reception with everyone singing Happy Birthday, and I had no reason to believe that its success would not be as great as the previous two years' had been but I was only halfway up the hill between the conference centre and the Highcliff Hotel, where my next engagement was, when Nick Wood from Central Office Press Department hailed me from behind. I walked back to meet him, still not scenting trouble.

Between pants to catch the breath he had lost running after me, he told me things were unravelling. The police were saying the policy was unenforceable. That surprised me until I found out that someone had rung up the Police Federation and briefed that the policy came without the resources I had fought so hard to get from Michael Portillo or the money from fines. I phoned the General Secretary, who responded with enthusiasm, but the damage was done. For that I blamed myself. I should have touched base with the Federation the night before and run through the policy in detail, crucially giving them an update on resources but because the proposals had always been so well received by the police I had not foreseen any opposition.

For all the other consequences which flowed I did not blame myself. A rumour began circulating that I had made up the policy without getting any agreement, a blatant lie. Another rumour said I was planning dawn raids on student residences, another lie. The public appeared to think we were making possession a criminal offence for the first time because we had stressed so hard that we were not making cannabis a decriminalised offence for the first time. The middle classes feared their little darlings might find their lives and travel prospects blighted by a bit of student naughtiness while ignoring the poor, black, disadvantaged, truanting lads on the council estates whose fate was not The Priory but Her Majesty's prisons. The recreation of the educated keeps the dealers in business.

All that I could have countered but then my colleagues indulged in a knifing frenzy of which Brutus, Cassius and Casca could have only dreamed. Lord Cranborne, whom William had sacked as Leader of the Lords after he engaged in talks with Tony Blair, took to the airwaves and called for cannabis to be decriminalised. The briefings about the implications of the policy grew wilder as did the attempt to say I had made it up on the spur of the moment with mutterings that Michael knew nothing about the fines – a rather unlikely story, given that they would actually bring in money.

Michael and I, furious with each other, made a united attempt at thwarting the journalists as we took our seats on the platform for William's speech. We were sitting side by side and knew, as they aimed their cameras at us, that they were trying to get a picture of us looking in opposite directions as once their colleagues had of Charles and Diana. So we agreed to look the same way, which was easy once William was speaking, but beforehand took a conscious effort.

Then came the knife-wielding. Jonathan Oliver, a reporter, told Simon Walters of the *Mail on Sunday* that a senior party aide told him over a drink in the small hours of Thursday morning that half the Shadow Cabinet disagreed with the plan to target cannabis smokers. In fact, as the speech makes abundantly clear, I was targeting the entire range of drugs activity and never actually mentioned the wretched weed by name.

The aide then said, 'Ask some of them if they smoked dope when they were younger. I promise you will receive some fascinating responses.'

The *Mail on Sunday* found no fewer than seven who admitted to having smoked cannabis when young: Francis Maude,

Bernard Jenkin, Archie Norman, Peter Ainsworth, David Willetts, Tom Strathclyde and Oliver Letwin although he said he had been duped (and doped) and was furious.

James Arbuthnot, our Chief Whip, had instructed Shadow Cabinet members to tell the truth if asked. Otherwise he feared the papers would dig around and drip out a series of revelations. I understand the reasoning but the Labour Chief Whip told his people to refuse to answer the question and it does appear to have been the better policy.

This was of course irrelevant in any analysis of the policy. It was a criminal offence when my colleagues were young, was so then and would be after my own policy came into force. But it made a good story and I struggled to get any reporter interested in the policy itself. Simon Walters rang me up and pretended to be interested in the policy for two minutes, then asked if I had ever had too much to drink at university.

I remained friendly with Simon but never trusted him again.

The really sad aspect of all of this is that there is still no serious offensive against something which blights so many lives and funds crime. Most of us know somebody who has come to grief through drugs. Some propose that decriminalisation or legalisation would get rid of the dealers and enable the State to control the quality of the drugs, to say nothing of raising money by taxing the purchases. Let us look at that argument further.

First, it is necessary to decide if, under this proposal, the State should legalise only soft drugs or all drugs. The latter should be unthinkable because it would mean that people could buy heroin or crack cocaine and the health and social consequences would be immense.

The first scenario is the one more usually put forward: legalise soft drugs and leave the more dangerous drugs illegal. That would mean that all the dealers' profits would be vested in hard drugs and they would be peddled more energetically. Secondly it is common ground that if the barrier of illegality were removed more people would be willing to try soft drugs. As for a certain percentage soft drugs are the gateways to hard drugs, then the number of people taking hard drugs would rise, which is probably why a study by the University of Amsterdam found that a rise in soft drugs use is followed by a rise in hard drugs use. So too would rise the numbers of sufferers of cannabis psychosis, the numbers of crimes committed under the influence of cannabis and the numbers of accidents caused by driving while under its influence.

We already have enough health problems with tobacco and enough health and crime problems with alcohol so why add a third legal drug?

If William had told me to drop the policy there would have been enormous pressure for me to resign, an option I briefly considered at the height of all the fuss but quickly dismissed because there was still so much I wanted to do. Ironically, after the election when I was serving on the Home Affairs Select Committee and Labour was introducing spot fines, I asked the minister if he was thinking of including cannabis use among the list of offences. He said it was an interesting idea and he would look at it and there was not a single squeak of protest.

The re-classification of cannabis from a Class B to a Class C drug, which was subsequently brought in to much fanfare about 'enlightenment' was subsequently reversed, largely at the request of the police.

The fallout was short-lived in terms of headlines and we never did formally abandon the policy, but without being able to advocate it as a priority it withered away. For me the fallout was more durable. It convinced many people at Westminster that I was out of touch, reactionary and lacked judgement. The Portillo camp was convinced it had seen off a rival but in truth my support was always in the country rather than within the parliamentary party which, as I have acknowledged elsewhere in this book, thought me odd.

My support in the country barely faltered as *The Times*, its political team stuffed heavily with Portillistas, found out when it began a ring-round of all party chairmen to see if they would support me or Portillo. They abandoned the attempt when I was leading three to one, according to the journalist who told me.

I had begun the millennium year kneeling in Westminster

Cathedral as we welcomed the 2,000th year of Christianity and listening to the fireworks booming at the very different celebrations down by the Thames. We had looked at each other and smiled. 2001 began with much less of a fanfare but I knew it would be crucially important in my own life as there would almost certainly be a general election in which, for the first time, I would be in the front line.

After that I expected it to be a fight to keep William and hoped we would have enough seats to see off any challenges. There was a widespread presumption that if we did not I would be a part of any ensuing leadership election but even then I was not convinced. The party in the country had the final say but it was the MPs which reduced the list to the final two.

For the time being it would be more than enough to concentrate on the election in which Home Affairs would play a major role although Save the Pound was seen as a big cannon in our armoury. Our problem with the pound however was that people did not perceive it as being immediately under threat. With no outstanding proposal to join the euro, people believed they would have a second chance as the government had pledged a referendum before taking any action.

As the election loomed the political commentator Andrew Marr suggested that the fight between Jack Straw and me would be an interesting one as we were both taking a slightly different approach from our parties, by which I presume he meant that Jack Straw was tougher than Labour would normally be while I was emphasising rehabilitation. At least he had listened to my speeches, which Archie Norman clearly had not done when he proposed as a 'new' idea that I might like to talk about rehabilitation!

Inevitably we were accused of playing 'the race card' over my asylum proposals but immigration was a major subject and filled the letters which poured into Central Office. One of the big differences between being a minister and being in opposition is that the correspondence is being dealt with by the same people who are doing the research for speeches and policy formation, attending meetings, drafting press releases, answering the phones and accompanying the shadow minister. There is no dedicated 'correspondence section' and letters are answered very late, despite the use of standard replies and computer-generated paragraphs. Occasionally people complained that they had written a fortnight ago so I obviously was not interested!

My team was led by Adam Newton and during the election Damian Collins, now the member for Folkestone, helped me as I had once helped Michael Ancram. For both these young men, the helicopter rides proved a source of delight. Back in Central Office Nicole Hughes, a calm-nerved New Zealander, dealt with press while Matthew Gullick, the son of a judge who was himself to win a major law prize, and Chris Wilkins crunched statistics and dug out anything embarrassing to Labour, while James O'Shaughnessy looked after the website. And with that plus a bit of ad hoc help here and there we had to manage. The danger was always that if I had a good intern in my parliamentary office, then Central Office would snap him up, as they did with a young man called Jamie Devlin who then stood as a candidate himself, albeit in a safe Labour seat, at the next election.

As the election loomed we needed something visible, which we could use up and down the country and make fresh impact each time. Labour was closing down local police stations and the team came up with the idea of a large mat, emblazoned with the message: **PUT A POLICEMAN HERE**. I would take this mat all over the country and put it down in front of police stations either already closed or marked for closure.

How was I to do this? A helicopter was the only answer so that I could visit several different localities in a day. Arise, take up thy mat and fly, seemed to be the solution.

Unfortunately I have enormous height phobia. This has never manifested itself in a normal aeroplane as the portholes are too small to get a real sensation of the huge void and I enjoy looking out of them. There was an occasion, however, when flying Virgin first class to the States before 9/11, on which I was invited into the cockpit to see the descent into New York. I accepted with alacrity but, of course, the pilot's cockpit is a vast window on both sides. I descended into JFK Airport with my eyes closed.

During another flight, this time over Hong Kong, the guide, unfettered by any EU health and safety rules, simply opened the door so that I could see better! That was another trip with eyelids squeezed tight shut.

I solved the problem by never sitting in the front of the helicopter but always in the back and in the middle of the seat so that if we banked I did not suddenly see the earth below me. Adam Newton was delighted as he loved being in the front and watching the pilot work the instruments. I enjoyed the flights, even when we had a near-miss with an American airliner on one occasion.

Matthew Parris joined me for one day's flying and confided that he was nervous. 'Oh, it's great fun,' I responded chirpily. 'But do you mind if I sit in the middle?'

It was a punishing schedule. Take Sunday, 3 May, as just one example when the journalist with me was Alice Thomson of the *Telegraph*. It being Sunday I was later than usual leaving home and set off at 7.45 a.m. to the Millbank studios a little over a mile away to give media interviews, then I gave Alice a long interview before visiting an East End flower market whence I moved on to a marginal seat near Wanstead to place my mat outside a police station. Next I hopped into the helicopter and off we went to Reading, then Cardiff, followed by Barry where I was heckled so rudely by Labour supporters that the local press took my side, then we flew to Wolverhampton, followed by Manchester where the mat made another appearance, then Bramhope near Leeds where a post office had suffered an armed raid. After Leeds came Leicestershire, where the mat was unrolled in Castle Donington, then Peterborough for a Radio Five election debate. The light by now having run out, I travelled by car at 10 p.m. to my own constituency.

Helicopters are not always reliable. Stress levels rose when fog at Oxford prevented us flying only an hour before I was due in London for a major media event and on another occasion we were grounded when water got into the fuel supply. The police mat proved a wonderful success but then came the meeting with the police themselves. Jack Straw had been heckled and slow-handclapped and when I said that clearly there were limits to the resources we could promise and that we could not make undertakings on pay, Adam Newton became very concerned that I would suffer the same fate. He was positively grumpy when I said I was going ahead and would tell them the truth, afraid that I would be shouted down.

Instead I received a huge ovation and Seb Coe embraced me when we met not long afterwards. The lessons were simple: 1, it pays to be honest and 2, the Opposition will never be as unpopular as the government.

When I confronted Jack Straw directly in a three-way television debate, the cameras panned us from above and I was the only one not using notes. As usual people noticed and thought it impressive, but in truth it is more difficult using notes, which are often no more than a comfort blanket. I would take huge files into questions when I was a minister and not use them at all. It is rarely possible to locate the right page and right paragraph and absorb it before having to deliver the reply but an uncluttered lectern promotes clear thinking and fast responses.

It proved a good campaign for me personally and Labour had some unrelated difficult moments such as when John Prescott actually threw a punch at a member of the public and Tony Blair was challenged publicly about the state of the Health Service by a cancer patient's spouse as the PM arrived to campaign at a hospital, but as polling day drew nearer I felt my stomach knot. Surely, surely, we would get back those marginal seats, where so many candidates had given up their jobs or made other arrangements for a prolonged campaign in the pre-electoral months? Surely any seat won in the carnage of 1997 must now be safe?

The results were catastrophic with 620 seats remaining unchanged and a net gain to us of just one seat. Turnout was low, suggesting a large rate of abstention and Labour votes fell more than did ours but there could be no argument that the defeat was decisive and our result derisory.

It was an appalling night. As we finished our own counts, members of the Shadow Cabinet headed to London and Smith Square. William was not expected for hours and I collapsed, exhausted, on Michael Ancram's sofa. Portillo had a London count and could have been expected to be there promptly and to wait for William, but after a flying visit to 'the war room' instead waltzed off on holiday, flying to Morocco. Where Maude was, I do not know but he had a Sussex count and could have also been there. They simply disappeared and were viewed as rats deserting the sinking ship.

When William and Ffion finally arrived at around 7 a.m., he was resistant to all our arguments that he should stay on for a few months at the very least. I tried, as did Ancram and Andrew MacKay, Iain Duncan Smith and Tom Strathclyde but we argued in vain. Less than an hour later he had resigned and we stood leaderless in the morning sunlight.

William Hague is a man of great intellect, steady nerve and steadfastness of purpose but he came to the front too soon. That is not the wisdom of hindsight: I said it when he was elected leader but I have no doubt that he thought the opportunity should be seized as it might not come again.

I often wondered if I was indirectly responsible for that decision in 1997. William had decided to support Michael Howard when one evening I met his principal supporter, James Arbuthnot, and told him I was about to launch a major attack on Michael Howard. William reneged on his deal immediately afterwards and I wondered if James had told him he was supporting damaged goods. It is only fair to report that James denies this was so but I find it strange that William's first lieutenant would not have told him what he had learned. Of course if you believe in coincidences . . .

Over the next couple of days I divided my time between media, long, deep sleep and the question of whether I should throw my own hat into the ring.

Chapter Twenty-Six

DEPARTING (1)

Looking back at the press cuttings for that period, I realise just how prolonged and voluminous was the speculation that I would be a candidate, but I was already mentally prepared for not having much support. I had never canvassed it but I knew that there were some votes on which I could rely simply from some colleagues having urged me to stand. The claim by the BBC political editor, Nick Robinson, in a later documentary that I 'could not find a single MP willing to support me' was a piece of fiction that only he can attempt to explain. I was however fairly certain that my support was sparse and that even those who knew me were concerned about the caricature to which I was prone.

The party in the country was another matter altogether and the messages flooded in. The underlying assumption was that the fight would be between Portillo and me, whereas the choice eventually offered to the party was Ken Clarke or Iain Duncan Smith.

'Use the media,' urged Damian Collins and so I agreed that the *Sunday Telegraph* could come to the cottage and interview me. 'Ann Widdecombe Breaks Cover in Leadership Race' ran the headline as I became the first to put my head above the parapets.

When I told David Lidington I might declare imminently he was silent. So my deputy would not be supporting me. Gary Streeter, a fellow traveller in so many conscience questions, demurred, said he would call back and then announced he was supporting Portillo. James Cran told me I was 'head and shoulders above the others' but then said senior whips should not take sides publicly. Patrick McLoughlin said the hunting issue was too great a problem. William said yes and Michael Ancram said yes if he did not stand himself, but they too would not become publicly involved although William dropped that stance pretty quickly when Ken was in the final.

So it went on. Those who supported me believed they must stay above the fray and I would never have been able to put together the traditional photograph of heavyweights. As for the rest, some were reserving judgement till they saw the full list, many mentioned hunting (it was a free vote but that was irrelevant; they feared their supporters would leave), others thought the 'party needed to change', others, though too polite to tell me to my face, told colleagues that I looked odd and was too strident. I knew I had not a hope.

Had the rules worked in reverse and it had fallen to the country to reduce the list to two, nothing would have stopped me but I was not prepared to emerge with a derisory vote. Meanwhile Michael was being photographed in plush, modern surroundings which surprised me. His message would have been better portrayed if he had been surrounded by hospital porters.

Well, I at least could make it clear that the Conservative Party was about the underdog and also demonstrate why I had been so 'strident' on law and order, so I decided to make my announcement that I was not going to stand on the Arden Estate, a council estate within view of the City which had been badly neglected. The press was unlikely to go there of its own accord but for this it came en masse. The commentators knew I was not standing but may have hoped there would have been a last-minute surprise.

I addressed them thus:

Thank you for coming here today. This is the third time I have invited the press to join me here and each time for the same reason: that this estate, which is by no means the worst of its kind, encapsulates one of the nastiest aspects of life in Britain today and one which politicians of all parties acknowledge but effectively ignore.

On estates like this all over the country live huge numbers of people whom I have called the Forgotten Decent. They are people like us but with only a fraction of our resources and all they want to do is live normally but instead their lives are made a daily hell by drugs, thuggery, intimidation and degradation of the environment.

If we really want an inclusive, one-nation society then we need to revolutionise places like this where mothers can't let the kids out to play without checking for needles, where gardens are wrecked and windows are broken, where the vulnerable are intimidated and every agency shrugs. The police leave it to the councils and the councils leave it to the police. The courts can't or won't take effective action and patterns of desperately defective parenting are passed from one generation to the next. It is not politically correct to talk about zero tolerance, taking problem children into secure training and evicting the troublemakers.

I regularly meet people like those I have met here all over the country and none of them feels that anyone is sticking up for them. It would have been one of my top priorities and I would have brought a real and possibly politically incorrect will to it. Physical regeneration is necessary but on its own insufficient. I am often accused of being old-fashioned so let me use an old-fashioned phrase: the peace and tranquillity of the realm. Where are peace and tranquillity for the people who live here?

I then turned to the leadership and acknowledged the lack of support within Parliament despite widespread support in the country. I said I regretted that the membership at large would not have the chance to vote for me. Then I said:

whoever leads this party into the future is going to need to be honest, plain-speaking, spin-free and true to his principles if he is to re-engage the public with Conservatism ... he is also going to have to work on the principle that the party is both its right and its left and cannot just resolve itself into one or the other.

I proceeded to state that, Michael Portillo apart, I would have no difficulty serving under any likely contender but that not-withstanding I had decided to return to the backbenches. I had not done this from disillusionment as I believed that we could and must win next time but I wanted to devote time to my mother during such years as remained to her, I wanted to speak on a range of subjects and to be free from the confines of collective responsibility. I had been in office or shadow office with the exception of one year since 1990 and this was the time to make the change. Backbenchers and Parliament were being marginal-ised and I wanted to fight that vigorously.

I then ended with thanks to my supporters and my constituency.

Over the years which followed I was to revisit and to keep in touch with the Arden Estate although I never managed to get quite such a press turnout again! When Michael Howard became leader he went there himself and afterwards told me that they had plastered the walls of the small community centre with press cuttings of my visits. When, in 2007, I came to make a film about the hopeless conditions on London housing estates I approached the Arden and they said no, all was going well at last and they didn't want to upset anyone and prejudice their chances of fur-ther funding. That they reached such a stage was due entirely to the efforts of a resident, Audrey Villas, who with a tiny band of helpers set out to make a difference and did.

The *Telegraph* reported the event as 'Bitter Widdecombe Retires Hurt' but the last thing I was feeling after that announce-ment was bitter. I was relieved and felt as if a great burden had rolled away. Yet, I did not at that stage rule out ever returning to front-line politics. I was taking a break and told myself that tomorrow could take care of itself. I might or might not return. I never did.

In many ways this was a departure from my normal policy of just plodding on, the policy which had brought me to the point of being a possible leadership contender. Michael Howard did plod on and reaped the rewards two years later, but some-thing in me was changing, subtly but noticeably. I was tiring not of politics but of the political game, which suddenly I was genuinely content to leave to others. I still toured the country, speaking, but confined my parliamentary activity to those areas in which I had a real, active, driving interest.

Michael Ancram and William Hague had both expressed surprise at my failure to stand, the latter saying that he had expected me to be 'a substantial candidate' and that the 'party must be mad'. Ken did not declare immediately and I decided to back Michael Ancram. I was closest in viewpoint to Iain Duncan Smith but thought he lacked charisma and would not be impressive at the despatch box. I think he won because he wasn't Widdecombe, Portillo or Clarke. He had no controversy attaching to him, was a clear Eurosceptic and thought reliable.

Clarke knocked Portillo out of the running by one vote. I was profoundly relieved but saddened by the irony that, had he and his supporters behaved differently, I could have been that one vote, which instead went to Clarke. I dearly wish Ken had won but the time before he had come fresh from a senior position in the Cabinet and was trusted as effective and loyal but now the Europe issue was too big.

We hanker for politicians to be honest and say what they really think and Ken did: that he had not changed his views but could hardly impose them on a party which thought the opposite. The party wouldn't have it and, as I spoke at meetings for Clarke, all I ever heard was Europe, Europe, Europe.

Iain rang me after he had won to ask if I was still minded not to serve and I said I was sticking to my plans for a break. It irritated me that, despite having stated that intention in June, some sections of the media interpreted my refusal to join the new Shadow Cabinet as a personal rejection of Iain.

In my final days as Shadow Home Secretary, I arrived in my constituency headquarters to find the very efficient organising secretary, Sue Dishman, near-incoherent with shock. It was 'about the planes'. I could get little more from her so I rang Central Office and thus heard about 9/11.

My mother, who was ninety that August, was well both mentally and physically and financially independent. When people asked me how I managed to look after her I replied that I didn't:

she looked after me. She reacted to the events of that dreadful day by saying that if there was a war she was not 'being sent away into the country'. She was, she proclaimed, staying in London with me.

I explained that it would not be like the war she had known, that Bin Laden's planes would not come bombing London as had Hitler's. Yet we had a no-fly zone and the skies were uncharacteristically silent. The homeland of a NATO country had been attacked and war seemed inevitable. I looked at the pupils of the Maidstone Boys' Grammar when I attended a speech day and wondered if they would be called up in a future which was suddenly bleak.

Memories are short and I am often asked in public meetings why we had to go to Afghanistan, the erroneous view having taken hold that it is only American and British soldiers who are there. The basic tenet of NATO is that if one of us is attacked at home then we all consider ourselves to be attacked. That is how we were sheltered by the US during the Cold War: if Russia attacked West Germany, for example, then America would react as if Soviet troops had invaded New York.

On 9/11 the United States was attacked and so every NATO country was automatically involved. Germany has suffered losses of 53 soldiers, 3 policemen and 245 personnel wounded, the French 88 losses, Italy 52, etc. Our losses are greater and we have more troops committed but our involvement is not unique.

Mother had always wanted to go on a cruise but she did not relish hot climates so as a trial the year before we had joined Fred Olsen's *Black Watch* and enjoyed an eight-day cruise of the fjords. Now we were off on an Arctic cruise for fifteen days and it was bliss not to be 'on duty'. The only downside was that Louis Theroux, who was making a film about me, was to join us for a couple of days. By a dirty trick Theroux obtained an interview alone with my mother which in her innocence she didn't even realise she was giving. I was angry at the time but now it is one of very few films of my mother which I possess.

The Arctic was followed by a Baltic cruise in 2002 and then by one to Iceland and Greenland in 2003 and a second to the fjords but when we made a second cruise of the Arctic in 2005, Mother fell and broke her femur and from then on began to decline in health.

Her needs grew slowly: first my friend from London University days, Veronica Jagnanan, used to stay when I was away overnight, then a carer used to come a couple of days a week, then I had to have someone there all the time. The son of Amah came over from Singapore on an extended visit and helped in exchange for accommodation and meals, then my nephew, Sean, and then a full-time professional carer.

Disaster struck while Sean was looking after her. Mother was weak because she refused to eat and he and the carers spent most of the day just trying to get food in her in small doses. She had the same attitude to glasses of water and cups of tea and we had regular drips to rehydrate her. Mentally competent in many ways, she was confused about eating and would tell us she had just had 'a big meal'. Worried that something might be bloating her stomach I arranged for her to have an examination but all was normal.

Mother would come down each day on the stairlift, watched by Sean, and spend the day in the lounge. Whenever I left the house I would ring Sean, who slept on a different floor, to say he was now alone with Gran. One morning on my way to the BBC I could not rouse him. I tried again and again and wondered if I should simply turn the car round but Mother had been fast asleep and it was long before her usual waking time. As I emerged from the interview Sean rang me to say he had found her at the bottom of the stairs.

She had got up early to use the bathroom, which was en suite, but for some reason had decided to go to the one downstairs and had not used the stairlift. I tormented myself with reproaches. Why had I not turned round when I could not rouse Sean? Why had I not left the bathroom door open? Perhaps she had suddenly found the handle too difficult. Why had I not left the stairlift with the platform down so that she could not have tried to bypass it? Why? Why? Why?

Mother survived but was never the same again. The femur she had broken mended yet again and the physiotherapist came in twice a week but she was too weak to make the effort necessary to return to full walking capacity, although physically able to do so. She did not disappear into that frightening world of no longer recognising people and friends who visited but she lost interest in television and Scrabble and said she 'wanted to be with Jesus'.

On 26 April 2007, I was getting ready to visit Nepal the next day as part of my Gurkha campaign when the carer, Lolly, called me into Mother's bedroom. Her breath was coming in great rumbling snores and Lolly thought she needed oxygen but then everything returned to normal. When the snoring sound came again, I tried to wake her but without success. I rang the doctor but she died before he arrived. I thanked God it had not happened one day later.

I always knew that even if I had never left the house I might not have been by her side at the moment of parting. It could have happened while I was in the bathroom or making a cup of tea. Yet because I was so busy and away so much my biggest fear was that I might not be there. My mother had been at my grandmother's deathbed and she and I at my father's and my biggest comfort in the days which followed was that I was with her. She opened her eyes once and looked at me so I knew that she knew I was there.

I had so often wished in the years she was with me that I was the older child so that I might have already been retired and had more time to spend with her but at least I was not on the front bench.

Indeed in 2002, a year after leaving the front bench, I began to think about changing our lifestyle. As Mother grew less active and stopped going out on her own she was left too much with just me and the carers whereas in Haslemere she had been part of the local life and of an active church. I thought if we moved to the cottage as our main home she might see a greater variety of people and as she always enjoyed the gatherings of my friends after Mass on Sundays for supper I knew she would like it.

I made enquiries about extending the cottage but soon realised that I could not leave her alone there while I was in London. It was too far away in an emergency and I would not be home every night let alone be able to call in during the day as I often managed with Westminster so close by. Indeed I often worked from home, which would certainly not have been possible from the constituency. I abandoned the plan and rejected the compromise option of selling both the house and the cottage and buying something halfway between London and Kent for the same reason.

I considered whether I should retire early. It would mean a much reduced pension if I left in 2005 rather than 2010 as I planned (it could of course have been 2006 and 2011 if the Parliaments had run their full course) and I would not be able to draw it at all until 2007, but I would be able to cope. I suggested it and met with fierce resistance.

'You never know what might happen. I could be dead or gaga by then and what would you do after I've gone?'

I nevertheless kept the option open in my mind while setting out to ensure that she was happy meanwhile. Certainly she was happier now I had left the front line and that had nothing to do with my greater availability.

'You will ruin your health,' she would tell me when I booked alarm calls for 4.30 a.m. I had no fondness for such hours but they were a normal part of front-bench life along with early trains and late-night interviews. At least I no longer had to cope with red boxes.

'Rude, nasty people!' she would fume at the diary columns in the papers. True, they were usually wildly inaccurate but they were also trivial.

I had taken to asking the taxi to stop right outside the Kennington Tandoori where we often ate and the proprietor of which, Kowsar Hoque, was wonderful with my mother. It was on double yellow lines but meant Mother did not have to walk far. It duly appeared in *The Times* diary that I was breaking the law. I laughed but Mother was upset because she thought she had caused me a problem.

'They hate you,' she said when reading the *Telegraph*'s account of the machinations which had surrounded my drugs speech. I could not deny it and out went the paper, which she had read daily from her youth.

It is normal, I assured her, but she was not looking at it from the perspective of a practising politician. Perhaps, I thought, I had become too easily inured, too dismissive of everything which did not actually constitute a serious libel, but I had not the time and energy to bother and when I did summon up enough disgust to complain, it rarely made a difference.

I have never actually sued a paper, although occasionally I have come very close. This has both an advantage and a disadvantage: editors will apologise because they know that it is the end of the matter and I will not be ringing the lawyers but it also makes them careless in the first place because I am not on their 'litigious' list.

The myth that I had a policy of chaining up women in childbirth was repeated so often that I had to put legal warnings on the desks of the editors of all main papers. I sent a copy of the Hansard so that they could see the truth. Despite that I am regularly obliged to repeat the warning, whereupon they apologise.

'I am sorry you are still pursued by the clanking of these ghostly chains,' wrote one editor, when promising a retraction, and I laughed.

I did not however laugh when the prisons' correspondent for the *Guardian*, Eric Allison, insisted on the Jeremy Vine programme that I had 'approved a policy of chaining pregnant women to their beds during childbirth'. I told him it was libellous, he responded it was true. I said I could sue and he challenged me to do so. The programme naturally enough gave me the right of reply and so I had no desire to pursue the station.

Despite the evidence of Hansard, Eric Allison, uniquely among journalists confronted with it, still maintained his statement was true and reluctantly I began proceedings. Both my solicitor and my counsel told me the case was as open and shut as a case could be but it would be expensive and time-consuming unless Allison agreed to go before a judge rather than a jury. Even if he, an ex-convict had the money to pay up, I would have to fund everything up front and the trial might be used to open up so many areas of prison policy that it could be prolonged.

I was still angry but anger does not exclude rationality. I had the opportunity to respond on Jeremy Vine and if I was interested in vindication rather than damages then I need go no further. Did I want this hassle in my life? I did not and told solicitors to forget it. It does make me laugh when I hear journalists complaining that they are so limited in what they can say and how the libel laws are so weighted towards the complainant when the truth is that unless you are an Ashcroft or a Beckham you have the choice between putting up with libel or risking beggary.

Yet it is less the expense than the hassle which deters me. I have watched people having their lives taken over by litigation, sometimes over fairly unimportant matters. God surely expects me to find better things to do with my time!

Getting something corrected without resorting to law is challenging and itself time-consuming. In 2001 a BBC journalist, Mark Mardell, posted on its website a description of my drugs policy which claimed it meant 'locking up everyone using cannabis, using up huge amounts of police time and hugely increasing the prison population'. Mark went on to say that the next day Michael Ancram was talking about the policy as akin to fixed fines for speeding offences and that this was 'the very opposite of what had been intended'.

I do not suppose Mark was just making it up as he went along but he clearly relied upon memory rather than research. I sent him a copy of the BBC's own verbatim transcript of the speech which included the line about how the fines would work in the same way as those for speeding offences. Mark agreed he had been wrong and undertook to correct the piece. Two months later he still had not done so, so I wrote again. He assured me the correction had been made but a month after that it had not been. This time I wrote to Greg Dyke and then the offending material was removed.

If it takes all that time for a sensible and justly respected journalist to correct something about which there is no dispute and which was actually of some consequence, is it any wonder that politicians simply do not spend their time chasing every lesser inaccuracy? Yet of course once something is on the files and uncorrected it can be quoted ever after.

Sometimes I do not know where the stories have come from. In 1992 I was rung up by a gossip columnist to ask if it was true that I had secretly married a Mr Brown who was the head of a private detective agency. Laughing helplessly, I replied that I had not married a Mr Brown, Mr Black, Mr Green or Mr any other colour. The journalist was most disappointed. It had, he told me, come from a most reliable source.

Towards the end of my time in Parliament the *Sun* rang Conservative Central Office to say that I had been arrested in Kensington High Street for being drunk at the wheel of my car. Horrified, David Cameron's office rang mine. No, said my assistant. As far as he knew I did not have the car with me, I was certainly not due to be in Kensington and anyway it was Lent when I did not drink at all.

I emerged from dinner at the Carlton Club to find two *Sun* journalists waiting for me. I told them I could not remember when I was last in Kensington High Street, that I did not drink and drive and, anyway, it was Lent when I didn't drink at all. Despite having stood around for nothing they did see the funny side.

How does it happen? The *Sun* told me a policeman had rung up. Was it just a prankster and if so why? Or had someone staggered from her car and said 'Hallo, Oshifer? I'm Ann Widdecombe. Can't arresht me!' Or had a real policeman heard Whittington or Willingdon as Widdecombe? I shall never know.

There is only one rumour which, with the wisdom of retrospect, I wish I had taken more seriously. While I was in Social Security, the *Kent Messenger* rang up to ask if I was among those about to be named in Peter Tatchell's Outrage campaign. As I had never had a lesbian instinct in my life, I dismissed it as rot and my name did not appear but the rumour persisted though never in a form that asserted its truth sufficiently baldly for me to sue. Then in 2001 a group called Tories Against Hypocrisy made the accusation on the Internet, accompanied by alleged circumstances which went back to my early years in Maidstone.

At first I laughed at the absurdity, then tried to identify the people responsible but as often as the allegation was taken down it appeared again and they were impossible to find. My third reaction was that they had probably done me a favour. Every dirty digger in Fleet Street would now go dirty digging and come back with a shiny clean spade and probably frustration at having his time wasted. Indeed, after that the hints and innuendoes virtually disappeared as the truth that a woman may be both heterosexual and unmarried was finally accepted. Maybe if I had reacted more energetically the first time the issue was raised I might have discovered the source and squashed the libel earlier.

Inaccuracy is rife though often completely harmless. No, I did not wake up in hospital to find a bunch of flowers from my then boss David Hunt by the bedside. I had not then been in hospital since I was sixteen. No, I did not take a cat back to the shelter because it did not get on with my other cat. No, I do not wake up to Tom Jones tracks on my CD. No, I did not weight 17 stone (!!). No, I did not turn down an appointment at the Vatican to take part in *Strictly Come Dancing*. The list is vast.

Sometimes journalists even think they know what is in your mind better than you do. Daniel Johnson wrote in the *Telegraph* that I 'certainly' did not think Oliver Letwin should be Shadow Home Secretary, when I was a fan of Oliver's and always had been since he had been prepared to find money for my schemes when I was doing his job. Indeed when he had gone through a rocky patch during that election I had telephoned the Chief Whip in his support.

What were Johnson's grounds? None. Just gossip and speculation. Yet he too is a good journalist.

I could write a book – and one day may – about my life in press cuts. It is a parallel universe.

Released from the duties of Shadow Cabinet, I spent the rest of my parliamentary years pursuing causes. Among many were the Gurkhas, of whom more later, and there was the recurring theme of freedom of religious expression which was under threat from laws on equality and on hatred.

Gradually freedom of speech has been eroded in this country until we have arrived at a point, which once we condemned in the Soviet regime, where expressing a view which contradicts State orthodoxy means losing one's livelihood or facing disciplinary proceedings or even finding the police on the doorstep.

A couple in Lancashire was questioned for an hour and forty minutes after asking to place Christian literature in register offices, alongside the Council's own literature on civil partnerships. The Council could simply have said no, but instead actually complained to the police. So did listeners when Lynette Burrows, a respected children's author, said on the radio that she thought homosexual couples should not adopt and who was subsequently rung up by police, while Trafford Housing Trust demoted a man and imposed a 40 per cent pay cut just because he had written on his *private* Facebook page that he was not in favour of gay marriage and had in the words of the judge, who ruled his demotion unfair, expressed himself very moderately upon the subject. Those who had complained simply took the view that he had no right to express the opinion at all.

Then there has been the rising number of cases of people disciplined just for wearing a religious symbol or saying something as innocuous as 'God Bless' or offering to pray for someone. If a Muslim makes some religious comment in my presence I do not become offended. If, when I was a Protestant, a Catholic offered to say a 'Hail Mary' for me then I would have replied merely 'thank you'. Britain, once the most tolerant of nations, is becoming intolerant of one of the most basic freedoms: the right to express an opinion or to proclaim a faith, and more dangerously is moving to a point where its citizens can be forced to affirm that which they do not believe.

When I was growing up in the immediate post-war period, when people had lost lives and limbs and homes to the Nazis, the fascist Oswald Mosley was still allowed to make speeches and Colin Jordan to hold his vile rallies. During the Cold War when missiles were lined up and pointing straight at us and our spies were running daily risks, one could still proclaim oneself a communist and sell the *Morning Star* quite openly. For that matter it was lawful to put up communist candidates for Parliament.

I have no doubt that very many people were offended but we regarded liberty as more important. Whatever happened to that simple principle which politicians of all parties appear to have comprehensively abandoned?

Backbench activity was not, however, all. In 2002 I agreed to serve on the Home Affairs Select Committee and became immersed in an examination of asylum. My greatest joy came when I persuaded the Chairman, John Denham, also a former Home Office Minister, to agree to a study of prison regimes with the emphasis on work and education. Sadly I left the committee before the work was finished and with reluctance but the following year my mother had a bad fall. She was then still active but for the time being I was needed at home from where I did as much work as possible.

2002 was also memorable for three other reasons: two new cats arrived, my second book *An Act of Treachery* was published and I had the first major health scare of my life.

Chapter Twenty-Seven

GETTING A LIFE

A n *Act of Treachery* was always the book I had wanted to write first but it was set in Second World War France and I knew the research was huge. I had not finished a novel since I was eighteen and had written not a word of fiction for ten years when I began writing in 1997 so I knew I could not afford to be side-tracked by research. I had to concentrate on writing. That was why I began with *The Clematis Tree*.

It was just as well because whereas the publishers loved *The Clematis Tree,* they were very unenthusiastic about the next book. It did however do well enough to come 14th in the *Times* bestseller lists and, regularly reprinted, is now still selling, as are the other three books, all these years after publication.

Pugwash and Carruthers had been chosen from the cat shelter when my mother came to live with me. Carruthers was old anyway and had been starved at some time in his life. I chose him because I wanted to give him a good end to his life not because I expected him to be with us for long but Pugwash was a young, active cat. It was therefore a shock when he died at the beginning of 2002 a fortnight after Carruthers. My mother missed him keenly but we decided to postpone getting any more cats till after our annual cruise.

After we returned we obtained Pugwash II and Arbuthnot, a brown tabby, who our Chief Whip, James Arbuthnot, was certain had been named after him.

It being recess I made time that September to visit an old colleague, along with David Amess. Ivor Stanbrook was in a nursing home, having suffered a stroke which left him unable to speak. He just uttered the same 'wodja, wodja' sound whenever he was trying to answer us but it was clear he understood what we were talking about.

Sobered, we stood outside the home and commented that nobody could know when illness would come, that either of us could be struck down that very night. We said it but we did not really absorb it. It was only a matter of hours before I learned the lesson for myself.

I woke in the early hours of the next morning and my heart gave a great shudder as I sat up. The room was spinning round me. I lay there waiting for the sensation to go but it did not. I tried to get out of bed and fell over, the room still spinning at a rate of knots. I thought I was having a stroke and for the first time in my adult life called the doctor in the middle of the night. Perhaps instead I had been poisoned very badly by some food I had eaten at an office gathering. The only possibility I eliminated was heart attack because, despite the initial huge thump, there were no chest pains.

Farce then ensued. I woke my mother but she was afraid that if she opened the door to the doctor the new cats might shoot out and never be seen again. However there was a researcher, Michael Hogg, staying overnight so my mother tried to wake him, first by calling, then by thumping on the ceiling with a stick. There being no response, I tried to bang the stick on the ceiling too but, having no control over my movements, waved it in the air, narrowly missed my mother and fell over on the floor. My mother had just decided to climb the stairs and shake him awake when he heard the commotion.

He and she then chased the cats around and confined them to the lounge. There was nothing whatever funny in the aftermath. A series of tests confirmed no stroke and no Ménières but the viral labyrinthitis, which is how the attack was eventually diagnosed, lasted five months. I was told I would be able to drive after four weeks but did not even try for seven and did not succeed for nine weeks. It cost me a fortune in paying a local taxi firm to take me everywhere but that was nothing compared to the horrible feeling that the earth was tilting.

I had been told to keep active, which was sound advice, as I was effectively learning to balance *de novo*. Some people resort to bed rest because they feel so vulnerable but it is the worst decision one can make. Gradually I learned to walk upright without having to clutch on to something and to go upstairs without hauling myself by the bannister. Then I went outside with a stick and so on until gradually everything was normal except the funny horizon and the way the ground rushed up to meet me whenever I ran. I also still needed a table or lectern to hold when speaking.

One day in February 2003 I hailed a taxi which pulled up ahead of me and ran to get in. As I was settling in my seat it suddenly came to me that the ground had not risen to meet me and, almost fearing to hope, I looked at the horizon. The resulting yell of triumph and relief caused the taxi driver to jump in his seat. If readers wonder why I have dwelt on this episode, it is because every time it appears in the press that I have had viral labyrinthitis, I receive dozens of letters from fellow-sufferers asking 'When will it go?' to which the only reply is the very unhelpful 'sooner or later'. One of my friends had it for a year. Others are better in days or weeks.

I was blessed it had not come months earlier for it would have destroyed my major venture that year which was the TV series *Fit Club*. When the producers first approached me I was wary. The programme commanded a large audience and there was the potential to lose a lot of weight and become generally fitter but the single disadvantage was enormous – one could look very silly indeed and I had not yet written off a return to the front bench at some stage.

'At some stage' was a euphemism for when Mother had died, but I could never bring myself to phrase it in those terms, particularly then, when she was still such an active, joyful lady.

I came to an agreement with *Fit Club* that I would not be required to do anything I did not want to do and I was very glad I made that stipulation when, in the second episode, they said the next exercise was swimming. The idea of appearing in front of eight million people in my bathing costume was preposterous, so I went off and played tennis instead. The coach was first class and I wished I had received such tuition at school, where I had hated the game.

In those days *Fit Club* was sensibly paced over six months. The group met one Sunday a month so we could easily fit the programme into busy lifestyles. When I was invited back as a judge in 2005 the series was squashed into nine weeks with a weigh-in each week and I commented to Adam Carey, the series doctor, that very few people would keep off the weight in the long term if they lost it so fast and so artificially. Adam himself has now more or less abandoned television because, in their quest for drama and ever more shocking footage, producers home in on extremes as in *Supersize vs Superskinny*.

I lost eighteen pounds over that six months and had already that year lost the same amount in a two-month radio challenge so ironically I was leaner and fitter when I was struck with the labyrinthitis. However, what *Fit Club* did for me was not merely physical. It gave me my first major television profile and I would be stopped in the street and greeted as 'that MP from *Fit Club*'.

I often speak of *Fit Club* as the beginning of my television career but the next couple of years produced nothing significant on that front and I was occupied by Parliament and writing my third book, *Father Figure*.

I cannot say with any precision when the inspiration for either of the first two books first gripped me but I know well that *Father Figure* came about because of my observation at constituency level of how loaded the court system is against men in family break-up. I have enormous sympathy for Fathers for Justice if somewhat less for some of their antics, but without those rather dramatic demonstrations nobody would have put much energy into addressing their plight. My known association with their cause stood me in good stead when one Easter some activists climbed on to the roof of Westminster Abbey and held up a service. I managed to persuade them to abandon the demonstration as I peeped timidly out from the safety of a window, averting my eyes from the drop.

2003 was notable for the Iraq War, the dodgy dossier and the suicide of the weapons expert Dr Kelly. Blair was no longer seen as truthful and the nation hated the loss of life, but when we look at the decision to attack and depose Sadam Hussein, we have to look at what we knew at the time not what we knew later.

We were only in that silly position because we had not gone on to Baghdad at the end of the First Gulf War, thus sending the Iraqi leader a message that we were not as serious as we might have been. I understand all the reasons for that decision but Sadam's record was appalling, particularly with regard to chemical weapons which he had used more than once. Forbidden to develop weapons of mass destruction, his response was regularly to frustrate the weapons inspectors and to posture that he had a capability, which was certainly not found after the Second Gulf War. It seemed reasonable to conclude that the danger was becoming too great to ignore, particularly given that we were still in the aftermath of 9/11 and the terrorism trail. We forget sometimes that it was not Blair's solo decision to take us to war – Parliament endorsed it. Certainly he wearied of games being played at the UN.

Blair liked to be admired and was always very sensitive to public opinion. He backtracked on hunting after the massive countryside demonstration but he was adamant this time that we had to go to war whatever people may have thought. I watched his face throughout those parliamentary debates and questions and I know that, rightly or wrongly, he believed he had no choice.

Blair was weakened but we were in no position to take advantage of public disillusionment, not merely because we had supported the war but because we were badly under-performing. Towards the end of 2003, the dissatisfaction with Iain Duncan Smith's performance as leader of the party was coming to a head. He simply could not command the House and did not appear to the public as somebody to be taken seriously. Even the whips' office, which will normally defend the leader to the death, was fed up and making less than loyal noises. I rallied behind him but felt no doubt of the outcome, which was that he lost a vote of confidence that November with enough of the old-style way of conducting business to make sure that the defeat was not too humiliating.

A return of some old-style common sense told us not to have yet another bloodbath of a leadership election. This time there must be not a contest but a coronation and the most likely candidate appeared to be Michael Howard. Michael Ancram was supposed to have said that if anybody else stood, he, Ancram, would too with the aim of then withdrawing in Howard's favour.

Lots of pairs of eyes swivelled in my direction. Would I launch another attack? It was six years since I had destroyed Michael's hopes of the leadership and I had always said it was a quarrel not a feud. I had no appetite for another assassination and could not believe that Derek Lewis, who was leading a very successful life, would want to rake up the past again but I rang him as a courtesy, telling him that I believed that Michael would become leader anyway, that it was probably the right outcome for the party at that moment and that if we were to have any hope of landing blows on Tony Blair we did not need to land them on each other. He agreed.

The press began to ring up every five minutes so I devised a one-sentence response: 'I do not retract anything I said in 1997, including the famous phrase, but this is 2003 and I have no intention of rehearsing those matters again.'

It occurred to me that any journalist out to make mischief could ring Michael and omit all after 'phrase' so I rang him myself and read out the single sentence.

He pronounced it 'very generous', which as I was still effectively calling him something of the night seemed a trifle optimistic but I suspect the reaction stemmed from relief. He said we should meet and we duly did so in his room at Parliament. It was a cordial conversation but a strained one in which I told him Derek also wanted an end to the matter (so he need fear no external briefings) and refused to support him outright. Diplomatically, I said I wanted to be certain no one else was standing. What I really meant was that would be too much to ask.

On one matter we were however agreed: the imperative to sort out the Augean stables that was Conservative Central Office with its briefings and factions and conspiracies. He tackled the problem in his usual way by sacking people. The justice of one or two cases was not a matter of universal agreement, but it put the fear of God into that hotbed of disloyalty and a more disciplined approach was observable thereafter. If only the Portillistas had been treated as robustly.

The coronation having taken place, Michael performed the political manoeuvre of burying the hatchet by offering me a front-bench position at the same time as ensuring my refusal by choosing a brief I could never have accepted: Overseas Aid. I could hardly globe-trot given my responsibilities at home. I turned it down flat, whereupon his supporters briefed that I had snubbed him. It says all that needs to be said about my gradual disengagement from political ambition that my reaction to that was no more than a large yawn.

I had some hopes for the party led by Michael. He had a formidable brain, great determination and could think fast upon his feet. Having always been loyal to the leader, he had the right to demand loyalty. He had held high office and had all the necessary experience but the party's performance at the 2005 general election was disappointingly lacklustre and as I travelled around Maidstone on my victory tour, waving and thanking the populace, I learned that Howard had resigned the leadership.

He is a man who could have been a political giant had he only learned to distinguish between toughness and bullying or decisiveness and autocracy, if he had known when to stop in delivering punishment, if his smile did not always remind one of the face of the proverbial tiger, if humanity and humility had played a greater role in his personality. I would trust him with anything except people.

Often at Westminster we would pass judgement on a colleague by asking whether we would serve in the trenches or the jungle with him or her. I would indeed fight alongside Michael, knowing that he would never be cowardly in the face of the enemy or desert his fellow-soldiers. The difficulty is that if the battle went wrong he would immediately be looking for someone to court martial and shoot, or perhaps just shoot.

The vehicle in which I was carrying out my victory tour was nicknamed 'the popemobile' and was the same one I used in each election. It was a blue pickup truck, belonging to John Breach, a local fruit farmer, with a small platform in a box plastered with my posters and campaign balloons. I stood on the platform, held on to the side of the box and harangued the electorate and, between villages, the sheep. When the truck finally gave up the ghost, the box and platform were transferred to another.

I always felt safe which is one of the few advantages of standing five feet and one and a half inches high (and never forget the half inch). Taller mortals felt as if they might pitch head forward into the road. The exception was Paddy Mayhew, the former MP for Tunbridge Wells, who, at over six feet, stood up and developed a faraway look in his eyes, as if fantasising about his army days in a tank.

It was not a popemobile but a pope which dominated the 2005 election for me as I once more travelled the country supporting candidates. Pope John Paul II had died before the campaign and the cardinals were now in conclave at Rome electing a successor. St Peter's Square was full of young people tensely waiting for the white smoke which would herald a new pope. On one dramatic occasion it had seemed as if it had arrived but it was a false alarm and as the smoke turned black cheers turned to groans.

I was keenly hoping Ratzinger, known as God's Rottweiler and who was keeper of the doctrine, would succeed. He was an older candidate but I thought that after the hugely popular John Paul II we needed a quiet period of transition before having a younger pope who would have a long reign. Thus Edward Winstanley, who was head of my staff and accompanying me on the tour to keep a rein on logistics, was listening to the radio at regular intervals.

We were in Pudsey supporting the candidate Pamela Singleton when the news came that there was white smoke. Edward cried out in excitement and we both fell upon the radio. It was clear from the reaction of Pamela and her helpers that they had no idea what all the jubilation was about. Later as we were heading for Leeds station Andrew Pierce rang up and broke the news that the new pope was indeed Ratzinger. Eight years later he was to become the first pontiff for six hundred years to resign, feeling too frail at eighty-five to continue. It was a momentous decision which will almost certainly mean that future popes feel able to retire. After all, Ratzinger, keeper of the doctrine, has effectively given them permission to do so.

Only someone with his deeply conservative reputation could have abolished the doctrine of Limbo, which was one of his early acts. A modernising pope would have caused uproar had he done so but it went almost unnoticed and was accepted from a pope who re-instated Friday abstinence from meat – which had been modified in 1985 – encouraged the Latin Mass and brought the liturgy back to a more literal translation from that language.

I knew that I was now entering my last Parliament and in 2005 I sold my cottage. There were those who advised me not to put it up for sale before the election but it seemed deceitful to make a virtue of living in Sutton Valence only to sell the cottage as soon as I was returned so, as was my wont in my constituency, I acted honestly and put it openly on the market. I was also advised not to say it would be my last Parliament in case people thought I might be losing interest but again I rejected the advice.

My reward was a healthy majority in Maidstone of 14,856 votes.

I missed the cottage and the quaint village in which it was situated but I faced the fact that I was then hardly using it. Mother was now ninety-four and in failing health. Since I could not be away overnight at the cottage and tended to drive back to London no matter how late, it was of little use to me and therefore to the taxpayer and it made sense to sell it and to use a hotel on the occasions when I did stay overnight.

My last Parliament saw the final triumph in the campaign on behalf of the Gurkhas. I had been battling with ministers for years to give them something better than a P45 and a one-way ticket to Nepal at the end of fifteen years' service when anybody coming into Britain on the back of a lorry got better treatment. There were also issues about the extent to which their families could accompany them while based in Britain and fees for the children of serving Gurkhas in higher education.

I was first alerted to the situation by an officer in the 36 Engineer Regiment, which was stationed in Maidstone and which had a Gurkha attachment. Whenever the Gurkhas appeared in civic parades they earned a huge round of applause and Britain did not understand why they were treated so badly, a situation which had its roots in agreements made in the 1940s.

The turning point was not one of my adjournment debates or letters or questions but the appearance on the scene of Joanna Lumley, a demonstration if one were needed of the power of the celebrity in public life. Our own ministers had been every bit as keen as Labour ones to maintain the status quo but the surge of support around the Gurkhas persuaded the party to change its mind and on 29 April 2009 an Opposition motion forced a climbdown.

Outside Parliament the Gurkhas were celebrating and cheering. As I switched my eyes from where a group of them were feting Joanna I saw, standing just a few feet from me, one of those whom I had met often in the course of the campaign. As our eyes met he saluted me. I felt a momentary stinging of tears. *A Gurkha saluted me* would not be a bad parliamentary epitaph. Sadly too much enthusiasm and bad advice in Nepal meant that some Gurkhas arrived here poor and ill-equipped to manage, but justice had at last been done.

Meanwhile the party was once more becoming image-obsessed under the new leader, David Cameron. I had not supported him. He had been in Parliament for only four years when he stood as leader and, if I had worried about Hague's experience, this seemed madness. At least his opponents had some experience of government and had been around long enough to experience a whole range of different parliamentary situations. I thought him big-headed and dismissive of everything that had gone before and it did not help that he was an admirer of Michael Howard.

His last opponent still standing was David Davis, a friend of mine from student politics who, whatever advantages he may have possessed, was an uninspiring speaker and when the two went head-to head at the 2005 party conference, I stayed away from the event, knowing that unless Cameron threw it away he must surely win. He has presence and confidence and took a leaf from my book by walking about without notes. I could hear the excitement from where I was signing books in the foyer. Oh, how I would have loved to have been in such a contest!

Once he had won I tried to give him my loyalty, which in many ways was made easy by the way he began to look like a prime minister in waiting. We might just win, I thought, and cheered him on. Maybe he wasn't quite so big-headed, I hoped, when we had a cordial conversation. And if he was, so what? Churchill was hardly a modest man.

Yet the image nonsense wearied me and I did not attempt to hide my scorn of the manipulation of the candidate selection process. First there was the abominably arrogant treatment of former MPs, although to be fair, that did not start with Cameron: it merely grew worse.

I did not think that there was anything superior about those of us who survived the electoral carnage of 1997. We were privileged still to be in Parliament and it ill-behoved us to lord it over colleagues who had lost. Those who were sufficiently senior went to the Lords and those nearing retirement could, if they so chose, give up altogether but that left a sizeable body of former MPs who had served for years and who wanted to come back.

Once a man or woman who had been selected, elected and re-elected would be automatically on the candidates' list and free to enter the selection fray following a subsequent defeat. Yet now such was the desire to do away with the past that there was an attempt also to dispense with those who had been part of that past.

Jacques Arnold, who had represented Gravesham for ten years, had not run off to find a seat where the Conservative sun shone bluer, but stayed and fought again. In October 2005, he received this charming letter from Andrew MacKay, then responsible for overseeing candidate selection:

Dear Jacques,

The Candidates Committee have decided not to place you on the new List and I thought you should hear it from me as Deputy Chairman rather than them. This is an exciting time for the Party and there is much to be done so I hope you might consider working with us.

Please come in and see me so we can have a chat.
Kindest regards,
Andrew MacKay

Outraged, I took the letter to Cameron himself, who agreed it was 'quite inappropriate' and I could see that he was genuinely displeased but no apology was sent to Jacques.

'The grammar is awful, too,' I observed and Cameron laughed.

Former MPs were having to fill in the same forms as new applicants. I was asked to give a reference for Chris Butler, who was already in Parliament when I arrived. The form questioned what speaking experience he had and what sort of meetings I had heard him address and why I thought he was loyal to the party. It was ludicrous.

Most ludicrous of all was the A-list. Cameron wanted to broaden the party's image by filling its benches with women, homosexuals and those from ethnic minorities. I can safely say that nobody has ever told me on a doorstep that he or she was not voting for me because the party lacked women, gays and ethnics. However, given that is what Cameron wanted, there were many already on the list but he also wanted them new and exciting and was, crucially, unbothered about previous experience. As a result the realities of parliamentary life shocked some of them to the core. One of his A-listers, Louise Mensch, resigned her seat less than three years after the election, while another is a thorn in Cameron's side. They are gloriously wilful and high-five each other in corridors when they have defeated their own coalition, an unthinkable action for my generation which would have worn a more-in-sorrow-than-in-anger expression. Most ironic of all, such bias inevitably brought in a new urban element which has thwarted his plans to repeal the hunting ban.

As part of the attempt to bring in more women, constituencies were told there must be equal numbers of men and women on the shortlists. In other words regardless of merit, men must be left off in favour of women if there was not an equal balance. So supposing a constituency selection committee placed a woman at the top and then, in order of merit, five men and then another woman, three of the men placed above her would have to be discarded for the final. For a party which believes in fair competition that is blatantly manipulative, dictatorial and plainly unfair.

I have never understood how any woman can want positive discrimination. In the 1970s the attitude was robust: give us equal opportunities and we will show that we are as good as the men. In the 1990s that became: we can't manage without special measures to smooth our paths and we want advantages over the men in order to compete. I believe it is the right of every woman in Parliament and elsewhere to look every man in the eye and to know that she got there on exactly the same basis as he did. If not, then she has become a second-class citizen.

In 1997 when all the Blair Babes came in, many as a result of positive discrimination, one commented to me a few months later that it was dreadful that the men were so rude to the women. I responded that it was also dreadful how the men were so rude to the men but she had not thought of that, having just been given a hard time in the Chamber and assuming it was because she was a woman rather than that she just had not given a good performance. The culture of whingeing grievance is silly and sad. It lets down women and is hardly worthy of the heirs to the suffragettes.

I do not suppose I endeared myself to David Cameron by the loudness of my opposition to the A-list but I was loyal to him in other respects and sent him the occasional encouraging note. Today my concern is less that Cameron is big-headed than pigheaded. His haughty dismissal of the anguish his pursuit of gay marriage has caused to some of his most loyal supporters in the country has driven them into the arms of UKIP, and if they are not wooed back then the only beneficiary will be Miliband. So many colleagues tried to talk to him at Westminster and were brushed off.

Yet he is undeniably able. He needs only to add a touch of humility and generosity to that ability to win success but, as with his mentor Michael Howard, that does not come easily and he appears unaware of its importance. Iain Duncan Smith and Michael Gove are making the sort of changes the country can respect and it would be a pity if their efforts were to be vitiated by the Prime Minister's obsession with image and 'modernising'.

After my mother died I set about building what would be my life when I left. In 2007 I confirmed to the constituency that I did not wish to stand again but then had to refrain from making that public until we could be certain that Gordon Brown was not going to call an election to secure a fresh term for himself. Had he done so I would have stood rather than let my association try to find a candidate at the gates of a general election. My profound relief when Brown decided not to go to the country told me how much I was now desirous to go.

I had hoped to announce it at my sixtieth birthday party when Aled Jones came and sang 'How Great Thou Art' to a party of more than ninety friends and family members in the House of Commons. I remembered my mother and Cardinal Hume coming to my fiftieth in the same room and felt a twinge of sadness that both were now gone.

I was house-hunting in Dartmoor but my own London sale fell through and I was obliged to withdraw from the purchase of a house with glorious views across the moors that I had been hoping to make my new home. 2007 had been a bad year: I had lost Mother, then Pugwash II who succumbed to cat flu, now the house purchase. I nicknamed Arbuthnot Luke, after St Paul's famous statement in prison that *only Luke is with me now*.

2008 began as an improvement. I secured the sale of my London house and found that my prospective purchase was still on the market. I bought it for its views but knew I would have to destroy the inside of the house, which was elderly and covered with 1950s-style linoleum.

On the day of the move the House of Commons was facing a very close vote on the future of sub-post offices, so I left Edward Winstanley and my nephew Sean in charge while I voted and then joined them in the early hours of the following morning.

There were times over the next three years when I felt I had bitten off more than I could chew but gradually the massive renovation project was accomplished. I had the library I had always promised myself, fireplaces, a state-of-the-art kitchen and some of the best views on Dartmoor. I longed to settle there permanently but also felt a slight tug at the thought of leaving Parliament.

I rented a flat in London to see out the time left. I would have been entitled to claim second-home expenses on it but felt that as it was my choice and mine alone to move to Dartmoor, it was unfair to hand the taxpayer the bill. Some friends told me I was being prissy but in view of what was to come, I am glad I was.

I was writing for the *Express*, this time the daily paper, and enjoying it. My fourth novel, *An Act of Peace,* had come out in 2005 and now I was beginning also to make television documentaries and to appear on quiz shows. In 2006 I had a highly successful appearance as chairman on *Have I Got News for You* and was invited back again in 2007, when thanks to the vulgarity of Jimmy Carr, it was not successful at all. You are only as good as your last programme and I have not been invited back since.

The documentaries largely went well but in 2006 *Ann Widdecombe to the Rescue* illustrated some of the pitfalls. I had a brief, well-publicised, stint as an agony aunt with the *Guardian*. It was by no means the usual type of agony aunt column, going by the name of *Buck Up,* and dispensing robust, old-fashioned remedies. It was the brainchild of Ian Katz but I could not see why anyone would write in with the purpose of being told off. Few did. However the idea appealed to David Mortimer, head of factual entertainment at the BBC.

He asked me to do a series in which I travelled the country sorting out everything from a lady whose husband played too much golf to a child whose parents would not let him have a pet mouse. We made a pilot programme in which I advised a mother and daughter who rowed all the time. It was very straightforward and a bit like a grown-up version of *Supernanny*. The series was commissioned but somewhere along the line the nature of the programmes changed and the BBC tried to make it into a send-up of me.

Naturally they did not confide such purpose to me so I was hardly giving them the reactions which would have fulfilled the agenda. The programmes became neither fish nor fowl. Worse still, they crammed three problems into each episode and everywhere I went people expressed frustration that they could not see enough of any situation. Somehow programme makers have formed the view that the public cannot concentrate for more than five minutes and must be presented with constant change as if fractious children. It is a myth to which all television seems to subscribe.

The following year a more sensible series came along in the shape of *Ann Widdecombe Versus*. The episodes were longer and concentrated on a single subject: Ann Widdecombe versus benefit cheats, prostitutes and truants. I had already made a programme for *Trevor MacDonald Tonight* on hoodies and these were spawned from its success. The ratings were good and the producers pleased.

Some images still haunt me. In Peterborough we found a prostitute, Colette, who wanted to leave but could get no help. Like so many of her kind she was on the game to pay for a Class-A drug addiction. Like the others she regarded the distribution of Methadone by well-meaning authorities as a joke: it was regarded as a free hit, kindly supplied by the State, not a substitute for the real thing. We tried hard to make some arrangements for her to go to Scotland where she had a relative and gave her a mobile phone to keep in touch. Colette almost certainly traded it in for drugs because she went off the radar.

In Derby I met the Philpott family, which consisted of Mick Philpott, his wife, mistress and eleven children still at home, all crammed into a three-bedroomed council house. Known as 'Shameless Mick', he had a child each year by each woman, lived on benefits and was demanding a bigger house. I could say much but cannot for, at the time of writing this, Mick Philpott and his wife are on trial, charged with the manslaughter of six of the children, and I do not know what legal processes may still be in being when the book is published.

Also that year I made a cameo appearance in *Doctor Who*, which brings me fan mail even now. I also made an advertisement for Giovanni Rana pasta which was tongue in cheek but sparked a great deal of huffing and puffing about whether MPs should make advertisements at all. I received one letter from a British company to ask why I was promoting their competition. I told them to go out and make their own advertising.

2008 saw the beginning of a run of religious documentaries which remain my favourites. I made a programme on the Reformation, which was well received even by those who were usually critical, often at a personal level. That was followed by one on the Ten Commandments in 2009 and in 2011 by yet another on the future of Christianity.

The programme on the Reformation was memorable for my filming the Orange March in Northern Ireland and the Festival of Fire at Lewes where they burn the Pope in effigy. How the citizens of Lewes ever get away with pushing carts of burning wood through the streets within inches of spectators is inexplicable under health and safety legislation but the answer is probably the same as with the Appleby Horse Fair, where spectators stand within feet of flying hooves: some traditions are too powerful to be regulated.

The Orange March showed how far peace has progressed in Northern Ireland. This once most contentious of events, which rarely took place without violence or disorder, had taken on the character of a giant fancy-dress fete.

When making the programme on the Ten Commandments I took to the streets around the Inns of Court and pushed a microphone under the noses of lawyers to ask them how many of the Ten Commandments they could list. Oddly only one of them remembered *thou shalt not bear false witness against thy neighbour*! In one memorable encounter a young man replied, 'No, I'm Jewish.' I did manage to wait until he was out of earshot before muttering, 'But so was Moses.'

Naturally we went to Mount Sinai. My last visit to that part of the world had been to Palestine when the BBC's *Any Questions* went there for the millennium and on the panel was an ex-terrorist, who gave me a Christmas present. I put it in my case intending to unwrap it on Christmas Day.

The exit checks at Tel Aviv airport are extensive and the Israelis extremely jumpy. I was asked, in the course of quite a long inquisition about what I had been doing in Israel, whether I had anything in my luggage which I could not indentify. Yes, a present. From whom?

'Sallah al Tamari.'

They stepped back several paces and asked me to produce it. I did. They stepped back again and told me to open it. It turned out to be a cushion cover.

I understand the nervousness. That country is subject to regular attacks from Hamas but the world only seems to notice when the Israelis strike back. Alone in a sea of hostile states, Israel depends upon support from the United States to keep it safe.

Writing became squeezed out. I found it quite possible to write and be an MP and to make television and be an MP but not to do all three. The novels, I realised ruefully, would have to wait until retirement, which was drawing closer.

I knew there was much I would not miss but also much that I would. In this country there is an army of unsung heroes and heroines who give their all to help others and every MP has them in the constituency. I would look at two of mine, Pat McCabe and Pat Wilmshurst, and think *and for His dwelling and His throne chooseth the pure in heart.*

I should miss the campaigns and the sense of achievement when an intervention made a significant difference to an individual life and small things like the gatherings in the smoking room after late-night votes. I was glad I had spent my life as I had but it was time for change.

Then came an event which so soured that last Parliament that those of us leaving could not wait to do so and many others wished they had stood down too: the expenses scandal.

Chapter Twenty-Eight
DEPARTING (2)

It is impossible to overestimate the damage done to Parliament by the expenses scandal. The press and media elected melodrama over truth and the public preferred a witch-hunt to justice. Party leaders vied with each other as to whose shirt was hairiest and plenty of decent people were traduced. The only commentator who seemed to understand the real situation was the then Archbishop of Canterbury, Rowan Williams.

There were MPs who had been fraudulent, most of whom have paid the penalty and rightly so. There were many more who were greedy and were equally deserving of exposure but, even after four inquiries and the *Telegraph* revelations, the majority were neither frauds nor grabbers.

What do you remember most vividly? The duck house? The moat? The helicopter pad? Well, there was no helicopter pad at all and neither Peter Viggers nor Douglas Hogg claimed for the duck house or the moat. Surprised? Read on.

The helicopter pad was a family joke. It was a small patch where a table and chairs sat in a normal garden and which the Spicer family had dubbed 'the helipad'. The gardener was party to the jest and submitted an invoice for clipping 'the helipad'. Michael Spicer should have been more alert to the potential for trouble but that, not extravagance at the taxpayer's expense, was his only failing.

How many families have no in-jokes? My father's pride and joy in his retirement was his vegetable patch. He watched the produce grow and would often go out and see how the potatoes or courgettes or carrots were progressing. My mother always called this ironically 'surveying the estate' and some of the neighbours copied the phrase, also in fun. Estate? It was a vegetable patch fifteen feet long. Helipad? It was a bit of patio in the garden.

It was perfectly acceptable to send the fees office staff a schedule of all the maintenance work carried out in the year from which they could take their pick as to what was permissible and within the financial limits. The schedules often greatly exceeded the total sums allowed so under no circumstances could everything on them be said to be being claimed. Both the duck house and moat cleaning were in such a schedule.

I saved myself from a similar scandal just by being wary. On each bill for hotel stays which I submitted I wrote 'claimed' or 'not claimed' beside each item. Had I not done so any journalist looking at the bill could have said I was claiming for my drinks or having friends to dinner, because the chances of his noticing that the sum claimed was different from the sum of the bill would have been very low.

However, perhaps the most important questions are why were we allowed to claim for second homes at all and how did it all get so out of hand? The theory was simple: we had to live in two places throughout a Parliament and this could mean that for twenty or twenty-five years MPs were having to divide their time between Westminster and the constituency. If that constituency was Kensington and Chelsea that was easy enough, but if it was Penzance or Highlands and Islands that was rather different. Therefore we needed two homes. So we had an allowance for the second home but had to account for how we spent it and there were rules within which we had to operate.

We could buy a home, in which case we had to find the deposit and the capital repayments every month. Given that we would already be paying mortgages on our main homes this was a not inconsiderable extra cost. Some therefore chose to rent because there was no cost to the MP, but rents go up so it is not a good bargain for the taxpayer, as will soon become apparent from the new rules which prohibit buying. Others chose to use hotels or London clubs which is fine if you do not move the family around with you.

Any essential costs associated with the second home and which were within the limits were allowed so some people, like me, did everything from the allowances: council tax, water rates, fuel, repairs as well as mortgage in order to reduce the subsidies we would have to make otherwise. Richer members were more care-free. If their boilers blew up just as they approached the limit of their allowances they sighed and reached for the petty cash.

The rules were strict: we could charge repair but not better-ment so the myth that we could put whole new posh kitchens on the allowances was a nonsense. We could charge to have our grass cut but not to plant flowers. I had a beautiful garden and charged for not a petal. In short the theory was we could claim for anything which we had no choice but to do, in the home we would not have had to have, had we not been MPs.

Some readers will say that surely we could manage to run a second home anyway on the salaries we earn but an MP earns nothing like as much as a GP or head of a large school and how many GPs or heads do you know who run second homes? I have always believed that MPs should earn a more substantial salary and have no second home allowances and so do most of those who have held inquiries but they have dodged the issue because anybody who proposes a salary rise for MPs is howled down and derided.

MPs themselves have been no better at getting to grips with the issue, courting popularity and playing to the gallery rather than seeking sensible solutions.

So that was the theory: the second home was a necessary cost and therefore all necessary expenses associated with it must be allowed. Unnecessary expense was not. What on earth then happened?

The answer is two-fold. First it looks as if some MPs were encouraged to think of the second home allowances as extra income rather than cost-reimbursement and secondly the fees office had a habit of trying to help us by interpreting the rules flexibly in the early days when the allowances simply were not enough and continued the habit long after the allowances had become adequate and realistic.

In response to public outrage at what was seen as a massive spending spree at taxpayers' expense Sir Thomas Legg was asked to examine all our expense claims over four years and to assess if they met *the rules prevailing at the time*. On the day his report was due to be published I walked into the House of Commons utterly confident that I had nothing to fear, having observed the rules meticulously. An internal audit had already said my expenses were in order and the *Telegraph* had proclaimed me a saint.

It was Andrew Pierce who told me that rumour had it that Legg, far from applying the rules prevailing at the time, had decided to impose retrospective limits for gardening and cleaning. It was both unjust and illogical.

The injustice lay in retrospectivity, a very poor principle in legislation. It is as if a street has a 50-mile speed limit which is then changed to a 30-mile limit and then all the camera records are examined in order to prosecute everyone doing 40 when the limit was 50.

So while the rules said we could claim only for maintenance but not for enhancement, Legg imposed, retrospectively, a rule which said there were actual monetary limits. I asked Michael Howard if he thought it legal and he said probably not.

The illogicality lay in picking just gardening and cleaning. Why not repairs? Why not mortgages?

I was not much affected. In one year I had exceeded the new gardening limit by £230. Yet I objected to the principle. The Legg Report was also sloppy and inaccurate in that some of its figures were wrong and there was a laziness about the way letters went unanswered.

The public cared for neither injustice nor sloppiness nor for the wild inaccuracy of some of the reporting. The sound of the witch-hunt was deafening and the whips were afraid there might be a suicide. Children were told in their school playgrounds that their dads were thieves. Huge repayments were demanded in some cases and simple errors were magnified to look like theft.

My constituents were silent, having nothing about which to protest, but as I took to the airwaves to protest at Legg's methods some muttered that I should not criticise him. I retorted that I had spent the last five Parliaments fighting injustice and if I had done that for so many others I did not see why I should not do it for myself and for colleagues.

We stood up for ourselves to the extent of demanding an appeals procedure and Sir Paul Kennedy, a senior judge, was asked to consider our representations. He was used to operating without fear or favour, was moved neither by MPs' protests nor the public's thirst for blood and brought an impartial analytical approach to each and every case, overturning some decisions and absolving MPs who had been vilified for no abuse at all. The Chief Whip told me he would have liked such vindication but Cameron had forbidden his senior people to appeal. He was sacrificing justice to electoral appeal and he was not alone in doing so. The party leaders should have come together, expelled the real wrongdoers and insisted on individual justice but instead they tried to outdo each other with ever tougher measures. Some might say they had no choice given the imminence of an election but if they had acted together there would have been neither advantage nor disadvantage.

The reputation of Parliament was deeply damaged. That has ramifications beyond the moment. The public complains about the quality of MPs and it is right to do so but why would any serious person come into Parliament now? Why would a high-achieving man who wants to help run the country or deploy experience gained over a working lifetime decide to put himself in the firing line over every bus ticket? Or join a profession everyone despises as sleazy?

Two types of person will eventually come to make up Parliament: the millionaires who can afford to claim nothing at all and the career politician who has no experience to offer. The rest will make their contribution elsewhere and I could not blame them.

Parliament's authority figure is the Speaker and until that Parliament the Speaker was always regarded as above the fray but Michael Martin had encountered hostility from the start because after Betty Boothroyd it should have been the Conservatives' turn and Labour used its large majority to ignore the custom. This was in Labour's first Parliament when Blair was at his most arrogant, believing he could do as he pleased and that there was no remedy available to us. He had already, as noted, moved Prime Minister's Questions to once a week without consultation. Martin was always resented and there was regular grumbling.

The climax came over the arrest of Damian Green when police entered the House of Commons and, without a warrant, searched his office. The offence of which he was suspected was aiding and abetting misconduct in a public office by receiving information from a civil servant in the Home Office. Martin seemed to blame Jill Pay, the Serjeant-at-Arms, for letting the police enter the premises without a warrant.

The post of Serjeant-at-Arms is generally held by an ex-military man and Michael Martin had appointed Jill in preference to a brigadier, who would almost certainly have sent the police off to get a warrant, and the House did not like the sound of a buck being passed. From that moment on he had lost the goodwill which still existed towards him and when his own expenses were queried he finally resigned in 2009. I always found him genial and fair but that had become a minority view.

This time surely even Brown would not be silly enough to try and force another Labour Speaker on the House? He did not need to because a Labour-leaning candidate sat on the Conservative benches in the shape of John Bercow.

The rules stated that anybody standing for Speaker had to have three nominations from MPs of parties other than his own and the joke in the Commons was that it was lucky for Bercow that he did not have to find three from his own side. I had always been fairly friendly with him but had watched him currying favour with Labour over some years and knew that if he were elected there would be more grumbling and that if the House were to get into the habit of turning on the Speaker it would become a rabble.

Nigel Evans, who is now a Deputy Speaker, asked me if I would consider standing. Had this been happening two years earlier I would have been tempted but by then my retirement plans were simply too far advanced. Being without a house in London did not matter much as the Speaker has an official residence but I had a successor in place who had been working the constituency for eighteen months and I did not see how I could turn round to my association and say that I was staying after all. I said no.

Nigel sought me out again. He had been speaking to some Labour MPs and they thought I should stand as a temporary Speaker to clean up the mess after the expenses scandal and hand over to a new, cleansed Parliament. He said he would see if the idea resonated on our own side.

Meanwhile the letters and emails had started to come in. I must stand. I was respected in the country. I was fearless. I could clean the place up. I had seen these statements before, when I had been contemplating standing for the leadership of the party and ever since I had declined to do so, I had received letters asking why I had not stood. I thought that if I stood now and stayed in until eliminated I should at least prevent an avalanche of letters asking me why I had not stood.

That however was merely an ironic reflection and I now had to apply my mind seriously to the issue. Did I really want the job? What could I bring to it over a year that other candidates would not bring over two Parliaments?

I took soundings and told Nigel that, yes, I would stand. Kim Howells told me he would find votes on the Labour side. The Irish said they would support Patrick Cormack but transfer their votes to me if he went out, but enough people rang me up to urge me to stay on for another Parliament in order to secure their vote for me to know that I could not win on the temporary basis I was offering.

There was no shortage of candidates: Margaret Beckett, Alan Beith, John Bercow, Parmjit Dhanda, Alan Haselhurst, Michael Lord, Richard Shepherd and George Young.

Michael Lord, Patrick Cormack, Parmjit Dhanda and Richard Shepherd were eliminated in the first ballot so at that point I knew I could rely on the Irish votes transferring but my performance simply had not been strong enough and I knew I would also lose votes now to more likely candidates. At that stage I could have withdrawn but had decided that if I stayed in until eliminated nobody could say I had not tried so I stayed in the race to be eliminated in that ballot. If my own vote had held up then the Irish votes would have taken me through but even if that had happened I was still too far behind the front runners, John Bercow and George Young.

I still receive letters even now, asking why I did not stand.

In my speech on that occasion I said that we needed somebody provenly capable of connecting with the general public, whom the public knows and by and large trusts and whom the public recognises and listens to. I could fulfil those criteria which is why 'among these very trusty old serving senators here this afternoon, I put myself before you as the rather vulgar tribune'.

I then turned to more internal matters, pointing to my record in the fight for backbench rights and criticising the power of the Executive and the lack of scrutiny. I returned to expenses again at the end, stating that whatever had gone wrong we must always remember the core principle that people of modest means must not be deterred from entering this House.

Re-reading that speech again for the purposes of this book, I could not fault it.

That morning I was endorsed by *The Times* as the most acceptable candidate. There are worse notes on which to leave the House of Commons.

The departure came a year later. The expenses scandal still rumbled, Douglas Hogg (the moat man) refused to contest the next election, which was a major loss to the House. Anybody who doubts that should look at his speech against the Iraq War at a time when few in the party took his view.

In the run-up to the end of that Parliament I and other retiring members were subject to the usual offers of jobs and consultancies when we left. Roger Freeman stopped me to ask if I was interested in non-executive directorships and I said a very firm no. I did not want any more piles of paper to crunch, any more bulging briefcases. The *Catholic Times* asked if I would consider writing for it once again as I had done in the 1990s. I kept it on file.

To those who said they expected me to go to the Lords I replied that I should like to but that it was solely a matter for David

Cameron. To offers of consultancies I said thanks very much but I was already fully committed. I would keep their letter on file and bear them in mind if I were to be seeking such opportunities later. The file in which I did keep anything which I thought might appeal was regularly filleted and remained very thin. It did not contain the infamous Anderson Perry letter.

It was with head-scratching that my office tried to recall the approach when the scandal broke. Those leaving received a spoof letter from a non-existent firm called Anderson Perry soliciting their services. Those who pursued it were invited for interview in which it was made quite clear that this was a lobbying firm looking for and willing to pay well for influence and access. It destroyed a number of potential peerages and added to the general impression that Parliamentarians were corrupt.

I was naturally enough wondering what I would do next and in that final year I would have listed the greatest possibilities in order of likelihood as:

1. The Lords
2. LBC
3. The Vatican

There is no prescriptive right to go to the Lords and a place there is purely at the gift of the PM but there had to be a strong probability: I was a Privy Counsellor, had served in senior ministerial office, had been Shadow Home Secretary and was one of the biggest players in the Hague years. I had emerged clean from the expenses scandal and few did more to travel the country cheering the troops and raising funds. So it was natural enough for colleagues to tell me I was bound to be asked. Most of them did not believe me when I told them it wouldn't happen but I knew because I had received private intelligence from an unimpeachable source that Cameron had set his face against it. The leader of the Lords, Tom Strathclyde, said in front of a number of MPs that it was because of hunting but I cannot believe Cameron that petty or that much in the grip of the squirearchy.

I moved on to the next possibility. Jonathan Richards of LBC was keen for me to take on a regular slot after I had several times stood in successfully for his regular presenters including Nick Ferrari and James O'Brien. He had come to the office to discuss probabilities and I had said I would like a weekly slot as I intended to live on Dartmoor. However when I tried to finalise arrangements he had gone cold on the idea and kept putting me off until I in turn put LBC in the bin.

That left the Vatican to which I attached absolutely no hope at all. Francis Campbell had been a highly distinguished ambassador to the Holy See but was now nearing the end of his term of office. Various people were trailing my name as a successor but I could not believe that I would appeal to Cameron given how I had opposed him so vigorously over the position of Roman Catholic adoption agencies vis-à-vis homosexual couples. He was unlikely to want me representing any government he might form to the Catholic Church.

I therefore mentally wrote off the Vatican and thought that my retirement would be likely to consist of walking on Dartmoor, writing my Wednesday column for the *Daily Express* and producing a novel every other year. I could now at last concentrate on renovating my house and settling down on the moor.

My valedictory speech was given to the House of Commons on 30 March 2010. My opening paragraph speaks volumes about the atmosphere prevailing at that time:

> I had always imagined that when I was making my last speech and about to depart I would be sad. Instead I find that my uppermost sentiment is one of profound relief. I sincerely hope that future generations of Members of this House will be able to serve in an atmosphere free of the welter of public vituperation and vilification that this Parliament has been confronted with, and that there will once again be a recognition on the part of the public that the overwhelming majority of people who come here – on both sides of the House and in all parties – do so with some degree, and sometimes quite a lot, of sacrifice in terms of either finance or family. My hope for the future is that some calmness and some respect will again prevail.

I then returned to the themes which I had made my major concerns: the importance of the family, marriage and the situation of the non-working mother and then the Forgotten Decent on the big estates.

I was followed by Frank Dobson who paid tribute to the two 'veterans' who had spoken before him.

When the election was called I gave my staff a drink and we went out on to the balcony of my office and looked up at Big Ben as we drank a toast. Edward Winstanley was going to work for another MP but was staying with me for a couple more months to complete the 'wind-up'. My caseworker, Bobbie Brasier, had been in the House more than forty years and was retiring. My friend, Veronica Jagnanan, had recently lost her job in the spate of City redundancies and was helping us out after my main secretary Annalinda Riley had found herself a job and was already gone. Young Adam, an intern from Hull University, was packing up boxes.

Who Goes Home? I heard the traditional cry for the last time as Parliament dissolved. I do, I thought.

It was the end of an era. Little did I know what lay in store. The next few months were determined: Edward and I would be off round the country for the election, we would clear out the Maidstone offices, hand over files of outstanding cases and then Edward, Veronica and I would move to Dartmoor to finish off whatever boxes remained. Bobbie would work from home and it would all be over by the end of July. In September I would embark upon *Strictly Come Dancing* on which I expected to last about three weeks. Nobody in the office approved of my being on it at all.

Chapter Twenty-Nine

SUMMER 2010

Strictly Come Dancing had come to me every year for five years and asked me to take part and every year I said no. It seemed inappropriate for a serving MP to commit so much time and to lose so much dignity. In 2009 I felt it safe to say yes with my retirement so imminent but the BBC, mindful of its duty of impartiality and fearing an election that autumn, did not want a party politician in its flagship Saturday-night programme so we exchanged letters of intent for 2010.

Everybody who could be called a friend begged me not to do it. It would upset my fan base, I would look ridiculous, I would lose all credibility.

As I had quickly lost the habits of government in 1997 so I now lost the habits of an MP in 2010. I would no longer be in the House of Commons and it was pointless to behave as though I were: instead I must now make judgements as I would have done if I had never been an MP. Anyway the fiasco was not likely to last long.

The election ended in an indecisive result but Cameron almost certainly acted wisely when deciding to form a coalition rather than a minority administration when the economy was so parlous. *There is nothing left*, said the outgoing Treasury minister in a note to his successor. There never is at the end of Labour administrations.

I was driving along the M4 in my Ford Focus rejoicing in freedom when my hands-free phone rang.

'Miss Widdecombe, it's Number Ten, are you able to take a call from the Prime Minister?'

As I waited to be connected I wondered what it was about. The Lords? No, there would have been no need for more than a standard letter. Some commission? Into prisons, perhaps? No, it was too soon for that sort of initiative to have been approved.

A few seconds later the Prime Minister was offering me the post of ambassador to the Vatican. After responding enthusiastically I suddenly became suspicious. Was this really David Cameron? I had occasionally had hoax callers pretending to be John Major or William Hague but I knew their cadences too well from many a genuine conversation. I had however no real knowledge of how David sounded on the telephone and this was a mobile on a motorway.

'You are not David Cameron,' I said on the spur of sudden certainty.

He was taken aback, as well he might have been, but I told him I would call Number Ten to check and rang off, whereupon I pulled into a service station and telephoned Downing Street.

'Ah, Miss Widdecombe! The Prime Minister is expecting your call.' Cameron dined out on the story for months.

My first reaction was that this was splendid, but then reality set in. So much in the posting was attractive: access to Vatican scholarship, close connection to the highest echelons of the Church, audiences with the Pope, working for the Foreign Office, being part of the Diplomatic Service, three years living in Rome and so much serious work to be done between a highly secular government and the Vatican. In modern parlance what was there not to like?

God and Mammon both posed problems. I had to accept that trying to explain some of the decisions of the government I represented to the Vatican would be as difficult for my conscience as it would be for my diplomacy. Indeed had I accepted the post, I would be out there trying to explain the re-definition of marriage now.

Mammon reared its head when I went to the Foreign Office to meet the Head of the Diplomatic Service, Martin Donnelly. I was offered the same salary as I had as an MP, but I was going to have to give up everything else: my *Express* column, my TV appearances, everything except my novels. That I could manage but when I came back it would be to nothing except my pension and it was too early for that.

It was unsurprising that the salary was so modest compared with that of most ambassadors. There were no trade fairs, no consular function, no visa department. It was not a sought-after post.

The house was an even worse factor. When I took the call from the PM, the kitchen was without floorboards and outside a series of earth mounds showed where excavations were in progress. The loft was full of unsorted boxes of papers, so unlike other diplomats, I would not be able to let the house while I was away. It would not be habitable in any normal way for more than a year. It says much about the seriousness with which I took the offer that I did actually find someone willing to live in the chaos and supervise the renovations. But how on earth was I going to pay for them?

I visited Francis Campbell in Rome. He was keen for me to take the job and said it would spawn its own opportunities when I left and I should not worry about going back to nothing. In particular he believed it would gain me entry to America with its vast TV industry.

I returned undecided. Christ told us to take no heed of tomorrow, to journey with neither scrip nor staff, to place our faith entirely in Him. Should I be considering the practicalities so much? And if the Prime Minister offered one the post of a foreign embassy should not one take it for that reason alone? That the PM had asked?

I was veering towards taking it but asked God for a sign. He obliged but I wish He had not been quite so dramatic.

I occasionally had flashing lights in my eyes but had been assured by a consultant that this was a normal sign of ageing. He had examined the retinas and all was well. That was a year ago and now the flashes were returning but they were different, deep yellow and slower. As I sat in the Old Inn at Widecombe-in-the-Moor, waiting for Edward Winstanley to bring the drinks from the bar I became aware I could see cobwebs. By the next morning I could not see the right-hand side of my nose from my left eye.

I called a taxi, caught a train to London and made the appointments as I travelled. By the time I got to Paddington I had no sight in the left eye. At Moorfields I was seen immediately and told the retina was detached. Well, I said, trying to be brave, lots of people go through life with the sight of only one eye.

'Yes,' replied the surgeon, Lyndon da Cruz. 'But *you* won't have to.'

They were the most beautiful words I had heard in years.

He re-attached the retina in a successful operation and today I have normal sight in that eye. How blessed I am to live in such a country in such an age. How blessed also to have BUPA cover.

The aftermath meant lying on my side on a sofa for ten long days. I dictated letters and Edward and Veronica looked after me. As the sight returned I drew a long sigh of relief. I had been told I needed after-care appointments at regular intervals and that as the operation itself caused a cataract I would need that operation too in a year's time. Italy suddenly became a non-option and I wrote with regret to Martin Donnelly and David Cameron. The PM replied sympathetically.

I assumed *Strictly* was ruled out too (the Vatican post had been moved from September to January to accommodate *Strictly* so it was still in my diary). To my surprise Lyndon da Cruz said I could go ahead with two provisos. I could dance as vigorously as I pleased and carry out any moves I liked but I must not bump my head as a bad bang could re-detach the retina. That is why Anton never held me head down as he did Nancy Dell'Olio a year later and always spun me so I landed firmly on my posterior.

The other problem might be spatial cognition. As my right eye was dominant, it might not happen but judging space could be a problem following re-attachments. I might think a step was further down than it was or I might pour a glass of water and miss the glass. That obviously would have put an end to the venture, but the effects of spatial cognition were minor and short-lived.

So I went ahead with *Strictly* but had to pull out of a paid cruise for a travel article as I could not risk being more than three hours from Moorfields. If any re-detachment were not fixed immediately, I would lose the sight.

That September Pope Benedict was to make a four-day state visit to Britain, in the course of which he was to beatify Cardinal Newman. I had made a documentary on Newman which was to be shown the night before the ceremony on BBC 2 and I was to help cover the visit for Sky Television. All of this was to coincide with *Strictly* training and my diary looked as demanding as when I had been in Parliament.

The papal visit was attracting controversy and the media were looking for the usual melodrama, which they found largely in the scandal of child abuse in the Catholic Church. The Vatican, whose public relations are as bad as that of bankers in the City, was not doing much to put it in context or proportion.

One priest molesting one child is a serious scandal but the media frenzy was creating a view that most priests were involved when less than 5 per cent ever faced allegations let alone charges. There was a much more damaging view too that there had been a 'cover-up'.

Most of the allegations went back to the 1970s and 1980s so let us look at the state of our knowledge about paedophilia at the time and to begin with the unlikely figures of Harriet Harman and Patricia Hewitt, now exemplary mothers and pillars of the establishment, then officers of the National Council for Civil Liberties, which allowed affiliation from the national Paedophile Information Exchange (PIE). It stayed affiliated from 1978 to 1983.

In 1977 the National Council for Civil Liberties stated that it had no policy on PIE's aims but claimed the evidence showed that 'children are harmed if, after a mutual relationship with an adult, they are exposed to the attentions of the police ...'

Does anyone suppose from this that Harriet Harman and Patricia Hewitt back paedophilia and do not want the involvement of the police? No, it merely shows the state of understanding or rather lack of it that then prevailed. The same appalling ignorance is evident in Harman's response on behalf of NCCL to a bill that sought to ban indecent images of under-sixteens. The same body also wanted to decriminalise incest.

I was a Samaritan in the 1980s and we received special training on dealing with child victims but if the perpetrators rang up there was no suggestion we should call the police: confidentiality was essential. It was not until the 1990s that this country had a register of sex offenders and not long before that when we finally came to understand the addictive and repetitive nature of paedophilia.

The Church thought wrongly that if it detached a priest from the source of temptation that all would be well – as if he were attracted to a grown woman, not realising that the reaction would be simply to find another child. It was a disastrous policy but not unique to the Church.

Child abuse is a scourge upon the innocent. It is found in all manner of churches, in the Scout movement, in care homes, in schools, in choirs and most of all in families. There is nothing unique about the Roman Catholic Church but that does not excuse what happened: it just sets it in context. Some of the loudest condemnations came from the BBC, which thanks to the Jimmy Savile scandal, now appears to have been more heavily mired in this disgusting scenario than most.

Thus the papal visit was forecast to be a failure but the script had to be re-written on the first day when the sun came out along with 25,000 people to greet the Pontiff. When he arrived at Westminster Cathedral thousands of youngsters squeezed on to the piazza, kneeling on the hard stone for Mass. Before it started, some recognised me in the Sky box and there followed a stampede for autographs, with the boys and girls standing on each other's shoulders to reach the box and hand down the bits of paper which I had signed. The police, bless them, watched this very dubious demonstration of health and safety with amusement rather than intervention.

In Birmingham the weather was bad but the crowds were undeterred. At Westminster Abbey I saw a man outside with a banner proclaiming *The Pope is the Anti-Christ* and within a few feet of him a girl with a banner proclaiming *We love you, Papa, more than beans on toast.*

It was a wonderful four days even though for the most part I was on the other end of a camera lens and commenting from afar but in Westminster Hall the Pope addressed members of both Houses of Parliament and I went along on a ticket obtained by a friendly member. I arrived early and positioned myself next to the stone commemorating St Thomas More, patron saint of politicians. He was, I worked out, bound to stop there and he did within two feet of me. God's Rottweiler? He looked more like God's Old English Sheepdog.

When David Cameron said goodbye at the airport, Benedict XVI left behind an impact that was not so much of triumph as of healing and the restoration of goodwill towards the Roman Church.

The papal visit over, I could concentrate on *Strictly*, from which I had had to take a week away from training to carry out the Sky coverage, and my new friend, Anton du Beke.

Chapter Thirty

STRICTLY FUN

For those who doubt it, the celebrities have no idea, and nor do the professional dancers, who is to be paired with whom on *Strictly Come Dancing* before it is revealed in the first programme of the season. I had never followed the show so I did not know one dancer from another. Everybody told me to beware Brendan Cole, who is actually a nice chap, and to hope for Anton du Beke.

In the practice sessions I was paired with Vincent Simone for the group dance. We were well matched in terms of height and I thought perhaps that would be the decisive factor. We got on but if the group dance had been my only experience of *Strictly* then I would have left early.

I hated the chaos, the sexual innuendos of the teacher and the loudness. Perhaps I had made a mistake. Whatever had I let myself in for? Only the professionals tried to calm down the dreadful clamour. It gave me an early glimpse of who was taking it seriously and Felicity Kendal was certainly one. While I collapsed with a cappuccino she was practising the moves in front of a mirror.

Somehow the routine shook down into some semblance of order but we still prompted each other. 'Teapot,' I reminded Vincent. 'Three and turn,' he reminded me. When it came to the sexually suggestive moves I murmured to him, 'I don't do this' and he immediately produced a substitute move which would not be too incongruous. I thought we should get on famously if eventually paired, but all my friends were telling me I needed Anton.

'Which one is Anton?' I asked Patsy Kensit. That was the state of my knowledge.

As everybody told me to hope for Anton, I did. When the night came the four people remaining at the end were Anton and Vincent, Felicity and me. I was certain I should be paired with Vincent on height grounds but then I glanced at Felicity and suddenly realised that she was not tall either. I knew then it was Anton with whom I should be spending whatever time I remained in the competition and so it transpired.

The training happens wherever the celebrity lives so mine took place in Devon, in the nearby town of Newton Abbot at the Deborah Bond Dance Academy. Anton would stay in Exeter for three of our days as did the camera team and I would drive in each day or go by car provided by the BBC. As the series took off and I became the surprise sensation, local interest grew and the snappers lurked outside both the academy and the coffee shop, called The Pharmacy, where we lunched nearly every day. When people ask why I didn't lose weight on *Strictly*, I explain that Anton liked lunch and Victoria sponge for dessert.

We had three weeks to train for the first dance, the waltz, which meant two weeks for me as I had to spend one covering the papal visit. I mastered the waltz, which is to say the steps, fairly easily as Anton introduced me to double whisks and turns but when he suddenly increased the pace and whirled me round the ballroom as if only speed mattered I collapsed in a panting heap.

I also had a problem if he taught me steps in a different order from the one he wanted me to perform. If I always twirled at the far left end of the studio, it was no use telling me to do a double whisk there and turn somewhere else. Neither Felicity nor I could understand how we had such problems remembering sequences. She was used to learning several thousand lines of script and I to speaking without notes and neither of us expected to forget our words but we could forget a dance routine that lasted only ninety seconds!

The music for the waltz was 'My Cherie', which I hoped was not a political statement. It was old-fashioned, romantic and nostalgic. The lighting conjured up the same images as we took off, Anton with his usual smile for the audience and me with my usual look of intense concentration and clinging on to him for dear life.

The reactions to a bit of a galumphing dance astounded me. People were in tears, including Scot Maslen, one of my competitors. The audience responded with overwhelming applause, even by *Strictly* standards. In retrospect I understand it better. It was the friendly equivalent of 'and she wasn't used to that, poor girl'. Here was a grumpy old puritan spinster in the arms of one of Britain's most romantic men, waltzing to a romantic tune in a sparkly dress with glitter everywhere.

My own feelings more closely mirrored those of the first comment from the judges: 'Well, you got through it.'

I employed a technique I was often to use on *Strictly* by greeting Craig with the words: 'If you think my waltz was bad, you should see my salsa.' By advertising the next shambles I hoped to persuade people that it might be worth seeing, in which case they would have to ensure I stayed in.

The salsa showed Anton just what a challenge he faced. I would not wear short skirts, I would not wriggle my hips, I would not let him indulge in innuendo. It was all rather different from Laila Rouass, the actress who had partnered him the previous year. I must record that I was given a very different picture of the alleged racist incident between them by those who witnessed the event than I had gleaned from the press. The ordeal had made Anton wary of press interviews and it was some while before he would dance with me without the camera team present, recording every word.

He decided upon comedy and from then on we took the ballroom dances seriously and turned the Latin routines into comedy. Despite the lowest salsa score in *Strictly*'s history, we survived to dance the quickstep. We were never in the bottom two until we were eliminated.

The quickstep was perhaps my favourite of the ballroom dances but it was an appalling week.

A year earlier I had stood on a rainy, darkening day outside Parliament and casually answered a call on my mobile. It was from my brother to tell me he had cancer and had been given a year to live. The shock was indescribable. We came from a long-lived family and I had just assumed that he would be around while we aged together. Bristol was not a long way from Dartmoor and I hoped that when we were both retired we would see each other more often. Indeed my brother had been priest of the same church for forty-seven years and but for his illness I think he would not have retired before the fiftieth anniversary.

He was loving *Strictly*.

The Sunday after the salsa I received a message from Meryl, my sister-in-law, to the effect that he was very poorly. I interpreted this correctly as meaning that if I wanted to see him alive I should go to Bristol there and then.

He was past responding to me and I knew he was aware of my presence only when I was leaving and said quietly 'See you in the New Jerusalem' and he muttered suddenly what sounded like 'I'll be there'. He was only seventy-three.

Two days later, I took the call from my sister-in-law at the Deborah Bond Academy. I left the training studio to take it in private and was immediately surrounded by eager little dancers, wanting my autograph. I had not the heart to refuse them.

My first instinct was to withdraw from *Strictly*. It seemed gross to be dancing on Saturday when my brother had died on Tuesday, but the family was insistent. He had loved my performances so much that withdrawal would be the last thing he wanted. His daughter Fiona and her husband were due to be in the audience that Saturday and they were adamant that they would still be there.

I endured some mawkish rot from the press about how I was going to 'dance away my heartache' and I told Charlotte Oates, the celebrity manager, that under no circumstances were the judges or anybody else to mention it. If there was an aspect of *Strictly* I did not like it was all the public emoting.

My wishes were respected but a sensitive director made sure that our results were read out first and there was no suspense about getting into the next round. We were usually among the last to be told.

As I came up for air after the funeral, I had to face flying.

This had been Anton's bright idea when I had said we needed to do something unusual in order to stay in, given my pedestrian performances. Funny they might be, but unless we created an atmosphere of 'what next?', people might grow impatient.

No celebrity had flown on the programme before and the proposal was taken up enthusiastically. Having been away for the funeral and also having to spend time in the special flying studios at Borehamwood, where they fitted my harness and suspended me from a height, I did not have half the usual time to practise the dance itself, as was observed in Craig's comment, 'It all went well until you landed.'

I was relieved to land. My height phobia had meant I came from the lowest tier in the room but it was quite high enough for me. I look at the photographs of me descending with a big smile and I know just how false that smile was!

The following week we danced the paso doble to the song 'Wild Thing' and this time resorted to high comedy. The steps were easy enough because there is one called the *'appel'* which effectively is a stop so if you are on the wrong foot, you have a chance to get back on the right one. It was what Anton added that brought the house down. I jumped, was spun at speed and then whooshed on the floor and dragged. This time Scot Maslen's tears were of helpless laughter.

The paso was followed by the Charleston and then the foxtrot. The last was the only occasion on which we did not get a standing ovation and I thought perhaps the public was tiring of us. If so, it was a disappointing week for that to happen because whoever survived that week went through to Blackpool. This meant much to the dancers, not only because there was a bonus paid to all who reached Blackpool but because the famous Blackpool Ballroom was Mecca for them.

Having survived yet again, I joined the coach for the resort I had hitherto associated only with party conferences. Anton wanted us to dress fairly spectacularly and initially suggested costumes from *Priscilla, Queen of the Desert*. I had the foresight to look up the film on the Internet and decided no, we would not model ourselves on transvestites. What was finally produced was a dress which I promptly called Big Bird: bright, canary yellow with huge feathers around the bottom. Anton matched me in a bright yellow top with gold glittery trousers.

Earlier that week Charlotte Oates had approached me with a serious face. Did I have any religious objections to dancing to 'Heaven is Missing an Angel'? I imagined the angels would themselves laugh at such solemnity and so a pair of angel wings was embroidered on the back of my costume. Our routine was another display of spinning but this time we had to do so at high speed and then, at a nod from Anton, I was to drop on the floor still spinning.

Meanwhile one of the couples most likely to win, Artem Chigvintsev and Kara Tointon, were having a serious problem. A lift had gone wrong in training and Artem's neck was badly damaged. Stuffed full of painkillers, he was insisting on dancing and performing the same lift. Felicity and I tut-tutted to each other about the folly of youth. Health was more important than any dance competition. In such circumstances we would be much more sensible.

I wasn't. The spin drop had gone off without a hitch in training and indeed was to become a motif of both the tour and my first pantomime but as I performed the move in dress rehearsal, I felt an agonising pull. Afterwards the pain got steadily worse. I told nobody, gingerly feeling my stomach and hip, surreptitiously seeing what I still could and could not do. My own words about Artem rang in my ears but they rang unheeded.

As we approached the move in the show I was apprehensive but it was mercifully pain-free. The next day I had intermittent pain but nothing unbearable. I rested but on the Monday was due to travel to London and as I sat in the back of the car felt agonising cramps in my stomach. I began to wonder if I had pulled a stomach muscle or caused a hernia. I trained as usual over the next few days, which was easier than usual because we were dancing the rumba and Anton had designed a fairly gentle routine, in which all the spectacle would be provided by a skit on the *Titanic*.

I was to stand on the balcony with a wind machine blowing

back my hair and my arms stretched out like Kate Winslet. An iceberg was to be placed on the stage and Anton would appear from much mist to ring a ship's bell. Never mind the dance, the story was spectacular. As the song to which we were performing was a hymn to a dead lover we felt we should play not for laughs but for the aaahh factor. As we embraced in the final move and cheers erupted from the standing, clapping audience I murmured to him 'aaahhh'.

We survived again and had now reached week ten, the quarter final, and I was no longer in pain. The judges were in cheerful despair.

'You are like haemorrhoids,' moaned Len Goodman. 'You keep coming back more painful than ever.' In another expression of the same sentiment he told us that snow was exciting at first but after a while you just wanted it to go away. 'Dancing hippos,' snorted an exasperated Craig, which seemed to me a gross libel of Anton.

'Dancing hippos' was the least of the judges' insults, which included 'dalek in drag', 'the *Ark Royal*' and Len's wonderful observation that 'Dancing is movement to music. Well, there was movement and there was music but there was also no relation between the two.'

The public enjoyed my backchat with Craig, Len, Alesha and Bruno but controversy was now starting to rear its head. It would be the final itself in two weeks in which there were three places and there were four good dancers.

Kara Tointon, Matt Baker, Pamela Stephenson and Scott Maslen were each serious competitors for the famous glitterball. In a few of the previous competitions there had been only two likely winners but my year had produced a crop of talent and if Anton and I were to enter the final it could be only at the expense of a serious dancer. We had already seen capable dancers eliminated but there was no real resentment because, although they were better than me, they were not likely to have been in the final.

Strictly Come Dancing is much more than just a dance competition. If that were all it was designed to be then it would never begin with a range of competitor stretching from Kara Tointon to Ann Widdecombe, from Matt Baker to Paul Daniels, nor would it be on prime-time television but would be consigned to sport. It is family, Saturday evening entertainment, enlivened by the likes of John Serjeant, Russell Grant and Lisa Riley. I was saddened when Edwina Currie tried to follow in my footsteps and was first out because she had so hopelessly misread the programme, talking sex and showing her knickers like a naughty five-year-old.

Would I knock out a potential winner and would that create a backlash? Indeed there were signs it was already beginning as we learned that the *News of the World* was preparing to run next day with the headline 'Professional Backlash as Widdy Heads for Crown'.

I thought it unlikely that I would get to the final but I had high hopes of the semi-final as Gavin Henson was still in the competition and had been in the bottom two the week before. When he was the first to be pronounced through to the following week, I knew it was over. For the first time we were in the bottom two and the other one was Scott, whom I certainly could not beat if there was any justice in the matter.

Then came my only disappointment on *Strictly Come Dancing*. When I had joined they asked me which tune I would like played when I went out and I said 'Nellie the Elephant'. A few weeks later Charlotte Oates told me that it had been forbidden in case it looked as if they were mocking me. The audience would not know it was my choice and might think the BBC was being rude.

Well, I thought, that had never worried the BBC in the past. I selected a lively Gracie Fields number, 'Wish Me Luck as You Wave Me Goodbye'. As Anton and I were asked to perform our last dance that is what I expected but instead the band struck up a sentimental dirge, 'It's Over' by Roy Orbison. I was so disconcerted that I failed to dance, still waiting for Gracie. Anton picked me up and spun me and then I asked the audience to sing 'Nellie the Elephant' and those who heard me did.

Mawkishness and sentimental mush filled more than enough

columns while I was taking part in *Strictly* as well as the more acerbic sketches, which I vastly preferred. People could not accept that I was just enjoying myself, that no great revolution had taken place. I was retired and having fun.

The silliest piece of all was produced by Rebecca Hardy for the *Mail*.

I told her I had not had such a prolonged period of sustained frivolity since leaving Oxford. 'Oooh, that is so sad,' she trilled. I had not said happiness or contentment or anything similar. I was talking about fun and how many mortals, once they start earning a living and raising families, have three solid months of daily frivolity and uninterrupted jollity (bar, in my case a bereavement)? Three months with no responsibility? But she wrote it was sad given that I was sixty-three.

She then asked Anton if he had noticed any difference in me after my brother died. Anton gaped at her and I came to his rescue with a brief 'None'.

Inevitably she rattled on about Oxford, describing me on the basis of what evidence I do not know as being in my youth willowy and doe-eyed. She then declared as if it were fact that being in love at Oxford had put me off men for life. Where did she dream that up from? My entire political career was dismissed as one of ridicule and lampoons.

When I commented on how I felt no tug when returning to Westminster, that it was as though I had never been there, I meant to indicate detachment and lack of regrets. But to this woman that was 'sad' too.

I was exhausted by the end of this prying twaddle, which was becoming all too familiar. As Anton remarked at the end of one interview, 'She thinks you're unfulfilled because you are single but her idea of bliss seems to be divorced with a son away at school.'

I told Stuart MacDonald, the *Strictly* press officer, that I wanted no more such interviews. He was surprised, telling me he thought it a nice piece and that celebrities liked that sort of interview, but once he had got the message that I did not he batted the sentimental stuff away with good-humoured determination.

He was a bright chap who might have done well in a party polit-ical press office.

Even before I heard that Gavin had got through, I had sensed we had lost because there were some funny signals from the judges. Craig actually praised some of the moves and Len, meet-ing me in a corridor, said he hoped I had not found him too harsh because 'you have been fantastic'.

'Have been?' I queried. 'Is it curtains?'

He immediately denied it, but I suspect he did know.

However disappointed I might have been not to have lasted another week, I was glad to get my life back. Christmas was almost upon me, I was behind with my correspondence and the building works were over for the winter. I had friends coming to stay for the festive season and I needed to catch up with the family, for whom it would be the first Christmas without my brother. The small pang at waking up to a Monday morning with no training was as nothing to the huge relief of once more calling my day my own.

Losing an only sibling means losing the last link with the past. I call it *the goneness*. There is no longer anybody with whom you can share an old family joke without having to explain it, nobody who shares your memories and can understand immedi-ately what you are talking about. When the whirlwind of *Strictly* had died, the goneness hit me.

I had always imagined my brother enjoying the theological section in my library – or the thriller section – praying with me in my tiny chapel (created in a box room), or walking with me on the moors, but none of that would now happen. I had to divest the house of that hope.

I could however still laugh at the memory of a conversation I had once had with my mother when she and my father were in their mid-eighties. There was an oft-repeated scenario, when I was visiting, whereby the telephone would ring and my father would go out to the hall to answer it. We would then hear him say, 'Oh, my God! When?'

'Oh,' my mother would murmur. 'Who's gone now?'

Then my father would return to the lounge and say a name,

433

such as Connie Trigg, which was familiar from my childhood.

I told Mother that if ever I wrote a novel of old age I would call it *Who's Gone Now?* which amused her mightily.

There was not however much time for mourning for January 2011 looked to be even busier than the *Strictly* season.

It had been while I was training in Newton Abbot one day that I was rung up and asked to join the live tour that travels the country for five weeks, playing at big venues such as Wembley and the O2. I was surprised because Anton does not do the tour, preferring to do a private one with Erin Boag, but the organisers suggested I dance with Craig Revel Horwood. It was too funny to refuse.

The live tour was an education. Nearly everybody under the age of forty stayed out until 4 a.m. in the clubs and bars of whatever town we were in. Sometimes they got back at 7 a.m. and were often very drunk but, a few hours later, they would lift, spin and execute complicated steps without a single mistake, while I, stone-cold sober and with eight hours' sleep behind me, stumbled and blundered.

I also discovered why celebrities shop so much. Both Pamela Stephenson and I were writing books and therefore occupied but those who had to kill an afternoon away from home found a pastime in shopping. I did get a new blouse, but Craig bought an ottoman. The one who made the best use of the time on offer was Len Goodman, who, whenever we arrived at a new town, would book a taxi for several hours and ask to be taken to places of local or historic interest.

The set travelled with us. This had four steps, up which we ran when leaving the stage. However once we had to use the venue's own set which had three steps. I tried to run up four and would have fallen if Craig had not grabbed me. It was, he told me, called muscle memory.

The organisation was immense. The set and the catering had to travel before us and be ready for our arrival and we had to learn fresh geography between dressing room, stage, make-up and canteen every day.

Dancing with Craig was very different from dancing with

Anton. He is taller and stronger and I felt the difference when being spun. We performed a routine every night, while the audience was voting, which was half-*Titanic* and half-Charleston. He added a move of dragging me between his legs so when he wore a kilt for the New Year's Eve dance, everybody asked me the obvious question but I was unable to enlighten anyone because I had deliberately closed my eyes.

I often travelled to the venue with the judges and we dreamed up the insults they might deliver. Once I thought Bruno Tonioni had a brainwave when he suggested that my dancing deserved to be classified as one of the plagues of Egypt and we discussed whether it should come after darkness or frogs, but the organisers forbade it as 'too religiously sensitive and liable to give offence'.

Craig Revel Horwood is one of the kindest, most generous-spirited people in all showbusiness. He is unfailingly considerate and I have never once seen him lose his temper or become irate when directing. Those who read his autobiography, *All Balls and Glitter*, which is absolutely not for the faint-hearted or under-eighteens and should be kept higher than the average person can reach, will find an episode in which he was taken on foreign travel by an older man who used him as a rent boy. As he needed his parents' permission to travel they deceived his mother about the purpose. Most of us would call such a man a pervert but Craig writes that he is 'a nice guy'. That level of forgiveness is rare in today's world.

Inevitably I am asked how we manage to get on but why should we not? I would no more want to engage with his raunchy, sex-fuelled world than he would with my maidenly, church-going one, but that does not mean that we should retreat into those worlds and throw up a rampart. As long as someone is kind and humorous and cares for his or her fellow beings what is the problem with friendship?

It was in the judges' car in Belfast that Craig suggested I join him in pantomime at the end of 2011. I agreed at once and thus found myself in Dartford playing Widdy-in-Waiting to his wicked Queen in *Snow White and the Seven Dwarves*. Inevitably we did a dance routine which had a hilarious consequence.

We were performing twice a day and one of the moves was the spin-drop. As we were approaching the thirty-second show I remarked to Craig that I was beginning to feel a bit bruised from continually falling on the floor so he suggested we abandon the drop and that instead he should pick me up and spin me. I asked if, given that he was in drag and wearing high heels, we should practise that which we would have both been confident about in normal circumstances. He said no, he could manage in heels.

When the moment came for me to turn into him for the lift I heard a heartfelt 'Oh, oh, Gordon Bennet!' in a tone that suggested a much stronger curse. When I asked him what had happened he explained that while we had thought about heels neither of us had thought about the false bust and it was only in the very act of picking me up that he realised he had no idea whether to hold me above it or below it. Trying first below, he then had to haul me above when I had already clamped my arms and weight into position.

Having made a name for myself by not being able to dance, I am always surprised at the number of times I am invited to dance for charity. On one occasion money was raised by bidding for me to dance with Peter Mandelson and he managed that lift in one go, although not of course with Craig's disadvantage on that occasion in pantomime. In my view, Peter should have been on *Strictly* but not in government.

The pantomime sold out and Craig and I reprised the role last year in High Wycombe to equally good audiences. There however arose a complaint that it was inappropriate in a family show to dress the servants in bondage gear. Initially I had not identified the men's outfits as such until a chance remark alerted me, but clearly the citizens of High Wycombe were less innocent than both me and those of Dartford or perhaps they had been reading *Fifty Shades of Grey*. Thereafter the men wore capes over their tops.

On that occasion Muddles was the ventriloquist Steve Hewlett, whose dummy is Pongo the Skunk. Why they are not on television I do not know.

Pongo brought back poignant memories. My brother was as likely to laugh at childish lavatory jokes at seventy-three as he had been at seven, still finding them hilarious when the rest of us were smiling feebly. Standing in the wings watching the act and hearing the audience convulsed, I imagined how he would have enjoyed it all.

Everyone who came backstage observed that performing twice a day must be hard work. When I was working seven days a week, clearing red boxes until the early hours, leaving Westminster at 3 a.m. and then getting up to be interviewed on the *Today* programme, nobody called it hard work but acting daft and making children laugh and having no responsibility for anything except getting on stage on time and delivering the right lines must, apparently, be exhausting. Sometimes such comments amuse me but sometimes they make me angry on behalf of MPs.

During 2011 I achieved what had always been my ambition: my own quiz show. I had long wanted to chair one or to be the quizmaster. Indeed each time *Countdown,* on which I had appeared in dictionary corner on many occasions, lost its chairman my agent put my name forward but without success. The channel was probably right but if the directors had taken me they would have had one chairman after Des Lynam instead of three.

Now Splash TV was anxious to capitalise on my public profile and devised a quiz programme called *Cleverdicks*. Their first thought was to offer it to the BBC and a large team came to watch it. They all sat with unmoving faces and I knew it would not be commissioned. I also was not surprised: the format was too dull, with my sitting at a table reading out questions.

As once I had done with party conference, so now I tried with *Cleverdicks* putting in movement and abandoning the sheaves of notes. When I explained what I was going to do on making the presentation to Sky Atlantic there was a great deal of nervousness but it worked. It worked also because the Sky team, which was a quarter of the size of the BBC's, reacted with enthusiasm instead of haughty reserve and of course interaction with the audience is meat and drink to me.

Sky Atlantic wanted to experiment with a home-grown programme. The quiz was intelligent with very few questions on pop music and many instead on history, geography, science and literature. The audience for such a channel is small and judging the ratings is always difficult but we were sometimes top of its evening's figures and we gained an audience not dissimilar to the channel's great hope, the heavily promoted *Mad Men*.

A booking was pencilled in for the studios and everyone confidently expected a follow-up show but Sky dropped it. We were told that some research had shown that Sky Atlantic viewers did not think the programme belonged on that channel. The real reason may well have been office politics, as Elaine Pike, who commissioned the series and had faith in it, went on maternity leave.

I know it could have been successful, just from the number of people who still stop me to ask when the next series will be coming and who are so disappointed when I tell them it will not be. I am saddened not by the loss of an ambition but by the loss of the programme. *Cleverdicks* could have had a serious future and I mourn its demise.

So *Strictly* had led to a tour, two pantomimes and a quiz show but the strangest consequence of all came when Rosemary Scoular, my media agent, phoned me and said that she had received a bid for me to appear at the Royal Opera House in, naturally, a spoken role. The opera was Donizetti's *La Fille du Regiment* and the part was La Duchesse de Krakentorp, a rude, autocratic old lady.

I agreed and for seven nights had the enormous privilege of playing at the Royal Opera House but it was nearly a massive failure. As with Anton du Beke and Craig Revel Horwood before them the directors *heard* me when I said that I could not hear music but did not *understand* me. They still expected me to pick up musical cues, which was quite impossible. Whereas Anton and Craig, used to dealing with amateurs, quickly adjusted, these rarefied mortals dealt only with consummate professionals and simply could not absorb my limitations. We all began to despair and it was suggested as we departed for Easter that I might have to be dropped.

I sent an email to Rosemary but she was not about. I could just imagine the publicity, about which the team at the Opera House seemed hopelessly complacent. 'We'll manage it. It won't be a problem.' I began to wonder that such innocence still existed.

Over the Easter I set about analysing the problem and on return was adamant. If I could not do it, I should not be asked to, so let me act and everyone else carry on with the music. If they were moving in a gentle sway to notes, La Duchesse could stand impatiently tapping her foot. I must react to visual not musical cues.

As ever, once the audience began responding all went well and I heard for the first – and almost certainly only time in my career – shouts of 'bravo!' The directors could hardly disguise their relief.

It is now understandably assumed that I am building a career in showbusiness but the truth is that I am not consciously building a career in anything: I am retired. I am doing what I think might be fun (panto) or enjoyable (Royal Opera House) or worthwhile (*Cleverdicks*) but I am not taking any decisions based on what will or will not advance a career.

The greatest compliment paid to me while I was doing *Strictly* was when a lady stopped me at a station and told me that every time the show came on air her four-year-old would say, 'Where's that granny, Mummy? I want that granny to win.'

Another said her small boy would lie on the floor, hold up his arms and say 'Pull, Mummy, pull like lady.'

'I voted and voted for you and it was the first time I have been allowed to watch it,' wrote Tony Newton in that year's Christmas card.

There are worse ways to spend one's life than bringing laughter and gaiety into that of others. I resisted the attempts following *Strictly* to engage me with the celebrity lifestyle, refusing most 'red carpet' events. Piers Morgan laughed at me when I appeared on his show because I had asked for fizzy water and tissues in my dressing room. He told me that I should now be demanding champagne. In similar vein he thought my Ford Focus hilarious. It should apparently now be a Ferrari.

None of that means I am no longer serious. The religious documentaries give me great satisfaction. I did almost go as ambassador to the Vatican and I reacted seriously too when I was sounded out as a possible candidate for police commissioner in both Kent and Devon. I refused because I would only do it if I had powers close to those of Giuliani, being interested in action not bureaucracy. I still write weekly for the *Express* and of course am now returning to novels.

I may yet write about Charles II's escape after the Battle of Worcester, a real-life fairy tale if ever there was one. For six weeks he hid from Cromwell, travelling in disguise as a servant in his own kingdom, sometimes evading capture by the Roundheads with only minutes to spare and aided by an assortment of woodcutters, millers and servants. There was a reward of £1,000 on his head but nobody betrayed him. I have made two television programmes about Boscobel, made famous for his having hidden in a nearby oak tree while Cromwell's soldiers searched the ground below, and would like to do much more on the subject.

I do not know what the future holds but my life has been well blessed. I had a happy, secure childhood. My parents lived until I was myself nearing retirement and both they and my brother had long, happy marriages. I have enjoyed robust health both mentally and physically and have achieved my twin ambitions of a political career and writing novels, and now, released from major responsibilities, I am having fun and living in one of the most beautiful parts of the country, often welcoming my family as I watch five small great-nephews and great-nieces grow up. I look out over the rolling moors from my library window remembering a child in a white school tunic under the setting sun of Empire and I think, 'Did it really all happen?'

It did.

FINIS. DEO GRATIAS

INDEX

441